P9-CCL-769

WISE
TEACHING

WISE
TEACHING

BIBLICAL WISDOM AND
EDUCATIONAL MINISTRY

CHARLES F. MELCHERT

TRINITY PRESS INTERNATIONAL
Harrisburg, Pennsylvania

Excerpt from *Jacob the Baker* by Noah ben Shea. Copyright © 1989 by Noah ben Shea. Reprinted with permission of Villard Books, a division of Random House, Inc.

Excerpt from *The Book of Blessings: New Jewish Prayers for Daily Life, the Sabbath, and the New Moon Festival* by Marcia Falk. Copyright © 1996 by Marcia Lee Falk. Reprinted with permission of HarperCollins Publishers.

Excerpt from *Number Our Days* by Barbara Myerhoff. Copyright © 1978 by Barbara Myerhoff. Reprinted with permission of Penguin USA.

Excerpt from *Knots* by R. D. Laing. Copyright © 1970 by R. D. Laing. Reprinted with permission of Routledge.

Unless otherwise indicated biblical quotations are from the New Revised Standard Version (New York: Oxford University Press, 1989).

Copyright © 1998 by Charles F. Melchert.

All rights reserved. No part of this book may be reproduced, stored in a retrieval system, or transmitted, in any form or by any means, electronic, mechanical, photocopying, recording, or otherwise, without the written permission of the publisher.

Trinity Press International, P.O. Box 1321, Harrisburg, PA 17105
Trinity Press International is a division of the Morehouse Group

Library of Congress Cataloging-in-Publication Data

Melchert, C. F. (Charles F.)
    Wise teaching : biblical wisdom and educational ministry / C.F. Melchert.
        p.   cm.
    Includes bibliographical references.
    ISBN 1-56338-139-7
    1. Wisdom literature – Criticism, interpretation, etc.
  2. Education in the Bible. I. Title.
  BS1455.M45 1998
  223'.06 – dc21   98-9864

Printed in the United States of America

98 99 00 01 02   10 9 8 7 6 5 4 3 2 1

To my parents, Elmer and Virginia Melchert,
and
to my son, Tim,
who have waited a very long time,
and to Mark, in memoriam

Contents

PREFACE

Everything has to start somewhere. Where does a book on wisdom and education start? In one sense this book started in a dimly lit basement cubbyhole study in a rented house in St. John's, Newfoundland, Canada, in the fall of 1974, as I began reading Gerhard von Rad's *Wisdom in Israel*.[1] Yet it could not have started there, for something earlier must have piqued my curiosity and given me interest and skills. We are now on the slippery slope of "infinite regress," sliding from subject to subject, toward some infinitely receding prior state until ultimately we find ourselves at something we could call *Creation* or *God*. That "slide" is faithful both to the spirit of the wisdom tradition and also to the spirit of educational ministry as I understand it — and those are my starting points in what follows. (Can one start from two places at once?)

I shall be writing at the intersection of two sets of questions: Wisdom texts try to "make sense of" the puzzles and mysteries of human and divine behavior. What do we learn about human living and divine mystery if we listen carefully to these texts? Wisdom texts also try to "educate" their readers, for the authors, the sages, were themselves simultaneously teachers and learners. How can we conduct our educational ministry in a manner that makes such learning more likely?

A word of warning: To listen truthfully to these "wisdom voices," we must beware of reading our own educational assumptions into their words. If the words "school" or "instruction" or "teaching" occur in these texts, we cannot assume that they refer to practices with which we are familiar today. In order to benefit from this conversation with these sages and their texts, we must be prepared to imagine dramatically different educational arrangements. For example, some would have us seek to follow Jesus and his approach to teaching. Yet Jesus had no classroom, no textbooks, no curriculum materials, no program, and he is not known to have urged anyone to study anything. Jesus did

---

1. Gerhard von Rad, *Wisdom in Israel* (Nashville: Abingdon, 1972).

not even tell Bible stories, and he was a homeless itinerant. What of this should we emulate? To listen well, we may be required to envision educational approaches radically different from those familiar today.

Many teachers have contributed to this book in ways they may not recognize. Ron Hals and H. C. Leupold taught me to love the Hebrew Scriptures. Dr. Leupold taught us not only by his careful scrutiny of the text but as well by his quiet graceful kindness, by the care with which he heard and answered questions — often with head cocked to one side, a wry smile, a twinkle in his bespectacled eye, and one forefinger raised, slightly curled, as though he were expecting another thought any moment. B. Davie Napier and Paul Minear taught me to appreciate the depths of the human dimension in biblical texts. From my father and from a saintly friend and colleague of sixteen years, Lamar Williamson, I learned much about the congruence between the study of a text and the way one composes daily life. From Randolph C. Miller I learned that the processes of human experience and educational interaction can be profoundly biblical and theological. From J. C. Wynn I learned homespun proverbs that illumined my life within and beyond the academy, as well as the importance of patience, humility, and humor for being wise. From Sara Little I learned, above all, that being rigorously truthful matters, even when it hurts. From my students over the years — especially those at the Presbyterian School of Christian Education, at Lancaster Theological Seminary, and at the University of Birmingham, England — I have learned again and again the excitement of seeing familiar materials in new ways and how such learning can transform people (teachers *and* learners) as well as the teaching and learning process. To each I am deeply grateful. This is not as good a book as these mentors and the biblical wisdom materials themselves deserve, but it is as good as I can make it — until I become more wise.

I have also had the benefit of wise counsel from careful readers, though sometimes I have not followed their advice, and thus I am responsible for the errors they sought to help me avoid. For their patient efforts to steer me right, I am grateful to Bill Brown, James Crenshaw, Ginna Dalton, Ellen F. Davis, John Hull, Beth Huwiler, Sara Little, Susan Minasian, Pamela Mitchell, Richard Olson, Kurt Strause, Paul Walaskay, Bob Webber, and Lamar Williamson. No one has been more responsible for seeing this book to light than my friend, lover, wife, and soul mate, Anabel Proffitt.

ABBREVIATIONS

AB	Anchor Bible
AnBib	Analecta biblica
BJS	Brown Judaic Studies
BZAW	Beihefte zur Zeitschrift für die alttestamentliche Wissenschaft
Gosp. Thom.	*Gospel of Thomas*
HSM	Harvard Semitic Monographs
IB	*Interpreter's Bible*
JB	*Jerusalem Bible*
JSNTSup	Journal for the Study of the New Testament–Supplement Series
JSOTSup	Journal for the Study of the Old Testament–Supplement Series
KJV	King James Version
NCB	New Century Bible
NEB	New English Bible
NIV	New International Version
NJPSV	New Jewish Publication Society Version
NRSV	New Revised Standard Version
OBO	Orbis biblicus et orientalis
RSV	Revised Standard Version
SBL	Society of Biblical Literature
Sir.	Sirach
Song	Song of Songs
TEV	Today's English Version
Tob.	Tobit
WBC	Word Biblical Commentary
Wisd.	Wisdom of Solomon
WUNT	Wissenschaftliche Untersuchungen zum Neuen Testament

THEN, NOW, AND MAYBE

In the contemporary world, wisdom is often regarded as ancient, words from a long-gone simpler time. Proverbial sayings are often regarded as old-fashioned. We doubt their relevance or usefulness in a complex and technical world.

Once upon a time Wisdom (with a capital *W*) was believed to be a crowning glory and achievement of human existence. In the West, from medieval times through the Renaissance, one could not claim to be an intellectual unless one had written a treatise on Wisdom.[1] In the East, many of the most revered figures of history and legend were not prophets or military leaders but sages. Many Oriental countries trace the moral substratum of their social order back to the teachings of Confucius, the "Great Teacher" and Sage par excellence. Many highly regarded ancient texts are collections of wise sayings from sages, such as the *Analects* of Confucius, Lao Tzu's *The Way of Tao*, the biblical book of *Proverbs,* the teaching stories of Mulla Nasrudin. As many as twenty-four collections of proverbs have survived among prebiblical Mesopotamian texts, and there are numerous Egyptian texts as well.[2] Study of these stories, sayings, and texts was once regarded as an important part of learning how to live, especially (though not exclusively) for rulers and their advisors. Egyptologist Ronald J. Williams observes,

---

1. Eugene Rice, *The Renaissance Idea of Wisdom* (Cambridge: Harvard University Press, 1958).

2. Reviews of such works can be found in James Crenshaw, *Old Testament Wisdom: An Introduction* (Atlanta: John Knox, 1981), 212–35; and in R. B. Y. Scott, *The Way of Wisdom in the Old Testament* (New York: Macmillan, 1971), 23–47. Fuller treatment, with attention to instructional texts, can be found in William McKane, *Proverbs: A New Approach* (Philadelphia: Westminster, 1970). The classic source for the texts themselves is J. B. Pritchard, ed., *Ancient Near Eastern Texts Relating to the Old Testament,* 3d ed. (Princeton: Princeton University Press, 1969). Additional treatments of the sages in Egyptian, Sumerian, Akkadian, Iranian, and Ugaritic texts can be found in John G. Gammie and Leo G. Perdue, eds. *The Sage in Israel and the Ancient Near East* (Winona Lake, Ind.: Eisenbrauns, 1990), 3–116.

These didactic works were studied, copied, and memorized for many centuries. For instance, a scrap of papyrus dating from between Dynasty 26 and Dynasty 30 bears a portion of the text of the "Teaching of Amenemhet." This means that the little tractate was still being read and copied some fourteen to seventeen centuries later.[3]

Today, few take wisdom seriously as an educational goal. Most often today, *wisdom* seems to be used as a euphemism for something quaint or, at best, mildly desirable but likely unattainable. It seems to be regarded as something left over from old times or primitive ways that is properly left behind when progress and modernity arrive, or else it is regarded as too "New Age."

WHY SHOULD EDUCATORS STUDY WISDOM?

Philip Nel observes, "The most peculiar feature of that wisdom [of the ancient Near East] is its educational or pedagogic quality."[4] This dimension of biblical wisdom has seldom been attended to by educators, let alone biblical scholars.[5] These texts offer a remarkable array of literary styles, devices, forms, and patterns that often are designed to elicit or evoke in the reader the substance of the issues the author is seeking to address. The fusion of literary, dramatic, and poetic interests with theological, cultural, ethical, and educational issues is a remarkable feature of many of these works. Paying close attention to such procedures and content in this literature could suggest alternatives to the conventional, childish religion and ethic so endemic in the West.

One of the major liabilities of contemporary education is its tendency to become a series of isolated specialties that seem to have little to do with learning how to live one's daily life in the real world. Wisdom texts have an in-depth concern for the *whole* human condition. Focusing upon the everyday questions of the or-

---

3. Ronald J. Williams, "The Sage in Egyptian Literature," in *The Sage in Israel and the Ancient Near East*, ed. John G. Gammie and Leo G. Perdue (Winona Lake, Ind.: Eisenbrauns, 1990), 24.

4. Philip Johannes Nel, *The Structure and Ethos of the Wisdom Admonitions in Proverbs*, BZAW 158 (Berlin: Walter de Gruyter, 1982), 1.

5. There are notable exceptions to this: Crenshaw's description of the epistemology of the sages in "The Acquisition of Knowledge in Israelite Wisdom Literature," *Word and World* 7:3 (summer 1987), 245–52; Brueggemann's *The Creative Word: Canon as a Model for Biblical Education* (Philadelphia: Fortress, 1982), which is important even though his treatment of wisdom materials covers only twenty-four pages; and Donn Morgan's forthcoming work on wisdom and higher education.

dinary individual and community, wisdom texts can help us attend to and learn from birth, life, death, sex, polite manners, sensuality, doubt, pride, injustice, suffering, and other realities and joys of everyday life. These texts are both intellectually honest, as they deal with the puzzles and mysteries of human life and divine presence, and emotionally passionate, as they express and try to make sense of the pain, the incoherence, the sadness, the despair, and the exuberant joy of human existence.

Wisdom texts are ecumenical and inclusive. They pay attention to the rich and the poor, the religious and the nonreligious, those who are up and those who are down. In a world where it is difficult but imperative to understand religious traditions and cultures other than one's own, we find that biblical wisdom traditions have long done so. These biblical texts pay attention to their own cultural and religious tradition, but they also listen to (and borrow from) the Egyptians, Greeks, Sumerians, Babylonians, and others. Rather than simply reject other cultures as barbarian or irreligious, these texts assume we can learn from each other about how to live.

Wisdom texts are highly sensitive to the limits of the human understanding of God. The authors believe that God's miracles are not only what breaks out of the ordinary but are also the ordinary itself. Thus they do not try to say too much too explicitly and, instead, recommend humility. Furthermore, the sages pay serious attention to nature as an arena of divine presence, often showing readers a profound, contemporary, even ecological, spirituality without being explicitly "religious."

Wisdom texts such as Proverbs and Job and Ecclesiastes (and Song of Songs?) are part of the biblical canon, yet often they are not taken seriously or are misunderstood. They seldom are used as texts for today's preachers or as a source of learning for laypeople. Why? Exploring these texts may help us discover how narrow our own "canon within the canon" really is.

Wisdom texts are also part of the link between the worlds of the Hebrew Bible and the New Testament. A familiarity with wisdom thinking is essential to understand the unity of these two canons.

And why not study wisdom? One of the primary functions of education is to enable people to discover the joy and wonder of learning and knowing something new. That could be reason enough.

WHAT DO WE MEAN BY WISDOM?

The word "wisdom" often refers to biblical texts such as Proverbs, Job, and Ecclesiastes because *hokmah* (the Hebrew word for "wisdom") occurs more often in these three works than in the whole of the remainder of the Hebrew Bible.[6] In addition, sometimes texts such as Confucius's *Analects* or the Egyptian "The Instructions of Amenemope" are also called *wisdom literature*. Such texts differ markedly from prophetic, historical, and priestly texts, yet they do not form a single literary genre.

In the biblical literature the word "wisdom" often refers to a human quality or ability. Indeed, "wise" or "wisdom" is used for an incredibly wide range of particular abilities, for example, those (women and men) who crafted the priestly garments, the tabernacle, the ark, and other furnishings (e.g., Exod. 28:3; 31:6; 35:25–26, 31; 36:2) or the artisans building Solomon's temple (e.g., 1 Chron. 22:15; 28:21; 2 Chron. 2:6). Similarly, it is used in Psalm 107:27 of the skill of seamen. "Wisdom" is also used of magicians, such as those Joseph, Moses, and Aaron confronted in Egypt (e.g., Gen. 41:8; Exod. 7:11), where the magicians' wisdom is contrasted with the true wisdom of Joseph (Gen. 41:33, 39). It is also used to characterize a king's counselors (1 Chron. 27:32–34), leaders chosen by Moses to assist him (Deut. 1:13, 15), and frequently Solomon, as in his "wise and discerning mind" (1 Kings 3:12). Moses urges the people to observe the commandments, "for this will show your wisdom and discernment to the peoples, who, when they hear all these statutes, will say, 'Surely this great nation is a wise and discerning people!' " (Deut. 4:6).

Michael V. Fox concludes that the Hebrew word *hokmah* (wisdom) means "knowledge together with the reasoning ability to apply it" and can be attached to the person, the activity, the importance of the activity, or even the circumstances of its performance.[7] Yet, wisdom is not limited to human beings, since humans can learn to be wise by studying "wise" creatures (Prov. 6:6–8; 30:24–28).

Was there a special group of "professional" wise men or sages with distinct social functions, like groups such as kings, priests, and prophets? A text such as Jeremiah 18:18 seems to identify a spe-

---

6. R. N. Whybray, *The Intellectual Tradition in the Old Testament* (Berlin: Walter de Gruyter, 1974), 4.

7. Michael V. Fox, *Qohelet and His Contradictions*, JSOTSup 71 (Sheffield: Almond, 1989), 82.

cific group and activity of "the wise": "Then they said, 'Come, let us make plots against Jeremiah — for instruction shall not perish from the priest, nor counsel from the wise, nor the word from the prophet.' " R. N. Whybray first showed this is too simple a conclusion,[8] for as Fox also says, "When the book of Proverbs promises to teach wisdom, it is not claiming to teach professional skills, nor does it do so."[9] Yet Fox is surely right in observing that late in the tradition the term "the wise" does seem to refer to a group of authors and teachers who were learned in Scripture and who collected and composed literature of several types (see the titles in Prov. 10:1; 25:1; 30:1; Eccles. 12:9; Sir. 3:29, 8:8, 44:4b). But here the purpose of calling them "the wise" was not, according to Fox, to call attention to the group, but "to exalt the status of the ancient sayings, assuring us of their place in the national scriptural traditions."[10]

In some biblical texts wisdom is poetically personified. In Job, wisdom often appears to be a human quality, but in Job 28, wisdom seems more a "thing" that humans seek but cannot find. In Proverbs, in Ecclesiasticus, and in the Wisdom of Solomon, wisdom appears as a desirable and powerful woman, who is either with Yahweh or Yahweh's agent. She even is said to have led the people out of slavery, guided the prophets, and taken up residence in the Holy of Holies in Jerusalem.

"Wisdom" can also designate a broad approach to life practiced by wise people. Robert Gordis says it is a "realistic approach to the problems of life, including all the practical skills and technical arts of civilization."[11] Similarly, James L. Crenshaw says, "Wisdom is the reasoned search for specific ways to assure well-being and the implementation of those discoveries in daily existence."[12] These definitions call attention to the fact that "wisdom" has also come to refer to an approach to life, a mind-set, or even a traditional intellectual and cultural phenomenon that has endured through time.

---

8. Whybray, *The Intellectual Tradition in the Old Testament*, 15–54. While Whybray demonstrates "wise" and "wisdom" do not refer to a class or professional group of wise men in Israel, he does not deny that there was an intellectual tradition. What he denies is that this tradition can be linked to a professional group, such as advisors to the king, teachers, or authors. The tradition must be described on other grounds.

9. Ibid., 330.

10. Ibid., 332.

11. Robert Gordis, *The Book of God and Man: A Study of Job* (Chicago: University of Chicago Press, 1965), 31.

12. Crenshaw, *Old Testament Wisdom*, 25.

Since we will also use it in this way in what follows, it may be useful to characterize this way of seeing life.

The threefold division of the Hebrew canon provides a handy way to compare traditions and to identify three distinctive mindsets: the Torah or instruction, the Prophets, and the Writings, especially the portion we call *wisdom*.[13] We can illustrate the mindsets by comparing them to how a child experiences and responds to different authorities in life. First, the child knows the parent, and what the parent says is taken to be the direct and authoritative word, like from a "god." This is like Torah. When the parent says, "Thou shalt not cross the street," the child knows she is to obey and does not seek another opinion. But, second, when the child's baby-sitter says, "Don't cross the street," the sitter speaks with authority derived from the parent. This is like the prophet, who transmits God's word and whose authority is derived from Yahweh. Third, after the child has moved out into the world on her own, she cannot depend solely upon the authority of parent or baby-sitter. Now she must learn from her own experience, not just from listening to others or reading books. As the years go by, her experience grows. She learns directly about the real world from her successes and from her mistakes. Then when she has learned something, she does not repeat the "god's" words, nor does she transmit another's word. Now she knows what she herself has learned directly, and she says, "I say to you...." If she has learned well, she speaks what is true. That is like the way of wisdom.

We shall, in what follows, often use the term "wisdom" to indicate a tradition or mind-set, but in doing so we shall also speak of "wisdom traditions," in the plural. This is to call attention to the fact that such wisdom takes differing forms with a life of their own. For example, some biblical wisdom is likely a product of an educated elite, perhaps linked with the royal court (Solomon, Hezekiah), yet other biblical wisdom is more likely attributed to folk wisdom, which is characteristic of nonliterate (oral/aural) cultures or peasant societies, as Carole Fontaine and Friedemann Golka have shown.[14] Literate wisdom and nonliterate folk wis-

---

13. Brueggemann, in *The Creative Word*, uses the canonical approach to distinguish three characteristic approaches to education in the Hebrew Bible. The illustration that follows is drawn from a presentation by Balmer Kelly, professor of Bible at Union Theological Seminary in Virginia, audiotaped in class presentations in the summer of 1979 at the Presbyterian School of Christian Education, Richmond, Va.

14. Carole R. Fontaine, *Traditional Sayings in the Old Testament: A Contextual Study*, Bible and Literature Series 3 (Sheffield: Almond, 1982); Friedemann W.

dom can coexist within a culture and complement or conflict with each other.

Under the influence of Augustine, "wisdom" became a Christian theological principle. For Augustine, wisdom was not a human achievement but a gift of grace, a way of knowing the divine, whose crowning glory was not participation in civic and political life, but beatific contemplation of things divine. Aquinas allowed more room for natural human ability, and allowed metaphysics and natural theology also to be seen as wisdom, rather than restricting it solely to the grace of special revelation. Then, through their rediscovery of the ancient Greeks, renaissance writers again humanized and moralized the notion of wisdom, seeing it less as a contemplative ideal or as knowledge, and more as an active moral and civic virtue expressed in the governmental, political, and business life of the times.[15]

Somehow, somewhere, between the sixteenth and the twentieth century wisdom as an ideal has been seriously diminished.

Many features of contemporary life inhibit our taking wisdom seriously. For instance, the dominance of a scientific approach to everything places a high value on specialization, efficiency, progress, and novelty and simultaneously makes it difficult to value what is old, traditional, or inefficient. In religious scholarship, such dominance has taken the form of a fundamental commitment to the historical approach. In this century, neoorthodox theology claimed that what makes the Judeo-Christian tradition distinctive from other religions of the world is the presence of a "God who acts in history." But the categories of (prophetic) history make little sense in a biblical wisdom tradition that never refers to either a "God who acts" or to any of the events of a salvation history.

Old Testament scholars like John Bright and G. Ernest Wright, who have taken the historical as the essential distinctive feature of Israel's understanding of reality, have seen the wisdom materials as an anomaly in the Bible, as peripheral or questionable, for they did not fit prophetic and historical faith.[16] Others dismissed wisdom on more explicitly theological grounds, such as Walther Eichrodt, who saw it as "only loosely connected with religious faith," or H. D.

Golka, *The Leopard's Spots: Biblical and African Wisdom in Proverbs* (Edinburgh: T. and T. Clark, 1993). See also Claus Westermann, *Roots of Wisdom: The Oldest Proverbs of Israel and Other Peoples* (Louisville: Westminster/John Knox, 1995).

15. Rice, *The Renaissance Idea of Wisdom,* chaps. 1 and 2.

16. John Bright, *The Authority of the Old Testament* (Nashville: Abingdon, 1967), 136; and G. Ernest Wright, *God Who Acts* (London: SCM, 1952), 103.

Preuss, who denounced the wisdom tradition as "theologically illegitimate" and a "foreign body within the Old Testament."[17] On
the other hand, wisdom texts have been adopted by some as useful tools in a nonhistorical dogmatism, a theology suited to a God
who is eternal, unchanging, and who transcends history.

Modern society, with its commitment to progress and novelty,
its hurried fascination with youth, and its suspicion of anything
old (including old people), makes it difficult to find time to reflect, ponder, and wonder. In such a climate, wisdom is unlikely
to flourish. Even in the domain of contemporary schooling, despite
a natural affinity with a tradition that cares deeply about education, there is likely to be resistance to biblical wisdom's lessons
since there is little evidence that wisdom could be an "outcome"
of a standardized curriculum. In addition, schools may resist wisdom's expectation of practice in the ordinary world of everyday life
in the community and its insistence upon virtues such as silence,
reflection, reverence, and humility.

CAN WE BRIDGE THE GAP OF TIME AND CULTURE?

We will examine literary texts, but the culture within which they
functioned was dominantly oral/aural. Most Israelites (like most
people in the ancient world) were illiterate.[18] They communicated
not by texts but in face-to-face relations using the spoken word.
Indeed, the basic wisdom form, the proverb, is primarily an oral
phenomenon. Recent developments in linguistics, anthropology,
and literary studies have helped those of us who take literacy for
granted recognize what a profound difference literacy makes.[19]

---

17. W. Eichrodt, *Theology of the Old Testament* (Philadelphia: Westminster,
1967), 2:81, and H. D. Preuss, in his *Einführung in die alttestamentliche Weisheits-
literatur* (Stuttgart: Kohlhammer, 1987), both cited by Roland E. Murphy, *The Tree
of Life: An Exploration of the Biblical Wisdom Literature* (New York: Doubleday,
1990), 121.

18. William V. Harris, *Ancient Literacy* (Cambridge: Harvard University Press,
1989), estimates only 10 percent literacy.

19. Much of what follows is indebted primarily (unless otherwise specified)
to Walter Ong, *Orality and Literacy: The Technologizing of the Word* (London:
Methuen, 1982), especially the first four chapters. See also Ong's *The Presence of
the Word: Some Prolegomena for Cultural and Religious History* (New Haven: Yale
University Press, 1967); Werner Kelber, *The Oral and Written Gospel: The Her-
meneutics of Speaking and Writing in the Synoptic Tradition, Mark, Paul, and Q*
(Philadelphia: Fortress, 1983); and Paul J. Achtemeier, "*Omne Verbum Sonat*: The
New Testament and the Oral Environment of Late Western Antiquity," *Journal of
Biblical Literature* 109:1 (1990), 3–27.

In a literate culture, people tend to think of words as marks on a page. Words are all there at once, filling space; we can study them. And if we do not remember them, we can look them up again. In an oral/aural culture, words are necessarily sounds, not visual objects. Sound words come one at a time, in order. When a word has passed, it is gone unless it is remembered. Sound words cannot be studied like written words, so memory is more important in an oral culture. There are no libraries or reference works except those that exist in people's memories. In a literate world, if I want words, I can find a book and read silently. In a sound word world, if there are to be words, some power (a speaker) must be present to produce the sound. Thus an oral/aural culture presumes and requires face-to-face presence in a way that a literate world does not. Indeed, even reading usually begins as an oral/aural process.

In a sound word world, most of my words depend upon the physical presence and cooperation of others. That necessarily means I cannot control the words the way a reader can choose to open or close a book and go back over them as often as he chooses. This ability in a literate world to study things is what makes possible careful analytical distinctions, clarity, and abstraction. It also leads to a desire for novelty and a denigration of repetition. On the other hand, in an oral world, brevity, repetition, metaphor, and the timely use of alliteration and assonance help ensure remembering. For example, the familiar proverb "Look before you leap" is memorable because it is brief, repeats the *l* sound, and uses interesting metaphors ("leap" is not meant literally) and because we have heard it in contexts in which its use helps makes sense or offers counsel. This latter is what is called the proverb's *performance context*, that is, the proverb performs or is passed on and learned by its use or performance within a particular social interaction, which also conveys and specifies the message or meaning of the proverb.[20] We learn and know what "Look before you leap" means because we have heard it used when someone was about to do something impulsively, without considering possible consequences. Apart from such timely social use, the saying can seem trite or meaningless.

Listening, unlike reading, is also intrinsically a public affair, for the sound must be "out there" to be heard. So a congregation or a class or an audience is those gathered to listen collectively, as a

---

20. See the careful study by Fontaine, *Traditional Sayings in the Old Testament*, 48–53.

group, bound together by attention to a common source. Reading, on the other hand, separates rather than unites. There is no collective word for readers.

We who are schooled in literate societies tend to forget how small a minority we are in both time and the present world.[21] We also tend to forget that the bulk of what we know, especially what we know how to do in living our everyday lives, we, too, have learned and confirmed orally and experientially, rather than from reading. Much of what we do daily continues to make use of orally acquired learning. We seldom look to "special revelation" or literary productions to provide us with the know-how we need to brush our teeth or to drive our automobile, to make sense of conversations, or even to learn to use computers. So we say, "My mother always said . . . " or "As Grandpa often said . . . ," or our children say, "My teacher said. . . . " We repeat these sayings not only out of nostalgia or a sense of tradition but because while they have been gleaned from the past, from an authority with experience, they have been confirmed in our experience as true. Our oral and experiential traditions continue to live alongside and amongst our more self-conscious literary accomplishments.

Similarly, the biblical wisdom materials, while literary products, often reflect the spirit of an oral culture. For example, the phrase "Listen, my child" occurs often in Proverbs, despite the fact that it must now be read, not heard. Biblical wisdom materials retain an interest in ordinary, everyday living and how to make sense of the events that occur in our lives and also presume that readers will be familiar with traditional material likely acquired orally. They also presume educational patterns characteristic of oral cultures.

WHAT ARE OUR TASKS AND METHODS?

How does an educator explore the interface of biblical traditions with educational concerns? We know too little about Israel's early pedagogical practices to historically reconstruct them. Clearly we cannot proceed with the naivete of the earlier quests for the historical Jesus and his teaching methods (or those of the sages). Most scholars would agree that we cannot write a history of education

---

21. Ong, citing Munro Edmondson, reports that of the thousands of languages that have existed in human history, only 106 have been sufficiently committed to writing to have produced a literature. Of the 300 spoken languages that exist today, only 78 have a literature. Ong, *Orality and Literacy*, 7.

for the first century (let alone earlier) because we have insufficient evidence. Still, three things can be said.

First, biblical wisdom borrowed from other cultures of the Middle East, and we do know something about their educational patterns.[22] Perhaps Israel's ways were analogous. However, such analogies might also mislead, for Israel borrowed selectively and often transformed what it did borrow.

Second, just because ancient sages did (or did not do) something is not, in itself, a reason for us to do it today. For example, for centuries, sages and other teachers used physical beatings as a familiar and accepted form of instructional discipline. Should we follow suit? Ancient schoolmasters used tedious rote memorization and oral recitation. Should we? Jesus was an itinerant teacher in sandals making up parables. Should today's teachers imitate him? If so, how? by wearing sandals, by becoming itinerant, or by making up stories? On what basis do we judge which practices should be followed and which should be improved upon? On the other hand, if neither the sages nor Jesus left explicit instructions about pedagogical procedures, perhaps what methods we use is not so important. No matter what we know of earlier practices, we still must make our own value decisions about what and how to teach today.

Third, the lack of direct historical evidence about ancient pedagogical practices may not be as decisive as it first appears. We do have texts that the sages used for educational purposes, and those texts permit some cautious inferences about teaching and learning if we look with care. Surprisingly, pedagogical questions have seldom been asked of these texts. If we ask the questions, what might we expect to learn for educational ministry? Clearly, we should not expect quick-fix solutions to today's problems. This study will not result in a program with which to reform the church's educational ministry.

How can a dialogue between pedagogy and biblical texts proceed so that each has a fair opportunity to say what is most important to it while being heard by the other? We need to provide

---

22. See especially McKane's introduction to the instructional genres of Egyptian and Babylonian-Assyrian literature in *Proverbs*, 51–208. Also Ronald J. Williams, "Scribal Training in Ancient Egypt," *Journal of the American Oriental Society* 92 (1972), 214–21. Andre Lemaire adds archaeological evidence and extensive bibliographical notes in "The Sage in School and Temple," in *The Sage in Israel and the Ancient Near East*, ed. John G. Gammie and Leo G. Perdue (Winona Lake, Ind.: Eisenbrauns, 1990), 165–81.

critical rigor in our study, yet remain hospitable to our educational interests by identifying questions we bring as educators to these texts. Therefore, rather than using historical methods to try to recover the pedagogical practices used by the sages or Jesus, we shall use something like a *transcendental method* (though without the Kantian overtones of necessity). We begin with the texts we have, not with historical reconstruction. The wisdom texts often use certain characteristic literary forms and devices (e.g., proverbial sayings) as they present their observations about life. Thus we can ask, (*a*) What do the literary forms of these texts, as well as their content, presuppose, entail, or imply about reader-learners and about learning and teaching processes? (*b*) Are some teaching-learning approaches more suitable than others for these texts or more likely to foster engagement with particular themes? We shall not assume that because they are suitable, they are therefore necessary. Nor shall we make historical claims that ancient teachers used educational methods familiar in later centuries. We shall not even assume that these teachers were more consistent than today's teachers. Using this approach, we can focus upon the texts we have and what they require or expect of reader-learners.

In order to focus upon pedagogy, we shall use variants of an approach that, in literary studies, is called *reader-response criticism*. We shall not confine ourselves strictly to any one version of this variegated approach, though the work of Stanley Fish and Wolfgang Iser have been instructive.[23] A "readerly approach" (to use David Clines's felicitous term)[24] seeks to bring readers explicitly into the process of interpreting texts and to slow down the reading process so we can attend carefully to what a text expects of and does to readers in the process of reading. Such an approach can help us identify the demands the text places upon

---

23. The best introduction (with annotated bibliography) to the various proponents and principles of this approach is Jane P. Tompkins, ed., *Reader-Response Criticism: From Formalism to Post-Structuralism* (Baltimore: Johns Hopkins University Press, 1980), see especially the introduction and chap. 12 for a historical review. An interesting critical introduction to literary criticism as a whole is Terry Eagleton, *Literary Theory: An Introduction* (Minneapolis: University of Minnesota Press, 1983).

24. See David A. J. Clines, *What Does Eve Do to Help? and Other Readerly Questions of the Old Testament* (Sheffield: JSOT, 1990). Readers will also find examples of Clines's use of this approach in his commentary *Job 1–20*, WBC 17 (Dallas: Word Books, 1989). Stephen D. Moore critically reviews use of these approaches in New Testament studies in *Literary Criticism and the Gospels: The Theoretical Challenge* (New Haven: Yale University Press, 1989).

reader-learners and what the text assumes about reader-learners.[25]
It stresses the interaction of text-subject and learner-subject, since
the teacher/author is now resident only in the text. A readerly approach is quite consistent with how we must now engage wisdom
texts whose original author is anonymous (or is a community),
where even the most adept scholars cannot reconstruct a particular
historical-cultural context with any confidence.

Are we asking questions of these texts that they cannot answer?
Perhaps. While these texts are pedagogical, they never directly reflect upon their own pedagogy. So we are about to ask questions
for which there are no direct answers in the text. That is a risk
most readers of ancient texts must take. If we do not take that
risk, we confine the text to its own time. One corrective is to allow
the texts to question us back. We may, living in our time and culture, ask questions and have expectations that lead us astray. If we
listen carefully, we may find in these texts new questions that are
even more fruitful than our original ones.

In this procedure, I am assuming (correctly, I think) that these
texts are not closed but open. Biblical texts have often been
thought to be closed, that is, "a complete, completed literary object
containing a defined set of words in a specific order with a single,
definitive, discoverable meaning."[26] Clearly some texts do intend
such control by their authors. But many wisdom texts seek more
to evoke than command. Even when they command, they play with
the minds and hearts of reader-learners and expect reader-learners
to bring something to the text and do something with it.

Our method is quite simple. We will ask each text four basic
pedagogical questions, questions that have been asked as long as
learning and teaching have existed.

1. What is worth learning? This question, addressing what we might
   now call *curriculum content*, has usually been asked in the form,
   What is worth teaching? Since our texts are focally concerned that
   the reader learn and/or construct something that may be said indirectly or not said at all, we will seek what the text expects the
   reader-learner to find worthwhile learning, assuming that it also is
   worth teaching.

---

25. One implication of this methodological decision should be mentioned,
though it is obvious. Since I must presume the learners in question are readers,
perhaps even thoughtful readers, I shall pay no attention to learning among the
very young. I make this explicit because many assume that educational ministry is
something largely for the young.

26. Edwin M. Good, *In Turns of Tempest: A Reading of Job* (Stanford, Calif.:
Stanford University Press, 1990), 179.

2. How is that to be learned? This question addresses what we now call *methodology*. We shall not assume, as these texts also do not assume, there is always one right way or even one best way to do it. We may discover contemporary approaches that are more consistent with ancient texts than the pedagogical practices most familiar in that time in history.

3. Why learn and teach? Or what is the point in engaging in the kind of learning and teaching characteristic of how these texts affect readers? We might now call this line of questioning *aims*.

4. What counts as education? Addressing what we might call *conceptual study*, this question seeks to determine what kind of educational approach is characteristic of the biblical wisdom traditions and whether there are ways to view the educational enterprise as a whole that fit the wisdom texts. It will be addressed in the last chapter.

All through this study, we seek to be responsible both to biblical scholarship and also to pedagogical inquiry, but we are using biblical scholarship for the sake of pedagogical understanding. This may mean readers interested in biblical texts will find much more pedagogy than is usual in biblical studies and those interested in pedagogy will find more biblical study than is usual in pedagogical texts. Like wisdom, this text is necessarily interdisciplinary. Wisdom texts typically make readers stretch. As we have noted, wisdom texts are interested in learning in real life, and life does not occur in segments marked off in accordance with the categories of scholarly disciplines.

The way in which we ask these questions of a text will vary with the style of a particular text. Since the proverb is so basic to this whole tradition, we shall begin with the Book of Proverbs and then move chronologically through other texts. You, the reader, are invited along on this journey through the thickets. Perhaps we can discover together some of what the wisdom tradition meant then and what significance it might have for educational ministry now — maybe.

Why maybe? Listening to the sages encourages humility. The sages of old struggled with difficult questions. They experienced recurrent surprises, pervasive wonder, and mystery. And often they were not taken seriously about matters that were of ultimate seriousness. Should we expect less?

A caution about reading: Proverbial sayings and wisdom texts are not meant to be quickly skimmed. Here the hurried pace of contemporary life misleads. We must learn to slow down our reading. In what follows, it is important that you pause — examine the biblical texts — don't simply scan through to the conclusions of the author. Don't try to read long sections; think through each proverbial saying before going on. Learn to pay attention more closely and more slowly. This text may be slow going, but according to the sages wisdom takes time. It is unwise to be impatient!

Michael V. Fox's feelings about Ecclesiastes suit this text as well:

> [T]here is tremendous interpretive pressure to raise the valleys and lower the hills, to make the way straight and level before the reader. But a reading faithful to this book, at least, should try to describe the territory with all its bumps and clefts, for they are not merely flaws, but the essence of the landscape.[27]

---

27. Fox, *Qohelet and His Contradictions*, 28.

CHAPTER ONE

"LISTEN, MY CHILD"
Proverbs

The Book of Proverbs, the oldest biblical collection of wisdom, is not an easy book to read through. There is no story line or plot and little structural or thematic cohesion. Actually, the Book of Proverbs is not a book at all, but a collection of collections of sayings. So before we focus upon what is and is not being taught in Proverbs, we need to form some picture of these texts.

WHAT KIND OF TEXTS ARE THESE?

The texts of Proverbs are poetry, not prose; proverbial sayings, not narratives; and they are literary productions, not folk proverbs. While Archer Taylor's classic 1931 study *The Proverb* insisted it is impossible to give *the* definition of "proverb,"[1] one contemporary definition captures some essential features: "A proverb is a short, generally known sentence of the folk which contains wisdom, truth, morals and traditional views in a metaphorical, fixed and memorizable form and which is handed down from generation to generation."[2] This description is especially apt for the one-line proverb, or *folk saying*.

While biblical proverbs sometimes feel alien today, we are familiar with the use of proverbial sayings: "How time flies!" "Practice makes perfect." "Out of sight, out of mind." "All that glitters is not gold." "Better late than never." We know what such proverbs mean because we know how they will function in some context. "Practice makes perfect," for example, may encourage a child who is tiring of doing the same task over and over. Today, advertising

---

1. Archer Taylor, *The Proverb* (Cambridge: Harvard University Press, 1931), cited by Wolfgang Mieder, *Proverbs Are Never out of Season: Popular Wisdom in the Modern Age* (New York: Oxford University Press, 1993), 4.
2. Mieder, *Proverbs Are Never out of Season*, 5.

slogans often are used proverbially, such as, "Just do it" or "You only go around once."[3] Advertising pioneer Fred Barnard actually invented the saying "A picture is worth a thousand words," describing it as a Chinese proverb to increase its credibility.[4]

Folk wisdom or *folk proverbs* are typically oral and often expressed in pithy single-line sayings (see Gen. 10:9 or Jer. 13:23) in parable-like stories (see the political impact of Jotham's fable in Judg. 9:8–15). The meaning of such sayings, when written, is largely determined by their performance in the narrative context.[5] For example, David, trying to convince King Saul he meant him no harm, cut off the skirt of Saul's robe while he slept. When he showed it to Saul later, David said, "As the ancient proverb says, 'Out of the wicked comes forth wickedness'; but my hand shall not be against you" (1 Sam. 24:13). David used the proverb to reassure Saul concerning his intentions. David says, in effect, "It is not in my nature or character to be wicked, and therefore I am no danger to you." Here the *context* determines the proverb's meaning, for were David not holding the corner of Saul's garment to show that he could have harmed Saul but did not, the same saying could be read as a threat.

While some sayings in Proverbs may have been expanded from oral folk sayings, most are *literary wisdom*, some of which are arranged in thematic groupings or longer poems. However, most are single two-line poetic sayings, and unlike folk sayings, there is no narrative context to help determine meaning.

All the older wisdom texts, except Ecclesiastes, are written in poetry form, so we must understand something about Hebrew poetry and also appreciate the pedagogical implications of poetic form:

> In general, poetry makes up in allusiveness what it lacks in precision ... [for] it is deliberately formulated in such a way as to permit a variety of interpretations and applications which go beyond its "literal" meaning but which are equally legitimate and which make it relevant to different circumstances and different ages. ... It may also be that the authority of the wisdom instruction and the wisdom proverb depend less on logic and argument than on persuasion through the actual forms of the language which they use: the per-

---

3. Ibid., 68–72.
4. Ibid., 137–40.
5. See the excellent study by Carole R. Fontaine, *Traditional Sayings in the Old Testament: A Contextual Study*, Bible and Literature Series 3 (Sheffield: Almond, 1982).

suasive power lay in the sound of the words themselves, and in the pictures which they created in the mind of the listener.[6]

Hebrew Biblical Poetry

The poetry we find in the Hebrew Bible was formed by two, or sometimes three, parallel lines marked by rhythmic beats and often by alliteration and assonance, rather than by rhyme, as we expect in English. Thus, even though written, these lines expect to be spoken and heard, to be performed.

These paired lines take several different forms. Sometimes they are *synonymous* or complementary. That is, the second line says much the same as the first, as though reinforcing the first line's meaning by varying the expression. Most sayings in Proverbs 16–22 are synonymous in form, as is this example from Proverbs 16:16:

> How much better to get wisdom than gold!
> To get understanding is to be chosen rather than silver.

"How much better" leads readers to expect a comparison, but when wisdom is compared with gold, it may evoke surprise and puzzlement. First, there may be surprise that reader-learners are expected to compare things that are measured differently — gold is commonly measured quantitatively, while wisdom is measured qualitatively. How are they to be compared then? We might know some ways to get gold, but how does one get wisdom? Second, assuming reader-learners are young, are they really expected to value gold less than something as intangible as wisdom? Clearly these values belong to the world of the teacher or the sage, and readers are being invited to share them. We know gold and what it is good for, but what is wisdom, and what is it good for?

In the second line, reader-learners find these values are not simply conferred (as in "get") but are chosen. Here the pedagogical implication is not simply that wisdom and understanding are chosen by the community, though that may be true, but they are "to be chosen." This choosing is yet to come. Indeed, reader-learners are expected to do the choosing. So two brief and relatively straightforward lines can evoke considerable effort and thought for reader-learners, even when the two lines mean much the same thing.

---

6. R. N. Whybray, *Proverbs*, New Century Bible Commentary (Grand Rapids: Eerdmans, 1994), 13.

Sometimes the two lines of a poetic saying oppose or contrast with each other, so the second line reinforces the sense of the first by contrast or by opposition. (Most sayings in Proverbs 10–15 are of the contrasting or *antithetical* form.)

> The lips of the righteous feed many,
> but fools die for lack of sense. (Prov. 10:21)

Notice the surprise evoked by the reversal of expectations of "lips." Lips are used to take in food, but here they are said to "feed" or nurture. So immediately we know we are in the land of metaphor: we are not really talking about lips, but of what comes out of the lips — words. The image here is perhaps that of a mother bird who feeds her young from beak to beak. Those who are "righteous" nurture or strengthen others with what they say.

The second line reinforces this notion by contrast and by heightening the effect. First, the "righteous" are compared, not with the unrighteous or sinners, but with "fools." In the wisdom texts, "wise" and "fool" are often polar opposites, and the fool is regarded as the equivalent of the sinner. The sages assume it is wrong to be foolish. We are responsible for lacking sense. Second, the image of the mother bird feeding her young is completed, for we expect that if she does not feed her young, they will die, for they depend on her. But the image is reversed. The lips or words of the fool are not said to lead to the death of others, but the fools themselves "die for lack of sense." This contrast also heightens the impact of the saying, for it is not just a bland comment upon how good it is to help others. This is a life or death matter. Life or death for whom? It could be a teacher or a learner or anyone who has the potential to be a fool. The stakes are high!

Sometimes the second line of a poetic saying, rather than saying the same or opposing the first, will extend, complete, or intensify the thought of the first:

> Bread gained by deceit is sweet,
> but afterward the mouth will be full of gravel. (Prov. 20:17)

Here the second line is a sharp, vivid picture with perhaps a more harsh effect than the first line might have led the reader to expect. Notice that the harmful effect of deceit is described as falling, not on those being deceived, but on the one doing the deceiving. So these instructional sayings evoke thought but also serve to warn reader-learners.

Pedagogically, notice *how* these sayings express thought and stimulate learning. The first line of each saying can express a complete thought. The second line is never identical, yet they form a couplet; they are intended for each other. Does this suggest that every complete thought comes in at least two versions? Or does it suggest that each thought is naturally seen from two points of view or framed in two equally "right" expressions of truth? Or does it mean that as a couplet these differences will form a single more complex and nuanced thought? Perhaps the form itself invites all three interpretations. So without the text or the teacher saying so directly, reader-learners come to understand there may be no one final formulation that settles the matter.

Wolfgang Iser, the literary critic, speaks of "gaps left by the text itself" that require readers to create connections to "fill in the gaps."[7] This is an apt description of how proverbs work. The reader must decide not only what each phrase means but also how those phrases constitute a meaningful single line and then how the paired lines relate with one another. Does the first line determine the framework within which the second line must be understood? Does the second alter the significance of the first? The poetic text does not so much "communicate a precise concept or judgment, prepackaged as it were" but "provoke thought rather than supply answers."[8] Since the gaps between the phrases and the lines can be filled in different ways, each text and saying are "potentially capable of several different realizations, and no reading can ever exhaust the full potential."[9] So even if a teacher dictates the text aloud to be memorized, and does so in an authoritative manner, the text itself suggests, "Now look at it this other way as well." That also invites the notion of *contest*, with its oral argumentation and confrontation, which is a prominent feature of education in an oral culture.[10]

Longer Wisdom Poems

The Book of Proverbs opens with a series of ten extended poems (Prov. 1–9; though 22:17–24:34 and chaps. 25–31 are also longer poems). Here a larger thematic frame helps shape the meaning

---

7. Wolfgang Iser, "The Reading Process: A Phenomenological Approach," in *Reader-Response Criticism: From Formalism to Post-Structuralism*, ed. Jane P. Tompkins (Baltimore: Johns Hopkins University Press, 1980), 55. My attention was directed to this text by the provocative study by Elizabeth F. Huwiler, "Control of Reality in Israelite Wisdom" (Ph.D. diss., Duke University, 1988).

8. Dermot Cox, *Proverbs: With an Introduction to Sapiential Books* (Wilmington, Del.: M. Glazier, 1982), 11.

9. Iser, "The Reading Process," 55.

10. See Walter Ong, *Fighting for Life: Contest, Sexuality, and Consciousness* (Ithaca, N.Y.: Cornell University Press, 1981).

of each couplet. These longer units are often explicitly instructional, intended to teach the young to follow the right path and to avoid evil.

In these poems, the reader-learner is often urged to pay attention, much teaching and learning language occurs, and reasons or motives are often offered for behaving a certain way. The language is often imperative, the language of command, with the familiar feel of classroom or parental instruction. Here learners are told what to do (or more often, what not to do).

Individual Sayings

In Proverbs 10:1–22:16 the tone is quite different. Here most of the couplets are independent of one another, rather than connected thematically. There are no admonitions to learn or listen and few commands. More often in these chapters we find indicative or descriptive statements, pithy observations about what reality is like, with little moralizing or direct persuasion. For example,

> Well meant are the wounds a friend inflicts,
>   but profuse are the kisses of an enemy. (Prov. 27:6)

Is this a warning or just an astute observation? It seems to be gleaned from bitter experience of the different kinds of hurts friends and enemies can inflict and so might help one discern the intentions of another more accurately. Yet there is nothing in the saying or the context to tell the reader-learner when or how to use it. It simply reports, "This is how things are. Watch."

> A soft answer turns away wrath,
>   but a harsh word stirs up anger. (Prov. 15:1)

As a teaching, this is indirect instruction at best. A reader might conclude either "If I want to avoid anger, here is one way" or "If I want to provoke anger, here is a recipe."

ARE THESE COLLECTIONS EDUCATIONALLY SIGNIFICANT?

In Proverbs, pedagogical language occurs over and over again. This may not imply schools, as it usually does today, but it does suggest conscious pedagogical intent. This is vividly clear in the opening verses of Proverbs:

> The proverbs of Solomon son of David, king of Israel:
> For learning about wisdom and instruction,
>   for understanding words of insight,

> for gaining instruction in wise dealing,
>   righteousness, justice, and equity;
> to teach shrewdness to the simple,
>   knowledge and prudence to the young —
> let the wise also hear and gain in learning,
>   and the discerning acquire skill,
> to understand a proverb and a figure,
>   the words of the wise and their riddles.
> The fear of the LORD is the beginning of knowledge;
>   fools despise wisdom and instruction. (Prov. 1:1–7)

This text seems to draw a reader up through the lines to a climactic statement of intent in verse 5, continuing on a plateau in verse 6, then settling gently onto firm ground in verse 7. Here the teachers state that learning proverbs will impart knowledge (content?), discernment (an ability or skill?), and understanding, so the "simple" or ignorant can learn to be less simple, overcome their ignorance, and thus act and live prudently, justly, and wisely (thus laying foundations for a righteous social order). Proverbs (and teachers of proverbs) also offer "gain" and "skill" to those already wise, no matter their age, what today we might call *lifelong learning*.

We also see here again the sages' love of wordplay. In contemporary literature, repetition is regarded as boring, and expansive or flowery language is avoided. Here repetitive and expansive language is used to heighten impressiveness. Now we value conceptual clarity and precision, while the ancient sages often preferred to "circle around a subject," as though to throw light on it from all sides by variations on the theme. Here in five verses, we are told what wisdom is or entails fourteen different ways. Reader-learners are not expected to easily or quickly read this text, which virtually requires reading, rereading, and pondering. Even the form of the text, with its clauses climbing "upward," lures a reader-learner to exert sustained effort toward a complex wisdom that no one simple summation or slogan can encompass.

Several technical terms appear here for intellectual activities: learners study proverbs, figures (or epigrams), the sayings of other sages, and riddles so they can enhance their skills of discernment, or in the wording of another translation,[11] to learn "to be adroit" (v. 5b) and for "acquiring the discipline for success" (v. 2b). This is very intentional activity, wherever it occurs.

---

11. The New Jewish Publication Society Version, 1988.

In What Settings Might Proverb Learning Naturally Occur?

There are few direct descriptions of where proverbial collections were used, so much of what follows is based upon either inferences from the text or from historical reconstruction.

FAMILY. The recurrent phrase "Hear, my son" (RSV) or "my child" (NRSV; see Prov. 1:8, 10, 15; 2:1; 3:1, 11; 4:1, 10; and others) sometimes refers to parental counsel:

> Hear, my child, your father's instruction,
>   and do not reject your mother's teaching. (Prov. 1:8)

A familial setting for wisdom instruction is clearly depicted in the second-century Book of Tobit.[12] Tobit is a colorful "book of pious fiction" intended to "provide religious and moral instruction in the form of an adventure story."[13] In the fourth chapter, Tobit, who is poor, blind, and expecting to die, prepares his son Tobias for a journey by giving him moral instruction about how to live, punctuated with imperatives and by repetition of "Remember, my son." Tobit urges his son to remember the Lord and his commandments and concludes saying, "So now, my child, remember . . . [my] commandments, and do not let them be erased from your heart" (4:19). Tobias is to remember both God's and his father's commandments.

These familial settings for instruction are quite ordinary, but in a society where there is little literacy, almost all significant instruction is done orally and informally, as everyday life gives occasion. (Indeed, this is also true even in a literate society.) Special occasions and celebrations — such as births, deaths, marriages, anniversaries, reunions, holidays, and festivals — all bring forth memories and provide occasions for sharing traditions. Such learning is not only cognitively fruitful; it is a rich, holistic, embodied, sensory, and emotional experience that makes for lasting memories.

SCHOOLS. The phrase "my child" in Proverbs is ambiguous and could be used as a form of address by a teacher acting *in loco*

---

12. Tobit, part of what is called the *Apocrypha*, was apparently very popular, since there are versions in Greek, Latin, Syriac, Hebrew, Ethiopic, and Aramaic. Fragments were found at Qumran as well. It was widely used among Christians during marriage ceremonies beginning as early as 1085 in England and was used in the wedding of King Louis IX of France in 1234. Luther praised Tobit highly, and it was used in Protestant traditions as diverse as the original Book of Common Prayer (1594) and the Old Order Amish of the U.S. See Bruce M. Metzger, *An Introduction to the Apocrypha* (New York: Oxford, 1957), 31–41.

13. Ibid., 31.

parentis. For example, one who has been complaining is warned, "And now, my child, listen to me":

> You say, "Oh, how I hated discipline,
> and my heart despised reproof!
> I did not listen to the voice of my teachers
> or incline my ear to my instructors.
> Now I am at the point of utter ruin
> in the public assembly." (Prov. 5:7, 12–14)

Clearly the text here assumes a school context of some sort, but what kind of school?

During the early centuries of Israel's life, what we now would call *informal pedagogy* was dominant. Indeed, there is little firm biblical or archeological evidence that schools even existed in Israel until about the second century B.C.E., well after the period in which the wisdom texts were written. Even two hundred years later, in the time of Jesus, it is doubtful that schools existed widely, despite the regulations concerning such schools in later rabbinic sources.[14] Yet some scholars insist that we can infer that schools existed from texts like that above, from archeological evidence, and mostly by inference from Israel's neighbors, who influenced Israel in so many ways.[15]

---

14. The later rabbinic writings observe that Simeon ben Shetah (ca. 103–76 B.C.E.) ordered children to go to school, while the high priest Joshua (63–65 C.E.) ordered that teachers be appointed to elementary schools in every town and that children go to school at the age of six or seven. (Does their ordering it mean it was so? Or does it mean that they had to order it because it was not yet so?) Yet, if such schools existed, it is odd that neither Philo nor Josephus mentions them. See the judicious discussion by John P. Meier, *A Marginal Jew: Rethinking the Historical Jesus*, Anchor Bible Reference Library (New York: Doubleday, 1991), 1:271–78. See also William V. Harris, *Ancient Literacy* (Cambridge: Harvard University Press, 1989), who argues persuasively that literacy in the Graeco-Roman world was quite rare and limited to the elite. He estimates that even in classical Attica the literacy rate was no more than 10 percent (114).

15. See the ongoing debate between James L. Crenshaw, "Education in Ancient Israel," *Journal of Biblical Literature* 104:4 (December 1985), 601–15, who cautiously concludes that neither textual nor archeological evidence will permit us to confidently affirm there were schools; and Andre Lemaire, "Sagesse et ecoles," *Vetus Testamentum* 34 (1984), 270–81; "The Sage in School and Temple," in *The Sage in Israel and the Ancient Near East*, ed. John G. Gammie and Leo G. Perdue (Winona Lake, Ind.: Eisenbrauns, 1990), 165–81, who insists there is sufficient other evidence from which to conclude there must have been schools, despite the lack of direct textual evidence or description. See the recent review of the discussion by G. I. Davies, "Were There Schools in Ancient Israel?" in *Wisdom in Ancient Israel: Essays in Honour of J. A. Emerton*, ed. John Day, Robert P. Gordon, and H. G. M. Williamson (Cambridge: Cambridge University Press, 1995), 199–211. Bibliographies appear in each. All these scholars agree that if there were schools, they were few in number and for males only.

Even were we to assume there were schools in early days, they surely did not resemble today's classrooms. Sirach, a sage-teacher who lived several hundred years later than the time represented by the Book of Proverbs, advised pupils to attach themselves to someone who was wise and follow him (Sir. 6:34–36). This presumes that the learner chooses the teacher and thus has an ability to recognize "who is wise" or to "see an intelligent person." Thus, the text may assume the learner is at least an older child and also presumes the learner is diligent about learning and able to devote the time required to "attach yourself" (like an apprenticeship), perhaps unlikely for most children, whose labor was needed to help with daily chores. It is likely that whatever schools existed were most fully used by the wealthy (whose children had more leisure) and by those in the royal court. But even here, pedagogy proceeded more informally than today.

INFORMAL GATHERINGS. Another setting where proverbial sayings occur naturally is in the informal gathering of friends. In Hebrew, the *sodh* was "a sitting together, either of friends familiarly conversing or of judges consulting together," where intimate secrets could be shared.[16] In Israel, men gathered in the marketplace,

> where the concerns of the day could be discussed, where judgment was passed on injustice done; here people entertained each other with stories and songs . . . [and] exchanged their life-experiences, and took pleasure when such experiences found fitting expression in sayings, similes, riddles, jests and mockery.[17]

We could as easily picture this *sodh* today, a relaxed gathering over drinks, or we could imagine similar conversations among women at the village well or in the market. Proverbial sayings slide easily into such contexts, providing the well-worn comfort of familiar phrases, yet allowing for fresh applications, discernment, and even newly minted lines.

ROYAL COURT. The legendary "wisdom of Solomon" (e.g., 1 Kings 9–10) testifies to the presence of wisdom in Israel's royal court. There

---

16. H. W. F. Gesenius, *Hebrew and Chaldee Lexicon to the Old Testament Scriptures* (Grand Rapids: Baker, 1979), 580. The familiarity of such a gathering is clear from the term's also being used to refer to a pillow, cushion, or couch upon which persons recline in familiar conversation. See references to the nature of such gatherings in Jer. 6:11 and 15:17; Ps. 55:15; Job 15:8; 19:19; and esp. Job 29:4, where it is also used to describe nostalgically Job's former intimacy with God.

17. Annemarie Ohler, *Studying the Old Testament from Tradition to Canon* (Edinburgh: T. & T. Clark, 1985), 168.

are also numerous references to counselors or wise counselors offering advice to rulers, both in Israel and in Egypt (e.g., David in
2 Sam. 17 or Pharaoh in Isa. 19:11–12). And Proverbs 25:1 identifies those who copied (and collected?) the proverbs in chapters
25–29 as "the officials of King Hezekiah of Judah."

In other royal courts in the ancient Near East, there were
schools taught by court officials to train those who would themselves become officials, using wisdom and instruction texts in that
training. *The Instruction of Ptahhotep* and *Amenemhet*, two Egyptian texts that predate the biblical wisdom texts by a thousand
years, both purport to be advice from an elderly pharaoh to his
son and successor. Both texts were still being used as copying ex-
ercises for schoolboys a thousand years later.[18] It is possible that
similar activities took place in Israel. While no biblical text explicitly refers to court schools in Israel, some proverbial sayings may
presume the royal court as their setting (Prov. 25:2–7; 31:1–9).

Proverbial sayings could be learned and used in all four of these
settings, but we must remember that we now have texts, either
created anew or representing the literary residue of such settings.
Therefore, one additional setting for learning and using proverbs is
their place in a collection of texts.

TEXT AS CONTEXT. Individual proverbs often gain meaning not only
from their use in a social context but by being arranged in proximity with other sayings. When the literary context of a single saying
is a longer wisdom poem, as in the first nine chapters of Proverbs,
the process of interpretation is familiar. The developing sequence
of lines helps shape meaning.

The importance of literary context has been shown by the studies of Claudia Camp, who argues persuasively that Proverbs 1–9
and 31 serve as a literary framework for the collections of proverbial sayings in chapters 10–30. Camp, drawing upon the work of
Carole Fontaine, Paul Ricoeur, and Gerald Sheppard, explains that
independent proverbial sayings originally "make sense" as they are
"performed," but when they become literary texts, they are intrinsically more independent of their original social context and more
aligned with other texts, which become both text and context.[19]
Thus the longer poems of chapters 1–9 and 31, likely added later,

---

18. William McKane, *Proverbs: A New Approach* (Philadelphia: Westminster,
1970), 51, 83.

19. Claudia V. Camp, *Wisdom and the Feminine in the Book of Proverbs* Bible
and Literature Series 11 (Sheffield: Almond, JSOT, 1985), esp. chap. 6.

become an interpretive framework that brackets the other collections. For example, Proverbs opens with the mother's teaching of 1:8 and Woman Wisdom, a teacher (1:20–33; chaps. 4, 8–9), and closes with Lemuel's mother's teaching (31:1–9) and the woman of worth of 31:10–31, who teaches wisdom and kindness — calling attention to the role of women and teaching in this text.[20]

The same may be true of sayings that were originally independent couplets. Sometimes, it seems the sages placed sayings alongside one another for reasons unknown or for no reason, but sometimes they gathered sayings that are similar or complementary, and sometimes they juxtaposed sayings that seem contradictory. In each case, proximity can influence interpretation, and perhaps the sages had reasons (pedagogical?) for those placements that are not always apparent to us now.

Royal Courtiers as Proverb Collectors

Proverbial sayings were collected and preserved, perhaps reshaped, by royal officials as noted in 25:1 and 31:1. Traces of these origins can also be found in the various instructions about how to get along within the royal court (23:1–5; 25:2–7; 29:2, 4, 12–14, 16, 26–27). Some have argued that these texts reflect a bias governed by the interests of the court — a concern for preserving the status quo, for "law and order," for stability of social institutions. Such interests are prominent in these proverbial sayings — indeed, the first seven chapters are heavily oriented to preserving, as can be seen in these frequent refrains: "do not forget my teaching," "hold fast," "do not forget," "do not forsake," "hold on," "keep my words," wisdom will "guard" and "preserve" you, and so on. While such interests may well suit the interests of the court, they are also interests built into the very nature of proverbial sayings, whose function is to preserve what has been learned from the experience of those who have gone before. Proverbial sayings are intrinsically conserving, but they are also, by nature, metaphorical, so even reference to a king might well serve as a metaphor for anyone who is "high and mighty" in demeanor. While some proverbial texts could have been used to teach royal courtiers how to get along in court (e.g., see 25:2–7; 29:2, 4, 12–14, 16, 26–27), these texts also could be applied more generically. Not only do they lack the specifically vocational tone of many of the Egyptian texts for courtiers; they also show a candid awareness that the

---

20. Ibid., 186–91.

royal court was not always a good place to be — hardly an apology for life in the court (see esp. 25:1–10).

WHAT IS WORTH LEARNING? WHAT IS THE CONTENT OF WISDOM?

Proverbs are not simply "knowledge" in the contemporary sense of a list of things one might know or have in one's head. Proverbs are to be learned, even memorized; thus one can (and should) possess them in that sense. Yet knowing proverbs is not itself the point: "One does not learn *from* them but *by means of* them."[21] Still, in a largely nonliterate culture, proverbial sayings preserve and conserve what earlier generations have learned from their experience, observations, and reflections. Transmitting this lore is important both for survival of the culture and for forming the social identity of a people. Therefore, we can infer from these sayings what the sages considered worth learning. What follows are selected themes that are both fundamental to these texts and of pedagogical significance.

Creation, Order, Retribution, and Two Paths

Proverbs has been described as secular, though Israel could hardly imagine separating what is religious or sacred from what is secular. Proverbs seems more secular than other biblical books because neither God nor the cult appears often in the text and neither seems to do much.

Much theology portrays God as both Creator and Redeemer but insists upon the primacy of the *historical* quality of biblical faith (compared with other religions). Walter Brueggemann observes that when God is discerned only in the disruptions that come upon us in history, the side effect is to "devalue" ordinary daily living and human culture.[22] Roland Murphy insists, rightly in my view, that the traditional theological picture that judges wisdom from the vantage point of God's revelation in history is biased: "The basic assumption [of this bias] is that Israel's understanding of the Lord as working in the historical communal order is somehow more orthodox, more Yahwistic as it were, than her understanding of the Lord through nature or by human experience."[23] If history

---

21. Cox, *Proverbs*, 88 (italics in original).
22. Walter A. Brueggemann, *In Man We Trust: The Neglected Side of Biblical Faith* (Atlanta: John Knox, 1972), 27.
23. Roland Murphy, *The Tree of Life: An Exploration of the Biblical Wisdom Literature* (New York: Doubleday, 1990), 123.

(and thus narrative) is the normative center of biblical thought, poetry and Proverbs pose a problem for this paradigm, with several proposed solutions. H. D. Preuss simply declared wisdom to be "theologically illegitimate," while Walther Eichrodt saw wisdom as "only loosely connected with religious faith."[24] Gerhard von Rad depicted wisdom as "Israel's answer" to God's saving acts.[25] Claus Westermann speaks of the "two conceptual fields" of a saving God and a blessing God (who are nevertheless one).[26]

Samuel Terrien reversed this, subsuming history under wisdom, claiming that only a wisdom concept, such as "God as elusive presence," is comprehensive enough for a unified biblical theology.[27] Many today try to find ways to acknowledge how different poetic and proverbial wisdom is from prose and from historical or prophetic texts, while affirming their complementarity.[28] God was as much at work in the concrete details of everyday life "as in the heady experiences of Israel's history and liturgical worship."[29] In Proverbs, the covenant relation is not denied, only bracketed, while the sages sought lessons in their experience of God's world.[30]

Granted the covenant relation is important in the dialogue with God, the dialogue between Israelite and environment (human and "natural") is also a dialogue with God. In Proverbs, humans are trusted to exercise dominion, which includes being responsible for helping creation and community live and thrive, and that takes place in history as well. What does Proverbs think is worth learning from this dialogue with the environment?

THE MORAL ORDER AND RETRIBUTION. The prophets helped people "order their living" by reminding them of the stories and lessons of history — Sinai, exodus, and covenant. The sages drew analogies between items in the created world and human behavior (clouds, vinegar, wind, rain, promises, laziness, and so on), suggesting patterns or similarities that order our understanding and behavior.

---

24. Ibid., 121–22, where Murphy briefly surveys these issues.

25. Gerhard von Rad, *Old Testament Theology* (New York: Harper, 1962), 1:355.

26. Claus Westermann, *Elements of Old Testament Theology* (Atlanta: John Knox, 1982), 114.

27. Samuel Terrien, *The Elusive Presence: Toward a New Biblical Theology* (San Francisco: Harper and Row, 1978).

28. Carole R. Fontaine, "Wisdom in Proverbs," in *In Search of Wisdom: Essays in Memory of John G. Gammie*, ed. L. Perdue, B. B. Scott, and W. J. Wiseman (Louisville: Westminster/John Knox, 1993), 111.

29. Murphy, *The Tree of Life*, 124.

30. Ibid.

Von Rad described the ethic of the sages as ordering their readers' thoughts and behavior to follow "the forces of order" built into creation by Yahweh.[31] The "righteous man" is one who is "in order."[32] Thus creation is the source of an order of things basic to a wisdom approach, but there are different understandings of the nature of this order.

Some scholars observed that this concept of order is similar to and thus may be derived from Egyptian or Mesopotamian sources. All Near Eastern wisdom texts borrow ideas and sometimes quote one another (Proverbs may have adapted an Egyptian text, *Amenemope,* in Prov. 22:17–24:23).[33] Other Egyptian texts see the ethical concern for order as grounded in *Maat,* the goddess of order, justice, and truth, who was the ordering principle of creation and the giver of life. Her representative, the pharaoh, upholds this fusion of order with justice and truth so that the social order will be in harmony with this cosmic order.[34] Similarly, Israel also saw order within creation since God had conquered chaos — creating form out of a formless void, light and order out of the darkness of chaos (Gen. 1:1–4). God took the initiative, "concealing valuable truths within nature itself," yet it was "left to humans to search out these lessons from nature and human behavior" and then to live in community in harmony with them.[35] In Israel's wisdom tradition, this order may be reflected in sentences like

> Treasures gained by wickedness do not profit,
> but righteousness delivers from death. (Prov. 10:2)

---

31. Gerhard von Rad, *Wisdom in Israel* (Nashville: Abingdon, 1972), 78–82.

32. Ibid., 79.

33. Adolph Erman first proposed a close relation between Amenemope and Proverbs in 1924, and at first it was thought there was direct borrowing, but recently a more cautious assessment is common. Still, there is common agreement that there is substantial interplay among the wisdom of the various Near Eastern cultures. See the discussion in G. E. Bryce, *A Legacy of Wisdom: The Egyptian Contribution to the Wisdom of Israel* (Lewisburg, Pa.: Bucknell University Press, 1989). More recently, Whybray concluded that while it "cannot be denied" there is much in this section of Proverbs which has affinities with Egyptian instructions, yet the idea of a "close dependence on Amenemope must be given up." See the discussion in his *The Composition of the Book of Proverbs,* JSOTSup 168 (Sheffield: JSOT, 1994), 132–45.

34. See the succinct summary of this discussion in James L. Crenshaw's tribute to Roland Murphy, "Murphy's Axiom: Every Gnomic Saying Needs a Balancing Corrective," in *The Listening Heart: Essays in Wisdom and the Psalms in Honor of Roland E. Murphy, O.Carm.,* ed. Kenneth G. Hoglund et al. (Sheffield: JSOT, 1987), 1–17.

35. James L. Crenshaw, "The Acquisition of Knowledge in Israelite Wisdom Literature," *Word and World* 7:3 (summer 1987), 247–48.

> Whoever digs a pit will fall into it,
> and a stone will come back on the one who starts it rolling.
> (Prov. 26:27)

Here the order and moral order alike seem a natural con-
sequence of the physical realties of the creation, rather than a
punishment brought on by some outside agency, thus anticipating
Jean-Jacques Rousseau and John Dewey by several millennia.[36] The
one who digs the pit will "fall into it," rather than be pushed into
it; the stone rolls back, presumably as a result of gravity, not as
the direct result of some divine push or act of retribution. In this
proverbial saying, as also in Rousseau and Dewey, the warrant for
such sentences is found in the self-evident quality of their experienced claims, not in the authority of the teacher or divine agent
who stands behind them. Piety brings about prosperity just as dig-
ging a pit makes a hole in which to fall. No explanation concerning
divine intervention is needed:

> Those who are kind reward themselves,
> but the cruel do themselves harm. (Prov. 11:17)

God is portrayed in other sayings (e.g., 10:3; 11:20–21) as an
actor in reward and punishment.[37] Either way, this doctrine of retribution is familiar and basic in Israel, especially in the prophetic
and priestly interpretations of the covenant, which insist that when
people sin, divine punishment can be expected. Within the wisdom tradition, retribution becomes a major issue of contention,
especially in Job and Ecclesiastes.

We still assume retribution. Parents and teachers alike use the
lure of reward and the fear of punishment in discipline. Could
we imagine teaching the opposite: rewarding bad behavior and
punishing good? We also assume and teach that there are *natural consequences* that follow good or bad actions. Indeed, science
is predicated upon the assumption that the universe is orderly

---

36. Jean Jacques Rousseau is often credited with originating the pedagogical
strategy of using "natural consequences," which he urged at length in 1762 in *Emile
or On Education*, bk. 2. Clearly proverbial sayings have also upheld this notion.

37. Klaus Koch, in a careful article, "Is There a Doctrine of Retribution in the
Old Testament," in *Theodicy in the Old Testament*, ed. James L. Crenshaw (Philadelphia: Fortress, 1983), 57–87, argues that retribution, strictly speaking, applies
only when punishment or reward results from some judicial process subject to a
previously established norm, so punishment and reward are not part of the nature
of the person or the action. He then argues that Proverbs speaks only of acts that
have consequences and never of divine retribution. On this, his reliance on circu-
lar reasoning makes his argument less persuasive. We'll return to these issues in the
chapters on Job and Ecclesiastes.

and will behave predictably as though governed by laws. This view of order as cosmic, or built into the universe, sees the order as "out there" so humans must discover it and learn to be in correspondence or harmony with it.

Other scholars disagree that biblical authors assume the explanations involving a cosmic order.[38] They acknowledge the affinities between Israelite and Egyptian modes of thinking, yet note that Israel seldom relies upon abstractions or explanations like *cosmic order* or *natural consequences* or other metaphysical or theoretical schemes. Rather than explain that humans are in a relation of correspondence with a reality built into the creation, "perhaps the wise of Israel seek to impose order on the attitudes and actions of their readers."[39]

To focus on how the texts motivate reader-learners to order their attitudes and actions clarifies several pedagogical features of proverbial texts.[40] For example, the sages "woo" reader-learners using graphic and seductive verbal "pictures" of attractive women — not so much to foster correspondence with cosmic order as to lure learners into ordering their own desires and behavior. Also, we shall find the sages seldom seek to control others or external events but seek self-discipline and self-control. We may also see why the sages' depiction of the two paths often seems simplistic.

THE TWO PATHS. One cannot miss the emphasis upon learning to choose the "right way" in Proverbs. Graphic verbal pictures paint the allure of "the wicked" or "sinners" or the "strange woman" (Prov. 1:10–19; 4:14–19; 5:3–6; 6:23–35; 7:6–27; 9:13–18). Alongside those, the sages place another set of pictures describing the benefits of loyalty to the path of the father/mother/teacher and Woman Wisdom (1:20–33; 2:1–19; 3:13–18; 4:4–9; 8:1–36; 9:1–12). The path of the wicked is portrayed as full of violence, thievery, drunkenness, sexual laxity, lack of discipline, poverty, discord, dishonor, calamity, lying, darkness, and it leads to death and Sheol. On the other hand, the right way is filled with security; insight; understanding; hidden treasures; integrity; righteousness; justice; truth; a love more precious than gold, silver, and jewels; healing; long life; happiness; and it brings favor in the sight of God.[41] (Such values would be quite at home in the royal court.)

---

38. See the sources listed in n. 33 above for this discussion.
39. Huwiler, "Control of Reality in Israelite Wisdom," 73–76.
40. Ibid., 76.
41. James L. Crenshaw, *Old Testament Wisdom: An Introduction* (Atlanta: John Knox, 1981), 82–91.

These pictures are not simply descriptive but are laden with moral evaluations and imperatives. The sages are convinced that reader-learners should learn to recognize "two ways" and to adopt their evaluations of those paths.

These lessons may seem somewhat simplistic, for the order assumed here is always a duality: there are two paths (one good and the other evil) and two kinds of people (wise and foolish). This duality may reflect the two-line form of the sayings, and it may reflect a pedagogical simplifying in order to clarify the basic choice in an otherwise complex situation. When teaching math to a child, we do not begin with all the complexities and ambiguities of set theory, calculus, and trigonometry but with addition and subtraction. But we need not stop there once the basics have been mastered.

Does Proverbs assume too simplistic a duality? Consider three ways the sages acknowledged the ambiguities and complexities in living in their collections of proverbial sayings.

First, the sages recorded proverbial sayings that are each clear and unambiguous by themselves but that evoke ambiguity by their being juxtaposed with one another. Does Proverbs 10:2–4 assume one order — or more than one?

> ²Treasures gained by wickedness do not profit,
> but righteousness delivers from death.
> ³The LORD does not let the righteous go hungry,
> but he thwarts the craving of the wicked.
> ⁴A slack hand causes poverty,
> but the hand of the diligent makes rich.

Here verse 2 seems to presume natural consequences, and verse 4 assumes that hard work itself produces wealth and laziness produces poverty. Verse 3 asserts that Yahweh actively thwarts the wicked, yet verse 2 acknowledges that the wicked have treasures. In this context, does verse 2 also acknowledge that the wicked, who have treasures, have been diligent (verse 4), or are there different paths to wealth? Then how did the righteous come to be "hungry"? As Elizabeth Huwiler observes, "If the purpose of the sayings were to find a universal explanation for the fact that some people prosper and others do not, this combination of sayings would confuse rather than clarify, and one might suppose that the sequence had been created by someone who neglected to observe or consider their apparent contradiction."[42] Yet these sayings clearly affirm for reader-learners that the values of piety and diligence are

---

42. Huwiler, "Control of Reality in Israelite Wisdom," 137.

better than wickedness and "a slack hand," while recognizing ambiguities in real life, presented here in the juxtaposition of sentences
rather than by explicit statement. Reader-learners are expected to
notice these juxtapositions.

Second, the sages often made use of the duality of how things
are compared with how they seem or appear, which suggests
awareness of more ambiguity than a simple black and white. For
example, some proverbs reflect an awareness that life in the royal
court has a dark side (e.g., Prov. 16:5, 8, 10–19). The sages used
irony and skepticism to show an awareness that things are not
always what they seem (see 30:1–4), and they used riddles and
enigmas to point to the complexity of things that "are too wonderful" for simple dualities (Prov. 30). The sages also offer astute
glimpses of order in a person's *inner* world:

> The heart knows its own bitterness,
>   and no stranger shares its joy. (Prov. 14:10)

> The human spirit will endure sickness;
>   but a broken spirit — who can bear? (Prov. 18:14)

Third, there is even some ambiguity about God's order. As we
just saw, God is said to "thwart" the wicked, yet these sayings also
affirm:

> The LORD has made everything for its purpose,
>   even the wicked for the day of trouble. (Prov. 16:4)

Does this reassure? It does express a monotheist conviction (God is
responsible for all that exists), yet it also implies that God planned
ahead for "the day of trouble" by creating a "purpose" for the
wicked. What could that purpose be? Was it to create learning opportunities? No explanation is offered, yet the next verse makes
plain that the ways of the wicked also have consequences:

> All those who are arrogant are an abomination to the LORD;
>   be assured, they will not go unpunished. (Prov. 16:5)

So retribution holds, but apparently God's order includes the ambiguities created by those whose ways even God finds to be an
abomination!

Since wisdom instruction is for adults as well as for children
(1:4–5), it is not surprising that we find sayings that seem simplistic while others tease readers into more complex ways of perceiving
and reflecting. The sages may have expected order among humans, because of the presence of God in creation, but that also

meant that, like God, order was not always self-evident. It needed discerning.

Education and the Fear of the Lord

To do justice to the theology of the Book of Proverbs, we must account for the infrequent appearances of God,[43] the importance of the use of the phrase "the fear of the Lord," and the importance of Woman Wisdom as an agent of God and as an educator (this latter theme will be treated in chap. 5). Explicit references to God are frequent in some chapters (e.g., ten times in chap. 3 and eleven times in chap. 16) and altogether absent in others (e.g., chaps. 4, 7, 13, 26–27). Some scholars have claimed this uneven distribution results from a later editorial process, a "Yahwistic reinterpretation" that places a more acceptable theological cast on older, more secular material.[44] Others point out, rightly, that just because God is not explicitly mentioned does not mean that God and covenantal themes are not implicitly present.[45]

Still, those familiar with other biblical texts might well be surprised that Proverbs mentions none of God's mighty saving acts and largely ignores cultic ritual and prophetic and priestly interests. Proverbs seldom makes claims about what God is like, though inferences about God can be drawn from the sayings. For example, God is said to care about justice and righteousness (3:32–33) and fair business dealings (11:1; 16:11), to favor humility (3:34; 22:4), to hate evil (6:16–19) and lying (6:17; 12:22), and to keep watch (5:21; 15:3). Yet more important is the repeated assertion that wisdom itself is grounded in loyalty to God:

> The fear of the LORD is the beginning of knowledge;
>   fools despise wisdom and instruction. (Prov. 1:7)

This verse is particularly important. First, it is repeated (with variations) more often than any other single verse. Second, it often occurs at critically important junctures in a text. For example, in Proverbs 1:7 it concludes the opening purpose statement for the

---

43. Out of 915 verses in the book, "The Lord" (Yahweh, the distinctively Hebrew designation for the liberating God) appears fewer than 90 times (and several of those are inserted by translators where they do not appear in the Hebrew text), and "God" only appears 6 times.

44. McKane, *Proverbs*, 10–17; Artur Weiser, *The Old Testament: Its Formation and Development* (New York: Association Press, 1961); and others. For a brief but telling critique of this view, see von Rad, *Wisdom in Israel*, 68 n. 12.

45. Kathleen A. Farmer, *Who Knows What Is Good? A Commentary on the Books of Proverbs and Ecclesiastes* (Grand Rapids: Eerdmans, 1991), 131–35.

whole collection describing the educational aim of the sages. It also closes the collection in the first section of Proverbs:

> The fear of the LORD is the beginning of wisdom,
>   and the knowledge of the Holy One is insight. (Prov. 9:10)

The saying occurs only once in the Book of Job, at a critical interlude just after Job and his three "friends" have completed their cycle of speeches and just before Job launches into his definitive defense or challenge to God (Job 28:28). In Sirach, this verse and variants occur five times in the first chapter alone (1:14, 16, 18, 20, 27), along with seven other reflections upon "the fear of the Lord" (1:8, 11, 12, 13, 25, 28, 30).[46] This verse has programmatic and theological importance in Sirach, which we shall explore in chapter 4.

Sometimes this verse has been treated simplistically, and even used as a justification for instilling fear in children. Today, educators are rightly suspicious of the use of fear as a pedagogical tool. While fear may temporarily motivate, continued use of fear will eventually curtail interest in learning by making learners defensive. So how can fear be regarded as training or teaching or the basis for understanding wisdom? What pedagogical import has this notion?

Von Rad claims this verse (and its variants) is important because it "contains in a nutshell the whole Israelite theory of knowledge."[47] "All that can be said either for or against Israelite wisdom is expressed in this statement."[48] Unlike contemporary views of knowledge, the Israelites believed that all human knowledge is grounded in commitment to God. What might that mean?

We ought not simply impose contemporary psychology on "the fear of the Lord." Fear, in its most literal and basic sense, is a natural response to overwhelming force. The Israelites are said to have experienced fear (or terror) in the face of the thunder, lightening, and earthshaking encounter with the Lord at Sinai. Such fear is not altogether misplaced. But along with the terror, there is an attraction or fascination.[49] But it is not just that there are other aspects to the experience of fear, but that "the fear of the Lord" may have

---

46. Other ancient (later) manuscript variants record additional instances of both phrases in this first chapter, in verses 5, 7, 12, 21.

47. Von Rad, *Wisdom in Israel*, 67.

48. Ibid., 68.

49. See the classic description by Rudolf Otto, *The Idea of the Holy: An Inquiry into the Non-rational Factor in the Idea of the Divine and Its Relation to the Rational*, 2d ed. (London: Oxford University Press, 1950), esp. 12–41.

other uses, with which we may now be unfamiliar. Would we say
the following?

> Happy is the one who is never without fear,
>   but one who is hard-hearted will fall into calamity. (Prov. 28:14)
>
> The fear of the LORD is life indeed;
>   filled with it one rests secure and suffers no harm. (Prov. 19:23)

These sentences suggest that being with fear is the opposite of
being hard-hearted and that being filled with fear gives rise to security, protection, and life. Here fear is a blessing, not a punishment.

So the fear of the Lord is not simply an emotional or psychological reaction to the presence of God. Rather, most often it means
simply knowledge of and obedience to God.[50] But neither is this
an exclusively cognitive knowledge, a proposition to be memorized or a doctrinal truth that functions as the premise for all that
follows. Perhaps it functions pedagogically much like the frequent
admonition in Proverbs 1–9 to "Pay attention! Be alert!"

Divine order cannot be completely grasped. It eludes mastery:
"The attitude of the wise man was perhaps more of wonder than of
praise, although this is a very fine line, as Psalm 104 indicates."[51]
The fear of the Lord is more like an attitude or posture, a standing
expectantly on tiptoes in the presence of the holy. Such a stance is
a "knowing" (that God is near or present) and, at the same time,
an emotional response to that knowing. This cognition (knowing)
is inseparable from the emotion (awe) because of God. Twentieth-
century educators and psychologists not only distinguish cognition
and emotion but tend to separate them so that objectivity can be
gained. The ancient Hebrews could hardly imagine an objective
posture before God. If one knows God, one is involved, and if
that involvement is "fitting," it would find expression as wonder,
praise, humility, and so on. Two sayings even treat the fear of the
Lord and humility as synonymous (15:33; 22:4).

Paul Holmer aptly characterizes this knowledge-emotion called
the fear of the Lord:

> To know that God is to fear him. Without the fear of God, one
> could not quite be sure of correct knowledge of him. But a word is
> needed about that fear. Certainly it is more like awe and regard, a
> kind of wariness, probably the sort that would mean watching your
> step in his presence.

---

50. Ibid., 66.
51. Ibid., 120.

Two aspects are discernible here. When God is characterized as worthy of fearful regard, one learns some theology, something about God. It would be very odd to be an expert on God without experiencing this fearful aspect. Those of us who are apt to ask for the objective teachings first, the plain teachings, without the emotional and subjective side, are easily misled here. It is not as if you can have the objective teachings on one occasion and then, as a matter of preference, decide to be fearful on another occasion. Nor is the fear separable in quite that way. For to know that God is fearful is already to fear. Thus the teaching about God cannot be entertained correctly without fear's being part of the mode of assimilating the meaning.[52]

In such a view, all education intrinsically and necessarily involves educating and cultivating the emotions as part of its cognitive interests. Because emotions and cognitions can be conceptually distinguished does not mean they can be separated, especially in learning to cope with daily living and with God. This is true not only for religious education but for all education.

To learn anything requires a basic attitude of being or becoming open to what is unknown or not known. To learn, one must respect "what is there" even when it is not yet fully comprehended. This entails a certain degree of risk, for what is there is not yet known, even as it claims our attention. If a fundamental attitude of attention and reverence for what is there underlies all educational activity, then both teachers and learners must continually expect the unexpected, or not be too surprised at being surprised. Too often teaching and learning are experienced as thoroughly predictable. This undermines both curiosity and a genuine sense of participating in a journey (a path) where neither the destination nor the route is completely known ahead of time. Thus this journey on a path is a faith journey, for trust and anticipation (hope) are both intrinsically necessary.

What is worth learning cannot be exhausted by identifying the doctrinal or theological content to be taught, nor can that content be treated as exclusively cognitive. For the sages, "it is not the theoretical expression of belief that is the heart of the matter," yet the sages point to "a faith response that is not explicitly related to a particular historical revelation of God."[53] If this insight plays it-

---

52. Paul Holmer, *Making Christian Sense* (Philadelphia: Westminster, 1984), 54–55.

53. Murphy, *The Tree of Life*, 126.

self out in our educational ministry, our knowledge may take less rationalistic forms, and this attitude and commitment may, in the words of von Rad, "liberate knowledge" to take its proper place in human activity.[54]

As the sages discerned the ordering presence of God, they sought to express it in language. They paid careful attention to *what* they said (or wrote) and to *how* they said what they said (or wrote), and their texts affirm this as a discipline highly worth learning.

The Mouth, Lips, Tongue, and Silence

Language and speech were very important to the sages, and while they did not use abstractions such as "language" or "speech," there are many astute observations about "word," "tongue," "mouth," and "lips." These have power in the sages' view; they affect others, for good or evil, so one must learn to use one's tongue, mouth, and lips wisely. This is not only true in Israel but is common to the wisdom of the ancient Near East. For example, the Assyrian scribe Ahiqar says:

> My son, chatter not overmuch so that thou speak out every word that comes to thy mind; for men's eyes and ears are trained everywhere upon thy mouth. Beware lest it be thy undoing. More than all watchfulness watch thy mouth.... For a word is a bird: once released no man can recapture it.... For the instruction of a mouth is stronger than the instruction of war.... Soft is the utterance of a king; yet it is sharper and stronger than a two-edged knife.... Soft is the tongue of a king, but it breaks a dragon's ribs.[55]

Words are powerful, so sages were concerned with both the content (the *what*) and the form (the *how*) of what is spoken and written:

> A word fitly spoken
>   is like apples of gold in a setting of silver. (Prov. 25:11)

"A word fitly spoken" may imply the right word at the right time. Both the content and the timing have to fit, but it also must be framed (a setting) so that it will be heard and received for what it is. The imagery here is visual as well as oral and temporal and may imply aesthetic standards as well. One's speech and writing should be true, but gracious and aesthetically pleasing as well.

---

54. Von Rad, *Wisdom in Israel*, 68.
55. "The Words of Ahiqar," in *The Ancient Near East: An Anthology of Texts and Pictures*, ed. James B. Pritchard (Princeton: Princeton University Press, 1958), 1:246.

If words have power, one must learn restraint. Words can wound or heal, preserve or destroy life, so they must be used with care:

> Rash words are like sword thrusts,
> but the tongue of the wise brings healing. (Prov. 12:18)

This theme is echoed in a New Testament wisdom text, James 3:5.

The pedagogical relevance of such observations is embarrassingly obvious. How often have adults used the tongue to wound children? How many adults can remember casual remarks seared into consciousness and recalled years later, such as "I always knew you were stupid!" or "Can't you ever do anything right?" How often do learners recall a remark by a teacher, perhaps offered in passing in the hall after class, that leads to significant insight?

The sages knew that telling the truth is indispensable in education and in the community. When learners come to believe that teachers do not tell the truth, they feel they have grounds for not paying attention. That undermines learning. If teachers do not seem to know the difference between what is true and what is not, or do not care, or when they are self-deceived, why should learners listen? For the sages, deceiving others and deceiving oneself have the same effect:

> It is the wisdom of the clever to understand where they go,
> but the folly of fools misleads. (Prov. 14:8)

McKane's translation makes the sense more explicit:[56]

> A shrewd man's wisdom illumines his way,
> but the folly of fools is self-deceit.

The "folly of fools" deceives themselves; it also misleads others. This is as true for teachers as for political or religious leaders (Prov. 17:7; 29:12).

Deceit, especially the misuse of language, is described as a form of hatred or contempt for others, which undermines both learning and community:

> A lying tongue hates its victims,
> and a flattering mouth works ruin. (Prov. 26:28)

Careless (i.e., undisciplined and untruthful) use of language can not only harm an individual but also can destroy community. Is this hyperbole? If language forms the bonds between individuals and

---

56. McKane, *Proverbs*, 231.

within a community, what one does with language is not a private affair but has public effects.

One simple way to discipline self and language is silence, and in Egyptian wisdom texts, the "silent man" is an important ideal for the sage. Not so in Hebrew wisdom.[57] In Proverbs, silence can be a sign of wisdom, even if it is adopted by a fool:

> Even fools who keep silent are considered wise;
>   when they close their lips, they are deemed intelligent.
>   (Prov. 17:28)

But more often, restraint rather than silence is advised:

> Do you see someone who is hasty in speech?
>   There is more hope for a fool than for anyone like that.
>   (Prov. 29:20)

Here reader-learners are asked to notice the difference between the wise and the fools and to pay attention to those who tell the truth, for those who deceive are unreliable.[58] Self-discipline can take the form of not being too hasty. (How hasty is "too hasty"? Judgement is required.) Haste makes mindless words public; then the harm is done. Self-restraint allows one to consider more carefully what is the most truthful thing to say and how best to say it.

Language and silence are inextricably linked. In an oral culture, when language is sound, it interrupts silence. Silence participates in truth by being part of what is given in the created order.[59] In a literate culture, as librarians insist, language and silence can coexist. Yet in a literate world as noisy as ours, silence now interrupts sound. In both worlds, then, an interruption is an opportunity for truth. One who teaches must seize the opportunity for truth, whether it comes in "a word fitly spoken" or in a moment of silence.[60]

Virtues: Hard Work, Discipline, Self-Control, and Humility

The sage-teachers constantly urged reader-learners to hard work, both in manual labor and in the process of learning. The learner is

---

57. Nili Shupak, *Where Can Wisdom Be Found? The Sage's Language in the Bible and in Ancient Egyptian Literature*, OBO 130 (Göttingen: Vandenhoeck and Ruprecht, 1993), 177–82.

58. Huwiler, "Control of Reality in Israelite Wisdom," 234–35.

59. See the thoughtful reflections of Max Picard, *The World of Silence* (Washington, D.C.: Regnery Gateway, 1948, 1988).

60. Parker Palmer's *To Know As We Are Known: A Spirituality of Education* (San Francisco: Harper and Row, 1983) offers useful suggestions about the use of silence in teaching in the section titled "Silence and Speech," 79–83.

admonished to be diligent, not to despise discipline and correction, and not to sleep too much. These lessons can be learned from the created order, from the ant (6:6) and other animals (30:24–31), as well as from reflection on the land and people:

> I passed by the field of one who was lazy,
>   by the vineyard of a stupid person;
> and see, it was all overgrown with thorns;
>   the ground was covered with nettles,
>   and its stone wall was broken down.
> Then I saw and considered it;
>   I looked and received instruction.
> A little sleep, a little slumber,
>   a little folding of the hands to rest,
> and poverty will come upon you like a robber,
>   and want, like an armed warrior. (Prov. 24:30–34)

Here we can imaginatively reconstruct how a sage formed wise observations: One day he passed by an overgrown field. Did he know the owner had a reputation for laziness? Perhaps he thought there may be a connection between the owner's stupidity, his laziness, and the condition of his field. So he "considered" the field, describing it with language that could apply (metaphorically) to the owner as well: "overgrown," weed covered, "broken down." Then the sage imagines how the owner rationalizes to himself as he folds his hands and slips into slumber, so "poverty" becomes the actor, in place of the owner.

Here is description without explicit moral or exhortation. Still, the sage, in characterizing the owner as stupid and lazy and by personifying poverty, does implicitly evaluate. Yet ironically, though poverty is an armed robber, poverty itself is not blamed. Instead, the reader-learner is left to infer that this robber, poverty, has been invited by the laziness of the subject.

Yet the sage does not claim to have *constructed* this insight; rather he "looked and received instruction." From whom did he receive it? From the field itself — the created order "speaks." Is this, as James Crenshaw suggests, an empirical investigation by a teacher who has "learned a valuable lesson from experience" by discovering a relation between cause (laziness) and effect (poverty)?[61] Michael Fox insists the sage has not "discovered" something, has not "looked for the cause" of the field gone wild,

---

61. James L. Crenshaw, "Wisdom and Authority: Sapiential Rhetoric and Its Warrants," in *Supplements to Vetus Testamentum* (Leiden: Brill, 1981), 15.

but rather his experience "sparked a meditation" and is used to support a viewpoint he already knows (on some other basis).[62] His value judgment has been formed by the community ethos within which the text is read, and that ethos now seeks confirmation within the experience of reader-learners. Either way, the warning here is not that God will punish the lazy one, but that one's actions have consequences.

The virtue of hard work is part of a larger concern for discipline and self-control, which are an essential part of both the educational process and the sages' notion of what it means to become and be wise. Many teachers stress "getting control" of their pupils from the beginning so they will learn to gradually assume self-control. This approach is present in proverbial sayings as well — especially in the familiar sayings about disciplining children and beating them with a rod for their own good (13:24; 24:13–14). But more often sayings urge self-control and self-discipline *by those in authority*. We saw above that controlling one's tongue (13:3; 21:23), restraining words (10:19; 17:27), and keeping secrets (25:9–10) are the wiser path, and these are things one must do for and to oneself.

One of the quintessential characteristics of a fool and foolishness is the lack of self-control, and this is dangerous:

> Like an archer who wounds everybody
>   is one who hires a passing fool. (Prov. 26:10)

Such virtues are not accidental or "sometime" characteristics but express character, so that an absence of self-control cannot be easily rooted out:

> Crush a fool in a mortar with a pestle
>   along with crushed grain,
>   but the folly will not be driven out. (Prov. 27:22)

Being foolish and lacking self-control lead not only to self-deception and misreading of reality but, thereby, to misjudging God. Psalm 14:1 ("Fools say in their hearts, 'There is no God' ") even claims that "folly is practical atheism."[63]

Self-control is also expected of kings (and all in authority). King Lemuel's mother urges her son:

---

62. Michael V. Fox, *Qohelet and His Contradictions* JSOTSup 71 (Sheffield: Almond, 1989), 91.
63. Von Rad, *Wisdom in Israel*, 65.

It is not for kings, O Lemuel,
    it is not for kings to drink wine,
    or for rulers to desire strong drink;
or else they will drink and forget what has been decreed,
    and will pervert the rights of all the afflicted.
Give strong drink to one who is perishing,
    and wine to those in bitter distress;
let them drink and forget their poverty,
    and remember their misery no more.
Speak out for those who cannot speak,
    for the rights of all the destitute.
Speak out, judge righteously,
    defend the rights of the poor and needy. (Prov. 31:4–9)

Her admonition to self-discipline was more than motherly concern and conventional moralizing. Her motive clauses in verse 5 claim the king needs self-control lest he forget to fulfill his communal responsibilities to speak for the silent, the poor, the needy, and champion the rights of those left desolate (vv. 8–9). Self-indulgence in a king harms the whole community. But Lemuel's mother does not lay the same expectation upon all. While she urges her son, the king, not to drink, she also urges him to give drink to the poor and oppressed so they can forget their misery for a while.

How does one gain self-discipline? Partly it is learned from the support and discipline of a family as found in King Lemuel's mother and the "father and mother" referred to constantly in Proverbs 1–7. But self-discipline must become part of one's own character, so eventually self-control and self-discipline must be earned by practice. It is described both as a gift (from God and from Woman Wisdom) and also as an accomplishment that comes from earnest and lasting effort by the learner (chaps. 2–7).

In the sages' understanding, the virtues of hard work, self-discipline, and self-control over one's own language and behavior are properly seen as closely related to another virtue: humility. In Israel and in Proverbs, humility is intrinsic to being a *creature* (which implies acknowledging a *creator*). It is presumptuous for a creature to claim too much responsibility for being what one is — physically, intellectually, socially, spiritually. By definition, a creature cannot be self-made. In Proverbs, the opposite of humility is pride or taking too much credit for oneself or being haughty:

When pride comes, then comes disgrace;
    but wisdom is with the humble. (Prov. 11:2)

> Pride goes before destruction,
>   and a haughty spirit before a fall. (Prov. 16:18)

While pride is correlated with and precedes disgrace or destruction, the texts do not claim that pride causes them. Neither should this be read as a warning against self-esteem. On one hand, remembering how much we are created by significant others, including parents and teachers, is a source of humility. On the other hand, as creatures, we also create. Not only do we create artifacts, but more importantly, in choosing the good paths, we help create our own lives, and in so doing, we shape and influence the lives of those around us and those who follow after.

How to Be Happy without Being Religious

The Book of Proverbs offers a collection of traditional *commonplaces* or conventional stock responses to everyday situations. Despite their location in a sacred text, this advice often does not seem particularly "religious." Scan through a typical chapter (e.g., chap. 13), and what we see are sayings on the value of discipline, guarding the mouth, laziness, lying, pretending to be rich, insolence, respecting the commandment and the teaching of the wise, a bad messenger, being careful with whom you associate, and so on. God is not mentioned, though sin and being righteous are. Cultic or temple or covenantal responsibilities are rarely mentioned (3:9–10).

Mention of the commandments in Proverbs is especially revealing. Proverbs 13:13 says that "those who respect the commandment will be rewarded," yet 13:14 says that "the teaching of the wise is a fountain of life." Similarly, Proverbs 19:16 says, "Those who keep the commandment will live," yet 19:17 says, "Whoever is kind to the poor lends to the LORD." All other mention of the commandments occurs in chapters 1–7, where they do not refer to the Decalogue. Rather the father consistently admonishes his children to keep "my words," "my commandments," and "my teachings" (Prov. 2:1; 3:1; 4:1–5; 6:20, 23; 7:1–2), as we saw earlier in Tobit as well. Each father passed on his own "commandments" — the sum total of his insights and wisdom gleaned from years of living.

There is no reason to believe that this father's commandments are inconsistent with God's commandments, yet Proverbs "never identifies the *miswot* (commandment) of the sage with that of God, not even implicitly."[64] This is so for several reasons. First, these commandments are never treated as though they are "divinely revealed."[65] Secondly, the father's commandments are linked with Woman Wisdom, and there the benefits to come from keeping the father's commands are the same as those promised to come from keeping the covenant (cf. Deut. 6–7; Prov. 3:1–2; 4:4–9; 7:1–5). In Proverbs, happiness and life and blessing come with being in continuity with one's tradition, one's family, the larger community, and especially by seeking Woman Wisdom (see esp. 3:13–18). Thirdly, Proverbs 7:3 even uses familiar Deuteronomic language of binding commandments and writing them on the heart (Deut. 6:6–8), but here the binding is to the father's commandments, and obedience to them leads to insight and wisdom.

No wonder proverbial advice seems so very practical: happiness is to be found within the precincts of becoming wise in common, daily living. Satisfaction in life comes to individuals as a communal achievement rather than as a covenantal or cultic reward.

WHAT PEDAGOGICAL WORK DO PROVERBS DO?

Learning and Teaching Proverbial Sayings

Today we normally learn proverbial sayings orally and informally, in face-to-face real-life situations, just as in oral and nonliterate cultures. But here we are dealing with texts and written, poetic proverbs. In ancient Israel, even among the literate, there was very little written material. Rarely, if ever, would students take a scroll off by themselves to read or study. Rather, if written texts even were present, they were deeply embedded in face-to-face group interactions. In ancient cultures, there were two basic approaches to gaining mastery of an authoritative text: recitation and memorization.

RECITATION. First, texts were read aloud by the teacher and repeated by the students, out loud in unison, over and over, perhaps with rhythmic movements, until they had mastered the text for themselves. Still, with some teachers, recitation could become a boring process, and a pupil's attention could wander occasionally, thus calling forth physical "reminders" from the teacher. Second, as we know from archeological finds of copybooks, students would write

---

64. Fox, *Qohelet and His Contradictions*, 321.
65. Ibid., 319.

sayings over and over, either from memory or as they were recited aloud by the teacher. Copying aided memory.

When a teacher recites or reads aloud from the text, it is clear who has the authority. In an oral culture, the very presence of a text, its use by the teacher, and the echoing responses by learners suggest that certain basics must be learned from authority figures and from the texts they mediate. Here originality and critical thinking are not valued highly.

MEMORIZATION. We often underestimate the powers of memory of an oral culture, where memory is the only library. For example, among Muslims, the Koran itself is not considered a text but a "recitation" of the words of God and thus is to be learned by repetitive recitation. Recent folklore studies reveal that verbal memory in completely oral cultures neither requires nor leads to *exact* replication. Rather the oral recitation of long works from memory is actually a creative, though tradition-bound, process. An oral singer or poet works with a standard meter or rhythm, into which he fits formulas of traditional content. Thus the poem's meter remains constant, while the content varies. Originality is a matter, not of introducing novel material, but of re-creating the poem, story, or song by fitting the traditional materials to the audience and occasion.[66] Indeed, one researcher found that learning to read and write actually disabled the oral poet, by leading him to think of a text that controlled the narrative and that interfered with his oral composing.[67]

On the other hand, *exact* or rote memorization presumes texts, and recitation of a memorized text is more reproduction than re-creation. Textual accuracy is more important than creatively adapting to the audience or occasion. Memorizing a text affirms its value, suggesting this is a text to be taken seriously. Memorizing a proverb also makes it possible to find suitable occasions for its use, but the sages knew that accurate recitation is not enough:

> The legs of a disabled person hang limp;
>   so does a proverb in the mouth of a fool. (Prov. 26:7)

Then what do proverbs do?

---

66. Walter Ong, *Orality and Literacy: The Technologizing of the Word* (London: Methuen, 1982), 57–68.

67. Ibid., 59.

Proverbs as Invitations

Proverbial sayings differ in both form and content, inviting differing responses from reader-learners. If I say to you, "Shut the door" (using the imperative form), I expect you to take a certain kind of action (move toward the door). If I were to say instead, "Shut the window," I expect a different action (move toward the window). Both sentences are commands or directives, which specify an expected response. The form of the two sentences is the same, but the content changes;[68] thus, they expect different responses. Sometimes the form changes as well. Instead of using the imperative form, suppose I said to you, "The draft from that open door is making me chilly" (using the indicative).[69] In form, this statement hardly seems an invitation, for it simply reports how I feel (though the context, my tone of voice, our prior relations, may all influence meaning and reception of the statement). Here the form of the saying itself puts greater responsibility upon the hearer to take the initiative in judging whether and how to respond. You may not respond (judging the matter of insufficient importance), or you may respond by shutting the door — or by handing me a sweater. Similarly, I propose, different forms of proverbial sayings may evoke or expect differing responses from reader-learners.

PROVERBS AS COMMANDS: INVITING OBEDIENCE. Some proverbs are prescriptive in form, using imperatives to command, prohibit, or exhort:[70]

Do not quarrel with anyone without cause,
    when no harm has been done to you. (Prov. 3:30)

They often are characterized by direct address:

My child, if sinners entice you,
    do not consent. (Prov. 1:10)

---

68. In a face-to-face, oral exchange, as depicted here, one also communicates by inflection or tone of voice. One could say these words with a tone that suggests a gentle invitation or with a tone more like an imperious command. Such changes might also evoke differing responses among hearers. But in written texts, as we have here, such oral inflections either are no longer present or must be discerned in other ways. One of the most familiar ways of discerning such inflections is by attending to the context in which the utterance is set. But most often in the Book of Proverbs, we have no indication of context.

69. Again, in a face-to-face situation, the directive force can be conveyed by tone of voice, even while using an indicative form. In a literary text, that can sometimes be detected by context, if context is supplied.

70. I am accepting here McKane's descriptions of these two genres without necessarily accepting his use of them to fashion a historical reconstruction of what he sees as the wisdom tradition's "secular" origins and later "pietistic" reinterpretations (McKane, Proverbs, see 1–22, 413–15). It should be noted that he is less rigid about this sequence than his critics take him to be (see pp. 373–74).

This prescriptive genre was also used widely in Egyptian instructional literature.[71] Prescriptive sayings often tell the reader-learner explicitly what to do or what not to do and thus are similar to commandments. While proverbial sayings are not attributed directly to divine revelation, or seen as universal prescriptions, they prescribe or proscribe behavior, and sometimes attitudes, and thus presume the teacher or author has authority to do so, presumably as representative of the community's experience encapsulated in the saying.

The advice offered in these commands is plain and seems to require little interpretive effort by reader-learners. We are invited to follow or obey:

> Put away from you crooked speech,
>   and put devious talk far from you. (Prov. 4:24)

Here the reader-learners are told quite explicitly what to do. On closer examination, perhaps the invitation requires more than passive or submissive obedience. Look again at the last three proverbs quoted. If people invite me to do something interesting, how do I know if they are enticing me or if they are sinners (1:10)? If I am tempted to quarrel, how do I learn to stop and tell myself there is no cause or "no harm has been done" (3:30)? When I am speaking, will I always recognize my own "devious talk" (4:24)? We all know how self-interest, self-deception, and other temptations can inhibit honest self-awareness. Even direct commands require a reader-learner to be able to "correctly" interpret both the text and the situation, to enable the advice to work as intended. Knowing the saying is not enough.

Imperative proverbs also frequently follow a directive with motive clauses — reasons, warnings, threats (1:32), or promises (1:33) — to show why one should respond as expected. (Look for a "that" or "for" or "so that" followed by a reason or motive for the "right response.")

> Listen, children, to a father's instruction,
>   and be attentive, that you may gain insight. (Prov. 4:1–2)

> Hear, my child, and accept my words,
>   that the years of your life may be many. (Prov. 4:10)

---

71. Ibid., 6–10, and especially his lengthy descriptions of Egyptian wisdom texts, 51–150.

Sometimes these reasons are subtle, sometimes they are so plain as to seem simplistic, and sometimes they bring religious sanctions to bear:[72]

> Do not envy the violent
>   and do not choose any of their ways;
> for the perverse are an abomination to the LORD,
>   but the upright are in his confidence. (Prov. 3:31–32)

In such sayings, reasons are offered by which reader-learners may learn judgment. This suggests that these imperatives are not universal, nor are they to be followed simply on the authority of the parent or teacher. Here there is no appeal to "Do this because I say so!" Rather offering reasons suggests a pedagogical purpose that the learner may come to *understand why* the right path is to be preferred.[73]

Sometimes the sages were so concerned about giving reasons that they even dropped the imperative form (see Prov. 2:1–15, a series of "if...then" clauses). While the reader-learner is urged to "accept my words," the "if...then" form seems to invite the reader to try it out — to practice seeking and then he or she will understand. In other words, even the most prescriptive and directive of the proverbial sayings presumes that reader-learners must learn to form their own judgments about how to interpret a situation, to make sense of their reality, and to know what leads naturally to what. Such sayings are misused if they are taken solely to invite obedience to rules or universal absolutes, for they invite the reader-learner to understand reasons and motives as well.

PROVERBS AS DESCRIPTIONS: INVITING TO SEE TRUTHFULLY. Many proverbial sayings compile, conserve, and transmit the lessons gleaned from the experience of the community over time. These lessons may be as basic as what makes for physical survival or may be astute observations about social behavior, etiquette, and how to be successful. These observations are not imperatives but are *indica-*

---

72. Using a scheme like Lawrence Kohlberg's patterns of moral reasoning to examine these motive clauses, one would find all four stages of the first two levels ("a-moral" and "conventional") of moral thinking explicitly represented and perhaps some fifth-stage "principled" thinking implicitly represented.

73. This approach is quite consistent with the research of Basil Bernstein, which explores the difference between parental language codes that rely on simple authoritative commands and those that give reasons for directives. Bernstein has shown that the latter is educationally and linguistically more productive. Basil Bernstein, *Class, Codes, and Control* (Boston: Routledge and Kegan Paul, 1977).

tive statements. They do what von Rad has called "cataloging the real."[74]

Consider the following proverbs:

> Clouds and wind, but no rain;
>   a man who boasts of a non-existent gift. (Prov. 25:14)[75]

> The north wind produces rain,
>   and a backbiting tongue, angry looks. (Prov. 25:23)

Both sayings offer concrete, vivid descriptions of an aspect of the created world. The proverb then lays alongside that another observation about some aspect of human behavior. The juxtaposition itself invites reader-learners to "fill the gap" so that each observation interprets the other, whether the link is analogical (25:14) or causal (25:23).

Here it is assumed that worthwhile lessons can be gleaned by attentive reflection. Since human beings are part of the created order, the orders seen in creation will have analogues in human behavior. Von Rad contends that in ancient societies such regularities are not just illustrations or pedagogic devices but are discoveries that catalog and advance the knowledge of a people trying to make sense of the world (natural and human) in which they live.[76] They then can conserve that learning in proverbial sayings by encapsulating what has been learned in memorable and evocative images.

While such observations may have ethical import, they are not grounded in an explicit "word of the Lord," nor do they derive from a covenant relation. They are not commands, and sometimes they do not imply an unequivocal ethical "ought." They are astute and valuable observations of what is real and true. Consider the following:

> The poor are disliked even by their neighbors,
>   but the rich have many friends. (Prov. 14:20)

> "Bad, bad," says the buyer,
>   then goes away and boasts. (Prov. 20:14)

While these proverbs offer no explicit ethical directives, they may be *used* to imply that, while this is how things are, they ought not be. But that would depend, in part, on when or how the proverb is said.

---

74. Von Rad, *Wisdom in Israel*, 123.
75. Ibid., 119.
76. Ibid., 115–23.

Accurate descriptions of reality are important because if one is to make viable ethical recommendations or prescribe how people can best live together, one must first of all get the facts straight and see clearly the world and human beings "as they really are." Perhaps these sayings aim more directly at fostering understanding as a basis for decisions about what to do.

Israel's early sages, unlike the ancient Greeks or modern thinkers, seldom expressed these behavioral principles in abstract form. If there are rules, they are to be inferred from particular, concrete observations and juxtapositions.[77] Nor is there here any attempt to systematize these observations into an explicit theory of any sort.

Pedagogically, this form of wisdom statement proceeds by *indirection* using analogical and metaphorical thinking — "This is like that."[78] This invites reader-learner participation.

> Like vinegar to the teeth and smoke to the eyes
> so are the lazy to their employers. (Prov. 10:26)

Here reader-learners are expected to know (or find out) what vinegar feels like on the teeth and how smoke irritates the eyes. How precise this observation is! It draws attention, not to the taste of vinegar, but to its effect on the teeth! And linking smoke and eyes is not a lesson reader-learners can master vicariously — the only way to know how smoke affects eyes is to have experienced smoke in one's own eyes. Only then can one "see" how a lazy person affects an employer. But the text does not precisely define that relation for readers. Each learner has to figure out the analogy herself. These proverbs invite full and experiential participation by reader-learners.

In many ways, the longer didactic or prescriptive poems we observed above are much simpler to interpret, partly because they seem so much less ambiguous. Von Rad observes, "The single line [proverb — composed of two parallel sections] often enough

---

77. Von Rad makes the contrast with the sages of Greece: "Israel, with great openness, gave precedence to the contingent event over the *logos* achieved by means of abstract calculation." Ibid., 311.

78. Ibid., 29–30, 49–50, 310–19. See Leo G. Perdue's recent summary of the metaphorical process and its utilization in wisdom literature, "Job's Assault on Creation," in *Hebrew Annual Review*, ed. Reuben Ahroni, vol. 10 (Columbus: Department of Judaic and Near Eastern Languages and Literature, Ohio State University, 1987), 297–301.

makes higher claims and demands a greater degree of intellectual participation than a developed didactic poem."[79]

PROVERBS AS NARRATIVES WITHOUT STORIES: INVITING IMAGINATION. Reader-learners will have observed that proverbial sayings are not narratives or stories, but they do make use of narratives in a different and pedagogically important way. For example, Proverbs 10:5:

> A child who gathers in summer is prudent,
>   but a child who sleeps in harvest brings shame.

Here is no explicit story, but the saying will make little sense unless the reader's own imagination fashions a mini-narrative in which two children have different attitudes, do different things, and thus get different results. The narrative frame needed might look something like this: One child diligently and prudently (with forethought) gets out of bed all summer in order to work in the fields. This child thereby has a fruitful crop to show for the effort when harvest time comes. The other child is depicted as sleeping through the harvest (and perhaps sleeping through the summer as well? see Prov. 24:30–34), missing the opportune time, and thus brings only a harvest of shame, shame that reflects not only on the child but also on the rest of the family. In these two lines, the "gap" is to be filled with a story (which leads to understanding). The saying implicitly invites reader-learners to construct a narrative based upon their own store of narratives gathered from daily living.[80]

The sage could have used the imperative, "Don't be lazy." Rather, this narrative-proverb offers concrete, sensual, real-life language, with which anyone can identify, indirectly appealing to the imagination and experience of reader-learners and pointing toward a judgment by evoking a narrative. In doing so, these teachers demonstrate their trust of reader-learners and stimulate creative thinking. Indeed, if the teacher takes too strong a role and directly provides the lesson or moral or point to be drawn from the proverb, both the proverb and the learner are cheated of their active roles in learning. In this regard, teaching with proverbial sayings is not unlike using parables and riddles.

PROVERBS AS "TEASING THOUGHT": INVITING REFLECTION AND WONDER. One of the intriguing effects of the use of irony, ambiguity, and riddles in

---

79. Von Rad, *Wisdom in Israel*, 27.

80. For an interesting perspective on the importance of this phenomenon in educational ministry, see Diane Hymans, "The Role of Play in a Cultural-Linguistic Approach to Religion: Theoretical Implications for Education in the Faith Community" (Ed.D. diss., Presbyterian School of Christian Education, 1992), esp. chap. 3.

Proverbs is not just that they tease reader-learners into significant cognitive activity, but that in so doing, they also evoke a sense of mystery, wonder, and awe.

Contradictions. Contradictions are often seen as "mistakes," and when they occasionally appear in these sayings (e.g., Prov. 26:4–5), they are sometimes "explained" by assuming the sages were just collecting two proverbs, without judging them. On the other hand, since the collectors managed to set these two proverbs next to one another, it would seem they meant the contradiction to be noticed. Contradictions may also be seen as a pedagogical practice: they puzzle and tease reader-learners into reflection. For example,

> A bribe is like a magic stone in the eyes of those who give it;
> wherever they turn they prosper. (Prov. 17:8)

> The wicked accept a concealed bribe
> to pervert the ways of justice. (Prov. 17:23)

These sayings are both in the indicative. The first points out the advantages of bribery (to the giver), and the latter, its disadvantages (for the community). Which is true? Both? How better to portray the realities of economic life truthfully than to preserve both sayings and arrange them close to one another so even casual readers will notice — and thus be faced with the complexities of real life. Here the juxtaposition of texts nudges in both directions, so reader-learners must judge, perhaps by imagining or constructing mini-narrative frameworks. Does it depend upon where one stands in the story — whether one is giving or receiving a bribe?

Contradictory indicative sayings may also reflect an ongoing debate between different perspectives on reality and morality among the sages and people of Israel. In Israel, poverty is sometimes regarded as divine punishment, sometimes it is to be abolished, but often it is simply taken for granted as a fact of life.[81] In Proverbs, there is little trace of the prophetic desire to "change the system." Instead, poverty and riches are often seen as the fruits of individual effort:

> The appetite of the lazy craves, and gets nothing,
> while the appetite of the diligent is richly supplied. (Prov. 13:4)

Here, riches are quite acceptable when they result from hard work. While wealth is not despised in Proverbs, still "not a single virtue

---

81. R. N. Whybray, *Wealth and Poverty in the Book of Proverbs* (Sheffield: JSOT, 1990).

is attributed to 'the rich,' " and a wealthy person is never held up as someone to emulate.[82] (This includes the king!) Some proverbs regard wealth as ephemeral and not to be trusted (11:28); others encourage ambition to wealth (11:16), while others approve being content with little (16:8; 17:1; 27:24), and another sets the whole issue into a larger context:

Two things I ask of you;
  do not deny them to me before I die:
Remove far from me falsehood and lying;
  give me neither poverty nor riches;
  feed me with the food that I need,
or I shall be full, and deny you,
  and say, "Who is the LORD?"
or I shall be poor, and steal,
  and profane the name of my God. (Prov. 30:7–9)

One effect of this way of arranging sayings is that it can evoke a sense of the ambiguities of life, a sense of the ironic, the comic, or even the satirical, depending upon how one reads. Sometimes the critical message is strikingly direct, and the only ambiguity is what "the ruler" will make of it:

Many seek the favor of a ruler,
  But it is from the LORD that one gets justice.
                    (Prov. 29:26; see also 29:4, 12–14, 16; 31:2–9)

Riddles and Enigmas. Samson's wager with the young men of the Philistines provides the only fully quoted riddle in the stories of the Hebrew Bible (Judg. 14:14). But the Hebrews understood "riddle" much more broadly than we do today. The Hebrew term for "riddle" can also be translated as "dark saying" or even "parable."[83] These forms demand even more reader-learner participation.

Riddles use ambiguous language, with literal, metaphoric, and symbolic meanings, which requires reader-learners to figure out (hidden) clues that would make sense of the whole.[84] Riddles are a "test."[85] Indeed, usually there is an implicit ban against telling learners how to make sense of a riddle: that would acknowledge

---

82. Ibid., 18–23.
83. See Ps. 78:2 and 49:4. James G. Williams, "Proverbs and Ecclesiastes," in *The Literary Guide to the Bible*, ed. Robert Alter and Frank Kermode (Cambridge: Belknap Press of Harvard University Press, 1987), 272.
84. James L. Crenshaw, *Samson: A Secret Betrayed, A Vow Ignored* (Atlanta: John Knox, 1978), 99–100.
85. Ibid., 105.

their failure. Indeed, the riddle may be less a particular form of proverb and more a quality characteristic of proverbs themselves. Riddles serve especially well when a larger truth cannot be read directly and simply from surface appearances. Then ambiguous or equivocal language serves both to express truth yet preserve mystery.[86]

Riddle forms are especially appropriate to the task of learning how to discern order or truth implicit in or hidden behind the seeming chaos and confusion of appearances. Parker Palmer says, "Education would not be necessary if things were as they seem,"[87] suggesting education can be seen as a process of puzzling things out, discerning the clues, or working at the riddles of life. Egyptian wisdom texts speak of proverbial sayings as "knots," so the one who comes to understand is described as "one who loosens ropes" or "unties knots."[88]

The *numerical sayings* of chapter 30 of Proverbs do not tell the reader what they mean or how to solve the puzzle of their sense, just as Jesus' parables most often do not tell the reader one right way to interpret them: "Three things are never satisfied" (Prov. 30:15); "Three things are too wonderful for me" (30:18); "Under three things the earth trembles" (30:21); "Four things on earth are small, yet . . . wise" (30:24); "Three things are stately" (30:29). The reader is left to ponder what is so wonderful about "the way of an eagle in the sky, . . . a snake on a rock, . . . a ship on the high seas, and . . . a man with a girl" (30:18–19). Here earth, sea and sky, bird, reptile, and inanimate object are joined with human behavior under a common description. That itself is almost "too wonderful" and stretches the mind. Since no answer is offered, different readers may discern different ways in which these four exceed understanding.

Proverbial riddles not only call forth creative thinking by the reader-learners; they evoke reflection and wonder at two levels at once: first, wonder about the subject of the riddle (e.g., wonder that an eagle, a ship, a snake, and a man may all have something in

---

86. Ibid., 103–4. Crenshaw also claims the riddle sets a trap or misleads or partakes in a mood of malice. This may be true of Samson's riddle. Yet Crenshaw also claims that revelation in the Hebrew Bible was normally via riddles, citing Num. 12:8. If that is so, then while it may be appropriate to speak of the need to discern more than appearances, it is not clear why malice and the intent to deceive are necessary ingredients of a riddle.

87. Parker Palmer, *To Know As We Are Known: A Spirituality of Education* (San Francisco: Harper and Row, 1983), 19.

88. Shupak, *Where Can Wisdom Be Found?* 316.

common) and second, wonder at the delight or joy of the learning task itself. When learners accept an invitation to puzzle out a riddle or enjoy an ironic observation, observe how much energy and imagination emerge in the process. This is not a pedantic, passive, or boring way to learn.

We have seen what the sages considered worth learning and how it was to be learned using proverbs. What is such learning for? Why do it that way?

WHY? WHAT IS THE POINT OF LEARNING THUS?

Roland Murphy claims that in Proverbs 1:5, "The hermeneutical key to the entire work is given; all that follows is to provide guidance (or "steering," Hebrew: *tahbulot*)."[89] Walther Zimmerli agrees: "Wisdom is *per definitionem tahbuloth*, the 'art of steering,' knowledge of how to do in life."[90] The Tanakh translates the verse: "The discerning man [*sic*] will learn to be adroit" (1:5, NJPSV). What could be a more fitting description of the purpose of wisdom than learning to steer one's way adroitly through the mazes of court and daily living? Indeed, this may not only describe the task of reader-learners in approaching the texts; it also implicitly describes how the sage functioned in the royal court, adroitly discerning and evaluating what is going on below the surface while not arousing the king's ire.

To Learn to Read Life

Since these are texts, one of the early tasks of an educational process must be learning to read. But reading texts is not an end in itself. Today's pedagogical language speaks of "mastering the basics," "getting the facts right," "finding the right answers," "pursuing truth," or "preparing for the job market." Proverbial sayings speak of reproof and correction, listening, understanding, loving and pursuing wisdom, discerning the good path, justice, and the fear of the Lord.

By concentrating on ordinary life and by requiring of reader-learners active learning, these texts imply that the purpose of learning to read texts is to become able to read life more clearly, more truthfully, with a sense of solidarity, humility, and awe. The

---

89. Murphy, *The Tree of Life*, 16.
90. Walther Zimmerli, "The Place and Limit of the Wisdom in the Framework of the Old Testament Theology," in *Studies in Ancient Israelite Wisdom*, ed. James L. Crenshaw (New York: KTAV, 1976), 317.

texts assume and intend that as one learns to read the ways of life, one learns to discern the ways of God.

To Steer the Right Way and Pedagogical Authority

Learning to see the right way is necessary, but seeing it is not enough. The texts tell reader-learners what to look for, how to recognize good and evil. Sometimes they tell the reader-learner *what to do* (which is the teacher-author's task), but more often they tell the reader *how to steer* (which is the learner's task). They make observations and invite or tease readers into drawing their own conclusions, to be practiced and tested in life experience, which learners must do for themselves.

In prophetic and priestly texts, teaching authority is seen as speaking directly on behalf of God, either in priestly transmission of the Torah consensus or in a prophetic revelation from the Lord that challenges that consensus, saying, "This is the word of the Lord."[91] Unlike the priest and prophet, the sage offered no appeal to a specific divine commission,[92] but rather the sage appealed to the communal tradition of the people and their families ("Hear, my child, your father's instruction") or to the created order ("Consider the ant [or lilies]") or to the listener's own experience of reality (Ps. 19:2). As Crenshaw has shown, the prophet constantly found himself in conflict with hearers who challenged him to show whether his was true or false prophecy. To vindicate their message, the prophets appealed to a call or visions or to covenant tradition, or they just argued with the people.[93] Such disputes polarize speaker and hearer, defining the conversation as "attack and defend," thus inhibiting reception of a new message. In defending themselves when a prophet exposed injustice, people often deflected the debate to the claim to prophetic office and away from the validity of the message. The question addressed (often implicitly) to the prophet was, Can you prove that you have the right to be *in* authority?

By comparison, Brueggemann observes, the wisdom texts "do not seem to hold much authority."[94] Perhaps what is being pre-

---

91. See Walter A. Brueggemann, *The Creative Word: Canon as a Model for Biblical Education* (Philadelphia: Fortress, 1982), chaps. 2–3.

92. Von Rad, *Wisdom in Israel*, 309.

93. James L. Crenshaw, *Prophetic Conflict: Its Effect upon Israelite Religion* (New York: Walter de Gruyter, 1971), 49–61, 103–6, 121–22.

94. Brueggemann, *The Creative Word*, 67. Zimmerli also spoke of a "deficiency in authority" in the wisdom texts; see his "Concerning the Structure of Old Testament Wisdom," in *Studies in Ancient Israelite Wisdom*, ed. James L. Crenshaw (New York: KTAV, 1976), 183–85.

sumed in these texts is not a lack of authority but a rather different approach to authority in pedagogy than some conventional approaches allow. The sage rather made observations about reality and social life and how to make oneself happy, prosperous, and moral and left validation of the message up to the listener by trying it out. The sage claimed no "office." Besides, his message often seemed quite noncontroversial.

The prophetic message may have had a greater impact because of the conflict and the necessity of making decisions both about the peoples' guilt and about the external political situation. The sage, on the other hand, may not have evoked such defensive behavior, thus leaving people more free to hear the message, yet perhaps it was easier to ignore altogether.

Educationally, values can be seen in both. Learning necessarily involves conflict, for to learn something new or different, one must often give up or change what one already knows. Yet educationally, conflict naturally evokes defensiveness, which inhibits short-term effectiveness.

The educator also can learn about the dangers of getting sidetracked to the issue of *being in* authority. Is one relying exclusively on someone else's authority? For the educator, it is much more important to be recognized as *having* authority, which happens when one demonstrates one's own competence in the teaching-learning interaction and when the subject matter being taught is not only effectively handled but also turns out to be true to life and reality.[95]

To Encourage Reflection: Conserve or Change?

Reflecting upon and learning from experience is one of the primary principles that Proverbs teaches. But that creates an interesting puzzle (which the texts of the wisdom tradition themselves must face): What if what we learn from experience contradicts the lessons urged in this text?

Let's briefly consider explicit proverbial sayings on three subjects: (*a*) how to act in the king's presence, (*b*) disciplining children,

---

95. Recognizing this distinction between "having authority" or "being *in* authority" and "being *an* authority" illumines how the appeals to authority differ between the prophets of Israel and her sages. The appendix to Crenshaw's *Prophetic Conflict*, 119, claims that prophet and sage spoke with the same amount of authority, though with differing perspectives (i.e., the prophet's outlook is vertical, while the sage's is horizontal). Perhaps the sage focused more on being *an* authority while the prophetic and priestly roles were, by definition, focused upon being *in* authority, so the issue is not "quantity" of authority but what type authority is operative.

and (c) women. Can the Book of Proverbs' teaching on these matters still be considered sound advice to guide contemporary behavior? Should it?

Proverbs frequently advises readers how to live with the king (Prov. 16:10–15; 20:6–9, 26, 28; 22:11; 23:1–3; 24:21–22; 25:2–7, 15; 29:12–14; 31:1–9). What do we do with such sayings? At the most simple level the question is, How can we take these texts seriously if we live in a democracy? If these are unchanging divine directives, must we first establish a kingdom? Or if we no longer live in a kingdom, shall we ignore such texts? Or shall we reinterpret them as advice to be applied metaphorically not to kings but to presidents, governors, or perhaps even teachers, pastors, and others in positions of authority? But if we thus reinterpret, how far can we go? How can one reinterpret texts that assume hierarchical authority and power relations antithetical to the basic principles of a democracy? If we interpret sayings about behavior with kings metaphorically, shall we do the same with other sayings?

Regarding the second subject, many readers are wary about the advice on child discipline offered in Proverbs. Some advocate this proverbial advice quite literally (while they ignore proverbial advice about kings). On what grounds is one set of teachings adopted while another ignored?

Some take the proverbial sayings on child discipline so seriously that they assume that "spare the rod, spoil the child" is a biblical saying.[96] The sayings most frequently quoted are

> Those who spare the rod hate their children,
> but those who love them are diligent to discipline them.
> (Prov. 13:24)

> Do not withhold discipline from your children;
> if you beat them with a rod, they will not die.
> If you beat them with the rod,
> you will save their lives from Sheol. (Prov. 23:13–14)

A later wisdom text is much more detailed:

> He who loves his son will whip him often,
> so that he may rejoice at the way he turns out.
> . . . .
> Pamper a child, and he will terrorize you;
> play with him, and he will grieve you.

---

96. Actually it comes from Samuel Butler's poem "Hudibras" of 1664. See Philip Greven, *Spare the Child: The Religious Roots of Punishment and the Psychological Impact of Physical Abuse* (New York: Knopf, 1990), 227 n. 3.

> Do not laugh with him, or you will have sorrow with him,
>   and in the end you will gnash your teeth.
> Give him no freedom in his youth,
>   and do not ignore his errors.
> Bow down his neck in his youth,
>   and beat his sides while he is young,
> or else he will become stubborn and disobey you,
>   and you will have sorrow of soul from him. (Sir. 30:1, 9–12)

Such texts are sometimes cited in manuals on child discipline and are used to justify corporal punishment in families and in schools. Some parents who take their religion very seriously feel these texts command them to punish their children, even if they are reluctant or ambivalent about doing so.

The historical studies of Philip Greven[97] and the detailed historical and psychoanalytic analyses of Alice Miller[98] have made us aware of the many effects of child beating, even that which is justified on religious grounds. There is persuasive evidence that such beating can turn children into murderers, bigots, suicides, and other distortions of divine intent. Others insist that contemporary society is too permissive and these texts guide us to more effective forms of child rearing. Are these texts relics of an earlier, uninformed age, or are they warnings about being too permissive?

The physical discipline of children is part of the wisdom tradition, as it was of the cultural ethos. Is this a part of the tradition we want to retain? We have not retained the arbitrary and coercive rule of kings, preferring instead more rational and participatory ways of decision making. Could the same be said for arbitrary and coercive child discipline?

Perhaps there is a prior question to be faced. Is it possible to adopt such texts directly without first taking into account the considerable difference in cultural standards such texts presume? Anthropologists have given us clear descriptions of the differences between today's Western cultures and those of the ancient Mediterranean. The approach to child rearing presumed in a text like Proverbs is based upon a fundamental distrust of the child and the fear that evil tendencies may erupt into evil deeds. To prevent this, and to make a boy into a "man," love must be coupled with the

---

97. Greven, *Spare the Child.* See pp. 47–49 for his treatment of proverbial material, but the whole work is relevant and sobering.

98. Alice Miller, *For Your Own Good: Hidden Cruelty in Child-Rearing and the Roots of Violence* (New York: Farrar, Straus and Giroux, 1983).

infliction of physical pain. This is done to accomplish the separation of boy-child from maternal care (at age seven or eight) and to induct the boy into masculine social norms. In such a culture, it is not the physical punishment that makes the discipline work so much as its being coupled with such societal values as subordination to (paternal) authority, strict family loyalty, in-group solidarity, and family honor/shame.[99] Obviously, these are cultural values not uniformly shared in Western democratic societies. What happens when the discipline practices are transferred without the support of those correlative social values?

Often proverbial sayings that directly command ("Do this") or prohibit ("Don't do this") also provide motive clauses, which offer reasons for obeying (Prov. 3:1–6; 4:6, 10; and others). The intent, as we have seen, is to cultivate in learners the practice of learning from their own and others' experience, as well as from newer paradigms for social relations. Just that poses the dilemma.

In the case of kings, our accumulated experience and new understandings of what makes leadership effective have convinced many cultures that the divine right of kings was not a right embedded in the nature of things. Instead, gradually, with much pain, it was decided there was not, or ought not to be, such a right. In an analogous fashion, the experience of historians, psychiatrists, and social-science researchers suggests that following the advice to beat children is not the best way to bring about the desired results. Responsible studies by reputable scholars substantiate the claim that brutality to children impedes, rather than encourages, moral maturity.[100] Violence breeds more of the same, and violence to children can help form violent adults who become abusive and too readily confuse pain and violence with the power to control others, with erotic stimulation, and even with religious duty.

If one of the basic principles of proverbial wisdom is to learn from thought and experience, what do we do when our thought and experience (especially when it is systematized and documented scientifically) tell us that some proverbial sayings may be mistaken?

---

99. John J. Pilch, " 'Beat His Ribs While He Is Young'(Sir 30:12): A Window on the Mediterranean World," *Biblical Theology Bulletin* 23 (1994), 101–13. See also Bruce Malina, *The New Testament World: Insights from Cultural Anthropology*, rev. ed. (Louisville: Westminster/John Knox, 1993).

100. This point is common in the many Kohlberg empirical studies, which show that reinforcing the lower levels of moral reasoning impedes movement to more complex modes, but a similar point can be made from several different developmental schemes.

What principle do we follow when one body of experience contradicts another? This dilemma is built into the wisdom tradition itself, since the central figures of both Job and Ecclesiastes used experience to question the theological tradition of the elders, and both are in our canon. Interestingly, a careful look at the way the text of Proverbs handles the role of women in an androcentric society may provide us with some clues about how to handle these questions.

Indisputably, these proverbial sayings are expressions of an androcentric culture. These are lessons primarily intended for boys and men. Never is a woman or girl explicitly intended to be the learner in these texts. Still, if we look carefully, we may notice the presence of a self-critical principle intrinsic to the texts of this tradition.

First, in wisdom texts from other Near Eastern cultures, the mode of address is *always* father to son, whereas here it is often father advising son to listen to both him and the boy's mother. Indeed, Proverbs 31:1–9 is unique among Near Eastern texts in that a queen mother instructs her son how to be king.

Second, while the feminine motif was used to hold the attention of male adolescent learners in Proverbs, Woman Wisdom is portrayed as responsibly and deeply involved with Yahweh from the beginning, not only as an ordering principle of creation but also as intrinsically necessary in learning and discerning the right path. This is most clearly evident in Proverbs 2–4 and 8–9. Indeed, she is even described as offering the blessing of "long life" and as a "tree of life" (Prov. 3:16, 18), which resonates with or parallels the blessings of God in both the Decalogue and the creation story.

Third, the Book of Proverbs uses powerful women to "frame" the heart of its message.[101] Not only are the opening chapters structured by the parallel appeals of two (metaphorical) women, but they also frame the rest of the book as a choice of two ways — one foolish and one wise, both depicted as women! This frame is completed in chapter 31 with reflections upon another strong, capable, or "valiant woman" (a better translation than the traditional "good wife").[102] This woman not only organizes and oversees the planting but works the fields, markets the merchandise, and is

---

101. See Camp, *Wisdom and the Feminine*, chap. 6.
102. See the excellent discussions in Elizabeth Huwiler, *Biblical Women: Mirrors, Models, and Metaphors* (Cleveland: United Church Press, 1993), 21–22; Farmer, *Who Knows What Is Good?* 123–27; and Camp, *Wisdom and the Feminine*, chap. 4.

generous to the poor, while her husband lives off her efforts and reputation (31:23). This is an idealized but remarkable picture. Such textual patterns, woven into the text alongside less-flattering portrayals of women, depict women as either the worst or the best, as long as women remained liminal figures. There are few realistic portrayals of women. Still, today, these idealized portrayals suggest the presence of alternative (biblical!) paradigms in gender relations that can be used to question conventional androcentric convictions.

How then do we interpret wisdom advice when newly discerned wisdom questions or contradicts older or more traditional wisdom? First, we must acknowledge that the texts themselves urge such critical reflection and decisions upon us, for it is in making such judgments that we learn to be wise. Second, if experience is one of the basic principles to which appeal is made in wisdom, then experience must be used in deciding between new and old versions or in finding how they are compatible. But in these texts, experience is neither a subjective, individual feeling, nor is it an authoritative pronouncement for all time. In wisdom texts, experience is a collective, communal consensus that has been tried and tested over time, even generations. Communal consensus does not come easily or without controversy, discussion, and hard work, as the prophetic writings surely testify. Yet consensus also changes. (Remember, in 1 Samuel 8–12, Israel came to a new consensus about wanting a king — even against God's "advice.") The issue is not how old the advice is, or who gave it, but how thoroughly it has been tested, whether it works, and for what or for whom it works. Third, *all* bear responsibility for that ongoing testing and learning and for the judgments that follow. Such judgments are a prime means of education and becoming wise.

Indeed, if we remember our history, this is what the texts of the Hebrew and Christian Bible have themselves done repeatedly. For example, as Michael Fishbane has shown, the Hebrew biblical text (*traditum*) has been repeatedly modified (*traditio*) by scribes down through the centuries with the intent of making the received text more accessible to readers or making it theologically more compatible (with the views of the scribes or copyists). This has happened in all genres and styles of texts. In each case, the intent is to reinforce the authority of the tradition (*traditum*) by means of changing it (*traditio*).[103] Indeed, Fishbane concludes, "A *tradi-*

---

103. Michael Fishbane, *Biblical Interpretation in Ancient Israel* (Oxford: Clarendon, 1985), 78–87.

tum always exists by virtue of its *traditio*."[104] In other words, this process of revising the biblical text, both as text and as theological conviction, can only be faithfully preserved by changing it faithfully. If this is true even of Torah texts and prophetic texts, how much more the wisdom texts?

Today, as in the biblical texts, there will be controversy and disagreement, which require judicious and prudent decisions. These decisions will be based on tradition, on what the texts recommend, *and* upon what we now know to be true. Indeed, if discernment and the ability to see below the surface are one of the primary goals of wisdom instruction, this is exactly what we should expect. A true sage should never be completely satisfied with what has already been learned. Neither should an educator.

If these texts intend to enable "steering through the maze of experience, seeking not to dominate, but to assume responsibility,"[105] then preserving the guidance of those who have steered the course before is wise. But steering also requires paying close attention to where course corrections may be needed, for the underwater shoals of the river may have shifted over time.

To Teach Virtues and Form Character

Proverbial sayings, oriented to living life, assume a broad understanding of what it takes to engage in living. In Proverbs, that includes the virtues of hard work, self-control, humility, courage, and just plain good sense. One must acquire, shape, and reshape such virtues. Proverbial sayings do not simply catalog virtues but promote adopting such virtues, with the knowledge, emotions, and attitudes they require, so that they form central character traits in each person.[106] Education in almost all cultures until the twentieth century was more about acquiring character than it was about acquiring knowledge. For example, we noted above that, pedagogically, acquiring knowledge is intrinsically related to an eagerness to learn, including an openness to correction and a willingness to learn from one's mistakes, even from people and situations that

---

104. Ibid., 88.

105. John White, "The Sages' Strategy to Preserve *Shalom*," in *The Listening Heart: Essays in Wisdom and the Psalms in Honor of Roland E. Murphy, O.Carm.*, ed. Kenneth G. Hoglund et al. (Sheffield: JSOT, 1987), 307.

106. See the careful descriptions by William P. Brown, *Character in Crisis: A Fresh Approach to the Wisdom Literature of the Old Testament* (Grand Rapids: Eerdmans, 1996), 23–35.

did not intend to teach — in other words to *humility*, which is not cognitive.

Interestingly, while Proverbs frequently admonishes reader-learners to resist taking the easier paths and to persist in the right way, courage (a virtue common in Greek and Roman wisdom) never is mentioned. Still, courage is often necessary in acting wisely, though courage need not be seen as a lone individual "standing tall." In these texts, courage is relational and takes form within trust. It begins, as we have seen so often in the opening chapters of Proverbs, with the trust of a child in parents and teachers. It reaches out to trust in Woman Wisdom and Yahweh (3:5).

Even reader-learners must begin with trust in a text because in order to learn, they must open themselves to the new, to what they do not know and to correcting what they thought they knew. They also must be open to recognizing self-contradictions. Since others can see our contradictions more clearly than we do, we must learn to trust others to help us see ourselves truthfully. That requires both humility and a courage rooted in trust in God and parents (3:11–12).

This sense of trust in parents, in God, and in others is grounded in a child's earliest sensual experiences, as psychologists and educators have often observed.[107] Here the threads of character begin to be formed — and integrity begins to take shape. As William Brown has effectively shown, this is not an individual achievement since the sages' "path can only be formed by the passage of many feet."[108]

> Those who trust in their own wits are fools;
> but those who walk in wisdom come through safely. (Prov. 28:26)

In Proverbs, character is communal rather than individual.

To Act Wisely, with Integrity

To become wise, intelligence is necessary but not sufficient. Even the fool can sometimes seem wise (17:28). (The wise fool has a long tradition.) The joke of the wise fool is more than funny; it often has a telling point best heard with humor. However, many of the proverbial sayings reach beyond words or intelligence to

---

107. Erik Erikson's *Childhood and Society*, 2d ed. (New York: Norton, 1963), is a classic description of how important this basic trust is in individual and social development.

108. Brown, *Character in Crisis*, 34.

actions that show integrity. Integrity is a sense of coherence and wholeness of life, a condition in which speech, attitudes, actions, and character are congruent with one another. In Proverbs, acting with integrity is a security better than wealth:

> Better to be poor and walk in integrity
> than to be crooked in one's ways even though rich.
> (Prov. 28:6; also 10:9)

One's integrity is evident not so much in what one thinks and says, but rather, one's thinking, character, and wisdom are manifest in what one does. This is as true for those who teach as for those who learn:

> The righteous walk in integrity —
> happy are the children who follow them! (Prov. 20:7)

Did the sages themselves follow their own advice? Did they "walk in integrity"? Brueggemann seems to think not, arguing that the sages of Proverbs were co-opted by the court and royal interests, functioning "as the intellectual brain trust for policy formation, as ideologues for social justification, and as pedagogues for the young who must inherit the monopoly."[109] In so doing, they provided "a rationalization for present systemic inequity and exploitation."[110] This entails a judgment that the sages lacked integrity, for they not only benefited from the status quo, they trimmed their message to maintain it, sustaining injustice while teaching justice.[111] This view either charges the sages with lacking integrity or with just not being very smart, not seeing their own self-contradictions. That seems inconsistent with what we have seen in these texts. Further, if these texts show reader-learners how to quietly adjust to the interests of those in power, how do we then account for wisdom texts that are critical of the status quo, even

---

109. Walter A. Brueggemann, "The Social Significance of Solomon as a Patron of Wisdom," in *The Sage in Israel and the Ancient Near East*, ed. John G. Gammie and Leo G. Perdue (Winona Lake, Ind.: Eisenbrauns, 1990), 125.

110. Ibid., 131.

111. Ibid. It should be noted that Brueggemann is not making a historical claim, but a claim that the texts reflect a "remembered Solomon" and thus also an ideology that permits exploitation of the poor for the sake of the rich. It should also be noted that Brueggemann speaks directly here only of the text of 1 Kings, but his argument applies as well to other texts by implication. See Walter Brueggemann, "The Epistemological Crisis of Israel's Two Histories (Jer. 9:22–23)," in *Israelite Wisdom: Theological and Literary Essays in Honor of Samuel Terrien*, ed. John G. Gammie et al. (Missoula, Mont.: Scholars, 1978), 85–105.

of the ethics of the court (e.g., Prov. 29:4, 12–14, 16, 26), but especially Job and Ecclesiastes?[112] Where did they learn such critical discernment?

The sages of Proverbs claimed to teach the ability to discern, to be shrewd, to understand riddles and enigmas (Prov. 1:2–6), which required seeing truthfully through surface appearances. They also counseled prudence. How does one "steer adroitly" through a social context (e.g., the royal court) in which one fosters equity and shrewdness among the "simple" without stirring up the wealthy and powerful? Is it possible that these sages prudently constructed their teaching to appear thoroughly conventional, acceptable to royal interests, while using patterns of learning and teaching that evoke quite different effects? To imagine that the sages were blind to the effects of their sayings because they were pawns of royal ideology does not seem consistent with the subtle brilliance we have noted in their arrangement and use of proverbial sayings in these collections. Nor does it seem consistent with their occasional critiques of kings and the wealthy. Huwiler suggests there is "a muted subversive message in the sentence wisdom," seen in these critical sentences.[113] Such sentences suggest that those in power sometimes "don't measure up."

As we have repeatedly seen, sentences can be subversive not only in content but also in form. Teachers who invite reader-learners into activities that foster new seeing or insight, which encourage a discerning critique of conventional order and thinking, may recognize that not all reader-learners will "get it," though perhaps some in power will. There is possible danger.

To conclude, the evidence suggests we assume these sages were prudent, shrewd, *and* pedagogically subversive. This is not only more in keeping with how these proverbial sayings act on reader-learners; it also better accounts for the emergence of the even more sharply critical thinking displayed in later texts like Job and Ecclesiastes.

---

112. Brueggemann accounts for them by concluding that Solomon (and "Solomon remembered") also had an emancipatory dimension as well, in the despair reflected in Ecclesiastes. See "The Social Significance of Solomon," 131–32. Perhaps the whole scheme is too simplistic, especially as it seems to presume an older notion of "ideology" as beliefs that make their holder selectively blind. On this view, only some have ideologies, while those who expose the ideologies of others are mysteriously exempt from this condition.

113. Huwiler, "Control of Reality in Israelite Wisdom," 79.

THREE EDUCATIONAL PRINCIPLES OF PROVERBIAL WISDOM

Three general observations about the style and attitude of a proverbial educational approach may hold true for the wisdom texts in
following chapters as well.

The Doctrine of the Proper Time

Schoolmasters have traditionally been firmly committed to the *law
of noncontradiction*. Indeed, the history of Western philosophy
and logic, from Plato, Aristotle, and Euclid on, is dominated by
a concern to identify ways of making clear and certain distinctions
between what is true and what is false, and since contradictions
cannot be true, they are to be avoided.[114] Logic helps to determine what went wrong and to correct the false inference. Children
are taught early to search for the right answers and to fear wrong
answers.

How then are we to deal with Proverbs 26:4–5?

> Do not answer fools according to their folly,
>   or you will be a fool yourself.
> Answer fools according to their folly,
>   or they will be wise in their own eyes.

Here we have two proverbs that offer contradictory imperatives.
Are we to answer or not answer fools? Is one of these wrong? If so,
which one? This problem is not limited to ancient texts. Today we
say both "Look before you leap" and "He who hesitates is lost."
These proverbs also offer contradictory advice, yet we have no dif-
ficulty affirming both. We do not regard one of them as wrong,
only as used at the wrong time or under the wrong circumstances.
Each may be right *under certain circumstances*. This is an important principle basic to all ancient Near Eastern wisdom, which von
Rad called the "doctrine of the proper time."[115]

> To make an apt answer is a joy to anyone,
>   and a word in season, how good it is! (Prov. 15:23)

The most familiar and explicit expression of this doctrine is
Ecclesiastes 3:1–8.

---

114. Eastern thought, especially that influenced by Confucius, operates on quite
different assumptions.

115. Von Rad, *Wisdom in Israel*, 138 ff. "Proper" is used here, not to indicate
that there is some conventional or proper thing to do that will determine what to
say or do, but to indicate that judgment is called for concerning what is appropriate
or fitting or even needful. It may be that sometimes the proper thing to do is not
"proper."

For the sages the issue is not which proverb is the right answer but which proverb is the right counsel for the right person,
at the right time, in the right situation. Should I advise Jim to act
quickly while there is opportunity ("He who hesitates is lost"), or
should I counsel him to take time to carefully think through the
possible consequences ("Look before you leap")? Choosing which
proverb to use will depend upon a host of prior judgments. For example, I must judge wisely about Jim's character (does he tend to
act without thinking, or does he typically dither endlessly?), about
the social circumstances (is there really a hurry?), and so on. Here
wisdom (as used by ordinary people in ordinary circumstances) is
defined as making such judgments with enough reflection and attention to previous experience that our decisions are sound and do
not consistently lead to further trouble.

Pedagogically, the task is to help learners ask for themselves:
What time is it? What is it time for? Which path shall I take? Judging the proper time can be very complicated and sophisticated. Yet
it is a process we all use every day — and which we do not learn
only in schools or from someone else's teaching. I suspect the Hebrew sages would have agreed with Aristotle: these are matters that
can only be learned well by practice. The teacher can help a learner
discern accurately what is real, what is at stake in this judgment,
what can be learned from the community's experience and traditions, and then can offer support for having the courage to try
it out.

Proverbial Sayings as Playing with Metaphors

J. G. Williams observes, "Metaphoric play is the most important
element of Wisdom poetics."[116] It also is one of the most important
educational dimensions of biblical wisdom writings. A metaphor is
an intrinsically playful or imaginative way of making sense out of
something. The simile

> Like a city breached, without walls,
> > is one who lacks self-control. (Prov. 25:28)

suggests we can better understand an undisciplined person by
thinking of how he or she is like a city without walls. But the
text does not tell reader-learners how to imagine this similarity.
For example, we could think, walls hold in the city, and thus a
city without walls has no boundaries; it spreads indiscriminately.

---

116. Williams, "Proverbs and Ecclesiastes," 275.

Similarly, an undisciplined person may be one whose attention wanders without boundaries. Or we could focus on the idea that this city had walls, but they have been damaged. Is there a breach in this person that needs repair? Or are both aspects to be noticed at once?

A metaphor works because of both the similarity *and* the dissimilarity of its two parts. A city is not literally a person, so a city and a person must be both like and unlike. Repairing an object (a wall) is different from repairing a subject (a person), and we had better honor those differences. Reader-learners using their own experience and imagination must make sense of what is like and unlike. This means reader-learners may well make more than one valid inference about a saying's meaning and use. A metaphor necessarily leaves gaps, which the hearer must fill. These gaps can never be completely eliminated, yet only by filling the gaps can one make sense of the text. If we make the metaphor too clear, if we settle the ambiguity in our drive for clarity and precision, we destroy the metaphor (turn it into an allegory), stop the metaphoric play, and thus inhibit the learning possibilities. However, to allow the reader to fill the gaps presumes that the text (and the author/teacher) places considerable trust in the capacities of reader-learners.

These metaphors are also an invitation. They invite reader-learners to see themselves in certain imaginative situations, trying something out in imagination before trying it in reality. In Proverbs 2:1–15, for example, the reader-learner is invited to picture herself walking down a path (metaphorically) where she must repeatedly decide which way to turn. The right way is not always self-evident; it must be searched for. Yet if she listens attentively and searches diligently, insight, understanding, and wisdom are given. Thus she learns what to look for, how and where to search (and where not to search). The picture here presumes that this kind of understanding comes, not just in the safety of a classroom preparation for the journey, but on the way, where there is danger. Here both teacher and reader-learner must work hard, for one must have "sharp eyes and an active mind in order to be able to distinguish good from evil."[117] Similarly, it may be hard to do the good even if and when it is recognized.

The mood or style of an educational approach appropriate to such texts must reflect something of this playful or ambiguous

---

117. Von Rad, *Wisdom in Israel*, 80.

manner, which may also invite one to create her own metaphors, contemporary and relevant, seeking community testing and affirmation, which may be offered to future generations. This approach will also enable learners to become more discerning about the metaphoric quality of like biblical texts. The educated learner will learn to discern which metaphors are important or dominant in a text's way of seeing the world. As we shall see later, the intrinsic ambiguity of metaphor is an especially apt way to express the necessity of a sense of mystery in our talk of things divine.

Embracing the Ordinary as Learning How to Go On with Life

The sages believed God's hidden order and will are all around us, and we must be constantly attentive, receptive, and able to use the community's experience in our own reflection to discern the clues. Reader-learners cannot constantly interrupt their living with "Please wait while I go ask my teacher." But often what is being reflected upon in proverbial sayings is not (or is no longer) "mountaintop experiences" or divine oracles or major turning points in national history. The right way is being sought in mundane matters like table manners, making loans, gossiping, making money, going to work, living with a neighbor or spouse, friendship, when to keep silent, and so on. Proverbial wisdom can be fascinating to study for its own sake, but like Ludwig Wittgenstein said of philosophy, it is intended to help one know how to go on with living life.

CHAPTER TWO

THE PRESENCE OF ABSENCE
Job

The Book of Job displays a genius that has stimulated readers for centuries. The long list of artistic works (novels, dramas, poetry, music, dance, paintings, films) it has stimulated is tribute to its power and lasting appeal.[1] Yet seldom has its pedagogy been examined carefully, perhaps understandably, since unlike the direct instructional intent of Proverbs, the Book of Job teaches quite indirectly.

Proverbs tells no stories, although readers are required to imagine narratives to make sense of the sayings. In Job, we find a loose narrative frame, not about God's saving acts in history, but a frame for poetic arguments about faith, suffering, and God's justice. Some educators may feel more at home here as the text tries to solve problems, offer explanations, interpretations, and arguments in the search for right answers or a more complete truth. There are surprises as well.

For reader-learners, the move from Proverbs to Job can feel like a seismic lurch. On the surface, there are many familiar features. Proverbial sayings are quoted, there are admonitions to self-control and humility as well as appeals to tradition, experience, and the created order, with competing reflections upon justice and the rewards of being righteous. Yet some familiar elements are missing. There are no more miniature enigmatic descriptions of "the real" or admonitions to hard work or reflections upon how to behave

---

An earlier version of portions of this chapter was presented as "The Book of Job: Education through and by Diversity" to the International Seminar on Religious Education and Values (ISREV) meeting in Banff, Alberta, Canada, 23–28 August 1992; and published with the same title in *Religious Education* 92:1 (winter 1997), 9–23.

1. See the five-page, single-spaced listing by David J. A. Clines in his commentary *Job 1–20* (Dallas: Word, 1989), cviii–cxii.

in the presence of a king or how to succeed in business. Worse, there are rumblings underneath, which keep throwing readers off balance, as familiar convictions seem to shift inexplicably. Israel's confidence that consequences and actions go together, often seen in Proverbs, is under siege in Job.

The seismic shift is especially felt in the shift from the cool, dispassionate atmosphere of Proverbs to the white-hot emotional turmoil of Job. If pain and suffering are mentioned in Proverbs, they are justified, for they happen to those who do not follow the right path, the fools, with whom the reader should not identify. In Job, things are not so simple.

THE STRUCTURE AND CHARACTERS OF THE BOOK

While the literary composition of the book is complex and controversial,[2] the structure of the book is simple. The book begins (chaps. 1–2) and ends (42:7–17) with prose narrative (to set up and resolve the drama), and in between all is poetry and argument. The prose prologue introduces the story of Job's afflictions — his loss of children, wealth, social standing, and health. The poetic arguments debate why this happened and what should or could be done about it. In the prose epilogue, Job is restored to health, wealth, and family and lives to a ripe old age with the blessing of God.[3]

An omniscient narrator begins the prologue:

> There was once a man in the land of Uz whose name was Job. That man was blameless and upright, one who feared God and turned away from evil. There were born to him seven sons and three daughters. He had seven thousand sheep, three thousand camels, five hundred yoke of oxen, five hundred donkeys, and very many

---

2. See the critical literature reviews included in the commentary by Clines (*Job 1–20*) or in J. William Whedbee, "The Comedy of Job," *Semeia* 7 (1977), 1–39.

3. Many scholars have argued that the present book is likely a composite work, incorporating legends, poems, and material that may have originally existed independently. That may well be so. Often this line of thinking has been used to resolve the tensions presented by the text. This approach is aptly described in the irony of Robert Gordis, a Jewish master of the wisdom literature: "The assumption is made that a conglomeration of separate documents, unrelated and at times even opposed to one another, were either haphazardly or deliberately manipulated to produce a masterpiece." See Gordis, *The Book of God and Man: A Study of Job* (Chicago: University of Chicago Press, 1965), 15. Despite the obvious fractures or gaps in the existing structure, we now have it as a literary whole, which is how reader-learners encounter it. Therefore, we shall seek to understand it as it is, not as it might originally have been.

servants; so that this man was the greatest of all the people of the east. (Job 1:1–3)

Reader-learners are thus introduced to the central character of the story (not an Israelite!), who is pious, wealthy, a great man, and thus has been blessed — an attractive figure.[4] The fourfold characterization (blameless, upright, feared God, turned from evil) assures readers this is a truly good man. Reader-learners then discover that Job is so scrupulously pious that he even offers sacrifices on behalf of his children, just in case they had inadvertently sinned during one of their parties (1:5).

Thus, as in any story, reader-learners are invited to accept not only the main character, Job, but assumptions necessary for the story to "work." The first premise is that Job is blameless and righteous and feared God. (Here some readers will have to suspend, at least temporarily, their belief that no human is completely blameless.) It is so important to the story that readers adopt this assumption that it is repeated by God in 1:8 and in 2:3, accepted as true by the adversary, and reiterated by the narrator twice more (1:22; 2:10).

The scene shifts from earth to heaven, and reader-learners find two new characters: *ha satan*[5] (if translated in English, "the adversary") and "the Lord" (Heb. *Yahweh*). The adversary, portrayed as

---

4. Part of the power of the book can be traced to the author's ability to abstract his characters from a particular historical and geographical setting. Job is not a Hebrew name, and he comes from Uz, outside Israel. Indeed, only Elihu bears a Hebrew name, yet he is ignored by all other characters, including the narrator. While "the Lord" (Heb. *Yahweh*) does speak, the generic name "God" (Heb. *Eloah*) is used most often.

While the book most likely took its present shape in the postexilic period, it may incorporate older (non-Hebrew?) Job legends. Several ancient Near Eastern texts are significantly similar to Job in subject matter, characters, or even wording, ranging from the Canaanite poetic epic "Keret" to the Egyptian "Dialogue of a Man with His Soul," the Babylonian "I Will Praise the Lord of Wisdom," and the Sumerian "Man and His God." See James B. Pritchard, ed., *The Ancient Near East: An Anthology of Texts and Pictures* (Princeton: Princeton University Press, 1958), vol. 2 for texts, or for summaries and comments, see Clines, *Job 1–20*, lix–lx; Roland E. Murphy, *The Tree of Life: An Exploration of the Biblical Wisdom Literature* (New York: Doubleday, 1990), 151–81. Job deals with issues that are historically and culturally concrete, yet not historically and culturally specific.

5. The presence of the definite article *ha* assures the reader that this is not a proper name (just as one would not say "the David"). Thus, rather than transliterate the word as though it were a name ("Satan"), it should be translated, for example, as "the adversary," as does the NJPSV. This text does not describe the adversary character as personified cosmic evil opposing God. It was John Milton who fused the serpent of Genesis and Lucifer from Isaiah (neither of which is called *satan*) with later notions of the devil and Satan in his *Paradise Lost* (1667), and from Milton we derive many of our popular notions of the devil. It is anachronis-

one of the "sons of God," whose job it is to keep an eye on what is happening on earth, has apparently not noticed Job until the Lord, seeming to boast, calls his attention to him:

> "Have you considered my servant Job? There is no one like him on the earth, a blameless and upright man who fears God and turns away from evil." (Job 1:8)

Here reader-learners are invited to adopt a second assumption: God initiated and is responsible for what follows. The adversary questions the Lord's description of Job, posing the fundamental challenge of the prologue and epilogue: "Does Job fear God for nothing? You've made him rich. Take it away and we'll see about his piety" (Job 1:9–11 paraphrase). Is the question real or rhetorical? Does the adversary truly not know what Job will do, or does he suspect Job fears God because of what he gets out of it? What does the Lord character think? While the Lord does not say directly, the adversary is given permission to proceed against Job, so reader-learners may presume either that the Lord does not know and allows the test to find out or that the Lord assumes Job will continue to be faithful. So Job's children all die, as do his servants and all his cattle. Job is bankrupt and in deep mourning.

How are reader-learners to respond? Are we not invited to feel empathetic with Job and feel some wariness about divine beings who play so loosely with human lives? Should humans like Job be used as pawns in a divine contest for bragging rights? Very subtly the narrator has invited readers to turn toward Job and away from the other two characters, at least out of a sense that "this isn't fair."

The other characters that the narrator introduces in the prologue play supporting roles: Job's children, servants, and wife. They are to be the means by which Job's suffering is made credible to the reader. It is striking that while's Job's agony is later described in great detail, the suffering of Job's children, servants, and wife is not even mentioned.[6] Indeed, an attentive reader may think to ask

---

tic to read such notions back into this text. See Peggy L. Day, *The Adversary in Heaven: Satan in the Hebrew Bible*, HSM 43 (Atlanta: Scholars, 1988).

6. Indeed, the treatment of Job's wife through the history of reflection on this text is worse than being ignored — she is often unjustly condemned and abused. Augustine called her the "devil's assistant," and Calvin "Satan's tool," and Aquinas thought Satan spared her in order to use her against Job. Yet in the text she echoes the speech of both the adversary ("curse God") and that of Yahweh ("Job persists in his integrity"). Her comment is truly ambiguous: the Hebrew has no interrogative. Is she recommending that Job curse God to continue his integrity or to give up

about the fate of these other characters. If Job is blameless, are they as well? But if *they* are being punished for sins, that turns the question away from *Job's* motives for being faithful. If the reader-learner is to continue exploring the adversary's question, he must also assume, at least for now, that the guilt or innocence of Job's wife, children, and servants is not an issue; otherwise, his attention may turn to questions about God: What kind of God would kill (or give permission to kill) children, servants, and cattle and torment a father and mother, just to answer an adversary's question? Does God not know how it will come out? If not, God is not omniscient. If God is all-knowing, why allow the adversary to pursue it at the expense of these innocent people? What kind of God is this? Or does the text intend for reader-learners to surmise that the adversary's question poses a double challenge: Are both Job and God being tested?

Through all this, the character Job remains oblivious of the heavenly contest between the Lord and the adversary. Once again the Lord asks the adversary, "Have you considered my servant Job?" (2:3), and boasts, "He [Job] still persists in his integrity." Then the Lord explicitly accepts responsibility for destroying Job: "you incited me against him, to destroy him for no reason" (2:3). Still, the adversary and the Lord again focus the readers' attention on Job and his motives for being faithful, and further testing ensues. Even Job's wife serves to direct the reader's attention to Job rather than to God, but Job persists in his faithful loyalty to God, as the narrator confirms, "In all this Job did not sin" (2:10).

By now, reader-learners have surely begun to feel empathy for this tragic figure and to feel a sense of conflict or tension — that something serious is wrong here. Conventional Jewish and Christian religion teaches the belief that God rewards good and punishes evil, which is a theological and ethical commonplace. This is so because God is both just and powerful. Wealth and social approval are signs of divine blessing, while suffering is a demonstration of

---

his integrity? See discussion in William P. Brown, *Character in Crisis: A Fresh Approach to the Wisdom Literature of the Old Testament* (Grand Rapids: Eerdmans, 1996), 58–59.

Terrien even suggests her plea may be "inspired by love and common sense...the desperate and bewildered woman, still confident in her husband's integrity, unable to hope for his healing, and profoundly sympathizing with his plight, found her only recourse in the idea of euthanasia, and prescribed for her husband a theological method of committing suicide." See Samuel Terrien, *Job, IB* 3 (Nashville: Abingdon, 1954), 921. Also see the discussion of the history of interpretation of this text in Clines, *Job 1–20*, 50–55.

divine disapproval (i.e., is punishment). This, too, is a common-place throughout the Bible and is taken for granted by the sages of Proverbs. Yet the story rests upon an empirical fact: Job is suffering despite the fact that he has been a pillar of righteousness as far as any can see. If this fact is true, there is something wrong with the belief. If the belief is true, this fact must be false. This is the dramatic tension that pulls the reader-learner through the book looking for resolution. Which must give — belief or fact?

The author presumes that the reader-learner shares the belief. (It is what most parents in most cultures assume in raising their children: "It's only fair.") The author underlines the veracity of the fact regarding Job for the reader by having it affirmed repeatedly.

The crafting of the story has invited reader-learners to entertain a theological and ethical dilemma, which then becomes the topic of poetic debate throughout the rest of the work. While this is indirect, rather than direct, pedagogy, it certainly does enlist the reader's own beliefs, imagination, and feelings to create in his or her mind a question about the orthodox doctrine of retribution: Is good always rewarded? Is evil punished? If not, why not? And even more, allowing reader-learners to listen in (as though secretly) to the dialogue between the Lord and the adversary puts them in a privileged position, where they know more than does Job about what is going on. The effect on readers is to help forge a sense of kinship with Job and a correlative suspicion about these divine characters, who do not seem to be playing fair. In other words, we have been made accomplices in being suspicious of God!

While Job mourns the loss of his family, servants, and wealth, three new characters appear: Job's "friends," or comforters, arrive. With the introduction of these characters, the scene shifts from heaven to earth, where it remains for the rest of the book. As this happens, the adversary drops out of the story, never to appear again! Apparently the adversary character has served his sole purpose in the story: to help pose the double challenge for readers. The author also drops the third-person omniscient prose narrative and strikingly turns to first-person poetic lament, thereby inviting the reader-learner to see everything that follows in the next forty chapters through Job's eyes, thoughts, and emotions!

In the process, in a subtle way, the double aspect of the central question emerges. Job, not being aware of the heavenly discussion of his own motives (as the reader is), asks, "Why me? Why suffering?" This can be read as Job's asking, "I have been as righteous as I know how to be. I have been faithful, and thus I expected to have been blessed in return. Why am I suffering?" Does that presume the adversary was right? Is Job's piety self-interested? Is he primarily interested in what he gets back from God?

On the other hand, Job's *why* question not only may be about his own confusion but may also be a question about the nature of God: "Why does God keep the bitter alive and fence them in? What kind of God is this? I thought I knew, but now I am not so sure" (cf. 3:20–23). Do Job's questions hint that he wonders if God is living up to God's own moral standards?

Reader-learners stand in two places at once — here in our contemporary world reading a story and yet simultaneously inside the central character of the story, feeling his (and our) anguish and his (and our) inability to comprehend what is happening. The ability of a story to pull the reader inside is a powerful pedagogical device, and here it pulls the reader-learner into a dilemma that subverts familiar assumptions about conventional moral order.

Job's friends have sat in silence for seven days, honoring the custom that the mourner must speak first (2:11–13). Now that Job has spoken, they begin their reflections and counsel, each offering his own explanations to resolve Job's enigma, yet the text insures that a reader-learner will read these explanations from the vantage point of "inside" Job. Do they have answers for Job's (and our) questions?

Enigma Explained

Each of the friends offers explanations to Job, but not because they feel the tension created by conflicts between belief and fact. They see no such conflict, for like Job and unlike reader-learners, they were not party to the prior conversations.

Job's friends all start with the obvious fact: Job is suffering. But each sees that empirical data through the lens of theological and ethical conviction. Thus they argue *backwards:* from conclusion to (hidden) premise. They reason: "Job is suffering; suffering is punishment. Therefore, there must be a prior condition (a hidden premise) that caused or accounts for that suffering; that is, Job must have sinned." Ironically, these sages seem to have learned their wisdom lessons well — they do not take things at face value. They use their ability to discern what is going on below the surface: despite appearances of being blameless, Job must have sinned. Though their feeling tone ranges from sympathetic to harsh anger and condemnation, their advice to Job is consistent: Repent and confess your sin (be prudent), and you will be right again.

When a fourth friend, Elihu, arrives, apparently unanticipated by the narrator, he offers a more directly pedagogical explanation. While he affirms retribution (34:12), Elihu echoes a theme from Proverbs 3:12 (hinted at by Eliphaz as well in 5:17–18) in explaining Job's suffering, not as punishment, but as God's teaching method. God terrifies to warn people to turn away from their misdeeds and from pride, to "spare their souls from the Pit" (33:16–18). Yet Elihu also refuses to believe Job's innocence:

> "You say, 'I am clean, without transgression;
> I am pure, and there is no iniquity in me.'
> . . . .
> But in this you are not right." (Job 33:9, 12)

How does he know this? Has he investigated? No, he knows this because "God is greater than any mortal" (33:12). Indeed, like Zophar, Elihu proposes things could get much worse if Job does not learn his lesson in time to avoid a God clothed in majesty (36:12–22; 37:1–24).

Elihu's notion of the pedagogical significance of suffering can be both true and dangerous. In the hands of friends like those counseling Job, this explanation can be used to add to the torment of the sufferer and to justify brutal pedagogical practices, since they are only part of the "necessary" pedagogical suffering.

Notice how awkwardly the text has now positioned the reader. On the one hand, the convictions being expressed about God and morality are familiar and taken for granted by many. God is powerful; who can contest with God? Yet the reader-learner, receiving these explanations from the dual vantage point of knowing what occurred in the prologue and of participating in Job's view, knows from the beginning they are all mistaken! The reader wants to say to the friends, with Job, "But you're not listening!"

The reader is also led to perceive that all these arguments are immune to evidence or counterargument. Each friend already knows the proper conclusion without investigation — no matter the evidence of Job's life and no matter what Job says. They say to Job, in effect, "Our theology and tradition tell us what is real and true, and if your life and your viewpoints do not fit that, you are wrong. You will have to make your experience fit this theology." This further induces the reader-learner to "take sides" with Job, but that also positions the reader against God!

How does Job respond? Job laments that not only is God terrorizing him, but his friends cannot be trusted, even when he begs for their honest words and when he wishes God would kill him (6:4, 8–9, 15–27). The reader-learner can feel the tension and anguish mount. Then Job moves beyond reflection and lament to protest directed to God:

> "Therefore I will not restrain my mouth;
> 　I will speak in the anguish of my spirit;
> 　I will complain in the bitterness of my soul.
> Am I the Sea, or the Dragon,
> 　that you set a guard over me?
> When I say, 'My bed will comfort me,
> 　my couch will ease my complaint,'
> then you scare me with dreams
> 　and terrify me with visions,
> so that I would choose strangling
> 　and death rather than this body.
> I loathe my life; I would not live forever.
> 　Let me alone, for my days are a breath." (Job 7:11–16)

In this first cycle of speeches (chaps. 4–27), Job speaks seven times of being bitter or of "bitterness of soul."[7] It is not surprising that Job is described as bitter, but when he expresses his bitterness in generalities, it leads to generic complaint (3:20; 9:18; 21:25). Yet in 7:11 (and again in 10:1), Job's language shows that he accepts his bitterness as his own: he speaks of "the bitterness of my soul." In each case, Job engages in direct address to God in the very next verse. It is as though when Job manages the courage to "own" his bitterness, he finds the courage to speak directly to the one responsible.

In 7:12–21 Job's direct address to God is couched in irony, saying in effect, "Am I some kind of monster that you have to watch me so closely? When I seek comfort in sleep, you invade my dreams. Why are my little sins so important to you? Haven't you anything better to do? Get a life! If my sin is so offensive to you, take it away! Let me be! I'd rather have your absence than your torturing presence!" Job again quotes the tradition. In a parody of Psalm 8, dripping with irony, he quotes Scripture to God: "What are human beings, that you inspect us so minutely? . . . Are you obsessing? What will you do with yourself when I am gone?" (Job 7:17–21; cf. Ps. 8:4). Here again, reader-learners find themselves in the midst, empathizing with Job's anguish, wondering why God

---

7. See 3:20; 7:11; 9:18; 10:1; 21:25; 23:2; and 27:2.

allows this, yet prudently not wanting to be quite as blunt as Job seems willing to be!

In chapter 9 legal language begins to emerge with greater frequency. Job uses words like *contend, innocent, appeal, mercy, accuser, summoned, contest, matter of justice, condemn, the judges, complaint, trial,* and *umpire.* Job acknowledges that the disparity between his own impotence and God's power makes it unlikely he will get a fair hearing, even though he is innocent (9:2–35). He briefly entertains the idea of a lawsuit but concludes it is futile:

> "For he is not a mortal, as I am, that I might answer him,
>   that we should come to trial together.
> There is no umpire between us,
>   who might lay his hand on us both." (Job 9:32–33)

Job finally decides he cannot rely on his friends and that his only recourse is to try to bring God to trial, to file a lawsuit, in effect, charging God with mismanagement of the universe, even though he knows the tradition says that no one can come face-to-face with God and live:

> "I will take my flesh in my teeth,
>   and put my life in my hand.
> See, he will kill me; I have no hope;
>   but I will defend my ways to his face.
> . . . .
> I have indeed prepared my case;
>   I know that I shall be vindicated." (Job 13:14–15, 18)

The climax to Job's case comes as he puts together his legal brief. He begins reminiscing about the good old days, when he and God were intimate and Job was honored and respected by others (chap. 29). He laments how far he has fallen and how God has caused his torment, even unto death (chap. 30). He rehearses his innocence by means of a rigorous code of honor and affirms his complete integrity (31:1–28). Finally, acting as his own defense attorney, he outlines his defense (though he has not yet been formally charged) and signs his legal brief (31:29–37). It is now up to God to declare him innocent. The narrator concludes, "The words of Job are ended" (31:40).

In filing his legal brief, Job explains that his suffering came, not because of his sin or the sin of his children, but because God has behaved unjustly, without cause. Job reaffirms his integrity and implicitly challenges God to respond, since tradition claims that not to respond is to admit guilt. Ironically, Job and his friends agree in their theological convictions, yet they draw radically different conclusions. Both accept retributive justice. Just as the friends *infer backwards* from a conclusion (Job's suffering) to a *hidden premise* (Job must be a sinner), so Job also *infers backwards* from a conclusion (he is suffering unjustly) to a *hidden premise* (God must be unjust).

What are reader-learners to do? There are several possibilities: (*a*) We can refuse to accept the premise of the prologue (that God could be responsible for innocent suffering), which might mean either to side with the friends (and find Job guilty of some hidden sin) or to refuse monotheism (evil must come from some source other than God). (*b*) We could stop reading the book (after all, it is only fiction!). Perhaps the book is unfruitful or implausible, since it presumes something about God that "we know" to be untrue (that God could be unjust) or since it assumes something about a human that we know to be untrue (that Job could be blameless). This particular response may be awkward for those who recognize this book (this fiction) as part of the Jewish and Christian canon, yet to take the book seriously is to be led to question some versions of orthodox theology and ethics. (*c*) We may proceed to wrestle with the dilemma as one made possible by an imperfect (finite) knowledge both of God and of other human beings. If we choose to wrestle, we are faced with the need to seek empirical evidence as far as it will lead us and, simultaneously, the need to reexamine some of our most deeply held convictions.

Even these choices pose dilemmas: The first two options arise because one has been sufficiently educated to be convinced that logical consistency is important in theological matters. Yet to accept either of these options is to stop the educational process. To refuse to play along with an author is to refuse to take the risk (new learning) that the text poses for a learner. Refusing to play along does not mean there is no risk, however, for in opting out, reader-learners risk being unable to grow beyond the dilemma to a new level of understanding. On the other hand, the last option, facing the dilemma, which seems to "know" less, leads to an ongoing learning process, yet with no assurance there will be a satisfactory answer at the end.

Ultimately in question are the conventional theological and ethical convictions of the Hebrew people (perhaps evoked by the experience of captivity and the destruction of Jerusalem). Israel had long believed that God would protect Jerusalem forever, as King David said: "The LORD, the God of Israel, has given rest to his people; and he resides in Jerusalem forever" (1 Chron. 23:25). Did the captivity mean that God broke a promise? The prophets had claimed that God was just and the exile was a punishment for sin. But the children who suffered most in the exile were suffering innocents. What kind of God would do that? Does God adhere to the same ethical standards God lays down for humans? Is God just or capricious?

Thus the author has faced reader-learners with a vivid picture of a radical crisis for Israel, indeed, for the whole Near Eastern understanding of world as coherent and just order. Covenant-oriented beliefs are threatened,[8] for a covenant presumes the enduring faithfulness of its guarantor. While the wisdom tradition appeals not to the covenant but to the created order, that too is threatened, for the stability of creation also requires the consistent maintenance of order by the Creator.

This crisis is not confined to ancient history. All contemporary systems of justice assume that evil acts call for punishment or retribution, while good behavior should be affirmed. Questions of retributive justice figure prominently among those attempting to make sense of racism and among liberation theologies of all stripes. If the conventional Deuteronomic theology and ethic are correct, people get what they deserve. What then becomes of the preferential option for the poor or the concern for the innocent and oppressed? This theology says they are getting what they deserve. On the other hand, if retribution is no longer operative, neither Job nor liberation theology has a basis for complaint. If God's actions are capricious and need not adhere to the principles of justice, what happens to the foundational principle for liberation theologies or, indeed, for the concept of covenant?

How can we choose? Surely there must be another view, a larger synthesis, that will reconcile this dilemma. Perhaps reader-learners can find it in the Lord's view.

Explanations Rejected

Since the third chapter, God seems a silent spectator, as though observing the other actors on stage. In chapter 38, it is as though God can no longer stand it and takes the stage, addressing Job di-

---

8. J. G. Williams, "Mystery and Irony in Job," *Zeitschrift für die alttestamentliche Wissenschaft* 83:2 (1971), 251.

rectly, with vehemence.[9] Now there seems only one issue, as the Lord speaks:

> "Gird up your loins like a man;
> I will question you, and you declare to me.
> Will you even put me in the wrong?
> Will you condemn me that you may be justified?
> Have you an arm like God,
> and can you thunder with a voice like his?" (Job 40:6–9)

It is as though God says, "Are you powerful and wise enough to stand up and challenge God? Demonstrate your qualifications before we go on! If not, get off the stage."

Suddenly, the terms of the discussion have changed. Job's friends had insisted the issue had to be retribution. Job had defined the issue as the justice of God. The Lord's language ignores both and asks about power versus impotence and knowing versus ignorance. The Lord does not recite the mighty acts of saving history known from covenant and redemption history but questions Job about stars, dawn, seas, snow, lightning, lions, mountain goats, the ostrich, horse, the hawk, and especially about Behemoth and Leviathan. This magnifies Job's (human) ignorance and impotence *and reframes the question.*

Job asked, What kind of God can we believe in? The Lord, who earlier (2:3; and again later, 42:10) acknowledged responsibility for Job's plight, expresses no empathy or concern for Job's suffering, nor does he mention Job's alleged sins. The reader-learner is bound to be at least perplexed: Has the Lord missed the point? As Samuel Terrien asks, "Why should he [Job] be forced to hear lessons in geology, astronomy, meteorology and zoology, while he is consumed by disease and unrequited love?"[10] Ironically, this is what Job had earlier predicted — that even if God appeared, he would not listen but would crush Job with divine power despite the justice of his pleas (9:16–19). God has "come on like a Divine Blowhard, a God-Almighty Wind, never really dealing with the questions, and parading his cosmic power apparatus in a way that fulfills Job's predictions."[11]

Having heard from the Lord, what does Job do?

---

9. Luis Alonso Schökel, "Toward a Dramatic Reading of the Book of Job," *Semeia* 7 (1977), 47–48.
10. Terrien, *Job*, 228–29.
11. Williams, "Mystery and Irony in Job," 247.

"I had heard of you by the hearing of the ear,
   but now my eye sees you;
therefore I despise myself,
   repent in dust and ashes." (Job 42:5–6)

He repents and withdraws (from the dialogue? or withdraws his lawsuit?). Reader-learners must now infer that Job's view is no longer viable. But why? Of what does Job repent? This feels too abrupt — but apparently Job sees something. What? The text does not say.

Thus the dialogue and differing viewpoints come to an end. But if the Lord's speeches have just now clarified for Job what the real question is, why should the discussion stop here? Is not this where the discussion should become most profitable? If Job withdraws at this point, does that not suggest that God's power and freedom permit God to play loose with justice? Are Job's discovery and withdrawal ironic? Has Job finally seen God clearly, or has he finally decided to accept the friends' advice? J. G. Williams asks, "What kind of a universe must Job now live in? Some suggest it must be a meaningless universe mismanaged by a chaotic, capricious, jealous Tyrant."[12] Many questions are left unanswered.

Where does this leave reader-learners? Is this just another wild-goose chase? The reader can hardly help feeling that nothing is as it appears here — we have beliefs and facts, we have truth and fiction, we have humans and sons of gods and the Lord God, and we have such discrepant pictures of what is really the case that it seems impossible to decide.

Do the last eleven prose verses help? The narrator returns and reports that the Lord declared (as we already knew) that the three friends (Elihu is ignored) had not spoken rightly of God, *as Job had* (42:7–8), and they were to ask Job to pray for them. As for Job, "the LORD restored the fortunes of Job when he had prayed for his friends; and the LORD gave Job twice as much as he had before" (42:10). And the book concludes: "So Job died old and contented" (42:17, NJPSV).

What does that settle? Still there is no telling what has changed the outcome. The enigma remains an enigma. What are we to draw from this about what is worth learning?

---

12. Ibid.

WHAT IS WORTH LEARNING?

Several of the themes we identified in Proverbs are developed or added to in the Book of Job.

The Search for Order

Whereas in the Book of Proverbs the sages roamed through the created order and human behavior using the image of a right and wrong path to help reader-learners learn how to steer through life, they did not anticipate that their commitment to integrity and to congruence between what one believes and what one does would find expression in anything like Job's conflict with the Lord! In fact, if we look for the voice of the sages of Proverbs in the Book of Job, we seem to hear it most clearly in Job's friends, whose message was rejected both by Job and by the Lord (and presumably by readers). On the other hand, Job, like the sages of Proverbs, is less interested in speculation about the universe than he is with how to cope with his own suffering. The Lord seems to insist upon lessons in cosmology, but even those seem more designed to humble Job than to teach him metaphysical truths. Job wants to know "how to read" his own life. The way of reading he has known before no longer seems to explain his experience. Yet seldom does Job ask God to explain God. And though the Lord rejects the explanations offered by the friends, he offers no alternative explanations.

What then are we to conclude about order from this book? At this point, only nonorder seems to hold. Clearly one thing has been rejected: retribution is not the ultimate explanation. Does this book suggest that neither God nor the universe can be reduced to the kind of order found in retributive justice? Perhaps reducing justice to a formula, especially one that confines or controls God, is unacceptable. That borders on magic.[13] Such formulaic and retributive justice may work *within* a legal system, where rights and wrongs are predefined. Is retribution as relevant when the issue is not legal but governance of the whole system?

A king or creator must be concerned about justice, but justice as governance differs from retributive justice. How does one apply retributive justice to a wild horse or to lightning? Indeed, not only is retribution too narrow a scope for God, but perhaps so is justice. Robert Gordis poetically suggests that the order and harmony of

---

13. Good, *In Turns of Tempest*, 193; James L. Crenshaw, *Trembling at the Threshold of a Biblical Text* (Grand Rapids: Eerdmans, 1994), 83–87.

the moral realm differs from that of the natural world and that beauty cannot be measured by the criteria of justice:

> The poet's ultimate message is clear: Not only *Ignoramus*, "we do not know," but *Ignorabimus*, "we may never know." But the poet goes further. He calls upon us *Gaudeamus*, "let us rejoice," in the beauty of the world, though its pattern is only partially revealed to us. It is enough to know that the dark mystery encloses and in part discloses a bright and shining miracle.[14]

If this is true, it asks the reader-learner to expand the notion of order one brings to thinking about God and the world alike. This, at least, the sages of Proverbs would approve.

Indeed, Carol Newsom has argued that the Lord's speeches, by ignoring the moral terms within which the dialogue has proceeded, draws the reader-learner into an alternative set of images and language.[15] Job and his friends have drawn their moral discourse using language that reaches from the family circle at the center to civic society (the city gate where Job was respected) to the margins (where reside the poor, the orphans, and widows who depend upon Job), arranged in a hierarchy of value. That Job experiences his suffering in terms of such language is confirmed by the images he uses for his pain and innocence in chapters 29–31. As the Lord describes the created order and asks Job if he comprehends it, Job is confronted with another realm of discourse that is not relational or familial and that requires him to contemplate the finite reality of another realm of subjects: snow, ice, horses, goats, and so on. None of these phenomena and creatures can be comprehended using the language of human relations. Nor are they presented in any predetermined order or status or hierarchy with each other. Yet the detail of description suggests that the Lord finds them fascinating, delightful, and worthy of contemplation. Does this suggest a reframing of the moral imagination? As though by contemplating the ostrich, Job might also stumble upon an answer to the Lord's questions concerning Job's own vocation and integrity: "Who are you?"[16] If the author intends a new form of order, it is left to Job and reader-learners to infer and construct.

---

14. Gordis, *The Book of God and Man*, 133–34.

15. Carol Newsom, "The Moral Sense of Nature: Ethics in the Light of God's Speech to Job," *Princeton Seminary Bulletin* 15:1 (1994), 10–15.

16. Brown expands Newsom's interpretation by considering the Yahweh speeches for what they portend for the "character" of God; see *Character in Crisis*, 91–103.

The Fear of the Lord: Justice and Mystery

While the phrase "the fear of the Lord" occurs only once in the Book of Job, the reality of that fear spreads all through Job's ruminations, those of his friends, as well as in the thundering of the Lord's climactic confrontation with Job. There is little doubt that the friends meant to frighten Job. And there is little doubt that Job needed no more terror, for that is how he already saw God's actions:

> "For the arrows of the Almighty are in me;
>   my spirit drinks their poison;
>   the terrors of God are arrayed against me." (Job 6:4)

Job initially cannot even dream of going to trial with the Lord for fear:

> "If he would take his rod away from me,
>   and not let dread of him terrify me,
>   then I would speak without fear of him." (Job 9:34–35)

Job expects the terror of God to descend on the friends for their speaking falsely for God and upon himself when he decides to go to trial (13:10–11, 14–16).

Such texts make it clear that to attempt to see in them only awe or reverence would miss the depth of Job's torment. Indeed, what most frightens Job is not just that he is being inexplicably visited by a malevolent God but that this God cannot be appeased by Job's obedience. This God has at one and the same time insisted upon Job's faithful integrity and yet terrorized him despite that. It even seems to Job (and his friends agree) that the longer he holds to his integrity, the worse his suffering becomes. Yet, ironically, to let go of his integrity is then to deserve punishment!

The Book of Job questions magical formulas by which good behavior controls God's responses or all suffering can be traced back to some previous sin. If God is transcendent, God cannot be confined to human explanations — not even those of justice. Job expressed this with his claim that God is not only a merciful and benign presence, but even to those who are his intimates, God can be a malevolent presence. That is a truly disturbing idea, but the Lord does not deny it. Instead, he declares Job has spoken rightly of God (42:7–8). This is especially disturbing if we cannot believe that God will always be just.

What are we to say to this? First, these thoughts are not Job's alone. We find them elsewhere in the biblical record and in the testimony of the faithful through the ages. Second, it seems incredibly trite, but perhaps the only thing to say is that this is acknowledging that ultimately God is mystery. Here we reach the limits of human understanding. Third, we (and Job) also know that God is gracious, which we also know by the faithful testimony of many. More to the point, perhaps, and possibly where Job arrived as well, is the recognition that we live in this world more by *trust* than by *knowledge*.

The Meaning of Suffering and How to Cope with It

Many have taken this book to be primarily about the meaning of suffering, especially the suffering of innocents. Surely this would have been in the mind of those Israelites caught in the turmoil of the exile. The explanations of Job's suffering offered by the friends were rejected both by Job and by the Lord.

One understanding of Job's repenting is that he stopped trying to read everything else and allowed himself to be read. The Lord's questions on Job's final examination on the universe and wild animals may have helped pull Job out of the isolation he describes in chapter 30, enabling Job to see himself more clearly — with a more limited role in cosmic affairs.[17] He did not have to be responsible for affairs beyond his competence, but that did not mean he was alone. Job's was no mean accomplishment:

> When humans no longer think themselves alone, masters of all they survey, when they discern the humility of their place in the vastness of God's creation, then that creation and its God can share the pain...[so they] can begin to understand the pain that cannot be avoided as a gift which teaches compassion and opens understanding.[18]

If we are to regard all this as an educational process, if teaching and learning are going on here, it surely is quite different from our familiar contemporary patterns.

HOW DOES LEARNING OCCUR?

We observed that the Book of Proverbs is directly and explicitly pedagogical. The Book of Job is more indirect. It seems to be narrating a story about someone other than the reader-learner. Yet

---

17. A. S. Peake, "Job: The Problem of the Book," in *Theodicy in the Old Testament*, ed. James L. Crenshaw (Philadelphia: Fortress, 1983), 107–8.

18. Erazim Kohak, *The Embers and the Stars: A Philosophical Inquiry into the Moral Sense of Nature* (Chicago: University of Chicago Press, 1984), 45–46; quoted by Newsom, "The Moral Sense of Nature," 26.

while Job and the other characters play out their roles in the story, reader-learners join in the debates.

Tradition, Experience, and the Use of Power in Teaching

Comparing the speeches of the friends with those of Job reveals some stark differences with pedagogical import. Both Job and his friends use the power of their respective expertise. The friends have theological expertise. They have studied God and how God works so thoroughly they know what Job needs, even without asking him. Eliphaz and Bildad appeal to the power of tradition ("the elders"; 8:8–10; 15:10, 17–19) and the power of social consensus to insist that Job should fall in line (4:7; 5:27; 15:7; 18:4). (Today this strategy would be called *domination*.)

Job feels the power of their position keenly. Yet he has spoken the truth as he sees it and pleads with his friends to teach him and help him understand: "Look at me; for I will not lie to your face" (Job 6:28). It is as though Job has gone to a physician who prescribed a treatment without ever engaging in any diagnostic procedure. The friends never ask Job, "What is the matter?" Their theological expertise has told them from the start that one diagnosis holds for all who suffer — and therefore the same remedy applies — regardless of specifics. Job is an object of their speeches. They do not need to know Job at all. They could have prescribed his lessons by computer modem from another country.

This is familiar pedagogical procedure. Teachers and other experts sometimes prescribe curriculum without regard to who learners are in their particularity, in essence saying, "You can't always ask students what they want to know — some things they just have to learn because they are true." Ironically, in this case, the friends' expertise is traditional, normative, communal truth — exactly the community standards of truth about God into which teachers are expected to lead students.

The Job character is learning he is no longer in control. He wonders if he can trust his traditional theology, and he reads tradition with ironic eyes. He is not even sure he is asking the right questions, for he keeps changing his approach. Job's expertise, what he knows most intimately and with certainty, is his own experience of suffering and his knowledge that he has done nothing to warrant such suffering. His expertise is a shattered worldview or theological picture that no longer makes sense. As reader-learners watch the drama unfold, they feel the pain his friends add by ignoring Job's personal experience and knowledge, denying their validity by refusing his experience and knowledge a voice. The friends represent tradition, social consensus, and theological expertise, which could become a resource for Job. Instead tradition, consensus, and expertise seem to prevent the friends from hearing the impotent one. They are puzzled by his ignorance, and they refuse his reading of tradition. Experts sometimes feel they need not learn from the ignorant and impotent. They know the answers.

Expertise is open to abuse, as is any power, and becomes doubly powerful when it is coupled with a genuine need on the part of the other, that is, the ignorant or impotent. The expert is tempted to regard the imbalance between need and expertise as a hierarchy, but within the teaching-learning interaction, a teacher's expertise exists for the sake of learners. The teacher is servant not lord. When a teacher's power is used to protect or enhance the teacher and the teacher's convictions at the expense of the learner, as in the case of Job, we see pedagogical abuse. The learner is being used.

Being Invited Inside Another

We observed the author's shift to first-person language in chapter 3, inviting the reader-learner to identify even more closely with the character of Job and to read the ensuing debate from inside his consciousness, including his incredibly intense emotional responses. While this happens infrequently in biblical texts, it is a familiar device in fiction. It is also a useful pedagogical procedure that can help a reader-learner to better understand views that are either outside one's own experience or are dramatically different from one's own views. Walking in another's shoes can enable a reader-learner to see what role those beliefs play in the context of another person's life. When we look from the inside, we can also discern that beliefs are not only intellectual arguments but also have emotional and behavioral dimensions that can deepen our understanding of the beliefs themselves.

In my opinion, one of the saddest aspects of much of the teaching that goes on in the name of religion is how little it seeks to understand those who believe differently.[19] Job's friends refused to try to see the world from within his consciousness, which made it easier for them to become abusive of Job, even as they saw themselves as helping Job! Here is another testimony to how thin is the

---

19. But see the recent work on the Continent and especially in England, for example, Robert Jackson's team of researchers and writers, whose approach is outlined in his *Religious Education: An Interpretive Approach* (London: Hodder and Stoughton, 1997).

line between help and abuse and how readily self-deception erases the line altogether.

Job's friends operate mostly at the level of intellect. When they get emotional, it is because Job has insulted the rightness of their ideas and arguments or refused to submit to their prescriptions (20:2–3). It is as though the only parts of their bodies that count are their cool heads. Perhaps they have learned the lessons of the proverbial sages about self-control very well. They seem afraid that Job's passions are not under control and that his emotions are getting the better of his theology (8:2; 15:5, 12–13). Job, on the other hand, has been touched — he has sores, physical pain, broken relations with loved ones, as well as his own psychological torment and spiritual anguish. Job's theological reflections are, not simply the product of his detached rationality, but are directly and inescapably related to the sores on his body and the scars on his soul.

Job's friends present him with a rational God who is both fair and placidly above our power to question. Job's God is as close to him as the pus on his arm and the ache in his heart where his children used to be. Job is asking himself: Where did the God I knew go? Is God a child killer? What kind of God can allow the torture of the innocent? Job's speeches are passionate because his theology cannot be reduced to cool intellect — it rises from and engages with his whole being. Theology is passionate because our passions show what we are most devoted to, what we have a passion for. Our passions determine what we contemplate, how we spend our time and order our lives. If a teenager has a passion for cars, he wants to spend as much time with cars as he can. He cannot leave them alone: he wants to look at cars, drive cars, take cars apart, put cars together, read about cars, talk about cars; he devotes himself to cars.

Job's passion is God — and he knows that passion in every fiber of his being. Look again at the range of body images in chapter 6 and 7: God is in the sores on Job's skin; God has poisoned his blood; God buzzes in his ears; God is in his bed and his dreams, in his breath, in his eyes, in his taste on his tongue, in his spit, in the marrow of his bones, in the bitterness of his soul. Is it any wonder he finds the instructions by his friends shallow and futile?

Do we, as educators, engage people's passions? Or have we become "educational docetists," treating learners as though they only *appear* to have bodies and passions? Do we dare touch their bodies and their sores in the process of learning God? By comparison, sometimes what we have constructed in educational ministry seems designed to make being religious convenient and not-too-upsetting-if-you-please. We make curricular materials as inexpensive as possible, not too difficult for teachers, and fun for the learners. We are eager to explore how the teaching can be entertaining via video or computer.

Being religious can be a profoundly intellectual challenge. It is also profoundly and passionately emotional, and it is incarnate and embodied. I think the Book of Job indirectly suggests that unless an educational process gets under learners' skin and at least makes them itch, it is unlikely to do much good. In order to be faithful not only to our religious traditions but also to how humans experience life, we must find ways of educating that people can taste, that follows them to bed and seeps into their dreams, that stirs their emotions and alters their passions and expands their visions. Were we to do so, we might be less likely to offer a disembodied faith in a disembodied God. We need to allow ourselves to be invited into our learners' lives so that we might see our people more clearly and know better what would heal their sores and save their souls.

Teacher and Subject Matter as Friends

The reader learns that the friends traveled from some distance to console Job and found him so altered by his suffering they could scarcely recognize him. This presumes they knew Job well, perhaps moved in his circles, perhaps were wealthy themselves, since they could afford long travel and stay away for days.

The word "friend" (Heb. *rea*) used here connotes a relation among neighbors or peers (16:21) or of some long-standing familiarity (Prov. 27:10) or even connotes a lover (Song 5:16). It suggests Job and his friends are of equal stature and thus might expect mutuality; friendship is not a one-way relation. Friendship is a common theme in the ancient world's wisdom literature, as seen in Plato's *Lysis, Phaedrus,* and the *Symposium,* as well as in Aristotle's *Nichomachean Ethics.* Though it is less apparent in the earliest wisdom literature of the Hebrews, it is treated at length in Sirach, and John's Jesus calls his disciples "friends." Martin Buber vigorously denied that friendship is an appropriate way to think about the teacher-learner relationship because it presumes a degree of mutuality that is impossible in a teacher-learner relation.[20] More

---

20. Martin Buber vehemently argued that if a teacher-learner relation became a friendship, it would destroy what he took to be a necessary "one-sidedness" within

recently Parker Palmer has argued that the caring hospitality and trust characteristic of friends suits the task of teaching well.[21] For Palmer, friendship between student and teacher comes about because the teacher has a prior friendship (even a love relation) with the subject matter. The teacher then invites the learner to become friends with this subject, to know it and be known by it.[22] Palmer insists that any true friendship is tested by conflict and is capable of incorporating creative tension into the relation, as in a lover's quarrel.[23]

It is doubtful that the relationships between Job and his friends survive the test. Job becomes convinced his friends not only are not kind but are even treacherous (6:14–18). He sees how his suffering actually frightens others. They hang on all the harder to their convictions, to their clean hands. Their fear cripples their ability to help the weak. Instead, they attack and add misery to misery.

Here is a graphic portrait of the pedagogical effects of fear — and not only on learners. The fears of the teachers prevent them from being able to help their learner. Their own fears evoke so much defensiveness they are unable to reflect upon the adequacy of their own convictions and hear what this learner is really asking. As Norman Habel comments: "A sufferer who has been attacked by Shaddai, the Archer, needs more than traditional answers to sustain him."[24]

Does Job's experience confirm the view that friends cannot be teachers? Friendship is a preferential relation.[25] Does that not conflict with the ethics of teaching? Is the problem here that these friends have chosen another over Job? Have they chosen to remain friends with their convictions, doctrines, and explanations at the expense of their friend Job? Indeed, is that not what faithfulness to God would require? One surely wouldn't change one's faith convictions to suit a human friendship. Must one choose? But if friendship is preferential, it is also mutual, and there is little trace of that in this text. These friends consider themselves Job's supe-

the mutuality that is a teaching-learning relation. See his *Between Man and Man* (Boston: Beacon Press, 1955), 95–103.

21. Parker Palmer, *To Know As We Are Known: A Spirituality of Education* (San Francisco: Harper and Row, 1983), 103–5.

22. Ibid., 104.

23. Ibid.

24. Norman Habel, *The Book of Job: A Commentary* (Philadelphia: Westminster, 1985), 148.

25. Gilbert Meilaender, *Friendship: A Study in Theological Ethics* (Notre Dame, Ind.: University of Notre Dame Press, 1981).

rior. They make no effort to listen to or learn from Job. Job speaks of his earlier relation with God as one of friendship (29:4), but even the Lord's speeches express neither friendship nor mutuality.

Still, might there be friend-teachers who do not insist upon always telling others what to do, friend-teachers who really listen attentively? Might a teacher-friend be able to be a learner-friend at the same time and not resort to conventional nostrums to dull or hide pain?

Questions in Teaching and Learning

Teachers know the importance of asking good questions. How do questions guide the reader through the text of Job?

First, the adversary's question structures the prologue: "Does Job fear God for nothing?" When the debates begin in chapter 3, the questions change and have quite different effects. Eliphaz also begins with a question: "If one ventures a word with you, will you be offended?" (4:2). This is the last *real* question any of the friends ask! A real question is an inquiry that does not already know the answer. All together the four friends ask Job eighty-four questions, of which this one is real, four are quotations of Job's questions, and seventy-nine are either rhetorical questions or impossible questions. A rhetorical question seeks no reply, for it is actually a statement, disguised as a question. When Bildad asks, "Does God pervert justice?" (8:3), he seeks no additional information, for he presumes there can be no other answer than no. Similarly, an impossible question is actually an argument, which "proceeds from consensus" about what is true and thus expects no reply.[26] For example, Bildad asks, "Can reeds flourish where there is no water?" (8:11). Such constructions allow a speaker to ask a question yet continue a monologue. They assume (without asking) assent from the listener or reader.

Job's use of questions is much more diverse than the practices of his friends. In the last five verses of chapter 7, the character of Job explodes with six questions:

> "What are human beings, that you make so much of them,
>   that you set your mind on them,
> visit them every morning,
>   test them every moment?

---

26. James Crenshaw, "Impossible Questions, Sayings, and Tasks," *Semeia* 17 (1980), 19–34.

Will you not look away from me for a while,
   let me alone until I swallow my spittle?
If I sin, what do I do to you, you watcher of humanity?
   Why have you made me your target?
   Why have I become a burden to you?
Why do you not pardon my transgression
   and take away my iniquity?
For now I shall lie in the earth;
   you will seek me, but I shall not be." (Job 7:17–21)

Job begins with a rhetorical question, but by parodying the question of Psalm 8:4, he turns the quoted question on its head to challenge the conventional understanding that humans are important to God. He then asks, "Will you not look away from me for a while?" No may be the presumed answer, but again, if it is rhetorical, it challenges the conventional assurance that the presence of God is good and to be left alone by God is a sign of displeasure. Here Job requests God's absence, at least long enough to swallow. Then Job explodes with a flurry of four anguished questions. They draw the reader further into Job's turmoil, bafflement, and pain at the continued torture. These are real questions begging for an answer and are painful because none seems forthcoming.

Sometimes Job's questions seek to understand God, but more often they are questions asking, "Why me?" Job rarely asks directly for explanations or justifications of God's actions (though see 3:20–23 and 21:7–26). More often he asks to know what he has done (6:24) or for self-justification.

Like Job's friends, the Lord peppers Job with seventy-four questions in four chapters, as in

"Who is this that darkens counsel by words without knowledge?
Gird up your loins like a man,
   I will question you, and you shall declare to me." (Job 38:2–3)

This must surely be a rhetorical question. Does the question seek simply to turn the tables in question asking, or does it try to intimidate, as seems suggested by the assertion in verse 3? Perhaps it is intentionally left to the reader to discern, yet the fact that this voice speaks "out of the whirlwind" (resonance with Sinai?) suggests unequal power.

What follows is a long list of questions that are either rhetorical or impossible, all having to do with some aspect of the mysteries of creation. Is this good pedagogical strategy? Would such questions inhibit or encourage searching? Not only do these questions *not expect answers*, but no space is allowed for a reply! The questions keep coming, one after another, until Job is silenced:

> "See, I am of small account; what shall I answer you?
> I lay my hand on my mouth.
> I have spoken once, and I will not answer;
> twice, but will proceed no further." (Job 40:3–5)

That is ironic; asking questions leads not to answers but to silence. Instead of prompting inquiry, these questions end it. There seems little connection between the questions and the answers.

Is the reader-learner to conclude with Job that someone seems to be withholding the answer? Or do some questions have no answers? (And, as a corollary, might some answers not have questions?) Or are some questions so misleading that it is better not to answer them, or even to ask them? Who is to decide that? Can we tell which is which before we ask? Surely, here we must resist the temptation to think we could catalog the kinds of questions we shall use, as though there could be some formula for that as well.

What are questions for? Do they serve only as a means to answers? When we get an answer, can we discard the question? Are questions used to pin things down and thus offer certainty and guarantees? Do we use questions as a means of closing off possibilities and restricting exploration of the mysteries of the universe and of God? Do we use questions as a way of controlling others — perhaps even ourselves? If so, should we? Would it make sense to affirm, with Wayne Robinson, that "questions are the answer"?[27] Can we use questions as a way of opening up what is new and wonderful and scarcely yet dreamed and, therefore, a little scary? The impossible question, much like the Zen koan, may be used to alter our conventional expectations and modes of inquiry, in favor of "evoking a sense of awe in the presence of mystery."[28] Perhaps some questions aim less at answers and more at worship. Can we use our questions as a way of opening ourselves up? Is that what happened to Job?

Irony, Sarcasm, and Pedagogy

Irony has not often been the subject of inquiry in educational ministry (perhaps, in part, because the field has focused almost exclusively on children and on direct, explicit instruction). Irony

---

27. Wayne Robinson, *Questions Are the Answer* (New York: Pilgrim Press, 1980).
28. Crenshaw, "Impossible Questions, Sayings, and Tasks," 19.

presumes a degree of maturity in the reader-learners because it
(*a*) is intended to stimulate recognizing an incongruity between
what is and how things seem; (*b*) presumes a vision of truth or
of a meaningful or moral universe, a sense of what ought to be;
and (*c*) sometimes presumes there is pain.[29]

Job's friends repeatedly use irony to direct attention to the discrepancy between his position (as a human) and what he claims to
be (innocent). Job returns their irony:

> "I also could talk as you do,
>   if you were in my place;
> I could join words together against you,
>   and shake my head at you." (Job 16:4)

This can be read as a straightforward rejoinder, or it can be an
ironic rejoinder that is critical of the friends' inability to see and
feel Job's predicament, thus a proclamation of how useless their
counsel is to him.[30]

Irony is usually designed to bring about recognition of a discrepancy but does it indirectly, by implying it. Thus it usually takes
an indicative form, requiring the hearer or reader to do the recognizing — and thus trusts the reader for that recognition. But
usually that requires some degree of detachment — which is a lot
to expect of one experiencing existential anguish. When one cannot remain detached, one may be tempted to lash out with sarcasm
more than irony.

The fine line between irony and sarcasm is crossed in the Book
of Job several times. Job lost hope in his friends earlier, even before
Zophar calls Job's words "babble" (11:3) and says,

> "But a stupid person will get understanding,
>   when a wild ass is born human." (Job 11:12)

Zophar's judgment is neither subtle, indirect, nor understated.
The only recognition needed here is that the stupid person is Job
himself. A statement like this may be in the indicative, but it
is a direct, personal attack, holding its object in scorn or contempt. That is sarcasm. Irony can induce humility; sarcasm aims
for humiliation.

Job replies in kind:

---

29. Edwin M. Good, *Irony in the Old Testament* (Philadelphia: Westminster,
1965), 30–33.
30. Ibid., 217.

"No doubt you are the people,
    and wisdom will die with you." (Job 12:2)

That alone might be read as either irony or sarcasm, but Job continues:

"As for you, you whitewash with lies;
    all of you are worthless physicians.
If you would only keep silent,
    that would be your wisdom!" (Job 13:4–5)

Verse 5 might be read as ironic, for silence could be wisdom (recall Prov. 17:28) if it stood alone. But in the context of these other unambiguous statements showing contempt for the friends for falsely defending God, the effect of the whole passage is sarcasm.

How do the use of irony and sarcasm affect the reader-learner and the one being criticized? If irony requires the recipient to discern or unravel the riddlelike language, it can presume respect for the reader-learner, but it is easily mistaken. There is risk, especially when the intent is not clear. The effect of sarcasm, on the other hand, usually is clear — the implicit contempt undermines the climate of trust necessary in a teacher-learner relation and with it, the motivation for learning. Thus, educators reject the use of sarcasm as pedagogically harmful.

What are we to make of the climactic Lord speeches of the Book of Job? They begin with a rhetorical question (38:2) and use impossible questions and irony — what about sarcasm? The answer will depend, as usual, upon how one reads the text. Is the text seeking to elicit humility from Job, or is it an extended put-down, trying to humiliate Job? Scholars have responded on both sides of that question. How do you read the speeches? (My own view will be clear in the last section of this chapter.)

WHY? WHAT IS THE POINT OF LEARNING IN THIS MANNER?

Job and reader-learners alike have been dragged through an intense learning process. What is this learning for? What can be inferred from what is worth learning and how it is to be learned?

Learning as Contest

The idea of learning as a battle or contest for truth (often taking the form of debate) has a long tradition that stretches back at least to the eighth century B.C.E. in both Hebrew and Greek literature.[31] In the ancient world, battles for truth were the common material of legend, myth, and actual ethnic and political conflict. The image of God as a divine warrior is a familiar theme all through the Hebrew Bible,[32] not invented by the author of Job. Battling for truth has been incorporated into the academic world in so many ways we cease to notice our many military metaphors: students "defend" their ideas from the "attacks" of others lest they "get shot down," and then the defender gets called "embattled." Teachers worry about discipline, seek to "empower" learners, and consider their "strategies" and "tactics," and so on. Ph.D. candidates must even "defend" their dissertation.[33]

When we think of contest, we naturally think in terms of power. In the Book of Job, while God's power is depicted as a warrior harassing and abusing Job, more often God's power threatens a fair judicial proceeding. Job feared his case could not get a fair hearing because God had too much power. God was the plaintiff, judge, and prosecuting attorney! Students in schools or children with parents sometimes have similar feelings. Job feared the Lord's power, but eventually he denied that God's power would change his own integrity and truth. Power can establish a winner, but it cannot establish truth, and thus education cannot be treated solely as a matter of power balances. However, power can lead both truth and people to hide, thus corrupting pedagogy.

Perhaps the most frequently heard objection to seeing learning as a form of contest is that in a contest or battle there must be winners and losers while, in principle, there is no necessity for anyone to lose. In this matter, the Book of Job is extremely interesting. In the final analysis, all the major players come out winners.[34] While we hear nothing either way about Elihu and the adversary, Job is restored, Job's friends are restored after Job's prayers, and the Lord decides the outcome.

---

31. Walter Ong, *Fighting for Life: Contest, Sexuality, and Consciousness* (Ithaca, N.Y.: Cornell University Press, 1981).

32. See Patrick Miller, *The Divine Warrior in Ancient Israel* (Cambridge: Harvard University Press, 1973).

33. Both Ong, Miller, and later Carol Gilligan, in her *In a Different Voice* (Cambridge: Harvard University Press, 1982), identify this approach as gendered and masculine.

34. This, of course, ignores the unfortunate role that Job's children and servants play — which is clearly unfair.

Learning as Seeing through Enigmas and Parables

Chaim Potok's novel *The Gift of Asher Lev* portrays the anguish of Asher Lev, an orthodox Ladover Jew and a painter, learning (through a lifetime) about communicating with paint and canvas. At one point, as Lev studies a painting by Picasso, he is approached by a figure at the edge of his consciousness, whom the reader soon discerns to be Picasso himself. Picasso challenges Lev to interpret what he sees and then brashly ridicules his reading of the painting. Picasso charges:

> You know about concealing things, Lev. But you are not yet really good at it.... Truth has to be given in riddles. People can't take truth if it comes charging at them like a bull. The bull is always killed, Lev. You have to give people the truth in a riddle, hide it so they go looking for it and find it piece by piece; that way they can learn to live with it. You tell people God is a murderer, they can't take it, they become angry, they kill you like you're a bull.[35]

Might this also be true when we are teaching about highly controversial and emotionally charged subjects like suffering, death, and God? Is this what the author of Job already knew?

Gordis reminds us that already in the Talmud Job is seen as a parable (Hebrew: *mashal*) for the human condition, for they recognized that not everything can be explicit and logical; sages have a predilection for "implication rather than explicit utterance," and they have an "affinity for riddle."[36] The text of Job invites the discerning reader-learner to see the whole enigma of Job as an extended riddle. Provocatively, in 30:19 Job says, "God has cast me into the mire, and I have become like dust and ashes" (RSV). Here "I have become like" (Heb. *wa'etmashal*) could also be rendered, "I have become a parable [consisting of] dust and ashes."

We have observed how the sages loved playing with riddlelike enigmas and words that evoke multiple meanings. The sages also used words with resonances that invite the reader-learner to remember other texts and thus discover new ways of seeing a text. Suppose we treated Job 30:19 as a pedagogically fruitful riddle inviting the reader-learner to play around with its clues and track down its resonances with other texts:

> "He [God] has cast [thrown, hurled] me into the mire [clay],
> and I [Job] have become like [a parable in] dust and ashes."

---

35. Chaim Potok, *The Gift of Asher Lev* (New York: Knopf, 1990), 192–93.
36. Gordis, *The Book of Job: Commentary, New Translation and Special Studies* (New York: The Jewish Theological Seminary of America, 1978), xxvii.

Or in the translation of Edwin Good:

> He has flung me to the muck,
> and I'm a cliché, like dust and ashes.[37]

By now, the reader-learner knows the feeling — we, too, have been tossed about by this text, by the arguments of the characters and the turmoil of their perplexities and pain, and we, too, have been changed.

The phrase "dust and ashes" occurs outside Job only one other time in the whole Hebrew Bible: in the mouth of Abraham in Genesis 18:27. There, Abraham argued with the Lord, challenging the wisdom of the Lord's decision to destroy innocent people in Sodom. Abraham asked the Lord not to destroy Sodom if there were fifty innocent people there, and the Lord changed his mind. Before Abraham presses further, he pauses, as though he suddenly realizes what he is doing. He is challenging the wisdom of God! As Abraham resumes his challenge, he says deferentially, "Here I venture to speak to my Lord, I who am but dust and ashes" (Gen. 18:27, NJPSV). He assures God that he knows his place, that he is treading carefully and politely even while challenging God. Perhaps Job's challenge is not without precedent. Indeed, this resonance is heightened when the phrase "dust and ashes" is used in Job's final response to the Lord (42:7), where Job, not the Lord, undergoes a change of heart.

In 30:19 the verb translated "cast" or "hurled" is *yarah*, where the basic meaning is "the hand, the finger outstretched to point the way,"[38] or "to show, to teach or instruct" by giving signals or directions. (Torah is derived from *yrh*, "to teach"; thus Torah may be understood as more teaching, in the sense of "guiding" or "pointing," than law, in the sense of "commanding.") Gordis notes that *yarah* is also used in 1 Samuel 20:36, where it refers to "shooting arrows."[39] The arrows are being shot as a message, a secret code (like a riddle?), between Jonathan and David (i.e., between friends) to warn David about the intentions of Saul. David must watch the arrows, listen to what Jonathan says to his servant boy, and then he will get the point or figure it out. If he reads the signals correctly, he can make sense of the message and thus know

---

37. Good, *In Turns of Tempest*, 131.

38. Nili Shupak, *Where Can Wisdom Be Found? The Sage's Language in the Bible and in Ancient Egyptian Literature*, OBO 130 (Göttingen: Vandenhoeck and Ruprecht, 1993), 40.

39. Gordis, *The Book of Job*, 335.

whether he needs to flee Saul. This is less learning the meaning of a verbal formula or conventional doctrine and more being shown clues or pointers that the learner must use to make sense of the message.

Perhaps Job 30:19 (*wa'etmashal;* "I have become like" or "I am a parable, proverb, or riddle") invites the reader to pay attention to the words, but also look at what Job does and see what happens to Job, and make comparisons, draw lessons, get the point, understand the enigmatic parable or proverb. Søren Kierkegaard once commented, "Perhaps, in an even stricter sense, we also call that one a teacher of men who had no doctrine to pass on to others, but who merely left himself as a pattern to succeeding generations.... Such a teacher and guide of men [*sic*] was Job, whose significance is due by no means to what he said but to what he did."[40]

How might Job himself be a parable? When Job comes to the end of his understanding (entering chaps. 29–31), suppose Job in his exhaustion says to himself something like this:

> I am back where I began. I know I am blameless (no one has convinced me otherwise). I am upright. I do fear God (surely I have good reason to, as anyone can see). And I have steadfastly departed from evil. Yet it is also inescapably true: *I do not understand.*
>
> If wisdom is a gift, from my experience, my tradition and community, from my God, then all I can do is offer this gift back, whatever I have of it. But what is my gift? What have I been given? The only gifts I have left are perplexity, physical pain, emotional torment, spiritual turmoil, social alienation, and an outraged sense of injustice — that's what I have been given by my tradition, my friends, my community, and my God. I have been given *the gift of my own inability to understand.* Can I find courage enough to be true to this gift? I must not pretend I have some other gift (such as the ability to deceive myself into thinking that everything is or will be all right). I must offer what I have been given, with all of its imperfections (after all, myself is in it) — offer it back to the Lord — "as is," not bent, folded, or mutilated, no coupons or discounts. Such is my gift. I have nothing else left but my lack of comprehension.
>
> Therefore, I must file my lawsuit for malpractice in governance of the universe.

---

40. Søren Kierkegaard, "The Lord Gave, and the Lord Hath Taken Away, Blessed Be the Name of the Lord," in *Edifying Discourses* (Minneapolis: Augsburg, 1944), 2:7.

Here I am. I put it all in the hands of the Lord, Allah, Master of the Universe, Great Spirit. To whom else can I turn? Lord, I believe, help thou my unbelief, my lack of understanding, and my lack of wisdom.

"Seeing" is a familiar but often unremarked theme in the Book of Job. It is also a familiar metaphor for learning from Plato onward. In 40:4–5 Job concedes he cannot answer the Lord's questions. Later Job withdraws, enigmatically saying,

> "I had heard of you by the hearing of the ear,
>   but *now my eye sees you;*
> therefore I despise myself,
>   and repent in dust and ashes." (Job 42:5–6, emphasis added)

In the very next verse, Job's restoration begins. What changed? What did Job see that changed his entire understanding? Why was hearing not enough? Was this seeing literal or figurative? Plato, in depicting the allegory of the cave, suggests that one person's seeing the light does not ensure either that others will also or that he will be able to communicate his insight to them.[41] Telling another what you see does not ensure he or she will also see. That is how parables work. A teacher cannot make the learner see things the right way. Often the teacher can only point.

The turning point for the character of Job came in his seeing things differently. That happened in a face-to-face encounter — a presence sensed. Some have said that God's presence is enough,[42] that Job discovered that if one has God's presence, one no longer needs answers. Perhaps, but the character of Job does not say what he makes of it. Perhaps Job saw that, like his friends, he was so busy arguing that he had stopped listening, until the Lord interrupted. Maybe now he can stop mourning (in dust and ashes) and protesting and go on with life.[43] Now he can find languages other than that of mourning and of justice and use the languages of creation, of freedom, of hope, of song, of wonder and mystery, and of thanksgiving.

Usually when we say we changed our mind, we also say what we changed our mind about. Job does not. Perhaps, as J. Gerald

---

41. Plato *Republic*, bk. 7.
42. See both Samuel Terrien and Paul Scherer, exegete and expositor of Job in *IB* 3, 1194.
43. This line of interpretation has been suggested by Habel, *The Book of Job*, 578–83; and Gustavo Gutiérrez, *On Job: God-Talk and the Suffering of the Innocent* (Maryknoll, N.Y.: Orbis, 1987), 86–97.

Janzen suggests, Job changed his mind, not about some*thing*, but absolutely.[44] Or perhaps we can say here what Ludwig Wittgenstein said of philosophy: it is to give us a clear view of what is hidden because of its simplicity and familiarity, with the result that "we fail to be struck by what, once seen, is most striking and most powerful."[45] So in one sense philosophy leaves everything as it is, yet if we see clearly what is striking and powerful, the philosopher is different![46] Is that not a helpful way to view the process of education? (That is a rhetorical question.)

Indeed, perhaps another resonance with Wittgenstein can also illumine Job's seeing. Wittgenstein's friend Drury, a physician, was having doubts about his vocation and his spiritual condition, and Wittgenstein counseled him, "I think in some sense you don't look at people's faces closely enough." Peter Winch takes this to be good philosophical and spiritual advice, for in Wittgenstein's *Philosophical Investigations,* the philosopher comments often that one must pay attention, and especially when another is in pain, for "the gods are there in each minute and unseen part" (quoting Longfellow).[47] But if one's hand hurts, it is not a body or a hand that has pain, but a person, the subject. So look not at the body but at the person, for "one does not comfort the hand, but the sufferer: one looks into his face."[48] Perhaps Job's friends (and some teachers?) see only ideas and arguments, not faces, and thus they miss the point.

Answers Are Not Always the Answer

The text of Job has led the reader-learner through many questions and answers, not to mention enigmas. The reader-learner has known all along that the friends' answers were missing the point, so it was no surprise when the Lord rejected them as well. Then the Lord also rejects Job's questions, and he withdraws his lawsuit against God.

---

44. J. Gerald Janzen, *Job* (Atlanta: John Knox, 1985), 255. Janzen suggests Job is called to accept his suffering within his "status" as a creation within the created order. Job is a suffering servant — in which case, his innocent suffering is more than abasement or punishment. Janzen also acknowledges that this is not said explicitly, for Job's self-understanding is left unstated — which, as we have seen, draws the reader into answering.

45. Ludwig Wittgenstein, *Philosophical Investigations*, 2d ed. (Oxford: Blackwell, 1958), 129.

46. Ibid., 124–29.

47. Peter Winch, "Discussion of Malcolm's Essay," in *Wittgenstein: A Religious Point of View?* ed. Norman Malcolm (Ithaca, N.Y.: Cornell University Press, 1994), 129–30.

48. Wittgenstein, *Philosophical Investigations*, par. 286.

The events leave the reader-learner with the Lord's viewpoint. That must be the right answer. Yet, as the Lord rejects the arguments of the friends, he says, "You have not spoken of me what is right, as my servant Job has" (42:7–8). So the reader is left with a puzzle: the Lord's view appears to be right, and the Lord says Job is right, but Job said that God acted unjustly. If the Lord affirms what Job said, does that mean that the Lord's views must also be rejected? Where does this leave the reader-learner?

Job is restored when "the LORD gave Job twice as much as he had before" (42:10). Why twice as much? In Exodus 22:9 we read: "In any case of disputed ownership involving ox, donkey, sheep, clothing, or any other loss, of which one party says, 'This is mine,' the case of both parties shall come before God; the one whom God condemns shall pay double to the other." Paying back double is both an admission of wrongdoing as well as restitution. Has the character of the Lord thus admitted wrongdoing to Job and made restitution? If so, does that not also imply that the Lord's dominating rejection of Job's pleas is wrong? Apparently all six explanations have now been rejected. Even more puzzling, once they have been rejected, each one is then reaffirmed as valid!

From the beginning this book challenges traditional orthodoxy, especially the Deuteronomic code and its convictions about suffering as punishment for sin and rewards for the righteous. Yet the Lord punished the friends for having spoken wrongly of God, while Job is rewarded for having spoken what is right. Does not punishing their speaking wrongly, and then commanding sacrifices, reaffirm the traditional priestly code that the friends argued for? Is the priestly code, through which these friends relate with God, thereby accepted as legitimate, though perhaps not as the only or ultimate explanation?

In this text, only the Lord brings about resolution, so somehow the two main characters, Job and the Lord, are both right, though each seems to have admitted error in some way. So the reader-learner arrives at the end of the book having explored a whole series of contradictions and discovering that each position is somehow wrong and yet also somehow true. The book ends with "And Job died, old and full of days" (42:17), thus giving the appearance of having wrapped things up rather tidily. We have learned a human can fear God without looking for something for self, yet, paradoxically, he is rewarded! We have learned that one can be innocent, challenge orthodoxies, and be vindicated, yet still repent.

The discerning learner-reader may also discover, after departing the book, that settled thought patterns have been permanently unsettled, that strongly held convictions might best be held with a slightly looser grip, that it might be wise to look for truth in viewpoints with which one disagrees.

IS GOD ABUSIVE? OR CAN ABSENCE BE A PRESENCE?

Job faced "the abusing God" repeatedly (chaps. 6, 9, 13–14, 16) in courageous, vigorous protest, climaxing in his reply to Bildad in chapter 19, protesting Bildad's attack and that of God, who not only attacked Job physically but isolated him from his family and servants, even making him loathsome to his intimate friends:[49]

> How long will you grieve my spirit,
> And crush me with words?
> Time and again you humiliate me,
> And are not ashamed to abuse me...
> Yet know that God has wronged me...
> I cry, "Violence!" but am not answered;
> I shout, but can get no justice. (Job 19:2–7, NJPSV)

Here "abuse" refers to Bildad, but is it too loaded a term for how Job describes God's treatment of him in this text? Might the term be used of the exile or of the Holocaust? What is abuse?

> Moments of abuse are characterized not only by deep human suffering but, most importantly, by the innocence of the victim. When a perpetrator acts abusively, the victim is innocent; when an abuser abuses, what happens to the victim is not in any way her or his fault. The victim usually has not wronged the perpetrator at all; however, even if the victim has wronged the abuser, the abuser's reaction is out of all proportion to the wrong committed. *The innocence of the victim, not the depth of the suffering or the cruelty of the perpetrator, is what makes the abusive behavior "abusive."* For this reason, we reject victimization of the victim.[50]

This seems quite an accurate description of how the text of the Book of Job describes the relation of God and Job. The horror of abuse is that presence is most real in the act of abuse, and then

---

49. David R. Blumenthal, *Facing the Abusing God: A Theology of Protest* (Louisville: Westminster/John Knox, 1993). See especially pp. 246–57 for his description of God as abuser and his treatment of Job's silence. I find the first more persuasive than the latter, but his treatment is thoughtfully grounded in the realities of abuse and the need for a theological response, as is the Book of Job.

50. Ibid., 248 (italics in original).

the absence is also filled with the dread presence of memory and of anticipation.

The ambiguities of presence and absence are also found in situations other than abuse. Religious communities and individuals alike often find themselves under siege by hostile cultural forces. We ask, as Job did, "Am I (Are we) important to God? Does God care if we live or die, prosper or suffer? What can hold us together and give us a viable identity under such pressures? What can we do to not only survive but thrive?" Often what lies just below the surface in such questions is the fear that the presence of God is no longer so clear. Sometimes it feels more like absence than presence.

One pedagogical response recently urged by many religious communities in the U.S. has been to insist that we go back to the basics and reaffirm the essentials of the tradition that is being forgotten or lost. They say, "We have to make sure that our children know the story, and thus we must create distinctive communities that hold on firmly to our unique denominational particularity." This is understandable, but adopting a defensive posture often squeezes out the subtleties necessary for vitality: a tolerance for ambiguity, mystery, and the reality of multiple answers to fundamentally important questions.

If Job has become a parable, it suggests that from the humble human view it is no longer clear that any *one* approach (be it fundamentalist, liberal, liturgical, doctrinal, biblical, aesthetic, social activist, and so on) has a total and exclusive claim on truth of God. This text may lead reader-learners to see that simplistic answers to complex questions seldom satisfy, and sometimes questions mislead. Might this also be true of some expectations of how God is present? Job remembered the presence of God as affirming, sustaining, and intimate. But he also knew of a presence of God that was quite different: malevolent, abusive, even seeking his death. In the midst of his torment and grief, he pleaded for absence, begging God to leave him alone. Yet somehow, how is not made clear in the text, Job — the parable — seems to have found a way to go on living with that ambiguity and still affirm the reality of God for himself, perhaps inviting the reader-learner to do the same.

As David Blumenthal and others make clear, "Intentionality is not an issue; the motives of the abuser are not relevant. Abusive behavior is abusive; it is inexcusable, in all circumstances."[51] Even when the abuser is God! We must find courage to say that "abuse

---

51. Ibid.

is unjustified, in God as well as in human beings"[52] as well as, with Job, "God is not always abusive."

In my view, one of the more lamentable characteristics of some contemporary churches and some contemporary believers is that being polite and keeping quiet have replaced speaking the truth in love. Too often have we become codependent supporters of those who unethically abuse people, alcohol, power, food, wealth, and other drugs. Job, like many of the Psalms, calls out for justice, protesting the abuse, calling God against God! Even in the hoped-for absence there is a presence, where one might at least imagine an abusive God giving way to the presence of a loving and just God.

The Book of Job leads us to acknowledge that simplistic and unambiguous approaches will often not be sufficient to cope either with the reality of human experience or with the reality of God.

---

52. Ibid.

CHAPTER THREE

THE ABSENCE OF PRESENCE
Ecclesiastes

The reader who moves from the Book of Job to Ecclesiastes[1] experiences a profound shift of mood. Job complained passionately about God's malevolent presence, preferring God's absence to such agony. In Ecclesiastes, Job's intense battles with human and divine antagonists are replaced with a cool, reserved skepticism. Here the one who speaks in the text seems unconcerned with the presence of God; indeed, God's presence feels indistinguishable from absence. This is unusual in biblical texts.

There is considerable debate about how to classify the literary genre of this text. Some argue it is highly structured by use of a complex web of numerical calculations (Wright, Murphy).[2] Others argue it is structured by the use of logical or philosophical categories (Coppens, Lohfink, Michel),[3] while still others suggest it is structured by the use of repetitive words and themes (or by repeated use of contradictory views; Loader, Fox).[4] Others have simply concluded this is more like a notebook in which are col-

---

1. When referring to the book, we shall use the title "Ecclesiastes," which is the Greek and Latin form of the Hebrew *Qohelet*. This term has to do with calling together a people, a congregation (Gk. *ecclesia*), and has been variously translated as "preacher" (Jerome, Luther, RSV), as "teacher" (NRSV), as "the philosopher" (TEV), and as "the speaker" (NEB) or simply transliterated as Qohelet, Qoheleth, or Koheleth. Here, when referring to the author, we shall simply transliterate the Hebrew, *Qohelet*, into English.

For further discussion, see commentaries by James L. Crenshaw, *Ecclesiastes: A Commentary* (Philadelphia: Westminster, 1987), 32–34; Robert Gordis, *Koheleth — The Man and His World: A Study of Ecclesiastes* (New York: Schocken, 1968), 39–42, 63–68; Roland E. Murphy, *Ecclesiastes* (Dallas: Word, 1992), xix–xxiii.

2. Addison G. Wright, "The Riddle of the Sphinx: The Structure of the Book of Qoheleth," *Catholic Biblical Quarterly* 30 (1968), 313–34; Murphy, *Ecclesiastes*, xxxix–xli.

3. See the review of these proposals in Murphy, *Ecclesiastes*, xxxv–xxxvii.

4. J. A. Loader, *Polar Structures in the Book of Qohelet*, BZAW 183 (Berlin: de Gruyter, 1979); *Ecclesiastes: A Practical Commentary* (Grand Rapids: Eerd-

lected a series of brief meditations, without a single structure to govern their arrangement (Zimmerli, Crenshaw, Whybray).[5] Robert Gordis suggests, "Koheleth would have been shocked, even amused, to learn that his notebook was canonized as part of Holy Scripture."[6] As a literary work, Ecclesiastes is perhaps best described as a collection of reflections or investigations or ruminations upon proverbial sayings and upon one individual's personal experience:[7]

> The book of Qohelet goes far beyond its predecessors in the importance it gives to the organizing consciousness of the sage. In other books, few sentences seem to reflect the situation or personality of a particular teacher. In most, the person of the sage disappears almost entirely, and we rarely if ever hear his "I" again, at least not until the epilogue.... The pervasiveness of the teacher's consciousness in the book of Qohelet is the main source of its cohesiveness.[8]

The Book of Proverbs was explicitly and directly pedagogical, yet it seemed quite unimportant to know anything about the anonymous teachers, except when the teacher was Woman Wisdom herself. In the Book of Job, no instructional intent is claimed, and the narrator remains anonymous. Ecclesiastes begins quite differently. Here there is no narrator but an author speaking in the first person (as in Prov. 8?), claiming to be king in Jerusalem, the son of David, yet he does not directly claim the name of Solomon. Why? From the opening line of the text, reader-learners are drawn

mans, 1986), 9–13; Michael V. Fox, *Qohelet and His Contradictions*, JSOTSup 17 (Sheffield: Almond, 1989), 16–17.

5. Zimmerli's view is described in Murphy, *Ecclesiastes*, xxxvii; see also Crenshaw, *Ecclesiastes*, 46–49; R. N. Whybray, *Ecclesiastes*, NCB (Grand Rapids: Eerdmans, 1989), 19–22.

6. Gordis, *Koheleth*, 131.

7. T. A. Perry likens them to Montaigne's *Essays*, which are pessimistic reflections expanded from maxims ("Annotating the Absurd: Kohelet's Maxims of a Maximal Discontent," [address given at the annual meeting of the Society of Biblical Literature, Philadelphia, November 1993]). I prefer Fox's parallel with Wittgenstein, who described his own work as "remarks, short paragraphs, of which there is sometimes a fairly long chain about the same subject" written over a period of sixteen years in which he was compelled to "travel over a wide field of thoughts criss-cross in every direction...my thoughts were soon crippled if I tried to force them on in any single direction against their natural inclination." As a result, the published "philosophical remarks are...a number of sketches of landscapes which were made in the course of these long and involved journeyings." See Ludwig Wittgenstein, *Philosophical Investigations* (Oxford: Blackwell, 1958), vii. Fox finds this "strikingly akin to that of Qohelet's 'philosophical investigations'...because the book is a report of a journey of a consciousness over the landscape of experience"; *Qohelet and His Contradictions*, 157–58.

8. Fox, *Qohelet and His Contradictions*, 159–60.

into a puzzle about the identity of the author that escalates into an enigma about the worth of anything and everything, including reading itself. Perhaps it is here we must begin.

HOW DOES LEARNING OCCUR IN ECCLESIASTES?

Engaging Reader-Learners

Upon reading that these are the words of the "king in Jerusalem" (implied to be Solomon, revered for wisdom, wealth, loyalty to the Lord, and leadership in Israel's golden age), the reader turns eagerly to discover what counsel this king offers:

> Vanity of vanities, says the Teacher,
>   vanity of vanities! All is vanity. (Eccles. 1:2)

What?! The reader pauses, catches his breath. The reader-learner is puzzled: he expected to learn from wise Solomon, yet the first sentence asserts that everything is vanity. If we believe the author, we might as well stop reading. Yet more text follows, inviting us to read on!

This opening salvo is repeated over and over again in the first two chapters, in effect saying, "I have seen it all, tried it all, and 'all is vanity and a chasing after wind'" (1:14; 2:17). The opening verse is repeated word for word in the book's conclusion (12:8), which suggests it may have thematic importance and function. Indeed, the phrase "all is vanity" (or "all is futile") is repeated seven times in just twelve chapters of this text, and this or that particular is judged as vanity or futile another seventeen times, reinforcing the notion that this may be a thesis statement offered the reader-learner.

The very next verse is equally perplexing:

> What do people gain from all the toil
>   at which they toil under the sun? (Eccles. 1:3)

This question is certain to get the attention of anyone with pedagogical interests. Education is often very hard work, and what makes it worthwhile is the hope of gain or benefit. How are reader-learners to read this question? If we assume the previous verse states a theme, we may take this question to be consistent with and to support that theme; that is, it is a rhetorical question that assumes a negative answer. Then it amounts to a claim: "There is nothing humans can do, no effort they can expend, no work they can do, 'under the sun,' or within a human lifetime, that will produce a gain or profit that really matters." No one committed to the educational process is likely to find that judgment attractive without further evidence or argument, but that might require more reading!

If reader-learners take verse 3 as a rhetorical question, we assume the author is setting forth a point of view, or a set of understandings, and the task of reader-learners is to discern and comprehend that view. Yet what is to be comprehended here contradicts or deconstructs that assumption! The fact that one is reading at all presumes that one hopes to gain something (at least pleasure) from the text. But these initial verses suggest there is no point in going on reading. What to do? Indeed, if "all is futile" is the message, why did the author write the book? Could he consistently claim that "all is futile" and yet also hope that writing (and reading) the book would make any difference?

The effect of the text's opening tactic is twofold. On the one hand, reader-learners are enticed to seek further evidence to support the claim that all is futile, which means we must both play along with, yet resist, that claim (temporarily) and go on reading. Or, on the other hand, we are enticed to pause temporarily and search our own experience and reasoning to assess the claim. Ironically, in taking either option, reader-learners must entertain the possibility that this initial claim may not prove true.

Proverbs and Job have led reader-learners to respect the authority of those who have gone before, whose collective experience the sage transmits for our edification and instruction. Now reader-learners are asked to question both the counsel that the sage offers and perhaps the sage himself. These dilemmas are only the first step in a radically new pedagogical approach fostered by Qohelet. Why would a teacher evoke such conflict so early in the process of reading?

Can Expectations Mislead?

A reader-learner's initial sense of conflict is reflected in the widely differing assessments of this book by interpreters and commentators from early times to the present. Scholars are deeply divided about the most fundamental issues concerning this book. Is the book fundamentally pessimistic or optimistic? Gerhard von Rad, one of the more astute Christian interpreters of Israel's wisdom, claims Qohelet seeks salvation in a world created by God, yet Qohelet discovers

The despair of a wise man at a life which he knows to be completely encompassed by God, but which has nevertheless lost all
meaning for him, because this God's activity has sunk down into
an unattainable concealment!...Very oddly, Ecclesiastes calls a halt
just before the point of complete bankruptcy....He does not recommend self-destruction: instead, he sees himself suspended over the
abyss of despair.[9]

On the other hand, Gordis, a wise Jewish interpreter of Israel's
wisdom, concludes

Every line in his book is instinct with the spirit of clear-eyed, brave
and joyous acceptance of life, for all its inevitable limitations....
That the basic theme of the book was *simchah*, the enjoyment of
life, was clearly recognized by Jewish religious authorities who thus
explained the custom of reading *Koheleth* in the synagogue on the
Feast of Tabernacles, the Season of Rejoicing.[10]

Such fundamentally divergent assessments of this work, by two
able and influential scholars, suggest that scholars, like other readers, bring differing expectations to the text and that the work itself
is legitimately susceptible to widely divergent interpretations.

Since it is the phrase "all is vanity" that disrupts our reading,
perhaps we need to begin at the most basic level, with the meaning of the key words. "Vanity" is the traditional (since the KJV)
English translation of the Hebrew *hebel*. *Hebel* is used thirty-eight
times in twelve chapters (with more occurrences here than in the
rest of Hebrew Bible combined) and often appears at key literary
junctures in the text. It is even doubled or intensified as *habel habelim* (vanity of vanities) in the introduction and conclusion (1:2
and 12:8), so *habel habelim* brackets the rest of the text. Clearly
this term is crucially important in this text. Yet observe the variety
of translations of *hebel* among scholars and translations:

1. "breath" (Scott; Farmer),[11] "puff of air," "vapor" (Davidson)[12]

2. "vanity" (KJV; RSV; NRSV; JB; Gordis; Leupold; Perry)[13]

9. Gerhard von Rad, *Old Testament Theology* (New York: Harper, 1962),
1:456–57.
10. Gordis, *Koheleth*, 130–31.
11. R. B. Y. Scott, *Proverbs and Ecclesiastes*, AB 18 (New York: Doubleday,
1965), 202, 209; Kathleen A. Farmer, *Who Knows What Is Good? A Commentary
on the Books of Proverbs and Ecclesiastes* (Grand Rapids: Eerdmans, 1991), 146.
12. Robert Davidson, *The Courage to Doubt: Exploring an Old Testament
Theme* (Philadelphia: Trinity Press International, 1983), 187.
13. Gordis, *Koheleth*, 195; H. C. Leupold, *Exposition of Ecclesiastes* (Grand
Rapids: Baker, 1962); T. A. Perry, *Dialogues with Kohelet: The Book of Ecclesiastes*
(University Park, Pa.: Pennsylvania State University Press, 1993).

3. "emptiness" (NEB)

4. "ephemeral" (Perdue),[14] "transience" (Fredericks)[15]

5. "futility" (Crenshaw; NJPSV),[16] "useless" (TEV)

6. "irony" (Good)[17]

7. "enigma," "mystery" (Ogden)[18]

8. "meaningless" (Loader; NIV),[19] "absurd, incomprehensible" (Murphy),[20] "absurd," "irrational" (Fox)[21]

The simplest or most literal translations are the first group, in which a literal rendering of *hebel* allows the author's own metaphor to show. "Breath" or "puff of air" or "vapor" simply replicates the metaphor, leaving it up to reader-learners to determine what the metaphor means. For example, to expand slightly upon a description first offered by the Scottish Bible scholar Robert Davidson: *Hebel* is like this. Imagine you are outdoors on a hot summer day. The temperature is 102 degrees and the humidity is 90 percent. There is absolutely no breeze and no air-conditioning. You are lying in a hammock but cannot muster the energy to make it swing or fan yourself. Ten feet away, a person walks by, and a few seconds later, you feel the slightest hint of a vaporous breath of air fleetingly brush by your inert form. That is *hebel*.

Once we have established the metaphor itself as a reference point, we must go on to do what most translations do: say what the metaphor means. How do we decide that? Translators differ in their approaches. Some choose to use the same word (vanity) each time *hebel* appears, if the context allows. Others try to choose a word that fits the particular context, whether it is the same English word each time or not. While consistency may be desirable, sometimes the usage in context demands different meanings. For

---

14. Leo G. Perdue, *Wisdom and Creation: The Theology of Wisdom Literature* (Nashville: Abingdon, 1994), 206–7.

15. Daniel C. Fredericks, *Coping with Transience: Ecclesiastes on Brevity in Life* (Sheffield: JSOT, 1993).

16. Crenshaw, *Ecclesiastes*, 57.

17. Edwin M. Good, *Irony in the Old Testament* (Philadelphia: Westminster, 1965), 182.

18. Graham Ogden, *Qoheleth* (Sheffield: JSOT, 1987), 20.

19. Loader, *Ecclesiastes*, 20.

20. Murphy, *Ecclesiastes*, lix.

21. Fox, *Qohelet and His Contradictions*, 31.

example, in English, in some contexts "step" means what you stand upon as you climb stairs, while in other contexts it clearly means what your legs do when you "take a step."

How does this work for *hebel*? For example, in 3:19 it says that since both humans and beasts die, neither is superior, for "both are *hebel*," or as the New Jewish Publication Society Version (NJPSV) translates, "both amount to nothing." In 8:14 Qohelet observes that since sometimes a scoundrel is treated as though he were good and sometimes the good are treated as though wicked, "that is *hebel*," or in the NJPSV, "that is frustration." In both these texts, the New Revised Standard Version has chosen to simply repeat "vanity." Presumably the Jewish translators decided that it is difficult to see how these situations could be expressed by using the root meaning of "breath" or "vapor" metaphorically, yet it is also not clear how they are situations for which "vanity" best expresses the likely meaning. Apparently the New Revised Standard translators decided to mark every instance of *hebel* with the same English word (vanity), letting readers make their own decisions about meaning in context.

These two approaches to translation agree that the meaning of the phrase is determined in part by context, which might suggest different nuances, but they differ on whether or not the translation itself should give voice to those nuances. How does that help us? If the author was seeking to transmit clearly and unequivocally his conclusions, why has he chosen words that are so ambiguous and open textured? Is it possible the author did not intend precision in meaning? If not, might that suggest a different way of reading this text?

What if this opening affirmation does not seek to be simply accepted or assimilated but seeks to arouse contention among reader-learners and thereby stimulate more testing by their own experience, evidence, and argument — perhaps even discussion? If that were the case, would it not be useful to choose a word that might well be read with different connotations, so as to allow or even encourage various assessments of the assertion itself? Indeed, is that not exactly what has occurred among the readers and scholars through the centuries? The text started a debate about the meaning of life and its various events that continues today. Instead of offering reader-learners a conclusion, suppose the text entices reader-learners to join in exploring conflicting views. If that were so, another strategy for reading is required.

Perhaps Roland Murphy is right: "The message of Ecclesiastes has suffered from excessive summarizing."[22] In an age that loves sound bites, we may find it especially difficult to exert the effort needed to understand a text like this. It challenges our expectations of texts. We expect a text to have a single, authorial point of view. Michael V. Fox argues that rather than try to harmonize the text's contradictions into systematic thought, or explain them as the work of redactors or different authors, we might recognize that the contradictions state problems rather than resolve them, without embracing the contradictions as paradoxes. Instead, Fox urges, contradictions are the lens through which this author views life. So rather than insist the text must be either consistently pessimistic or consistently optimistic, we should be faithful to the "uneasy tensions" that are characteristic of its thought.[23]

Let us return to the opening verses once more, this time not assuming the text offers a single view. Suppose the text offers reader-learners competing claims, evidence to support each claim, yet no unequivocal conclusions, as in a debate — within oneself and within the wisdom tradition. This time reader-learners might read the second and third verses, not as a single theme, but as two sides of a discussion. Now, verse 3 is not a rhetorical but a real question, asking, "What value is there or could there be? Is all really *hebel*? Let's test that." Verse 2 claims that all is vanity — there is no advantage to anything. Then verse 3 asks, in effect, "Is that true? Do people gain something from their effort? If so, what would it be?" A debate is joined.

What do we see in the text that follows?

> A generation goes, and a generation comes,
>   but the earth remains forever.
> The sun rises and the sun goes down,
>   and hurries to the place where it rises.
> The wind blows to the south,
>   and goes around to the north;
> round and round goes the wind,
>   and on its circuits the wind returns.
> All streams run to the sea,
>   but the sea is not full;
> to the place where the streams flow,
>   there they continue to flow. (Eccles. 1:4–7)

If we take this text as evidence for "All is vanity," it answers the question about gain by suggesting that since everything comes

---

22. Murphy, *Ecclesiastes*, lviii.
23. Fox, *Qohelet and His Contradictions*, 9–11.

around again and again, nothing is gained. On the other hand, if we stress the final clause of verse 4, then human generations go and come, "but the earth remains forever." What does one gain? We gain reassurance that something can be counted on despite human efforts and apprehensions. The earth "remains forever," the sun rises again, the wind returns, and the rivers "continue to flow." Not everything is vanity, for some things endure. Indeed, Leo Perdue suggests the Hebrew word often translated as "gain" in verse 3 (Heb. *yitron*) may well come from a different root, one meaning "to remain or abide." So instead of asking "What gain?" we ask, "What endures from the labor of life?"[24] What endures is what we stand upon and take for granted, not even noticing, so busy are we in our efforts to gain an advantage.

Here is the fly in the ointment: human dissatisfaction (v. 8). Humans strive for profit, to be able to say, "See, this is new." They are unwilling to return to what is lasting. But perhaps this suggests it may not be *things* that are *hebel*. If the meaning of *hebel* is influenced by its use in context, in what other contexts is it used in this text? Seven times the author offers a summative judgment that "this too is *hebel*" or "all is *hebel* and a chasing [striving] after wind (*ruach*)" (1:14; 2:11, 17, 26; 4:4, 16; 6:9). Here *hebel* is not simply synonymous with *ruach* (spirit or wind) itself but with "chasing wind," or a human activity related to wind. Here *hebel* and "pursuing wind" are not just metaphors but judgments on human dissatisfaction, on striving or seeking the new that is not worthy of such effort.

Here are two points of view in dialogue with each other: one affirming that everything is *hebel*, all human toil adds up to nothing; the other affirming that some things endure, but restless striving is not content with what is and what is given. Either interpretation is possible — we will need to read further!

In 1:12–2:23 the text describes extensive empirical investigations to test the proposal(s). The author, pictured as a wealthy king, tried it all: wealth, pleasure, power, building, farming, slaves, singers, mistresses, wisdom, folly, even madness (2:1–10). He explored every possible kind of profit or gain that one might claim resulted from effort. What did he learn?

> Then I considered all that my hands had done and the toil I had spent in doing it, and again, all was vanity and a chasing after wind, and there was nothing to be gained under the sun. (Eccles. 2:11)

---

24. Perdue, *Wisdom and Creation*, 208.

Here is where Qohelet makes one of his most distinctive and original contributions to the wisdom tradition. The teachers of Proverbs expected reader-learners to participate in acquiring wisdom by listening, acquiring the community's collective experience (tradition), making sense of sayings, and finding real-life uses for them. But learners were not expected to challenge or offer anything new. Job's friends appealed to the elders, expecting Job to accept that authority and reshape his thinking. They did not accept his challenges. Qohelet, on the other hand, does a radically new thing in this text. Wisdom here is not something to be learned, so much as it is a tool with which to investigate the world. His method was "to seek and to search out by [means of] wisdom all that is done under heaven" (1:13). He said to himself, "Come now, I will make a test of pleasure.... What use is it?" (2:1–2). He tested what he saw and heard from others "by wisdom" (7:23). This suggests he saw wisdom more as a procedure to be used than as conclusions to be mastered. Rather than ask the elders, he used his own body, not just for the sake of enjoyment, but as a means of answering a philosophical question, What is good for people to do? (cf. 2:3).[25] Unlike previous sages, his arguments start from empirical and sensory evidence, and then he infers his conclusions. Forty-six times he testifies to what he saw or observed, and eight times to what he remembered.

Qohelet summarizes his methods succinctly in 8:16–17:

> For I have set my mind to learn wisdom and to observe the business that goes on in the world — even to the extent of going without sleep day and night — and I have observed all that God brings to pass. Indeed, man cannot guess the events that occur under the sun. For man tries strenuously, but fails to guess them; and even if a sage should think to discover them he would not be able to guess them. (NJPSV)

Notice his language: he "set my mind to learn" and "to observe"; he "tries strenuously," "fails," and seeks "to discover" (even though he fails). This describes empirical procedure. When he arrives at a conclusion, for example, that "toil is *hebel*," then he validates that with additional evidence, taking the publicly observable data that death intervenes so that he who toils leaves the fruits to another to enjoy (2:21–23).[26] Clearly, Qohelet does not want the reader either to take his own or someone else's word for it. His

---

25. Ibid., 87.
26. Ibid., 89.

text and his procedure invite reader-learners into the process of investigation, argumentation, use of evidence and testimony, and so on. The procedures are public and can be used by all. In principle, we as reader-learners could offer additional evidence to support or contest his conclusions.

How does this affect reader-learners? To expect reader-learners to master the text's doctrines or lessons may be largely to miss the point. The value of the text may be not only the viewpoints espoused within it but the manner in which it seduces reader-learners into reflecting upon life *themselves*. A corollary principle is that universal conclusions are unlikely if the data base is one person's empirical experience. Is that a liability, or is it an apology for relativism? But empirical investigation is a perfectly legitimate and appropriate mode of inquiry for claims to universal truth. To use the familiar philosophical example, if someone claims, "All swans are white," finding a single black swan is sufficient to refute the truth of the claim. Similarly, if one were to assert that "the evil are never punished" or that "the righteous are always rewarded," only one Job disproves the claim. Analogously, "all is vanity" can be refuted by finding a single gain or profit. So Qohelet's approach is highly appropriate to his inquiry.

Many teachers and learners have asked their own form of Qohelet's question: "Is there any point in going on with this?" Teaching and learning, like reading, are predicated upon the hope that something worthwhile will result, though there has been debate whether the gain is to be found at the end (product) or along the way (process). Yet what we are taking for granted is already there, while we are looking for something else yet to come.

Reflection: Using Wisdom to See

The struggle to describe the literary genre of this text leads Murphy to note several distinctive features of the text that do not fit neatly into familiar forms. There are wisdom sayings (indicative and imperative proverbs), but often they are combined either with new aphorisms or with each other in a "yes...but" manner. There is also the repeated first-person refrain about what "I have seen." Murphy describes the text's "unusual style" as reflection "characterized by observation and thought, and hence [it] has a fairly loose structure," incorporating several literary genres.[27]

---

27. Murphy acknowledges adopting the earlier suggestions of Ellermeier and Braun; see Murphy, *Wisdom Literature: Job, Proverbs, Ruth, Canticles, Eccle-*

Rather than adopt the reflections of this author, we have suggested this text invites readers to do as the author has done, to engage in first-person reflection on the mysteries of life. How does it do that?

First, Qohelet quotes traditional thought, especially proverbial sayings, sometimes to support his view (5:3, RSV; 5:2, NJPSV), sometimes as a starting point for his own commentary (4:9–12), but more often to challenge the sayings with facts he has seen:

> The wise have eyes in their head,
>   but fools walk in darkness.
> Yet I perceived that the same fate befalls all of them.
>   (Eccles. 2:14–15; see also 8:11–14)

In Ecclesiastes 4:5–6 Qohelet pairs a conventional proverb (cf. Prov. 6:10; 24:33) with another proverb and then appends his own final phrase, as the NJPSV translation makes clear:

> [True,] The fool folds his hands together
>   and has to eat his own flesh.
> [But no less truly,]
> Better is a handful of gratification
>   than two fistfuls of labor which is pursuit of wind.

There is also the "yes . . . but" pattern, as in 3:16–22, which pairs Qohelet's observations ("I saw") with his reflections ("I said in my heart") and returns back to "I saw," echoing the author's internal debate and inviting reader-learners to participate. In each of these ways, the text draws reader-learners into traditional affirmations, then challenges them to reflection by posing alternatives. Here traditional conclusions are not the last word but are used as a means for constructive, creative reflection.

Qohelet also evokes reflection with his innovative use of startling aphorisms, which Jesus adopted later (see esp. chaps. 7, 9–10):

> Wisdom is more valuable than weapons of war, but a single error destroys much of value. (Eccles. 9:18, NJPSV)

> A little folly outweighs massive wisdom. (Eccles. 10:1, NJPSV)

> Whoever is joined with all the living has hope, for a living dog is better than a dead lion. (Eccles. 9:4)

Qohelet's use of aphorisms is characteristically distinctive from proverbial sayings. The proverb distills the collective wisdom of

---

the community, while an aphorism expresses a more personal or individual insight.[28] The proverb often gives no reason to support its claim to self-evident truth, for none is needed. Aphorisms also offer no reason — because none is possible.[29] Aphorisms offer the "wisdom of the counter-order," depending more upon the individual creativity and vision of the author than the collective judgment of the community.[30] In the words of Perdue,

> The aphorism is a subversive saying wearing the disguise of a proverb.... It attempts to challenge and perhaps even undermine the hearer's worldview in which they find meaning and continuity for living... sages use aphorism in their efforts to reorient their hearers to a new and different meaning system.[31]

In each case, the sayings (often in hyperbole) provoke reflection but settle no issue with a definitive word. They act as invitations to reader-learners to see if they see what the author sees. But since what this author sees is so very distinctive and based on his personal vision, reader-learners may find themselves asking what every learner must eventually ask about every teacher who leads them beyond what they already know: can we trust him?

Can We Trust This Author?

If the self-consciousness of this author is so central to the book, and if his method entails tests using his own body and his own personal experiences, what, if anything, does the text tell us about this person? Is he who he says he is? Can reader-learners trust him?

The book begins with a claim: "The words of the Teacher, the son of David, king in Jerusalem" (1:1), leading the reader to think of Solomon. The epilogue (12:9–14) describes Qohelet, not as a king, but as a sage (Heb. *hakam*, "wise man") who taught, studied, arranged proverbs, and wrote plain truth.

Yet the Hebrew of this text is centuries later linguistically than the time of Solomon. It is as though someone writing today, claiming to be a royal author of the time of King James I of England,

28. Williams, *Those Who Ponder Proverbs: Aphoristic Thinking and Biblical Literature*, Bible and Literature Series 2 (Sheffield: Almond Press, 1981), 47–55; see also John Dominic Crossan, *In Fragments: The Aphorisms of Jesus* (San Francisco: Harper and Row, 1983), 20–25.

29. Crossan, *In Fragments*, 25.

30. Williams, *Those Who Ponder Proverbs*, 47.

31. Leo G. Perdue, "The Wisdom Sayings of Jesus," *Foundations & Facets Forum* 2:3 (1986), 28–29. A very similar view was argued earlier by William A. Beardslee, "Uses of the Proverb in the Synoptic Gospels," *Interpretation* 24:1 (1970), 61–73.

used King James's English yet occasionally slipped in twentieth-century expressions. One could understand an author using ancient linguistic expressions (e.g., "thee" and "thou") to lend credence to his claim that his text was ancient, but how could one claim to be one of the ancients while using forms of language that only emerged centuries later? Indeed, the notion of Solomon as author is dropped after the second chapter, when the author's point of view is either distant from or critical of the king and when he seems to know more about how to respond to a king than about how to rule.[32] Perhaps not even the text expected reader-learners to take Solomon's authorship too seriously. Is that deceptive?

So who is Qohelet? T. A. Perry aptly describes this sage-teacher as "a man who without regard to orthodoxies states his experience with full awareness of his limitations, who delights in controversy and in being challenged and corrected."[33] Gordis suggests the author likely lived in Jerusalem, since he demonstrates familiarity with the temple and with the corruption of government and frequently mentions Jerusalem.[34] In addition, he probably belonged to the upper classes, was well informed on a wide variety of subjects, including history, the science of his day, and some Greek philosophical notions.[35] Gordis has also astutely observed that Qohelet was a sensual person with a passionate love of life.[36] He loved the sun (11:7), good food and wine, beautiful gardens (2:5), even all "delights of the flesh" (2:8). He used his own body in his empirical approach, which makes the trust question important. His body and his perceptions are not ours.

On the other hand, what drives the investigations and observations of these texts is Qohelet's passion for justice and truth, though he seems not to have been an activist.[37] Despite searching, he is unable to find evidence that justice is as universal as the older sages claimed, and therefore, his commitment to telling the truth leads him to question much traditional and conventional theology.[38]

Yet pedagogically, trust that the text (or a teacher) is telling the

---

32. Murphy, *Ecclesiastes*, xx–xxi. See 3:16; 4:1–2; 5:7; 8:2–4; and 10:4–7, 16–20.
33. Perry, *Dialogues with Kohelet*, 41.
34. Gordis, *Koheleth*, 76.
35. Ibid., 77–78.
36. Ibid., 78–79.
37. Ibid., 80–82.
38. Ibid., 81–82.

truth is very, very important to the success of education. Every learner knows that deception and self-deception undermine learning. Qohelet seems keenly aware of the limits of wisdom and of his own convictions and especially of the mysteries that surround all human ability to understand God. He is a keen observer of the human scene, who quickly spots self-deception and ideological cover-up, especially among those who uphold traditional religious sensibilities (see 7:23–29; 8:17). Can we trust him as he challenges what we have taken as true? In Job, God eventually declares Job has spoken rightly (even if that is a fiction), but Qohelet contains no such "vindication." Yet ironically, while Qohelet challenges traditional theology as profoundly as Job, he never argued directly with God or accused God of being irresponsible or capricious, as does Job.[39]

There is a reticence and respect for limits in this author-teacher and a willingness to explore, which might suggest this teacher will also respect a reader-learner and encourage honest explorations. Whether or not a reader-learner can trust this text and its author will be a decision for each, which is congruent with the spirit of this text as a whole.

WHAT IS WORTH LEARNING ACCORDING TO QOHELET?

Does Qohelet have a point of view or more than one, or does he only seek to provoke?

Does Death Negate Gain?

The driving question behind these experiments in truth is, "Who can possibly know what is best for a man to do in life?" (6:12, NJPSV). As Qohelet searches for what is good to do, he asks: "What does one gain?" or "What endures?" (1:3). What makes something worth doing? How lasting must some effort be to be worth doing? How could one measure that? As his yardstick, Qohelet uses death. In death's presence, is there any enduring value?

For Qohelet, death is the great leveler that haunts all human striving. Whatever dreams order or whatever aspirations drive peoples' doings, all will be leveled by death (2:13–19). When Qohelet strove to become wise, he realized, "What happens to the fool will happen to me also; why then have I been so very wise?"

---

39. Samuel Terrien, *The Elusive Presence: Toward a New Biblical Theology* (San Francisco: Harper and Row, 1978), 375–76.

(2:15). It is a fact, but it baffles him: "How can the wise die just like fools?" (2:16). Surely this is not just. "For the fate of humans and the fate of animals is the same; as one dies, so dies the other" (3:19). "No one has power over the wind...or power over the day of death" (8:8).

This is an extremely sharp challenge to Israel's basic conviction that life is good, and long life a blessing, no matter which tradition is consulted. Moses urged Israel to "choose life" (Deut. 30:19). Amos promised, "Seek the Lord and you will live" (5:6, NJPSV). Woman Wisdom cried, "Come...give up simpleness and live!" (Prov. 9:6, NJPSV). For Qohelet, it was not that simple, for life without justice is hollow.[40]

One might well expect this view to lead to despair, and many have regarded this as a book of ultimate despair. But actually, Qohelet is ambivalent about death, as seen in 9:1–6 where he laments the "injustice that is universal: death." "Equal fates for unequal persons is an absurdity which not even the fortunate are spared."[41] Indeed, while they live their hearts are sad, their minds are mad, and then they die! (9:3). But then Qohelet turns around affirming that the living, unlike the dead, have "something to look forward to" (NJPSV) or "have hope" (NRSV), and he offers an aphorism for support: "a living dog is better than a dead lion" (9:4). This unconventional saying affirms life, but with considerable ambiguity, seen in the ironic comparison of a live dog (a common scavenger, much despised, not today's house pet,[42] or a metaphor for a contemptible person[43]), with a dead (royal) lion. Is Qohelet aiming for logical consistency? He is telling the truth and both views are true. What makes the living better than the dead? "The living know that they will die, but the dead know nothing" (9:5). Crenshaw concludes, understandably, that this offers neither comfort nor any basis for hope.[44] While some commentators find a ray of hope in this passage, Fox observes bluntly, "knowing that one will die is not a 'hope' or a feeling of security, but rather something that can be relied on, something that one can be certain about."[45] Just as

---

40. James L. Crenshaw, "The Shadow of Death in Qoheleth," in *Israelite Wisdom: Theological and Literary Essays in Honor of Samuel Terrien*, ed. John G. Gammie et al. (Missoula, Mont.: Scholars, 1978), 206–8.

41. Fox, *Qohelet and His Contradictions*, 257.

42. Gordis, *Koheleth*, 305.

43. Crenshaw, *Ecclesiastes*, 161.

44. Ibid.

45. Fox, *Qohelet and His Contradictions*, 258.

while everything is changing, the earth remains and the rivers return (1:4–7), such a conviction is not much, but it is not nothing.
We might call this a "minimalist" approach. Leah Goldberg's poem
expresses it well:

IN EVERYTHING

In everything, there is at least an eighth
of death. It doesn't weigh much.
With what hidden, peaceful charm
we carry it everywhere we go.
In sweet awakenings,
in our travels,
in our love talk,
when we are unaware,
forgotten in all the corners of our being —
always with us.
And never heavy.[46]

Qohelet further did not entertain a notion of life after death,
where injustice is redressed. Even the hope of an afterlife may not
have eased his consciousness of the injustice of all this, for two
reasons. First, Qohelet is seeking to discover what is good to do
here on earth, among humans, within this life. He wants to know
what is of enduring value that will motivate human achievement
rather than drag us down to a lowest common denominator. Will
telling the oppressed to wait for justice after death help? Even if
true, it would not end oppression and injustice here. Second, to
urge that a just resolution of these inequities will come eventually
is perhaps to miss the point altogether in Qohelet's eyes.

To propose judgment after death as a solution entails agreeing
with one of Qohelet's main convictions arising from his search:
that "no one has power" — neither over the wind nor over death
(8:8). This entails two very important aspects of Qohelet's thought.
In the first place, humans, if ultimately impotent, cannot be as
central as we often imagine ourselves. In the second place, such
power is in the hand of God, and that, in principle, precludes or
negates human striving. In this matter, which seems to be one of his
rock-bottom basic convictions, Qohelet fundamentally agrees with
the conventional Israelite sages. And ironically, while his search
through empirical investigations may have turned up no contrary

---

46. Leah Goldberg, quoted in and translated by Marcia Falk, *The Book of
Blessings: New Jewish Prayers for Daily Life, the Sabbath, and the New Moon
Festival* (San Francisco: HarperSanFrancisco, 1996), 196.

indications, this particular conviction cannot be an inference from empirical studies. Qohelet's belief that all is ultimately in the hand of God is a principle of faith. Yet that does not lead Qoheleth to affirm life or justice after death, and to understand why that is so we must ask what Qohelet believes about God.

God and the Fear of God

Who is God for Qohelet? Job insisted upon addressing the Lord directly, even in the midst of his suffering at God's hands. Qohelet not only never addresses God; he never refers to "the Lord" (Heb. *Yahweh*), though he does refer to God (Heb. *Elohim*) thirty-three times. Like other wisdom writers, Qohelet neither refers to God's acts in history nor denies that this is the same God. Though covenantal traditions offer security, consolation, and reassurance about injustice, Qohelet never appeals to them.

Still, Qohelet has no doubt that God is in control of all: "I know that whatever God does endures forever; nothing can be added to it, nor anything taken from it; God has done this, so that all should stand in awe before him" (Eccles. 3:14). This awe before God is not imposed but grows out of our inability to comprehend what God is doing and why (3:10–11).[47] Nor does the fear of God sufficiently terrify the wicked to prevent their evil deeds; thus, Qohelet cannot affirm the doctrine of retribution. Or does he?

> Though sinners do evil a hundred times and prolong their lives, yet I know that it will be well with those who fear God, because they stand in fear before him, but it will not be well with the wicked, neither will they prolong their days like a shadow, because they do not stand in fear before God.
> There is a vanity that takes place on earth, that there are righteous people who are treated according to the conduct of the wicked, and there are wicked people who are treated according to the conduct of the righteous. I said that this also is vanity. (Eccles. 8:12–14)

How are we to read this? Does this text affirm that retribution holds or that it is an injustice (*hebel*) when it does not? Or is Qohelet here citing the conventional doctrine, while setting it alongside facts about sinners who prolong their lives, so the facts show the absurdity (*hebel*) of believing the doctrine?

---

47. Fox, *Qohelet and His Contradictions*, 195.

A reader-learner could legitimately take it either way.[48] Qohelet concludes:

> When I applied my mind to know wisdom...then I saw all the work of God, that no one can find out what is happening under the sun...even though those who are wise claim to know, they cannot find it out.
>
> All this I laid to heart, examining it all, how the righteous and the wise and their deeds are in the hand of God; whether it is love or hate one does not know. (Eccles. 8:16–9:1)

"No one can find out," yet all is "in the hand of God." No wonder humans must stand in awe — but here the awe is not Joban terror so much as it is a product of ignorance and lack of control. This carries over into advice about cultic duties as well. Qohelet warns readers to be cautious: "Do not be overeager to go the House of God" (5:1, NJPSV). He advises using few words in God's presence, not making too many vows, and fulfilling them promptly (5:1–5). A similar caution is appropriate in ethics as well:

> Do not be too righteous, and do not act too wise; why should you destroy yourself? Do not be too wicked, and do not be a fool; why should you die before your time? It is good that you should take hold of the one, without letting go of the other; for the one who fears God shall succeed with both. (Eccles. 7:16–18)

In Proverbs, Job, Sirach, and the Wisdom of Solomon, Woman Wisdom or God, or both, speak directly to people; "in Ecclesiastes, the heavens remain silent."[49] Thus there "seems to be no room for a personal relationship with God."[50] God's presence is absence. As L. Gorssen has said, "God is utterly present and at the same time utterly absent. God is present in each event and yet no event is a 'place of encounter' with God, since humans do not understand what his will is.... Events do not speak any longer the language of a saving God. They are there, simply."[51]

What Can Humans Possibly Know?

For Qohelet, death not only undermines all justice and striving; it is also an epistemological barrier. What humans know for sure

---

48. So do the scholars. For example, Gordis takes this as a quotation that Qohelet refutes, *Koheleth*, 296–98, while Fox takes it as affirmed by Qohelet, *Qohelet and His Contradictions*, 252–53.

49. Crenshaw, *Ecclesiastes*, 24.

50. Murphy, *Ecclesiastes*, lxviii.

51. Quoted in Murphy, *Ecclesiastes*, lxviii–lxix.

is, "Who knows?" And that holds for life and death equally, so
not knowing is not relieved by a belief in retribution in an afterlife: "For who knows what is good for mortals while they live the
few days of their vain life, which they pass like a shadow? For
who can tell them what will be after them under the sun?" (Eccles.
6:12). The popular saying "God only knows" might well have been
coined for Qohelet.

Still, there are some things humans can and do know. We can
know that the created order "remains forever" (1:4). We know
there is a regularity in "for everything there is a season" (3:1), although we cannot predict or control when that season will come.
Indeed, since nothing is really "new under the sun" (1:9), we can
be assured that the future will "echo the past,"[52] and if we look
at what there are seasons for (3:1–8), we recognize that all these
times continue to occur 2,300 years later, regardless of location,
date, and culture. Is that reassuring?

Still, Qohelet seems to "not know" more than he "knows." (He
says he does not know or "who knows" eighteen times, while he
only says "I know" three times.) But like Job, he does know that
retribution does not work as traditionally promised and that failure is "an evil I have seen." But unlike Job, Qohelet blames no one,
human or divine, for this.[53] Nor does Qohelet question whether
God exists. Indeed, he seems to know that God is "there," offers
gifts, controls reality, and expects awe.

Can one build an adequate pedagogy upon such a minimal epistemology? Qohelet insists we must not pretend to know more than
we do, which implies a humble epistemology, suited to human fini-
tude, as Job also learned. Qohelet honors mystery without letting
go of God and without insisting on logical consistency. Does knowing these things help us steer through life? What should we do?

What Can or Should We Do?

If death negates striving and if God expects awe but not understanding, is caution the only available counsel? There is in this
text another set of observations, which lead to strikingly different
imperatives, in a sharply contrasting mood.

In 2:18–23, Qohelet laments, then quietly affirms, something
else he saw: "There is nothing better for mortals than to eat and
drink, and find enjoyment in their toil. This also, I saw, is from the

---

52. Fox, *Qohelet and His Contradictions*, 102.
53. Terrien, *The Elusive Presence*, 377.

hand of God; for apart from him who can eat or who can have enjoyment? For to the one who pleases him God gives wisdom and knowledge and joy" (Eccles. 2:24–26). Similarly, right after affirming that humans "cannot find out what God has done," he quietly states, "I know that there is nothing better for them than to be happy and enjoy themselves as long as they live; moreover, it is God's gift that all should eat and drink and take pleasure in all their toil" (Eccles. 3:12–13). Again, after another lament over the "grievous evil that I have seen under the sun" (5:13–17), he reports, "This is what I have seen to be good: it is fitting to eat and drink and find enjoyment in all the toil with which one toils under the sun the few days of the life God gives us; for this is our lot" (Eccles. 5:18).

The text of Ecclesiastes lays conflicting descriptions and assessments of the human condition alongside one another, each in the indicative. Qohelet never tells reader-learners what to do about it or how to steer through such a life. How are reader-learners to make sense of these sentences? Could they be assurances that even when everything is in doubt, some things remain?

After another lengthy lament (9:1–6) comes a striking series of imperatives, in which Qohelet tells reader-learners exactly what to do:

> Go, eat your bread with enjoyment, and drink your wine with a merry heart; for God has long ago approved what you do. Let your garments always be white; do not let oil be lacking on your head. Enjoy life with a woman you love, all the days of your vain life that are given you under the sun, because that is your portion in life and in your toil at which you toil under the sun. Whatever your hand finds to do, do with your might; for there is no work or thought or knowledge or wisdom in Sheol, to which you are going. (Eccles. 9:7–10)

How are we to make sense of these directives? These passages hardly seem congruent with what has often been taken to be the overriding negative message of this book.

Are these compensatory reassurances, as though Qohelet were saying: "If you can't find meaning in life, you can at least enjoy eating and drinking. Go ahead; drown your anxieties." Such a reading would fit the interpretation that sees verses 1:2–3 as both affirming the same theme: "All is vanity." Is it that Qohelet is saying, "All is *hebel*, even, ultimately, eating, drinking, and making love, but they are surely better than sitting in gloom"?

Or, if 1:2–3 is read as two sides of a dialogue, might these passages affirm a positive answer about "what endures" despite the reality of death and uncertainties about what God is up to? Could the text be read in this way: "Just as 'the earth remains,' you can embrace what is most common — eat bread, drink wine, love a woman, enjoy your work. Enjoy simple things; we can all do that, no matter how wise"? Such a reading is consistent with not striving. Qohelet repeatedly calls these common realities *gifts* (from God), with no hint of any strings or conditions attached. They are not seen as a reward for or a profit from our striving! When we see eating, drinking, making love, working, as fruits of our own striving or as reflections of our social status or as a means to something else (e.g., a business opportunity), we miss the point. To see these common things as a means or as an accomplishment is to deny they are gifts, arrogating to our credit what simply is. Perhaps Qohelet implies that when we see gifts as means, they become a source of injustice, which is the "evil I have seen under the sun." Thus, we could paraphrase his advice:

> Be in your body. Eat bread. Drink wine.
> Wear clean clothes. Never be without perfume.
> Enjoy making love with one you love.
> Work hard. Enjoy your toil.
> Above all, do not burden yourself with expectations —
> life and love are a gift — enjoy.

Proverbs attended to daily living and common things, yet largely ignored death and the tragic element of life; thus, it did not see what Qohelet sees. Job showed what happens when the tragic dimension becomes central. Does Ecclesiastes suggest that even Job did not go far enough? The conventional sages stopped short of using *all* the evidence in their investigations — they did not include death or treated it as theologically neutral. With Job, death is viewed as a relief from torment, a wished-for end (3:11–13), or as a threat that when Job's death intervenes, the Lord will lose his favorite target (7:17–21). In this text, death threatens the meaning of everything and therefore illumines life.

It seems to this reader-learner that it requires considerable courage both to face truth as honestly and resolutely as has this author and to move from "We cannot know" to "Enjoy life!" It is a long journey from "You do not know" (11:6) to "Light is sweet, and it is pleasant for the eyes to see the sun" (11:7). Indeed, notice the sensuous imagery of this indicative sentence. The light of the sun is visual; the eyes see the sun, or they use the light of the sun to see more clearly "what is," as does Qohelet. The sun is also tactile as it warms the skin. And Qohelet here tastes light — it is sweet, which resonates, on the one hand, with the sensory enjoyment of God's gifts of bread, wine, love, and work, as well as with prophetic call. Ezekiel was ordered to eat the scroll filled with "words of lamentation and mourning and woe," and "in...[his] mouth it was as sweet as honey" (Ezek. 2:8–10; 3:3). He was then commanded to go speak those plain words, even though the people "will not listen to you" (Ezek. 3:7).

Both prophet and sage bring unconventional words to people in troubled times. Both found getting a hearing difficult. Perhaps both offer hope that may lend itself to fantasy, illusion, and speculation but that will only be tasted by those who see it as based in sober truth. Both offer God's gifts.

WHY LEARN IN THIS MANNER? WHAT IS THE POINT?

Qohelet has made reader-learners swim in treacherous waters, leading us round and round. It is not always clear how much of this is the author's intent. Could there be pedagogical intent?

Teaching as Challenging

The artist Reinhold Marxhausen, speaking of teaching art to students, once said, "Seeing truthfully is better than knowing what you are doing." This text may suggest that the point or purpose of teaching and learning has less to do with what you know or what you can do and more to do with coming to see the world truthfully. This text evokes truthful seeing by challenging virtually everything reader-learners bring to the text.

CHALLENGING CONVENTIONAL WISDOM. Qohelet is a wise man criticizing wisdom, for conventional wisdom offered more security than reality warrants. Following Job, Qohelet felt that "life is more complicated than the sages made it out to be."[54]

When the issue at stake is seeking to learn truth, to have decided ahead of time what ways of seeing are acceptable may prevent inquiry and take responsibility for learning out of the hands of the reader-learner. On the other hand, a text as ambiguous as this one not only offers unconventional notions that may upset reader-learners; it also cannot control the outcome of

---

54. Murphy, *Ecclesiastes*, lxiii.

their thought processes, and that entails risks. It necessarily presumes some maturity among reader-learners, while it also presumes trusting them.

Controversy emerges because two legitimate interests come into conflict. There is a desire to conserve what has been gathered from the experience of the past, which is a legitimate and important interest in any culture or religious tradition. There is also a desire to acknowledge that what is may change as cultures and questions change. These interests clash — and often each sees the other as a threat.

Qohelet acknowledges that he learned that seeking wisdom (whether conventional or new?) is also "chasing wind":

> For as wisdom grows, vexation grows;
> To increase learning is to increase heartache. (Eccles. 1:18, NJPSV)

Ironically, in the epilogue to Ecclesiastes, someone (not Qohelet) agreed that reading Qohelet is also chasing wind and sought to counteract the imagined dangers to reader-learners of the book:

> Of anything beyond these, my child, beware. Of making many books there is no end, and much study is a weariness of the flesh.
> The end of the matter; all has been heard. Fear God, and keep his commandments; for that is the whole duty of everyone. (Eccles. 12:12–13)

Here is the voice of a censor warning reader-learners not to take too seriously what has been said in the preceding book. In recommending that everything can be summed up in a one-line wise saying, he either profoundly misunderstands Qohelet's message(s), or else he seeks to mislead reader-learners.[55] He is saying in effect, "You probably don't need to read this book (it may make you weary), but if you must, see it as consistent with traditional teaching." That, in itself, is a testimony to the power of this text! This warning and Qohelet alike demonstrate that in chasing truth one often finds much wind.

CHALLENGING REASONING WITH TRUTH. There is no choice; all must and do begin with inherited wisdom. Long before any children arrive in

---

55. The summary offered in 12:9–14 reduces the powerful enigmas of this text to the most conventional outcome possible: "Fear God, and keep his commandments." Can that really be the original author's intent? That is a single conclusion, with little ambiguity or "riddle quality." Besides, the rest of the text never even mentions the commandments, let alone suggests that keeping commandments is a solution to his inquiries. For these and other reasons, the scholarly consensus is that these verses are the work of a later editor.

any teaching-learning process, they have already absorbed an enor-
mous quantity of conventional wisdom gathered and transmitted
by their language, their culture, and their family. They already have
lots of gifts. This text does not challenge the existence or usefulness of conventional wisdom — it insists reader-learners cannot
stop there.

If we accept Qohelet's account of his procedure, it seems he began with a question about the wisdom he had already acquired.
What was it worth? He set out to test it all (2:1–10; 7:25; 8:16).
His experiments with truth raise perennial pedagogical questions:
How do experience, empirical reality, and reasoning cohere? Are
they in conflict? Need they be? What is an optimum relation
among them? Qohelet reminds us not to run away from or try to
hide our contradictions, for they may be exactly the path we need
to pursue, the path to life.

Qohelet also recognized the role of human senses and bodies
in learning. In many cultures, perhaps especially in the culture of
schools and churches, there often seems to be a fundamental distrust of the body. The further learners go up the schooling ladder,
the more they are asked to "park their bodies at the door." Qohelet, on the other hand, did not presume that the answers or truth
he sought would always take the form of abstract propositions
or moral absolutes. Sometimes useful and profound truth comes
embedded in one's muscles, in a visceral sensation, in the taste of
bread, in a sunset, or in the reassuring feeling of the warm sun on
one's face. These things endure.

Qohelet also offers teachers and learners alike the humble recognition that the search for truth is just as finite and limited as is the
human condition. Sometimes the truth is "I don't know" or even
"We can't ever know." Qohelet was especially reticent to claim to
know the ultimate mystery, the mind of God. When teachers emulate such reticence, expect less often to be the answer giver, they
may discover themselves to be colleagues in learning and knowing. Is it possible that mutuality may take the form of collegiality,
that is, teachers and learners as colleagues standing before the mysteries of the universe? In Luther's graphic phrase, "Before God,
we are all beggars." What Qohelet and Luther both discovered is
that beggars may be particularly adept at spotting gifts among the
mundane.

WHAT ARE LIMITS FOR? The ultimate test question is death. In seeking to
discover "What is good for mortals to do? Does anything endure?"
Qohelet decided the answer must transcend death. What did he

find? One way of reading this text says that Qohelet found nothing transcends death. Death cancels all. So he answered, "*Hebel hebelim* [Superlative vapor!]. All is *hebel.* "

Another reading is equally legitimate: Is there anything that does not smell of death? Seeking ultimate answers and finding none (and being unwilling to make them up) can lead to such despair that even one's bread has no taste. Accepting death as a human limit, then focusing on common life within that limit, letting God take care of the ultimate answers, Qohelet proposed that bread and wine could taste good and that work and love might be seen as joyous gifts. Is it not ironic that sometimes one must face ultimate realities in order to see clearly common, daily realities? Perhaps, epistemologically, gaining clarity about what we cannot know offers clarity about what we can know and about what is of enduring value.

Education as Seeing

Job, in repenting, testified to what a difference it makes to turn from reliance on hearsay or second-hand learning to seeing face-to-face. Job also discovered that he saw pain, perplexity, and suffering differently when it was his own. When his perplexities were his own, he felt less ready to accept generic over-the-counter remedies and painkillers. He discovered anew that one size does not fit all. Qohelet seems to accept this and then goes further. He not only tests traditional notions; he tests the limits of the meaning of living and discovers new knowledge that never was in the tradition.

Both Job and Qohelet use the metaphor of seeing, often at crucial points in the text. In twelve short chapters, Qohelet used the word "see" more than forty times and refers to the sun thirty-three times, and this in a book of wisdom, where one might expect to focus on what has been heard of old. This is particularly striking also in a culture that is still largely oral/aural. Qohelet looked everywhere "under the sun" for the truth and reached into the dark places as well. He brought many things to light that may make some people uneasy, for they are aspects of reality we often prefer not to face.

Qohelet also reminds us that the seeing image becomes even more fecund if we allow more of the senses into the act. We can not only see the light; we can also feel the light on our skin; we can hear the light tones of music when compared with the heavy and dark tones that come with threats and somber moods. Even some smells can be described as more light than others. Qohelet even tastes light, and it is sweet, which then leads him to command the young to joy (11:9)! Is it not wondrous how many forms truth can assume? To see more truly, we need to open all our senses.

Learning as Receiving Gifts

Possibly the most important effect this text offers reader-learners is lessons in how to "let go." Many teachers need control — of learners and of the outcomes of the teaching-learning process. Many learners expend considerable energy resisting that control and asserting their own. Is this striving and chasing after wind? Some encourage teachers and learners to practice the ancient motto "Carpe diem" (Seize the day)! When we do, needing control, we stress *seize!*

What if everything were regarded as a gift (from God), not an achievement of our own striving? If work is a gift instead of an achievement or a means to something else, gratitude might replace pride. Is it easier to share gifts than what we have earned?

What has this to do with pedagogy? How much of what any individual knows is actually the product of his or her own single-handed effort? The vast majority of what we have learned is ours as a result of those who *gave* time, *shared* insights (perhaps in books), *gave* encouragement as we struggled to new ways of thinking and seeing, and *gave* praise for our meager accomplishments, thereby *giving* us confidence to go on by ourselves. Our learning is full of the gifts of others upon which we rely daily. If that is true and acknowledged, we have laid a basis for sharing with others in much the same way — rather than being stingy hoarders of knowledge for which we seek the sole credit. Such sharing might even lead to what Letty Russell has persuasively called "partnership as a mode of educational ministry."[56] When there are many gifts in a community and they are being widely shared, that community is moving toward *shalom*.

IS THIS MINIMALIST ACCOUNT ENOUGH?
CAN ABSENCE OF PRESENCE BE A GIFT?

Some readers of Ecclesiastes may feel Qohelet has reduced religion and life itself to its bare-bones essentials. It may not seem,

---

56. Letty Russell first suggests this in *Christian Education in Mission* (Philadelphia: Westminster, 1967), though she there calls it "participation." Later, in *The Future of Partnership* (Philadelphia: Westminster, 1979), she develops the theme more fully.

at first glance, a rich or fully textured description of what makes life meaningful. On the other hand, Murphy suggests that Qohelet "demonstrates that there is more to religion than salvation."[57]

Compared with the powerful, though malevolent, divine presence we observed in Job, Qohelet's world feels like a comparative absence of the presence of God. Instead of a prophetic or priestly God who pursues creatures in every moment of their existence, for good or ill, Qohelet's God seems a dim, shadowy, even remote, horizon. For Job, the absence of presence promised relief from torture. But is the absence of presence enough? Qohelet recommends we stop striving and go back to the basics: find joy in God's common gifts of bread, wine, work, and making love. That may be the beginning of hope.

Both life and pedagogy are grounded in hope. Both require a vision, a dream, some reason for going on with the hard work that is necessary and that sustains living, growing, and learning. Are Qohelet's common basics or gifts rich enough to sustain lifelong learning and abundant living? Is Qohelet's absence really so empty? Does it not depend upon what one's heart is looking for? If our life is filled with gifts of bread, wine, a lover, work, and joy, aren't these presents divine presence rather than absence? Can we see truthfully?

It is easy to view absence as negative and presence as positive. Human and divine reality may be more complex. It is striking that even in his lowest moments we do not find Qohelet doubting whether God is there or is in charge. While there does not seem to be a feeling of personal divine presence, neither is there a feeling of complete divine absence. How could we account for this? Is this pedagogically relevant?

Allow me an analogy: A lover can be intensely aware of the absent presence of her lover, perhaps as Qohelet is deeply aware of the absence of the immediate presence of God. Yet that absence, in both, does not nullify life; only death does that. For Qohelet and perhaps also for a lover, absence need not lead to despair; it may motivate a search. The paradoxical truth is, as many know, the absence of a loved one is more than simply emptiness. Absence itself can be filled with longing, with memories, with an eagerness for being together again, with hope for presence, and so on. In short, while the emptiness is real, it can also be quite full.

---

57. Murphy, *Ecclesiastes*, lxix.

In a quite similar manner, learners can be present in their absence in a teacher's planning. The educational endeavor as a whole can be seen as a process of planning for the eventual absence of the learners from the presence of the teacher. Ironically, viewing education in this manner can be a corrective for a temptation to foster dependence among learners, which cripples their educational efforts. Planning itself, even when done in the absence of the presence of learners, is fueled by hope. As the emptiness of a lover's absence can also be full, by analogy so can the learner's absence be for a teacher. Teachers ponder the meaning of a student's actions. They wonder what they can do to help this one gain more self-control, to help that one be more expressive, and to help another see the light in math. Teachers who take seriously the absent presence of learners while they plan may affirm by their actions, "Lo, I am with you always."

CHAPTER FOUR

SLEEPING WITH THE ENEMY
Education amid Culture Wars

As the authors of Job and Ecclesiastes tried to help the people of Israel steer through the suffering and cultural dislocation of the exile, Sirach (also known as Ecclesiasticus) and the Wisdom of Solomon addressed yet another cultural crisis, one framed by the following questions: Must faithfulness change when culture changes? Are being religious and faithful to God not eternally the same even as time passes and culture changes? How can we be faithful while living within a culture increasingly dominated by other values? This time the other culture was an increasingly influential Hellenism, that is, the language and culture of Greece. Both authors faced the same questions but answered them in radically different ways. Might we learn about our own cultural conflicts from these responses to a threat to traditional faith?

The exile had seriously weakened national and cultural autonomy, but after Cyrus's Edict of Toleration in 538 B.C.E., and the rebuilding of Jerusalem, a new reality gradually emerged. Instead of an autonomous kingdom, Israel became a temple-state governed by a priestly aristocracy (while paying tribute to Persia). Later, when the Greeks took over, priestly aristocrats governed under new management. Groups of *hasidim* (the pious) arose; these were largely lay nonaristocrats who sought to live more strictly religious lives. (In Roman times, the aristocratic priestly families were succeeded by the Sadducees, while the *hasidim* were succeeded by the Pharisees and the Essenes.)

Alexander's rule increased the influence of Greek culture in the Near East (ca. 334–330), for he had ideals that were different from those of the previous victors. Cyrus and the Persians had demanded political loyalty and payment of taxes from Judea, but they allowed indigenous ethnic and religious traditions among vassal provinces. Since Jerusalem was on the fringe of Persia's interests, it could remain relatively isolated.[1] To understand the encounter between the Israelites and Hellenism in this time period, one must comprehend the Hellenistic concept of *paideia*, the Greek word for both "education" and "culture."[2] Alexander sought not only political sovereignty but also the fostering of Greek language, institutions, values, and ideas. Education (*paideia*) was not just preparation for a career but the lifelong effort "to realize ever more perfectly the human ideal."[3] As such, *paideia* included not only the learning process but the ideals and products of learning, in other words, the ideal civilization itself. Thus for Hellenism, *paideia* was a human, social, and cultural commitment of religious significance.[4]

In newly conquered regions, Greek cities were founded with a Greek constitution and an elected council. These cities — with their Greek gods, Greek baths, theaters, and educational institutions — became administrative, commercial, and cultural centers for the region. As early as 270 B.C.E., Greek inscriptions reveal that Phoenicians from Sidon and Tyre (just north of Galilee) had been victorious boxers in Greek games, which shows they knew the Greek language and were educated in a Greek *gymnasium* (like our high schools, stressing both academic and athletic competition).[5]

When Alexander died in 323 B.C.E., Judea found itself no longer on the fringe but right in the middle of two warring factions. For the next century, the Seleucids in Syria and the Ptolemies in Egypt fought five wars on Judean soil. Equally important, some of Israel's social elite favored the new Hellenistic culture, while others opposed it, thus exacerbating polarization within Jewish society,

---

1. For further background on this period, see Rainer Albertz, *A History of Israelite Religion in the Old Testament Period*, vol. 2, *From the Exile to the Maccabees* (Louisville: Westminster/John Knox, 1994); and Martin Hengel, *Judaism and Hellenism: Studies in Their Encounter in Palestine during the Early Hellenistic Period*, 2 vols. (London: SCM, 1974).

2. H. I. Marrou, *A History of Education in Antiquity* (New York: New American Library, 1956), 143.

3. Ibid., 142.

4. The essential description of this Hellenistic pedagogical understanding is Werner Jaeger's classic, *Paideia: The Ideals of Greek Culture*, 3 vols. (New York: Oxford University Press, 1945).

5. Hengel, *Judaism and Hellenism*, 1:170. The classics scholar Moses Hadas suggests the best evidence of how effective the Hellenistic educational system was in conquered areas is the large number of writers and philosophers who came from non-Greek localities. For example, Zeno, possibly a Semite, founded the Stoic school of philosophy, with its passion for righteousness (which makes it natural to think of his being influenced by Hebraic traditions). Zeno's six successors came from Tarsus, Babylon, and Sidon. See Moses Hadas, *Hellenistic Culture: Fusion and Diffusion* (New York: Norton, 1959), 105–7.

not least between urban (more hellenized) and rural populations.[6] Urban families benefited from the prosperity brought about by the Ptolemaean rule and found it both useful and desirable to learn Greek, adopt Greek names, wear Greek clothing, and even participate in the festivals and games of Greek culture:[7]

> Jewish religious identity was taken for granted and was not yet fundamentally put into question, even if people could at times use polytheistic forms of greeting in business correspondence with Greek partners. But from the perspective of the lower class in city and country, who hardly came into contact with Greek culture in Judea, it must have seemed as if they were being exploited by a clique which not only did not care about the solidarity required by the Torah, but also increasingly drifting off into a suspect un-Jewish life-style that was alien to them. As a result of this cultural reshaping, the chronic class contrast developed such a potential for conflict that it only needed an occasion to turn it into a civil war.[8]

Not all who were open to Greek influence were willing to adopt the Greek lifestyle. Some respected members of the upper classes insisted on remaining faithful to tradition and sought solidarity with the poor and the more conservative members of society.

In 175 B.C.E., Jason (whose name is the Greek form of the Hebrew Joshua), a resident of Jerusalem and of priestly lineage, offered the Seleucid kings a bribe if they would appoint him high priest (which they did). Then he offered more money if they would convert Jerusalem into a Greek city, including a new, elected governing council, a new Greek *gymnasium*, and an *ephebion* (a school for military training). Two years later Jerusalem sent representatives to compete in the Greek athletic games in Tyre.[9] That Jason established a *gymnasium* shows that a Greek primary school must have already existed in Jerusalem, for a pupil entered the *gymnasium* at age fourteen or fifteen, and instruction was in Greek.[10]

While the Greek rulers, both Ptolemies and Seleucids, had allowed some ethnic and religious autonomy as a form of social

---

6. Hershel Shanks, ed., *Ancient Israel: A Short History from Abraham to the Roman Destruction of the Temple* (Englewood Cliffs, N.J.: Prentice-Hall, 1988), 177–79.

7. Albertz, *History of Israelite Religion*, 2:537–38.

8. Ibid., 538.

9. Ibid., 181–82.

10. Hengel, *Judaism and Hellenism*, 1:103.

control,[11] this ended abruptly with the invasion of Jerusalem by
Antiochus IV Epiphanes in 167 B.C.E. Perhaps in frustration over
being prevented from taking over Egypt, Antiochus raided the
temple treasury and then banned circumcision and all religious
observance of the sabbath and festivals. According to the ancient
author Diodorus, Antiochus went on to profane the temple by sac-
rificing a sow (a ritually unclean animal) in the temple, pouring
its blood on the altar, sprinkling pork broth on the holy books,
and forcing the priests and people to eat the meat.[12] Within a year,
there was an armed revolt, led by the Hasmoneans, especially Ju-
das Maccabeus.[13] After a guerilla war, an independent Maccabean
kingdom was established, with priest-kings, which remained until
the Roman takeover in 63 B.C.E. These and similar events shape
the cultural and political context within which Ecclesiasticus and
the Wisdom of Solomon emerge. Ecclesiasticus (ca. 180 B.C.E.) was
written in Hebrew in Jerusalem, and the Wisdom of Solomon (ca.
50 B.C.E.) was written in Greek, likely in Alexandria, Egypt, the
cultural capital of Hellenism.

Proverbs, Job, and Qohelet had borrowed from or adapted
Semitic or Egyptian sources — either directly or indirectly. Learning from other cultures and religions was never rejected by Israel's
sages, so why did it become such an issue at this time? Neither of
our authors explicitly addressed this issue, but the change from Hebraic ways of thinking to Greek ways of thinking, as we shall see,
was a profound shift, which altered concepts, social and cultural
values, pedagogy, and religion. Indeed, the case could be made
that theology itself only became a central concern when the shift
was made from Hebraic to Hellenistic ways of thinking about religion. Joseph Kitagawa, the eminent historian of religion, once
observed, "If you ask Asians to describe their religion, they will
tell you about their practices; if you ask Christians, they will tell
you about their beliefs. Judaism . . . is in this respect more like an
Asian religion than like Christianity."[14] So the issue was, Does the

---

11. See the rationale offered by the Greek historian Polybius (201–119 B.C.E.),
cited in James D. Newsome, *Greeks, Romans, Jews: Currents of Culture and Belief
in the New Testament World* (Philadelphia: Trinity International Press, 1992), 18.

12. Ibid., 19.

13. Ibid., 11, 36–42. Scholars debate whether Antiochus's "reforms" preceded
and instigated the Maccabean revolt or whether there had been a prior urban uprising to which Antiochus responded with new regulations to try to put down the
uprising. See Helmut Koester, *History, Culture, and Religion of the Hellenistic Age*,
vol. 1, *Introduction to the New Testament* (New York: de Gruyter, 1982), 208–19.

14. Quoted in Jon D. Levenson, *The Hebrew Bible, the Old Testament, and His-*

adoption of a foreign culture (Hellenism) threaten the Lord and Jewish tradition?

In Babylonian captivity, Israel asked, "How can we sing the Lord's song in a strange land?" Now, in Hellenistic Jerusalem, Sirach asked, "How can we sing the Lord's song in our own land, when the lyrics are in a foreign language and the harmonies are strange?" Sirach was willing to adopt newer cultural patterns to the extent that they did not change traditional ways. Yet in Hellenistic Alexandria, the Wisdom of Solomon asked, "Why not sing our song using foreign concepts and tunes? Aren't our ways superior even in new styles?" The Wisdom of Solomon was willing to modify traditional thought to fit into the new culture, using Greek concepts. Early Christians debated many of the same issues as Greek and Latin replaced Hebrew as the language of the new religion. The controversy has hardly died, though it takes new forms: Can the church adapt itself to the new media age, or is that to sell its soul? Should it adapt? Can the incarnate Word be communicated in cyberspace? Should it? Perhaps only now can we appreciate what a transformation took place when the Word took print form. Was that a blessing or a mistake? These issues are significant for pedagogy and religion, and these two texts can contribute reflective experience and wisdom to the discussion.

SIRACH

Ecclesiasticus was written in Hebrew, likely in Jerusalem in about 180 B.C.E. and later translated into Greek (in 132 B.C.E.) in Alexandria, Egypt, by the author's grandson. The author, Sirach, was a scholar (39:1–11) with a school in Jerusalem (51:23). He traveled widely (34:10–11), was respected as an advisor to public officials (38:24, 31–34; cf. chap. 39 and 51:13) and as a judicial consultant (10:1–2; 38:33; 39:4). While Sirach wrote in Hebrew, he used Hellenistic literary forms. He maintained distinctively priestly worship patterns and celebrated the Torah, yet rejected isolationist separatism and favored openness to foreigners.[15] Clearly this author wrestled with what is today called *multiculturalism*.

---

torical Criticism: Jews and Christians in Biblical Studies (Louisville: Westminster/ John Knox, 1993), 52. Levenson's chapter "Why Jews Are Not Interested in Biblical Theology" is helpful.

15. See the balanced and succinct review by John G. Gammie, "The Sage in Sirach," in *The Sage in Israel and the Ancient Near East*, ed. John G. Gammie and Leo G. Perdue (Winona Lake, Ind.: Eisenbrauns, 1990), 355–72.

In our previous texts, reader-learners have been pulled immediately into the experiences and feelings of the central characters.
Here we first encounter a prologue written by Sirach's translator, his grandson, who describes why his grandfather wrote this
book, when and why the grandson then translated it, and the difficulties of translating from Hebrew to Greek. Only then does the
reader-learner encounter the beginning of Sirach's text.

By calling attention to his own arrival in Egypt and the difficulties of translating, the grandson pulls the reader-learner's attention
toward the translator, rather than the text. We are told that the
purpose of the text is "so that... those who love learning might
make even greater progress in living according to the law," yet attention is drawn away from the reader's "progress in living" to
matters of text and translation. When reader-learners finally arrive
at the proverbial sayings, they must shift gears.

How Does Sirach Engage Reader-Learners?

Sirach's reader may feel quite different from the reader of our three
earlier works. Sirach offers many astute observations, much wise
advice, and new approaches to wisdom. Yet Sirach's approach to
wisdom is so shaped by his understanding and use of "the commandments" that his proverbial sayings most often take the form
of imperatives, and so does his advice. This tends to have the effect
of making reader-learners the object or target of what he thinks
we ought to do or think. In what immediately follows, we shall
observe *how* his text engages reader-learners in learning new approaches — especially in his commitments to piety, prayer, praise,
and travel. Much of the rest of his pedagogical insight is offered as
his conclusions, which he urges readers to learn.

PROVERBIAL SAYINGS. Sirach structured his book by creating thematic
poetic proverbial discourses like those in Proverbs 1–9.[16] Sirach
concurred with the content of Proverbs in many matters, including retribution, folly, and death, despite the discussions of Job and
Ecclesiastes.[17] While he assumed familiarity with Proverbs, rather
than just quote that text, Sirach "explained it and developed its
implications for his own day and his own society."[18]

---

16. Wolfgang Roth, "On the Gnomic-Discursive Wisdom of Jesus ben Sirach,"
Semeia 17 (1980), 74.
17. Jack T. Sanders, *Ben Sira and Demotic Wisdom* (Chico, Calif.: Scholars,
1983), 4–11.
18. Patrick W. Skehan and Alexander A. DiLella, *The Wisdom of Ben Sira*, AB
39 (New York: Doubleday, 1987), 43.

"Listen" and "my child" appear frequently in Sirach (as in Prov. 1–9), urging reader-learners to pay attention to elders and parents (e.g., Sir. 2:1; 3:1–20; 4:1). Yet where the "father" in Proverbs urged the reader-learner to remember "my commandments," the accumulated experience of the fathers, Sirach explicitly advises, "Remember the commandments" of Sinai and "the covenant of the Most High" (28:7). He also offers extended reflections about children honoring parents and remaining humble, affirming a familial hierarchy, for it reflects the "might of the Lord" which is glorified by the humble (3:20). So it is no surprise that he adopts the imperative (commandment) style of Proverbs 1–9 rather than the indicative style of Proverbs 10–22. Indeed, Sirach uses "Do not" over 140 times, showing how thoroughly he has imbibed the commandment form, inviting — or more strongly, commanding — a reader-learner's obedience. For example, Sirach frequently begins a command with "Do not say" followed by a quotation, usually followed by a reason for the injunction (5:3–6; 7:9; 11:23–24; 15:11–12; 16:17; 39:21; 39:34).[19] This form is rare in Proverbs but occurs frequently in Egyptian texts such as *Amenemope, Ani,* and *Onchsheshonqy* and in the Wisdom of Solomon.[20]

The literary form may reflect that there have been differing views, but Sirach leaves no doubt about the right answer. Sometimes one should "not say" something because God will punish the offender (5:3, 6); other times the imperative is absolute (11:23–24). The strong imperative tone of this text (and the relatively fewer indicative sayings) suggests less room for the reader-learner's own discerning and perhaps greater control by the author, thus representing Sirach's response to the threats of a new culture and news ways of thinking. The approach surely limits the range of responses expected from reader-learners and requires little reflection.

HYMNS AND PRAYERS. Sirach expands on hints in Proverbs (e.g., in Prov. 30:7–9), forging a much closer connection between study or learning and worship.[21] Learning and prayer flow together naturally for Sirach. Job and Qohelet stood in awe and even evoked awe within reader-learners, yet they did not include hymns or

---

19. Roland E. Murphy, *The Tree of Life: An Exploration of the Biblical Wisdom Literature* (New York: Doubleday, 1990), 72.

20. James Crenshaw, "The Problem of Theodicy in Sirach: Of Human Bondage," in *Theodicy in the Old Testament*, ed. James L. Crenshaw (Philadelphia: Fortress, 1983), 120–21.

21. James L. Crenshaw, *Old Testament Wisdom: An Introduction* (Atlanta: John Knox, 1981), 164.

prayers in their texts. Sirach seems less interested in evoking awe
in reader-learners than he is in showing readers how to pray
and praise God, recording long prayers, petitions for deliverance
(22:27–23:6; 36:6–14), prayers of thanksgiving (51:1–12), and
hymns of praise to creation (42:15–43:33).

Sirach's use of prayer, personal reflection, and praise blends
naturally with his advice, sometimes catching reader-learners off
guard. In 22:19 he begins with reflections on friendship, then
engages in first-person reflection (22:25) and self-examination
(22:27), and smoothly and naturally moves into a personal prayer
(23:1–6). Here wisdom much more clearly and explicitly emerges
from a prayerful relation with God, and the reader finds oneself
in the midst of prayer without warning (see also chaps. 35–36). It
almost feels like eavesdropping at times.

Sirach's last lengthy hymn (44:1–50:26), praising famous men
or human heroes, is quite striking and unusual as he borrows Hellenistic literary forms and values to celebrate historical Hebrew
figures:[22] Nowhere in Hebrew Scriptures are human heroes praised
unless it is a means by which to praise the Lord and call attention
to the Lord's glory. Yet Sirach explicitly affirms that the Lord gives
them the glory (44:2). Sirach praises kings, sages, prophets, musicians, the wealthy, those who were remembered, and those who
were not. What was the nature of their glory? They were "godly
men, whose righteous deeds have not been forgotten" (44:10). In
other words, unlike what is found in Greek praise of heroes, Sirach attributes their glory not so much to their virtues, courage,
strength, nobility, nor even their strength of character. For Sirach,
they are to be praised for their piety and for the way they and their
descendants "stand by the covenants" (44:12). In so doing, Sirach
unites wisdom with Israel's history (for the first time).

Sirach praises Enoch, Noah, Abraham, Isaac, Jacob, Moses
(five verses), Aaron (sixteen verses!), Phinehas, Joshua, the judges,
Samuel, Nathan, David, Solomon, Elijah, Elisha, Hezekiah, Isaiah, Josiah, Ezekiel, Zerubbabel, Nehemiah (but not Ezra), Enoch,
Joseph, Shem, Seth, Enosh, and Adam and concludes with twenty-
six vivid verses about Simon, son of Onias, high priest in Jerusalem
(50:1–26). In this selection of heroes, we see both Sirach's ori-
entation to the priestly tradition and his use of a Greek literary
form (the encomium) and values (virtues embodied in and ex-

---

22. Burton L. Mack, *Wisdom and the Hebrew Epic: Ben Sira's Hymn in Praise
of the Fathers* (Chicago: University of Chicago Press, 1985).

pressed by heroes) to serve his Hebraic commitments. We also see his revisionist interpretation of Israel's stories.

The list is also pedagogically interesting, for we might expect Sirach, the teacher, to expand upon Moses the teacher (Deut. 4:5; 6:1). Sirach affirms that the Lord gave Moses the commandments so he might teach Israel (Sir. 45:5), but Moses "exalted Aaron" to the priesthood. After a lengthy description of Aaron's splendor, authority, and glorious robes, Sirach says Moses gave Aaron authority to teach and enlighten Israel with his law (45:17)! In other words, Moses delegated his teaching office to Aaron, so the priestly office absorbs the teaching office.[23] Sirach concludes his hymn by locating virtually all Israel's religious offices in the high priesthood in Jerusalem, thus yoking learning, piety, and worship.[24] James Crenshaw rightly concludes, "Ben Sira places prayer and praise at the very center of the intellectual endeavor."[25]

Sirach also invites reader-learners to reflect upon the stories of his heroes (which he seems to assume are already known), suggesting reader-learners follow these examples of fidelity and piety:

> Sirach's educational example, however, is the pious man [sic]. This brings the religious components into the centre of the educational system. The man who strives for piety, the one who fears God, that is, the one who gives his heart to God, is man as God wishes him to be. To him alone are the sources of wisdom and knowledge open. It is, then, Sirach firm conviction that — to put it briefly — faith is also a factor in education. The fear of God is able to make something of a man. It improves a man both with regard to his knowledge of the world and to his behaviour towards others. It forms him, protects him and supports him. Put concisely, "Whoever seeks God receives instruction" (musar–paideia, 32:14).[26]

Is there not a certain irony in the fact that this rationale for a close link between faith, piety, and education — a rationale so familiar in twentieth-century Protestant denominational circles — is found most fully and explicitly expressed in a book that is excluded from the Protestant canon?

---

23. See also the contemporary description of how the priestly tradition bears a basic teaching function in Walter A. Brueggemann's *The Creative Word: Canon as a Model for Biblical Education* (Philadelphia: Fortress, 1982), chap. 2.

24. Ibid., 31–36.

25. James Crenshaw, "The Restraint of Reason, the Humility of Prayer," in *Urgent Advice and Probing Questions: Collected Writings on Old Testament Wisdom* (Macon, Ga.: Mercer University Press, 1995), 217.

26. Gerhard von Rad, *Wisdom in Israel* (Nashville: Abingdon, 1972), 260.

TRAVEL AND EXPERIENCE. Important sources of learning apparently emerged for Sirach from his own cosmopolitan experience:

> An inexperienced person knows few things,
>   but he that has traveled acquires much cleverness. (Sir. 34:10)

> I have seen many things in my travels,
>   and I understand more than I can express. (Sir. 34:12)

> [O]ne with much experience knows what he is talking about.
>   (Sir. 34:9)

Sirach has studied, but in traveling in foreign lands, serving the great and rulers, he "learns what is good and evil in the human lot" (39:4). Here there is no imperative or command to travel, but reader-learners may hear an implicit suggestion that travel could also be a source of learning, if used wisely.

Sirach also offers the fruits of his travel experience and reflections as lessons to be absorbed by reader-learners. For example, in his travels and his serving in foreign courts, he had occasion to participate in many banquets, and he offers observations and directives about how to behave both as a guest and as a "master of the feast" (thereby presuming another Hellenistic custom; 31:12–32:13). In typically cautious fashion, he urges moderation in both eating and drinking, but if the host insists and you "are overstuffed with food," he advises, "Get up to vomit" and thus find relief (31:21). In all this, there is no hint that one is to avoid eating what is ritually impure. Rather one is free to "amuse yourself there to your heart's content," although "above all bless your Maker, who fills you with his good gifts" (32:12–13). No banquet, either in Israel or in foreign courts, should prevent one from remembering the Creator. For Sirach, no matter what is learned in travel and experience, piety has the last word.

SCHOLARLY STUDY. Sirach was self-conscious about his own methods, approach, and commitments. He compared his own vocation as sage-scholar with other vocations, such as the physician (38:1–15), the farmer, the artist, the blacksmith, and the potter (38:25–30). These others all "rely on their hands," and while they were skillful and necessary to "maintain the fabric of the world," Sirach observed they were not sought out "for the public assembly" or as rulers or judges (38:31–34). In contrast,

> The wisdom of the scribe depends on the opportunity of leisure;
>   only the one who has little business can become wise. (Sir. 38:24)

Sirach detailed the tasks of the sage-scholar in what might well have been a self-portrait (39:1–5). While the law and prayer were major concerns for Sirach, wisdom comes from studying biblical texts. Indeed, the only biblical books to which he does not refer are Ruth, Ezra, Esther, and Daniel![27]

Yet Sirach took seriously the wisdom of *all* the ancients. Contemporary scholars have identified many of the non-Hebrew sources Sirach used, including Homer, Theognis, Euripides, Xenophon, Hesiod, and Sophocles.[28] While none of these are directly quoted, Sirach may have used an anthology of Greek writers or picked up their ideas and phrases from conversations with foreigners and those with Greek educations.[29] For example, friendship is not a familiar theme in previous Hebrew writings, though it did appear as a dramatic element in the narrative of David and Jonathan. (I do not count Job's friends as reflections on friendship.) Yet many Hellenistic works reflect extensively and philosophically about the nature and importance of friendship. Aristotle devoted two of the ten chapters of his *Ethics* to reflections on friendship. Sirach follows suit (6:5–17; 7:18; 9:10; 12:8–9; 13:21; 19:13–15; 37:1–6). Sirach was also familiar with Egyptian works and used as much as 15 percent of the writings of the Egyptian sage Phibis (found in *Papyrus Insiger*).[30]

In all this borrowing, Sirach does not adopt Greek or Egyptian conceptual patterns. Rather "when its suits his (Judaic) purpose, i.e., when he regards it as true, he claims it for Judaism."[31] Sirach is "entirely open to Hellenic thought as long as it can be Judaized. What he opposes is the dismantling of Judaism."[32] In Crenshaw's more graphic description, Sirach "attempts a marriage between Hellenism and Hebraism, between Athens and Jerusalem, although he saw to it that Zion wore a chastity belt, the keys of which had been entrusted to the Most High himself."[33]

Sirach's position on foreign ideas was not taken only in response to non-Hebraic writings. Sirach even resisted some who were part of his own wisdom tradition when they moved in ways unaccept-

---

27. Skehan and DiLella, *The Wisdom of Ben Sira*, 41.
28. See the balanced discussion of Sirach's use of non-Jewish sources by Skehan and DiLella, *The Wisdom of Ben Sira*, 46–50, 260.
29. Ibid., 47.
30. Sanders, *Ben Sira and Demotic Wisdom*, 97.
31. Ibid., 57.
32. Ibid., 58.
33. Crenshaw, "The Problem of Theodicy in Sirach," 128.

able to his own views. For example, Sirach firmly limited thinking, perhaps reacting to the works of Job and Ecclesiastes:

> Neither seek what is too difficult for you,
>   nor investigate what is beyond your power.
> Reflect upon what you have been commanded,
>   for what is hidden is not your concern.
> Do not meddle in matters that are beyond you,
>   for more than you can understand has been shown to you.
> For their conceit has led many astray,
>   and wrong opinion has impaired their judgment. (Sir. 3:21–24)

In Sirach's view, a scholar's openness has limits and is balanced with solid grounding in the biblical texts and with clarity about one's heritage and convictions. This permitted a disciplined ability to use materials from other sources as well. How does one acquire that disciplined ability?

DISCIPLINE AND SELF-DISCIPLINE; SPEECH AND SILENCE. The need for discipline and control of the tongue stood high on Sirach's list of advice for learners, though he adds little to the conventional advice in the Book of Proverbs:

> My child, from your youth choose discipline,
>   and when you have gray hair you will still find wisdom (*Sophia*).
> . . . .
> She (*Sophia*) seems very harsh to the undisciplined;
>   fools cannot remain with her.
> . . . .
> Put your feet into her fetters,
>   and your neck into her collar.
> . . . .
> [A]nd when you get hold of her, do not let her go. (Sir. 6:18–27)

This may seem a harsh approach and *Sophia* a stern taskmaster, yet notice that Sirach softens it by setting it in the context of reflections on faithful friends, which immediately precedes it (6:14–17). He does not so much command but urges reader-learners to choose discipline. In addition, the motive clauses offer rich promises. Not only will the diligent student find a "good harvest" and "eat of her produce" (6:19), but will also find rest, joy, security, a "glorious robe," and a "splendid crown" (6:28–31).

Sirach did not deny that harsh times come to the faithful, but he treated them as a necessary discipline that would be the means to a glorious outcome. The fool sees only the harshness:

> To a senseless person education is fetters on his feet,
>   and like manacles on his right hand. (Sir. 21:19)

The self-discipline and self-restraint manifest in good manners are
very important:

> The foot of a fool rushes into a house,
>> but an experienced person waits respectfully outside.
> A boor peers into the house from the door,
>> but a cultivated person remains outside.
> It is ill-mannered for a person to listen at a door;
>> the discreet would be grieved by the disgrace. (Sir. 21:22–24)

Yet when it comes to pursuing learning and wisdom:

> Happy is the person who...
> . . . .
> pursuing her [Wisdom] like a hunter,
> . . . .
> who peers through her windows
>> and listens at her doors;
> who camps near her house,
>> and fastens his tent peg to her walls. (Sir. 14:20–24)

Education in wisdom is too important to let good manners stand
in the way!

Sirach's advice on the tongue, mouth, and lips is also conventional but offered with humor:

> Some people keep silent and are thought to be wise,
>> while others are detested for being talkative.
> Some people keep silent because they have nothing to say,
>> while others keep silent because they know when to speak.
> The wise remain silent until the right moment. (Sir. 20:5–7)

But Sirach astutely observed what many teachers know: "there
is a cleverness that increases bitterness" (21:12). Some learning
does not produce wisdom. When skills and knowledge are used
only for one's self-interest, they are not as valuable as when
they are used to instruct others, for then "the fruits of his good
sense will endure" (37:23). What makes speech good is not just
knowledge; it must contribute to the life of the community.

The attentive reader-learner will have noticed how often Sirach's pedagogical manner is overwhelmed by his concern for right
matter. When Sirach is writing about *Sophia* or Israel's heroes or
when he is praying or singing hymns, his text is alive, but on
many other subjects the text feels heavy-handed, authoritarian, and
controlling.

What Is Worth Learning?

Sirach reached back to Proverbs in style and content but reached right over Job and Qohelet. If Sirach knows Job and Qohelet, Gerhard von Rad observes, "then the whole affair is all the more disappointing...[for] nothing has made sufficient impression on him to force him to rethink traditional teaching."[34] This may be evidence for how little sense of a discrete wisdom tradition there was in Israel, little sense that a sage needed to know a particular literature or discuss certain established views. Or it may be that Job and Qohelet evoked very little response in Israel — suggesting they were not widely known or influential. In light of Sirach's use and nonuse of other works in Israel's wisdom tradition, what does Sirach consider worth learning?

WISDOM, TORAH, AND THE FEAR OF THE LORD. Was Sirach trying to absorb wisdom into the frame of normative Yahwist theology by linking *Sophia* and Torah and Israel's heroes? Chapter 1 begins with third-person reflections on the nature of wisdom, which is frequently personified as *Sophia* (Woman Wisdom; the text is Greek, so we use *Sophia*). *Sophia* is eternal, with the Lord, created before all things by the Lord, who is the only one wise (1:1–7). *Sophia* is also part of the created world, generously lavished as a gift on "all the living" (1:4–10), bringing riches, health, peace, knowledge, and long life (1:17–20).

Sophia even seems synonymous with "the fear of the Lord" (here "piety," not "terror"), which is manifest as "glory and exultation," "a crown of rejoicing," gives "gladness and joy and long life" and "a happy end" (1:11–13). Then follow reflective and creative variations on a theme from Proverbs 1:7, "The fear of the Lord is the beginning of Wisdom":

> To fear the Lord is the beginning of wisdom,
>   she is created with the faithful in the womb. (Sir. 1:14)

> To fear the Lord is fullness of wisdom;
>   she inebriates mortals with her fruits. (Sir. 1:16)

> The fear of the Lord is the crown of wisdom,
>   making peace and perfect health to flourish. (Sir. 1:18)

> To fear the Lord is the root of wisdom,
>   and her branches are long life. (Sir. 1:20)

---

34. Von Rad, *Wisdom in Israel*, 238.

The changing metaphors evoke the richness and variety of both *Sophia* and the fear of the Lord. *Sophia* is with the Lord from the beginning and yet is created, and is also created "with the faithful in the womb." The metaphor of origin for *Sophia* (assuming something like a tree, as in the proverbial "tree of life," Prov. 3:18) points to the origins of wisdom among humans as well. It also specifies that wisdom comes to "the faithful" (and not to sinners, Sir. 15:7), thus reflecting the note of piety throughout Sirach's text. Yet Sirach, like Proverbs, is not satisfied with a metaphor of origins or roots alone but includes the whole metaphoric tree (cf. Prov. 3:18). What Sirach offers is no analytic or logically precise definition of either wisdom or *Sophia* or the fear of the Lord. Instead Sirach "circles round the phenomenon in the totality in which it can be experienced ... which removes it still further from a precise, conceptual definition because, no matter how much one tries to define it, it becomes lost again in mystery."[35]

Near the end of chapter 1, Sirach abruptly drops third-person reflections, directly addresses the reader-learner, and in so doing, makes eminently clear the text's pedagogical and theological interests:

> In the treasuries of wisdom are wise sayings,
>   but godliness is an abomination to a sinner.
> If you desire wisdom, keep the commandments,
>   and the Lord will lavish her upon you.
> For the fear of the Lord is wisdom and discipline,
>   fidelity and humility are his delight. (Sir. 1:25–27)

There are many wise sayings, but for Sirach they only come to fruition if one is godly, which apparently means "keeping the commandments." Indeed, this is later made explicit:

> Whoever fears the Lord will do this,
>   and whoever holds to the law [Torah] will obtain *Sophia*.
>   (Sir. 15:1)

> The whole of *Sophia* is fear of the Lord,
>   and in all wisdom there is the fulfillment of the law. (Sir. 19:20)

> All this is the book of the covenant of the Most High God,
>   the law [Torah] that Moses commanded us. (Sir. 24:23)

Clearly, the link between the fear of the Lord, the covenant, *Sophia*, and the specifically Israelite Torah, the commandments,

---

35. Ibid., 242.

has been forged much more tightly than in Proverbs. This links *Sophia* more closely with Torah and priestly interests, which is consistent with Sirach's interest in the temple and in Aaron, Phinehas, and Simon, the high priest. One might be tempted to conclude that the norms and commands offered derive, not so much from collective experience as in Proverbs, but from the Torah. Was Sirach trying to find room within the historical and covenant theology for wisdom? The priests and prophets proclaimed that covenant theology should lead to covenant behavior, but Sirach puts it exactly the other way around. Rather than wisdom being good because it followed from Torah, Torah is to be followed because it is wise: "If you desire wisdom, keep the commandments" (1:26). Thus, Torah is a means to wisdom! In the words of von Rad, "It is not that wisdom is overshadowed by the superior power of the Torah, but, vice versa, that we see Sirach endeavoring to legitimize and to interpret Torah from the realm of understanding characteristic of wisdom."[36] Wisdom is the center of Sirach's thought around which all else revolves.

The centrality of wisdom in Sirach's thought is also seen in how the book is structured — reflections on wisdom begin, end, and center the book. The first chapter begins describing wisdom; the final chapter reflects upon the importance of *Sophia* in everything Sirach did and wrote and invites the reader-learner to "put your neck under her yoke" (51:26). Right in the middle of the book is a lengthy hymn of praise to *Sophia* (chap. 24), concluding with reflections on Sirach's own teaching ministry, derived from *Sophia*, as he labored for "all future generations" and "for all who seek *Sophia*" (24:33–34).

As we saw earlier, Proverbs opened with a statement of objectives about wisdom, which concluded with the familiar "The fear of the LORD is the beginning of knowledge" (Prov. 1:7). There we inferred from its use that the fear of the Lord is simultaneously and inseparably cognitive and affective, so one cannot "know God" and not "fear God," in the sense of having an attitude of awe and attentive reverence.[37] This is true for Sirach as well, but there is also here a marked change. In Proverbs, the fear of the Lord means recognition of "dependence on God" and the "obligation to obedience in respect of the divine will."[38] Sirach, on the other hand,

---

36. Ibid., 245.
37. See pp. 36–39.
38. Von Rad, *Wisdom in Israel*, 243.

is more oriented toward human feelings,[39] or what Edmond Jacob calls "tones of interiorization and spiritual asceticism."[40] In this regard Sirach was more like the prophets than the older sages:

> For the fear of the Lord is wisdom and discipline,
> fidelity and humility are his delight. (Sir. 1:27)

Here fear, wisdom, humility, discipline, and fidelity (Gk. *pistis*, often translated "faith") are used as synonyms. Humility (an interior attitude or disposition) was a favorite theme for Sirach.[41] Humility is appropriate in the presence of greatness (4:7; 10:12–18), which includes the greatness of God (3:17–20). It is not for sinners (13:20), for it is linked with godliness or piety (7:17). According to Sirach, God chose Moses because of his fidelity and humility (45:4). It is not surprising then that such inner traits were often best expressed in prayer and liturgy for Sirach (1:28; 2:7–11; 17:25; 23:1–6).

RETRIBUTION. Sirach agreed with the traditional doctrine of reward and punishment or retribution assumed in biblical tradition, but he made God even more central to the picture and significantly modified how natural consequences work.[42] Like Proverbs and Qohelet, Sirach believed God determines everything and judiciously distributes rewards and punishments, but there is little recognition of Job's and Qohelet's questions, for Sirach says, "Do no evil, and evil will never overtake you" (7:1; see also 33:13; 51:30). On the other hand, Sirach also believed humans have considerable free will:

> It was he who created humankind in the beginning,
> and he left them in the power of their own free choice.
> If you choose, you can keep the commandments,
> and to act faithfully is a matter of your own free choice.
> (Sir. 15:14–15)

Sirach made no attempt to reconcile these apparently contradictory claims about determinism and free will.[43] Either he left that reconciliation to the reader-learner, or else he leaned upon his "doctrine of opposites":[44]

---

39. Ibid.
40. Edmond Jacob, "Wisdom and Religion in Sirach," in *Israelite Wisdom: Theological and Literary Essays in Honor of Samuel Terrien*, ed. John G. Gammie et al. (Missoula, Mont.: Scholars, 1978), 257.
41. Von Rad, *Wisdom in Israel*, 259 n. 26.
42. Hengel, *Judaism and Hellenism*, 1:143.
43. Murphy, *The Tree of Life*, 75.
44. Ibid.

> Good is the opposite of evil,
>   and life the opposite of death;
>   so the sinner is the opposite of the godly.
> Look at all the works of the Most High;
>   they come in pairs, one the opposite of the other. (Sir. 33:14–15)

Is this a metaphysical dualism to explain the dualities Sirach experienced? Such dualism is familiar in Hellenistic thought (and in the New Testament) but foreign to earlier Israelite thought. Yet Sirach did not adopt a complete Hellenistic response, which was to believe in an afterlife in which rewards and punishments are justly given. Sirach consistently rejected this option, and for him all retribution must happen before death (14:11–19; 41:1–4). Indeed, one must not even grieve too much for those who die, for

> Do not forget, there is no coming back;
>   you do the dead no good, and you injure yourself. (Sir. 38:21)

While Sirach regarded death as final, he also could moralize death and use it as a pedagogical device to influence present thinking and behavior (7:36; 11:24–26). Sirach added a psychologizing motif that again seems more Hellenistic than Israelite (and it is expanded in the Wisdom of Solomon): punishment may take the form of fears and anxieties:

> Perplexities and fear of heart are theirs,
>   and anxious thought of the day of their death.
> there is anger and envy and trouble and unrest,
>   and fear of death, and fury and strife.
>   (Sir. 40:2, 5; see also 11:27–28)

In these reflections, Sirach often brought great sensitivity to his descriptions of psychological states and motives (e.g., 34:1–8; 40:1–10, 28–30). Educators know that in more recent times, the psychologizing and interiorizing of motivations in teaching and learning have grown apace. All the emotions Sirach listed in 40:1–10 have since been used (and abused) by teachers and schools, sometimes with the same anxious effects on learners.

WOMEN, CHILD-REARING, DISCIPLINE, AND WISDOM. Each of our earlier texts showed some ambivalence about the value of women and children. Sirach does not. This text contains more harsh sayings about women, children, and discipline than any in the Hebrew Bible, even while raising *Sophia* to the pinnacle. If we are to fully appreciate Sirach's use of *Sophia* as a paradigm figure and the ambiguities of his approach to pedagogy, we must understand these sayings more fully.

At the outset, we must see Sirach's text in its cultural and historical setting, not to excuse it but to avoid judging it anachronistically
by twentieth-century or Western standards. Near Eastern cultures
generally were androcentric and patriarchal, according women few
rights. In such cultures, females were perceived as intrinsically
under the control of some male (first father or brother, then husband), so marriage was a process of disconnecting the female from
her family of origin and embedding her in her husband and his
family,[45] as can be seen in Sirach's descriptions of the "good wife"
(26:1–4, 13–18; 36:26–31). In these texts, the wife's value is measured solely by her effect on her husband. She will make him live
long, bring him joy, peace, social status, contentment, and good
cheer. Her beauty stimulates him sexually, she keeps the house
clean, and her silence is a "gift from the Lord." There are also
extended descriptions of an "evil wife" and the difficulties and dangers of daughters (42:9–10), with no corresponding descriptions of
good or evil husbands or the dangers of sons.

It is not possible to either hide or excuse Sirach's blatant misog-
yny.[46] Male adulterers were not to be punished as harshly as
female adulterers, even when the woman's motive for adultery
was to produce an heir for her husband (a high value) while the
man's motive was simply "hot passion," which showed a lack of
self-discipline (23:16–26). In this, Sirach seems both unjust and
self-contradictory:

> Better is the wickedness of a man than a woman who does good;
> it is a woman who brings shame and disgrace.
>
> (Sir. 42:14; also 25:13, 15)

Sirach is also the first to attribute the origin of all sin and death to
a woman (presumably Eve):

> From a woman sin had its beginning,
> and because of her we all die. (Sir. 25:24)

If women and children are troublesome, they are to be dealt with
firmly (to use the current euphemism):

---

45. See the discussions of the cultural anthropology of the Mediterranean world
in Bruce Malina, *The New Testament World: Insights from Cultural Anthropology*, rev. ed. (Louisville: Westminster/John Knox, 1993), esp. chaps. 2 and 5. While
this material treats the first century B.C.E., there is little evidence that the dominant
features in this picture had changed much in two centuries.

46. For more extended treatment of these texts, see Warren C. Trenchard, *Ben
Sira's View of Woman: A Literary Analysis*, BJS 38 (Chico, Calif.: Scholars, 1982).

He who loves his son will whip him often,

. . . .

Pamper a child, and he will terrorize you;
    play with him and he will grieve you.
Do not laugh with him, or you will have sorrow with him,
    and in the end you will gnash your teeth.
Give him no freedom in his youth,

. . . .

    and beat his sides while he is young,
or else he will become stubborn and disobey you,
    and you will have sorrow of soul from him. Discipline your son
    and make his yoke heavy. (Sir. 30:1, 9–13)

These statements are more harsh than any other biblical texts but not as offensive as some other ancient texts.[47] (That is *not* an apology for their bias but a recognition that this systemic bias against women and children was widespread.)

We have repeatedly suggested that using proverbial sayings in teaching expects considerable responsibility on the part of the reader-learner. Learning to become wise requires practicing making real-life judgments about what the sayings mean and when and where to use them, which also presumes that one will be open to correction and to learning from one's mistakes. Sirach can even say:

My child, honor yourself with humility,
    and give yourself the esteem you deserve. (Sir. 10:23)

This presumes that the child honors himself and gains self-esteem, which is actually deserved. This is not a source of arrogance or pride, for the task here is humility. But the child is expected to do something for himself, to be an agent in the process! Yet Sirach's child-rearing advice seems to presume that children never be allowed to make a mistake or take initiative on their own, for fear they will go wrong. Is this not simply a self-contradiction?

If women or children cannot be agents, it is neither necessary nor possible to educate them. Indeed, education is quite impossible

---

47. DiLella rightly critiques Trenchard for overstating his case concerning Sirach's "negative bias" compared with other ancient cultures, in Skehan and DiLella, *The Wisdom of Ben Sira*, 90–91, citing other examples, such as Semonides, a Greek in the sixth century B.C.E.: "Yes, this is the worst plague Zeus has made — women. . . . The man who lives with a woman never goes through all his day in cheerfulness." Or Hipponax, also in the sixth century: "The two best days in a woman's life are when someone marries her and when he carries her dead body to the grave."

if agency is required by this approach to learning yet denied to the learner. Yet Sirach repeatedly urged learning and also urged seeking *Sophia*, the most desirable and available woman. Sirach clearly considered *Sophia* an agent, even God's agent, for she took the initiative to reach out to human learners, acting as nurturing lover, wife, and mother (15:2–4).

Sophia, in Sirach's view, was simultaneously a gift from the Lord and also an achievement that came from striving and rigorous self-discipline. Both were true at once. Humans must strive, and God would be generous and merciful. While that may not resolve the contradiction, the text does hold both assertions as true at the same time. For Sirach, authentic piety is more important than logical consistency.

KNOW ISRAEL'S HISTORY. Sirach merged traditional historical material with wisdom themes and interests, thus forging a unified whole, as we have seen, and demonstrating that becoming wise requires mastery of traditional lore. He ends his praise of famous men by assuring reader-learners that

> Happy are those who concern themselves with these things,
>   and those who lay them to heart will become wise.
> For if they put them into practice, they will be equal to anything,
>   for the fear of the Lord is their path. (Sir. 50:28–29)

In other words, Sirach (foreshadowing a "great man" theory of history) used historical events as a form of moral education.[48] Reader-learners are to come to know these famous men not only in a factual way, for Sirach repeatedly calls them an example. That is, reader-learners are to lay them to heart and put them into practice and thereby participate in the path that is the fear of the Lord. For Sirach, knowledge is not valued for its own sake.

Why? What Is the Point of Learning?

Can we infer from what Sirach thought was worth learning and how it was to be learned some clues about what this learning was for?

PROGRESS IN LIVING ACCORDING TO THE LAW. According to the grandson's prologue, the purpose in both the writing and the translation of this book is progress in living according to the law, a view confirmed in Sirach's own words in the epilogue. Such progress is not casuistic adherence to legal minutiae but is faithfulness, fidelity, or loyalty

---

48. See Ernst Breisach, *Historiography: Ancient, Medieval, and Modern* (Chicago: University of Chicago Press, 1983).

to the tradition and thus to the Lord. Such fidelity to Torah (teaching) leads to the gift of wisdom. Sirach did have reservations about how far one's thinking should be allowed to roam, lest it lead one astray (3:21–24). (Was this a conservative response to the threat of foreign influence?) Despite these reservations, Sirach did not reject all foreign influence nor curb his enthusiasm for travel and for learning from foreign texts.

Neither Sirach nor his grandson spelled out in any detail what *progress* might look like. This may disappoint some who like to map out charts of progress in learning objectives and developmental levels that can be scientifically measured. But this reticence is quite in keeping with the wisdom materials, for what shape wisdom takes will depend upon the concrete particulars of a person's life and experience and will be shown in wise actions (such as those of the exemplars: Israel's famous men) more than in measured progress.

PIETY AND CHARACTER FORMING. Piety was essential in Sirach's wisdom. For Sirach, if one is to remain faithful to the Torah and the temple, one must know the history of Israel. But knowing the stories well is necessary but not sufficient by itself. Sirach brought historical persons and events into the wisdom discussion and showed how one can learn from them in one's own time. While these characters (including those anonymous others in 44:9) have not all made the same contribution, they are models of piety or fidelity, a blessing even into the present. Reader-learners become wise by laying them to heart and putting them into practice so reader-learners themselves will follow the path that is the fear of the Lord (50:27–29). In these texts, as in Proverbs, knowing is both cognition and participation in the affective "fear of the Lord," "taking to heart," and "putting into practice." The fact that he exhorts so explicitly on this matter shows that in Sirach's experience were some who "concern themselves with these things" yet who did not take them to heart or practice them.

The stories and practices of those who have gone before are an important part of Sirach's approach to character formation. Sirach was more inclusive than usual in his choice of exemplars. He mentioned kings, counselors, prophets, scholars, sages, musicians, poets, composers, priests, peaceable rich men, anonymous godly men, though no women. These exemplars live on because who they were has become part of who their children are, and thus they perpetuated loyalty to the tradition and to the Lord. Yet Sirach offered little description of their exploits.

Rather he used phrases like "Enoch pleased the Lord" (44:16), "Noah was found...righteous" (44:17), "Abraham was the great father" (44:19), and Phinehas was "zealous in the fear of the Lord" (45:23), stood firm, showed courage, and so on. What distinguished these heroes for Sirach was not just what they did but who they were, that is, the virtue of their character.[49] Such heroes showed loyalty to God's ways and faithfulness to Torah and the commandments (which is their piety) — these formed their children as well. For Sirach, that ongoing loyalty or piety is the pedagogically important aspect of learning the history of Israel, and that is the effect he hoped would be absorbed by the reader-learner (50:28–29). Such faithful loyalty was essential to Israel's identity in a multicultural world.

Loyalty is the one theme that runs explicitly through Sirach's frequent discussions of friends. Friends must be tested, lest they not stand by you in trouble (6:7–13); they may even become an enemy (37:2). The centrality of the virtue of loyalty is repeated over and over (7:18; 9:10; 12:8–18; 13:21; 37:1–6). The ability to be a faithful and loyal friend is directly related to fearing the Lord (6:17). Loyalty to friends, loyalty to God, loyalty to Israel, are all of a piece. Together they form Israel's identity.

If exemplars help form character, then we should consider as well Sirach's own example, his own piety. While earlier wisdom texts either ignored or played down participation in the temple or liturgy or prayer, for Sirach these were not only highly important aspects of wisdom, piety, and character; he was also quite self-conscious of his own role as a model. As we have seen, Sirach's humble piety was rooted in temple worship, priestly exemplars, prayer, study, and *Sophia* and often found expression in self-examination and extended hymns of praise. The naturalness of Sirach's fluid movement from commanding imperative to self-examination to prayer and praise is itself a demonstration of how he sees these as a unified whole, not disparate parts. And these are woven deeply into his identity and into Israel's identity as well. Judaism still regards study as worship.

For some today, those who habitually assume sacred/secular or church/state distinctions and who assume education is a form of "knowledge is power," Sirach's practice of linking prayer, praise, worship, and humility with learning and study may seem odd. But historically, pedagogy has long been more about forming charac-

---

49. See Hengel, *Judaism and Hellenism*, 1:140–41.

ter and piety than about gathering knowledge. Our pedagogical language itself reveals its roots in religious experience and communal commitment. What is of most worth? is itself a question about community commitments and leads naturally to worship, which refers to acts that presume and show what is worthy of respect, honor, or reverence or to what one is devoted. It is not unusual to speak of a teacher's being devoted to or loving her subject and enthusiastically endorsing its worth. Similarly, little moments of wonder are important in the process of learning and are highly akin to the states of awe and reverence so familiar in worship and religion.

This linking of piety and education carries dangers as well, some of them demonstrated by Sirach. When religion is viewed as transmitting the right answers or correct doctrine, teachers can constrain or even eliminate the spirit of open inquiry that motivates and enlivens education. Much contemporary education seeks to avoid such temptations by succumbing to its opposite. What is gained when a commitment or devotion to secularity is used to constrain or eliminate inquiry having to do with faith or religious truth claims? Let's look more closely at how Sirach used his own piety pedagogically.

AUTHORSHIP, AGENCY, AND GOD. One of the most striking aspects of this text (compared with other texts in the Hebrew biblical and literary corpus) is the degree to which the author emerges in the text as a character in his own right. Many have seen this as another of the signs of Hellenistic influence. In Proverbs and Job, the authors never speak in the first person. Qohelet does use his own experience self-consciously as a source of learning and teaching, yet Qohelet begins in disguise, making his first-person claims in the guise of a fictional character. Sirach's text demonstrates his pedagogical self-consciousness in his role *as author* and as transmitter of tradition. Sirach even saw himself as an extension of *Sophia*, a canal from her river (24:23–30). Like her, Sirach claimed his teaching was inspired, even prophetic, and he was quite conscious of his place in history:

> I will again make instruction shine forth like the dawn,
>   and I will make it clear from far away.
> I will pour out teaching like prophecy,
>   and leave it to all future generations.
> Observe that I have not labored for myself alone,
>   but for all who seek wisdom. (Sir. 24:32–34)

While Sirach humbly described himself as a latecomer and a "gleaner following the grape-pickers," he expected leaders to listen to him (33:16–19), for he knew that his message was sound:

> So from the beginning I have been convinced of all this
> and have thought it out and left it in writing. (Sir. 39:32)

As he summed up his lifework, Sirach described his writing and its benefits to reader-learners, again in implicit comparison with *Sophia:*

> Instruction in understanding and knowledge
> I have written in this book,
> . . . .
> and those who lay them to heart will become wise.
> For if they put them into practice, they will be equal to anything,
> for the fear of the Lord is their path. (Sir. 50:27–29)

Here, unequivocally, we see the contrast with contemporary understandings of knowledge is power. For Sirach, understanding and knowledge serve practical piety that is the fear of the Lord.

Sirach's use of his own experience and piety as an offering to the reader-learner is most explicit in the autobiographical conclusion to his book, where he rehearsed his life journey and made one last appeal to reader-learners to join his quest for wisdom and serenity (51:13–30). His own journey began in the temple, praying for *Sophia*, following her "straight path," grappling with wisdom, in strict conduct and in prayer. He "made progress in her," and therefore

> The Lord gave me my tongue as a reward,
> and I will praise him with it. (Sir. 51:22)

Then he turns in direct address to the reader-learners,

> Draw near to me, you who are uneducated,
> and lodge in the house of instruction.
> . . . .
> Acquire wisdom for yourselves without money.
>
> Put your neck under her yoke,
> and let your souls receive instruction;
> it is to be found close by.
>
> See with your own eyes that I have labored but little,
> and found for myself much serenity.

Hear but a little of my instruction,
and through me you will acquire silver and gold. (Sir. 51:23–28)[50]

Sirach concludes in the spirit of humility we have come to expect, deflecting all credit and praise for these benefits from himself to God:

May your soul rejoice in God's mercy,
and may you never be ashamed to praise him.
Do your work in good time,
and in his own time God will give you your reward.
(Sir. 51:29–30)

Note how this approach differs from that of Qohelet. While Qohelet used his own experience to gain understanding and then sought to evoke in reader-learners a similar process of gaining their own understanding, Sirach used his experience as a model for reader-learners to follow. He seemed to expect that if reader-learners would follow his lead, they would arrive at similar conclusions. Sirach and Qohelet arrived at radically different understandings of God and of the way to wisdom, perhaps in large part to radically different epistemologies.

The authors of Job, Ecclesiastes, and Ecclesiasticus each exercised considerable agency and originality: new ideas, new forms, a new sense of authorial importance, especially with regard to established conventional theology and tradition. But in each case, using new approaches was never an end in itself. There was no insistence that the tradition must get relevant. Each claimed that if the tradition did not come to terms with truth, it would die. But the truth that had to be faced — while known through personal experience, through the created world, and through new cultural forms — the truth at issue, was God.

We turn now to the Wisdom of Solomon, which also wrestled with Hellenism and Judaic religion, using different procedures and arriving at different conclusions. Let us compare.

THE WISDOM OF SOLOMON

Sirach asked, "How can we sing the Lord's song in our own land, when the lyrics are in a foreign language and the harmonies are strange?" He used the strange harmonies to tell forth the heritage, the wisdom, and the greatness of Israel and the temple and

---

50. Is the resonance of this invitation with Matthew's Jesus accidental? See Matt. 11:28–30.

made those harmonies sing hymns of praise to the Lord. Sirach's grandson took Sirach's book to Alexandria, Egypt, the cultural capital of those strange harmonies. There the grandson's translation served a large Israelite community living in diaspora — far from Jerusalem. A hundred years later, succeeding generations of Greek-speaking Jews in Alexandria found the Hebrew language less and less familiar.

Alexandria, a city of a million people, had a large Jewish population, who fully participated in the political and cultural life of the city. Alexandria had the world's largest library and a state-supported community of scholars. Here the Greek translation of the Pentateuch began in the third century, and later the rest of the Hebrew Bible was translated into Greek. Now known as the Septuagint, it was the Bible used in the synagogues of Diaspora Judaism, as well as in the early Christian church.[51] In Palestine, Greek was known, but Hebrew and Aramaic remained the language of religion and everyday life. In Alexandria, Greek was not only the everyday language but also the language of the synagogue liturgy, Bible reading, and Jewish literature. Thus did Hellenistic concepts and ideas introduce fundamental changes into Hebrew thought patterns. Religious rituals became thought of as symbolic and spiritual, and religious writings began to be thought of as philosophy and were interpreted allegorically.[52]

Sirach had used Greek literary forms to serve Israel's story, but now the question had shifted. Could Israel's religion be adapted to fit into Greek thought patterns and philosophical concepts? The anonymous author of the Wisdom of Solomon answered yes, offering his own revisionist interpretation.

How Does This Text Engage the Reader-Learner?

The Book of Wisdom (which is another name for the Wisdom of Solomon or Ecclesiasticus), like Sirach, addresses an elite readership: "Love righteousness, you rulers of the earth" (Wisd. 1:1; also 6:1–2, 9). While the wisdom tradition frequently used the fiction of royal authorship, here it is maintained more consistently through the text, though even when a king speaks directly (chap. 7), he stresses that he is essentially no different than any other common person. Thus the text claims there is no distinction in principle that

---

51. Newsome, *Greeks, Romans, Jews*, 9–15; Koester, *History, Culture, and Religion*, 1:222–25, 252–55.
52. Koester, *History, Culture, and Religion*, 1:224.

would restrict the reader-learners of this text to those who are of the aristocracy.

What Is Worth Learning?

The opening and closing lines of the first section of this text summarize several fundamental themes that are important for pedagogical understanding.

LOVE RIGHTEOUSNESS...THINK...SEEK. The Book of Wisdom opens in direct address to reader-learners using imperatives, "Love righteousness, you rulers of the earth, think...seek him [the Lord]." Immediately reader-learners are offered reasons why. Fifteen times in the sixteen verses of the first chapter we read either "because" (eight), "for" (six), or "therefore" (one), and most of these follow indicatives, not imperatives! Here reader-learners are not just expected to do what they are told (in the imperative). Rather, they are expected to want or need reasons for the commands and statements alike. Reader-learners are expected to engage in reasoning all through this text, "for perverse thoughts separate people from God" (1:3). A "holy and disciplined [Gk. *paideias*, "educated"] spirit...will leave foolish thoughts behind" (1:5). Indeed, the ungodly are said to have "reasoned unsoundly" (2:1) and were "led astray" by their reasoning (2:21). From the opening lines, the pedagogical task is laid before the reader-learner: piety requires learning to reason soundly, for "the ungodly will be punished as their reasoning deserves" (3:10).

Reader-learners may feel they are in a different thought world here. Even Sirach, with his doctrine of opposites, did not divide the world so sharply. Here wrong thoughts separate from God,

> But the souls of the righteous are in the hand of God,
> and no torment will ever touch them. (Wisd. 3:1)

The Wisdom of Solomon uses Hellenistic ideas — specifically dualism and other Platonic notions. For example, the good path begins with worthy thoughts (7:15), while

> the reasoning of mortals is worthless,
> and our designs are likely to fail;
> for a perishable body weighs down the soul,
> and this earthly tent burdens the thoughtful mind. (Wisd. 9:14–15)

Reasoning fails because of the body, which corrupts or burdens mind and soul.

For this author, "the idea of making idols" was the beginning of all evil (14:12, 27), and ignorance and mistaken ideas lead to murder, adultery, corruption, perjury, sexual perversion, and the defiling of souls (14:22–27). And just penalties will come to those who "thought wrongly about God" (14:30)! Just as in Platonic thought, ideas precede and determine all action and all moral evaluation, so also here. Such body-soul dualism is thoroughly Greek in concept and equally thoroughly un-Hebraic.

RETRIBUTION AND DEATH. The Book of Wisdom agrees with Sirach (against Job and Qohelet) that the Deuteronomic doctrine of retribution is clear, unequivocal, and just. Retribution fits neatly into this divided world where the ungodly are punished and the righteous are rewarded. Not only are the ungodly punished themselves for their bad reasoning, their misdeeds, their rebellion against God (3:10), but "their wives are foolish, and their children evil; their offspring are accursed" (3:12–13). According to the Book of Wisdom, the flaw in the reasoning of those who question the doctrine of retribution may be that they only think of *this* life. They say, "Short and sorrowful is our life" (2:1); "Our name will be forgotten" (2:4); and "There is no return from our death" (2:5). Therefore they say, "Let us enjoy the good things that exist" (2:6), resembling Qohelet even if not quoting him.[53]

In all our previous texts, death is the end of life, and most often it is value-neutral. It just happens. Only in Job is death valued (some of the time) as a possible form of relief (Job 3:17–19; 6:8–9; 7:13–15). In Ecclesiastes, death is ambiguous. While death is neutral, as an "equal-opportunity employer," it calls the doctrine of retribution into question. The impartiality of death for Qohelet is an evil, for it wipes out the meaningfulness of striving to be wise or righteous.

In the Book of Wisdom, death is also ambiguous. Sometimes it means a neutral physical death, which comes to all alike (4:7, 16; 7:6). At other times, physical death is not neutral but is punishment for wicked deeds or thoughts (2:24; 12:20; 19:1–5). And at other times, death seems to be not just physical death but separation from God (4:18–5:14).[54] This separation is seen as a form of punishment or torture because these ungodly dead are depicted as able to see the righteous "numbered among the children of God"

---

53. It has been argued, reasonably, that this author may be rejecting those views whoever speaks them, Jews or Greeks, rather than specifically targeting Qohelet.

54. Michael Kolarcik, *The Ambiguity of Death in the Book of Wisdom 1–6: A Study of Literary Structure and Interpretation*, AnBib 127 (Rome: Editrice Pontificio Instituto Biblico, 1991).

(5:5) and enjoying the Lord's care as their rightful reward (5:15), which the unrighteous do not share.

This ambiguity of death in the Book of Wisdom can be traced in part to the corollary Greek notion of "immortal" (Gk. *athanatos,* literally, "without or absence of death," "death-less"), which bridges Greek and Hebrew pictures of human beings. (Note: this is *not* the same as resurrection since immortal means "not dead.") The notion first arises in 1:15, "righteousness is immortal," which makes no claims about human nature. In traditional Hebraic thought, this would mean that God intends for people to be righteous, and thereby immortal, in that their righteousness lives on in memory and effect on the community and on other individuals. But this author apparently intends something different. Notice how the king corrects himself while describing his birth:

> As a child I was naturally gifted,
> and a good soul fell to my lot;
> or rather, being good, I entered an undefiled body. (Wisd. 8:19–20)

He first identifies the "I" with his body and then corrects himself, in better Greek fashion, that the "I" is the soul, who enters a body. Here the body is "undefiled," a rather neutral description compared to the Lord's affirmation in creation that "it was good." Hellenists (following Plato) valued the soul more highly than the body since the soul is immaterial and thus unchanging or eternal. The body, on the other hand, is material and corruptible — it can decay and must die, while an idea or a soul can be immortal, that is, nondying, like God. In this passage, the nonmaterial soul exists before and after the body. According to Plato, souls wait (in heaven) for a new body to come along, at which time one enters the body.[55] At the death of the body, the soul returns to wait for another new body.

In this conceptual framework, ideas and reasoning (and souls) are more lasting than behavior, thus shifting the pedagogical focus to sound reasoning and ideas, which are more important than judging the right time and place.

> Thus they reasoned, but they were led astray,
> . . . .
> and they did not know the secret purposes of God,
> . . . .

---

55. See Plato *Phaedo* 83–88. While this picture is familiar from several of Plato's writings, it is also common to many Hellenistic writings, often with embellishments.

for God created us for incorruption,
and made us in the image of his own eternity,
but through the devil's envy death entered the world,
and those who belong to his company experience it.
(Wisd. 2:21–24)

Physical death is neither the end of life, nor is it the same for all people. Here there is no Sheol to which all alike go (the Hebrew "picture of death"). Instead, death leads to a "day of judgment" (3:18) and a division — the souls of the righteous are with God (3:1), and the ungodly will be punished (3:10).

This new picture enables the author to offer a new form of the doctrine of retribution that avoids the arguments of Job and Qohelet. No longer is what "I have seen under the sun" evidence for the inadequacy of the conventional doctrine of retribution. Empirical evidence (which is temporal, not eternal) is no longer sufficient, for retribution comes *after* death in the form of being immortal and in the hand of God and of being loved by God (4:10). How then do humans gain immortality?

SOPHIA BRINGS IMMORTALITY. Concluding his appeal to learn to reason soundly, the author urges reader-learners to "desire wisdom (*Sophia*)" (6:9, 20). He launches into a detailed description (extending over the next four and a half chapters) of why *Sophia* is so desirable, beginning with a Hellenistic form of argument called a *sorites*, which beautifully lays out the plot for what is to follow:[56]

The beginning of wisdom is the most sincere desire for instruction
and concern for instruction is love of her,
and love of her is the keeping of her laws,
and giving heed to her laws is assurance of immortality
and immortality brings one near to God;
so the desire for wisdom leads to a kingdom. (Wisd. 6:17–20)

The sorites is a rhetorical form of persuasion using a thought chain. The last term of each line becomes the first term of the next line, until the reader-learner is led inexorably to the desired conclusion, which then seems reasonable. Reader-learners are led from a desire for instruction to immortality near God!

The importance of *Sophia* and her nearness to God in the thought of the Book of Wisdom can hardly be overstated, but it

---

56. This familiar Hellenistic rhetorical form is also found in Chinese (Confucius, Lao Tzu), Hindu (the Upanishads), and Egyptian (*Onchsheshonqy*) writings. For examples, see David Winston, *The Wisdom of Solomon*, AB 43 (Garden City, N.Y.: Doubleday, 1979), 154–55.

is expressed succinctly in a sequence of five powerful metaphors or images, which show how much further this author is willing to take poetic personification:

> For she is a breath of the power of God,
> and a pure emanation of the glory of the Almighty;
> therefore nothing defiled gains entrance into her.
> For she is a reflection of eternal light,
> a spotless mirror of the working of God,
> and an image of his goodness. (Wisd. 7:25–26)

These images lay the groundwork for the revisionist interpretation of Israel's history in chapter 10 and following.

Sirach had already reinterpreted God's mighty acts under the banner of "Let us now sing the praises of famous men" (Sir. 44:1). The Book of Wisdom now attributes these mighty acts neither to Israel's heroes nor to the Lord but to *Sophia*. The text explains these events by putting Israel's exclusivist nationalist traditions within a conceptual framework familiar to Hellenistic universalizing philosophical traditions:[57] *Sophia* protected Adam, delivered him, gave him strength, saved the flooded earth, steered Noah, kept Abraham strong, rescued Lot and Jacob, delivered Joseph, brought Israel over the Red Sea, drowned their enemies, and so on (see 10:1–21)! By the author's portraying these events as resulting from *Sophia*'s actions, she assumes attributes and activities often ascribed to God.[58] By the time reader-learners arrive at chapter 10, it can hardly be surprising that *Sophia* can save and rescue, since she has already been called the source of "immortality" (6:18; 8:13).

How Is This Content to Be Learned?

To engage reader-learners in Alexandria, the Book of Wisdom uses an even greater variety of Hellenistic literary forms and concepts than did Sirach.

IMPERATIVES, ARGUMENTS, AND EXPLANATIONS. Sirach and Proverbs both appealed to "the fear of the Lord" as a motive for obedience. The Book of Wisdom also links imperatives with "because" clauses that use fear as a motive, but "the fear of the Lord" is never cited. Rather the appeal is to fear of exposure (1:3, 7–9), fear of guilt (1:6), fear that the spirit of the Lord will reveal secret words (1:11), fear of punishment (3:10; 4:18–19), fear of judgment (4:4–5), and so on. Yet these motive clauses do not so much

---

57. Ibid., 33–38.
58. Ibid., 34.

evoke prescribed behavior but motivate reader-learners not to reason unsoundly. The issue here is not so much finding a time and
place to apply a proverbial saying, as it is to follow a line of
argumentation. Accompanying imperative commands with explanations shows reader-learners how important it is to recognize the
difference between good arguments and bad arguments. To do that
one must constantly seek instruction and learn to reason soundly.

DIATRIBE. Another way of fostering the ability to discern good from
bad arguments is to provide examples, as the Book of Wisdom
does in using the *diatribe*, another Hellenistic literary form. In a
diatribe, the author creates first-person speech as though he were
quoting an opponent. Thus an author can make opponents say
what he wants them to say, without risk. They always say what
he wants.

The diatribe is used, for example, in the second chapter, where
reader-learners are offered an extended example of how the ungodly reason unsoundly. To paraphrase, they reason thus: "Life is
short, full of chance, death comes from which there is no return
and no remembrance; therefore let us enjoy wine, perfume, spring
flowers, for this is what is given us" (2:1–9). Everything up to this
point could well have come from either Qohelet or the Epicureans without significant distortion. But in 2:11 the line of argument
(again in paraphrase) takes a harsh turn: "Let us oppress the poor,
the elderly and the widow, for might makes right and weak is
useless. Further let us torture and kill the righteous man for he em-
barrasses us." (Qohelet drew no such conclusion.) What the Book
of Wisdom finds wrong with this argument, as we noted above, is
that its users do not take into account the afterlife and God's just
retribution (2:21–24). In the diatribe, reader-learners have been
given a sample of bad reasoning, according to the author's view,
from which they can learn to spot similar examples in their own
lives. (This diatribe continues in 2:12–20, resonating strongly with
Psalm 22, Isaiah 53, and especially with the crucifixion scenes of
the Gospels, though written before Jesus' time.)

The use of the diatribe is pedagogically interesting. On the one
hand, it creates a sense of dialogue for reader-learners, showing
how the other side reasons. This lays upon reader-learners the responsibility for sorting out what is plausible about this reasoning
and what is not, and it allows them to ask, Why do we believe this
and not that? On the other hand, what opponents say can be controlled. This is similar to the teacher (or curriculum material) that
lets learners look at another viewpoint, as long as it is formulated

or articulated by the teacher. This can be effective; it can also be dishonest. There is sometimes a temptation to articulate the other view less plausibly than its proponents might do, not necessarily by deliberate distortion, but by omitting certain aspects. It is often intrinsically difficult to make beliefs of others fully plausible when one does not share them.

For example, Qohelet recommended seeing life as a gift and enjoying it without striving, but that was not mentioned in the diatribe. Never did Qohelet even hint at saying, "Since life is unfair, we might as well be unfair also." Never would he agree that might makes right. Perhaps the author of the Book of Wisdom has not understood Qohelet or has distorted his message. (He would not be the first nor the last.) Or perhaps he did not have Qohelet in mind at all. However, this illustrates a danger in using diatribe.

While a diatribe can be a useful and imaginative tool for creating a sense of dialogue in the pedagogical process, it must be governed by a rigorous sense of honesty if it is to serve truth. Caricature is a form of humor or entertainment but is of dubious value as a form of education.

THE USE OF METAPHORS AND REVISIONIST HISTORY. Poetry, proverbial sayings, and religious language necessarily use metaphors to communicate and evoke insight in the reader-learner. Metaphors *evoke* imaginative and intellectual activity by reader-learners. When the Book of Wisdom says of *Sophia* that "her radiance never ceases" (7:10) or that "she was their mother" (of all good things; 7:11–12), the text seeks to evoke the readers' own familiar associations with "light" and "mother" so they can illumine the attractiveness of wisdom.

Yet metaphors also involve subtleties that are pedagogically significant. The metaphors cited above are set in a descriptive or indicative context. The metaphor itself neither exhorts nor commands; it states how things are or how they could be seen. Similarly, the king in Wisdom 7 describes or testifies how and why he came to value *Sophia* so highly. In both texts, while there is a larger persuasive intent that governs the text as a whole (both want reader-learners to come to care for certain values and to choose the right path), the use of metaphors leaves considerable room for reader-learners to interact with and construct their own understandings and implications. Other texts use metaphors in contexts more sharply defined and governed by a persuasive intent. In such contexts, metaphors support a strategy of persuasion more consistent with the imperative or command language of the context.

For example, the unsound reasoning of the ungodly in 2:2 uses several evocative Hebraic and Hellenistic metaphors: "the breath in our nostrils is smoke" and "reason is a spark." Often in biblical texts, the metaphor of the breath is used as a metaphor for the life that is in humans because it has been breathed into them by God at creation and birth (Gen. 2:7). The metaphor resonates with God's blessings and with God's creative activity. But in this context the breath is not the breath of God or life but is "smoke," soon to be extinguished (2:3), and is also the breath the ungodly are using to reason unsoundly! Similarly, the spark is a familiar Hellenistic image, resonating with images of a divine spark, but here it will soon "turn to ashes" (2:3) and thus help provide a rationale for brutal exploitation of the righteous poor, widows, and the elderly (2:10). Are these metaphors chosen to suggest a flippancy about life and religious convictions that may turn reader-learners against the speakers? After all, reader-learners have been told earlier that these lines of reasoning are to be rejected.

A similar strategy is evident in the Book of Wisdom's revisionist view of Israel's history. Again the literary form is ingenious and highly attractive. The hermeneutical key is found in 11:5:

> For through the very things by which their enemies were punished, they themselves received benefit in their need.

The text that follows is divided into five sections (11:6–14; 11:15–16:15; 16:16–29; 17:1–18:4; 18:5–19:22), each with two parts, God's acts in history and in creation. In each section, the elements of creation that God used to punish opponents become the means of blessing for Israel.[59] Reader-learners are never left in doubt about which are the enemies and which are the good guys. It is a fascinating and unequivocal portrait of just divine retribution following rationales similar to those offered by Job's friends. Yet there are hints that this portrait has been retouched here and there. For example, in 16:20–21 the account of the manna provided Israel in the wilderness omits the murmuring and complaining reported in earlier versions (cf. Exod. 16 and Num. 11). Thus the reinterpretation not only adapts Israel's story to Greek ways of thinking but also glorifies Israel's leaders (see 18:24) and cleans up the people's behavior.

Admittedly, such reinterpretation is a familiar pedagogical practice in both religious communities and secular schools. Usually it is

---

59. Murphy, *The Tree of Life*, 90; see also Leo G. Perdue, *Wisdom & Creation: The Theology of Wisdom Literature* (Nashville: Abingdon, 1994), 310.

done with good intentions, for example, offering reader-learners good role models. Yet this approach is less than fully honest and presents unrealistic pictures of historical figures, which portray them as larger-than-life and thus even harder for learners to emulate.

PRAYER, GIFTS, AND PROMISES. In the Book of Wisdom, as the king describes his love of *Sophia*, he implies that he began his search for wisdom by praying to God, and as a result, "wisdom came to me" (7:7). Yet in the sorites (6:17–20) we examined, the text suggests that the beginning of wisdom is desire for instruction, and prayer is never mentioned. Again in 8:21 the king reports that despite his natural abilities he "would not possess wisdom unless God gave her to me," so "I appealed to the Lord," and then follows a prayer. Through the next nine chapters, the historical reinterpretation takes place within a framework of prayer addressed to God!

This repeated insistence that all is within the dominion of God is consistent with the thought of Sirach, Job, and Qohelet, yet here God is solely benevolent, loving, and caring to those who are righteous and faithful. Thus this text counters the questions raised by Job and Qohelet. Within the portraits painted by this text, the questions asked by Job and Qohelet could never even arise. Order is reestablished, and suggestions of counterorder are banished.

Will Qohelet's questions go away simply by insisting it cannot be that way? Do these prayers express more than the faithful piety of their author? Would Job's *ha satan* have sniffed a trace of self-interest, a need for control, in these prayers? While the king acknowledges *Sophia* is a gift from God, why does he want to possess wisdom? Can *Sophia* or wisdom ever be a possession? Do these questions point to a feeling similar to what learners sometimes have with teachers who seem to have everything under control, with those who have an answer for every question? Is that because they never ask a question for which they do not already know the answer?[60]

Why? What Is the Point of Learning in This Way?

This text, addressed to young Jews educated and knowledgeable in Greek ways, seeks to show that the old song can be sung, not

---

60. This is borrowed from the movie *Shadowlands*, where it is a question C. S. Lewis's wife asks her husband-teacher.

by borrowing a few new touches (as in Sirach), but by a thorough translation of the old into the structures of new harmonies.

TO KNOW GOD, AVOID IDOLATRY, AND REASON SOUNDLY. To be faithful to God while living in a culture that denies the importance of your God is difficult. In such a context, thinking about God can seem not just old-fashioned but simple-minded, irrelevant, or even unreasonable. For the Book of Wisdom, one of the things that can undermine being faithful to God is bad reasoning, so it is important to learn to recognize arguments that lead away from God or toward idols and foolish (false) values. Here idolatry, atheism, and agnosticism are foolish, for they make wrong inferences about what is seen, they keep searching, or they trust in their sight without inferring what is behind it (13:1–7):

> Yet again, not even they are to be excused;
> for if they had the power to know so much
> that they could investigate the world,
> how did they fail to find sooner the Lord of these things?
> (Wisd. 13:8–9)

In this view, what needs to be learned is how to infer God. This lesson is pressed home over and over in the sections on idolatry, which consists largely of faulty inferences or unsound reasoning, which the author parodies and ridicules (13:10–19; 14:18–31; 15:7–17). Ignorance and wrong thinking are the root of the worship of idols, the source of all evil — "they thought wrongly about God" (14:30; also 14:22–27).

Ironically, rarely does the Hebrew Bible place such confidence in human reason, although it is quite familiar in Greek thought. Plato and Aristotle, and many others, believed that what makes the human closest to the divine is the rational capacity. The irony is that placing such reliance upon thought as the root of both evil and the path to knowing God, on the one hand, prepares a rationale for education, but on the other hand, may lead people to expect more of education than it can deliver.

WISDOM OFFERS INTIMACY WITH GOD. We saw earlier how this text affirms that seeking *Sophia* leads to immortality, which brings one "near to God" (6:17–20), and this begins with and remains intimately connected with instruction, learning, and the disciplines and humility needed for the educational process. Strikingly, while this text seeks to control thought, it also uses metaphors that open thought to something less rigorous than logic and more akin to personal intimacy, which by definition is hard to control. As this text describes *Sophia*, the language conveys the need for trust or love, even for the intimacy of a close relational involvement (marriage?) with this woman (7:8–13; 8:2–9). This is not a purely human intimacy, for when *Sophia* "passes into holy souls," she even "makes them friends of God" (7:27). David Winston describes this as a "sense of mystical intimacy with the divine."[61]

In a culture that sees education as a form of information processing or behavior modification or vocational training, some will find such metaphors odd. Traditionally, marriage implies preferential, exclusionary, and permanent relations. How could it be a workable pedagogical metaphor or model for a teacher-learner relation? And a mystical relation is so contingent and unpredictable, so beyond the influence of teacher planning. What might be gained by using the image at all? Could we imagine that *Sophia* might engage in lesson planning? These metaphors challenge our frameworks.

Admittedly, history (e.g., classical Greece) warns that incautious use of love language, let alone mystical language, to portray pedagogical relations can lead to serious problems in teacher-learner relations. While teaching is both a relationship and a task, the latter defines the former. Teachers need a clear ethical sense of boundaries and responsibilities lest they succumb to the temptation to exploit their power and their learners. Teaching is more essentially defined by aims than it is by skills or roles,[62] and those aims entail a responsibility to help learners meet their own learning needs, not to use learners to meet a teacher's needs. On the other hand, such concerns may reveal as much about our own limited pedagogical imaginations as they do these ancient texts. Surely character formation (one contemporary as well as traditional purpose for education) requires sufficient interaction and intimacy (not unlike marriage?) to alter or form not only behavior and thoughts but also attitudes, emotional responses, moral judgments, dispositions, and whole perspectives on the world. What teacher has not experienced those transcendent moments within a teaching-learning interaction when suddenly, unexpectedly, and even inexplicably (and without prior planning) the whole atmos-

---

61. David Winston, "Wisdom in the Wisdom of Solomon," in *In Search of Wisdom: Essays in Memory of John G. Gammie*, ed. L. G. Perdue, B. B. Scott, and W. J. Wiseman (Louisville: Westminster/John Knox, 1993), 164.

62. See the careful reflections on these issues by R. S. Downie, Eileen M. Loudfoot, and Elizabeth Telfer, *Education and Personal Relationships: A Philosophical Study* (London: Methuen, 1974).

phere comes alive with a vibrancy, intensity, and delight that might aptly be called inspired? Such occasions might be rare, very brief, or rather more extended. They might lead to (or are the product of?) pedagogical breakthroughs with a learner or class, yet they feel significant and are often remembered with great clarity. Mystical language may not be inappropriate for such occasions.

Both Sirach and the Wisdom of Solomon (compared with earlier texts) seem to have a greater interest in or to exert greater pressure on reader-learners to come out in a particular place. Perhaps it is the fluidity of their cultural situation that makes them less willing to leave things too open-ended. If that is true, then their use of language drawn from friendship, love, marriage, and mystical relations can serve as a pedagogical corrective for too closely defined and predetermined outcomes. Further, such language can also remind both teachers and learners that one cannot always know from whence the transcendent may arise. All must learn to be open, receptive, ready, even expectant.

COMMITMENT TO HERITAGE. This text is convinced that while Greek culture may be more modern and sophisticated than the old Hebrew ways, when those old ways are translated into Greek modes of thinking (and cleaned up a little), the natural ethical and religious superiority of Hebrew ways will shine forth. And their worth will enhance commitment to following those ethical and religious paths.

ON EDUCATION, TRADITION, AND CULTURAL CHANGE

Dealing with cultural change, modernity, and needing both to change and yet hold on to what is true are very complex and conflictual matters. How can education maintain traditional values and religious heritage, support cultural and religious identities, while at the same time help learners live within the modern, ever-changing world? How can we proceed pedagogically when the surrounding culture does not support what educators seek to inculcate? Can different thought systems serve the same God? Can we be loyal to a tradition while changing it? Can we be faithful if we never change? Already in Sirach and the Wisdom of Solomon we see reflections of two of the oldest responses to such questions, both still in use today: Sirach adapted the new to conserve the tradition, and the Wisdom of Solomon adopted the new to modernize the tradition so as to preserve it.

Posing such questions in contemporary terms, we ask, which is figure, and which is ground? Does tradition modify modern ways, or do modern ways modify tradition? Or, which is more important, being modern or being traditional? Must one choose? Answers to such questions often give rise to interesting ironies. The author of the Book of Wisdom was willing to radically change Hebraic tradition to fit into Hellenism, yet he did so because he was convinced that Hebraic culture and religion were superior, which he demonstrated by offering derisive comparisons. Sirach, on the other hand, was equally convinced that Hebraic ways were superior, yet he never compared. He just went on doing what he knew was best. Ironically, Sirach was much more self-conscious of his own individual role and self-importance (a Hellenistic trait), while the author of the Wisdom of Solomon made nothing of his own individual thought or role in history.

One of the ongoing issues in our contemporary culture wars is the intractable polarizing we force on one another with our insistent urge to find the one absolutely right answer for all time and all peoples. The older wisdom tradition made much of finding the right time for a word to be spoken or a deed performed. This implies (as Job and Qohelet recognized) that theological and ethical interpretation is dynamic and open to ongoing change. Job and Qohelet engaged in an ongoing discussion about whether a particular traditional doctrine (retribution) was eternally right. Sirach was willing to relinquish purity laws for foreign foods, while retaining traditional Torah and temple. The Book of Wisdom, translating the Hebrew stories and convictions into a modern conceptual framework, adapted the right path/wrong path duality of Proverbs 1–9 to fit the dualism basic to Hellenistic thinking. The Book of Job depicts the Lord as tolerating many wild statements by Job, statements that surely would be condemned by Sirach or the Book of Wisdom.

Simplistic either-or or right/wrong thinking is found in many parts of the biblical record, but so are protests against that kind of thinking. Indeed, the Books of Job and Ecclesiastes suggest that simple dualities are incompatible with the complexities of God's nature and God's behavior with humans. Sirach and the Wisdom of Solomon made little use of the traditional doctrine of the proper time, yet both can be seen as an expression of what they consider the right word in their own right time. Perhaps the danger comes in the insistence by some that only right/wrong or either-or dualisms will be acceptable expressions of the biblical message and of divine ways.

Scripture includes works that seem mutually incompatible. Yet this fact seems highly compatible with an orthodox doctrine that God loves all human beings — even those who are themselves mutually incompatible with one another. If God can love those who are incompatible, and the canon can include works that are incompatible, does that not exhort us to be wary of always dividing up the world and people into we/they or in/out or saved/damned? On the other hand, Sirach and the Wisdom of Solomon also remind us that there may be times when simpler either-or ways of thinking are highly appropriate.

Despite their differing responses to the conflict that arose when Hebraic religious tradition met Hellenistic culture, Sirach and the Wisdom of Solomon agreed in three important judgments that contribute to pedagogical change and that we see reflected again in the twentieth century. First, in the face of cultural and linguistic pluralism, they responded by recommending education. Both presumed, with many today as well, that in the midst of cultural and social diversity, education can be a unifying force. But they perhaps differed on who is to be unified. For Sirach, the threat of Hellenism was not as pervasive; he seemed to believe that all persons in Israel could still be faithful, even though only some would come to his school. Sirach saw his education contributing as a part of the larger culture, perhaps assisting in shaping the way the culture wanted to go. The Wisdom of Solomon, on the other hand, could not assume that the larger culture of Alexandria would support his values. So he directed his attention to the few, perhaps an elite group of young men, who would be educated to represent loyal Israel as a minority within the pluralism of Alexandrian culture. The Wisdom of Solomon paid little attention to the interests of the larger culture, while using it to support the minority culture. Second, both focused upon the individual, as did Job and Ecclesiastes, and both pay more attention to the psychological. Perhaps this is the influence of Hellenism on their thinking, or perhaps it is also a tendency to turn inward and away from apathetic or hostile outside forces. Third, they also both upheld tradition by means of highly innovative uses of metaphors, of new literary devices and thought forms. Even more significant, in my view, is their highly innovative use of the traditional figure of *Sophia* and her greatly increased pedagogical significance. We turn to explore this figure more fully in the next chapter.

CHAPTER FIVE

WOMAN WISDOM
Education as Playing
in the Presence of God

Before turning to the New Testament, we pause to take a brief historical-critical look at an often overlooked figure of unusual pedagogical and literary importance for the New Testament. During this interlude, we gather some texts from our wisdom books, specifically texts and images of Woman Wisdom, which many of the authors of the New Testament used like "picture frames" through which they could see Jesus more clearly.

In our journey through wisdom texts, we have noted divergent depictions of women. While Proverbs presumes its readers will be males, Woman Wisdom is accorded near-divine status, and the strange woman is to be shunned. Job's wife lost all her children, wealth, and social status, yet no attention is paid to her suffering, and she is not mentioned in Job's restoration. Qohelet cannot find even one woman whom he holds in high regard (Eccles. 7:28). Sirach denigrates women,[1] yet he exalts Woman Wisdom. The Wisdom of Solomon addresses young men, while devoting a quarter of its text to the glories of *Sophia*. Let us look more closely at the portrait of Woman Wisdom in these texts, many of which regard her as pedagogically important. Since these texts are located within books we have already examined, we shall not repeat the pedagogical questions but will observe what in these portraits of Woman Wisdom is pedagogically distinctive.

---

1. Ben Witherington, *Jesus the Sage: The Pilgrimage of Wisdom* (Minneapolis: Fortress, 1994), 51.

WOMAN WISDOM IN PROVERBS

The older material in the Book of Proverbs (chaps. 10–29) is framed by chapters 1–9 and 31. These chapters place women and pedagogy in an extremely prominent place in shaping the reader-learner's understanding of the whole book.[2] Bernard Lang argues that these texts presume a school context because of their didactic rhetoric, though he can produce virtually no archeological or textual evidence that Israelite schools existed in this time period.[3] Teaching was likely conducted in the public arena, in the market near the city gates, as Lang contends, though that need not presume organized schools. As Lang himself suggests, for the young, "watching people do business is educational," as is watching justice dispensed in the city gates.[4] Woman Wisdom, appears in an urban context, where she "raises her voice" in the city streets and the public square (1:20; 8:1; 9:3), competing with others in the bazaar hawking their own goods. Her teaching is a public affair, and her wisdom is meant to apply to public affairs, as well as to private thoughts and behavior. Indeed, she claims that her wisdom is fundamental for economic affairs, matters of public justice, and government rule and that she is listened to by kings, rulers, and nobles (8:15–21).

The text of this first chapter also describes a loyalty contest between the appeals of traditional familial values and those of a "gang family" who offer treasure and solidarity:

---

2. Bernhard Lang, despite his pedagogical interests, follows von Rad in assuming that the Woman Wisdom passages in Proverbs are "completely isolated" and "unconnected with their surroundings" (*Wisdom and the Book of Proverbs: An Israelite Goddess Redefined* [New York: Pilgrim Press, 1986], 3–4). As argued in chapter 1, I find Claudia V. Camp more persuasive, *Wisdom and the Feminine in the Book of Proverbs* (Sheffield: Almond, JSOT, 1985), see chap. 6.

3. Lang, *Wisdom and the Book of Proverbs*, 7–12. The lack of either archeological or textual evidence for the existence of schools in Israel is highlighted by Lang himself, for the only supporting Israelite evidence he offers is a British newspaper report of an excavation in 1938, which showed the press "taking the existence of schools for granted" (8). Lang does refer to the research of Lemaire (which we noted in chap. 1) but takes no notice of the careful review of the evidence and negative conclusion by James L. Crenshaw in his "Education in Ancient Israel," *Journal of Biblical Literature* 104:4 (December 1985), 601–15. Lang draws upon analogies from Egyptian and other Near Eastern sources to support his contentions. Lang concludes, "It remains indisputable that the Book of Proverbs originated in the school and was being read there" (10), which inspires little confidence in his reasoning or his conclusions. This extends as well to his contention that Woman Wisdom was originally a goddess within early polytheistic Israel, the "divine patroness of the Israelite school system" (7) and the "divine patroness of rulers" (60), which he supports with equally dubious logic, use of evidence, and supposition.

4. Lang, *Wisdom and the Book of Proverbs*, 28.

We shall fill our homes with loot.
Throw in your lot with us;
We shall all have a common purse. (Prov. 1:13–14, NJPSV)

The father predicts that these will suffer the natural consequences
of their behavior — getting caught in their own nets and dying
(1:16–19). Then another voice, Woman Wisdom, mocks those who
listen to sinners (1:20–31) and refuse her advice. She, like the father, warns that "they shall eat the fruit of their way" (1:31),
a graphic metaphor for natural consequences and for assuming
responsibility for one's own behavior.[5] In the next chapter, the
contest continues, as the reader-learner is admonished to follow
neither the way of evil men (2:12–15) nor the "loose woman," the
"adulteress" (or prostitute, 2:16–19). In the third chapter, Woman
Wisdom returns with an attractive picture of her benefits:

Happy are those who find wisdom,
    and those who get understanding,
for her income is better than silver,
    and her revenue better than gold.
She is more precious than jewels,
    and nothing you desire can compare with her. (Prov. 3:13–15)

This contest motif is familiar in the teaching-learning patterns
characteristic of oral/aural cultures.[6] But the parental values depicted in Proverbs are neither narrowly nor exclusively familial.
There is only a single mention of finding a good wife (5:18) and no
talk of having lots of children or of settling down within the clan
and honoring familial values, and so on. (Compare the description
of the values of the Rechabite clan in Jeremiah 36.) The values espoused in Proverbs 1–9, even those of "father" and "mother," are
shared communal values and virtues of character[7] and most often
pedagogical values: knowledge, discernment, understanding, justice, foresight, the paths of the just, avoiding crooked speech and
evil, and above all, seeking or finding Woman Wisdom. In seven of
the first nine chapters of Proverbs, Wisdom acts and speaks as a
strong and desirable woman. In Proverbs 4:5–9 the reader-learner
is invited to acquire wisdom, to love her, to hug her, and thus one
will find both honor and wealth. James Crenshaw observes, "Because the students almost without exception were males, wisdom

---

5. Ibid., 49.
6. See Walter Ong, *Fighting for Life: Contest, Sexuality, and Consciousness*
(Ithaca, N.Y.: Cornell University Press, 1981).
7. See William P. Brown, *Character in Crisis: A Fresh Approach to the Wisdom
Literature of the Old Testament* (Grand Rapids: Eerdmans, 1966), chap. 2.

was described as a beautiful bride, and folly was depicted as a harlot enticing young men to destruction. In this way language became highly explosive, and the quest for wisdom suddenly took on erotic dimensions."[8]

These teaching passages are made lively and powerful by a poetic, metaphoric device called *personification*. A poet treats a thing or an abstraction imaginatively as though it could move and act as a person. The psalmists often use personification, for example, in "justice and well-being kiss" (Ps. 85:11, NJPSV) or "O gates, lift up your heads" (24:7, NJPSV). The poet invites the reader to see the gates as people who lift their heads, to see justice and well-being as kissing. Such imaginative use of language is more evocative, lively, and emotionally potent than saying, "Justice and well-being go together" or "The gates will rise." As Lang observes, "Languages whose grammatical structure gives male or female gender to 'things' invite personification. Hebrew is one of those languages." (So is Greek.) He adds that Hebrew likes to "link abstract concepts to action verbs."[9] Instead of saying, "Don't be wicked," the poet says, "Do not let wickedness reside in your tents" (Job 11:14). The sages also personify things:

> Three things are never satisfied;
>   four never say, "Enough":
> Sheol, the barren womb,
>   the earth ever thirsty for water,
>   and the fire that never says, "Enough." (Prov. 30:15–16)

Lang and others claim that the personification of Woman Wisdom is evidence that she was originally a goddess. Admittedly there are precedents in Canaanite, Egyptian, and other Near Eastern goddesses. However, Lang's own descriptions of the wide-ranging use of personification within Hebrew literature provide a simpler explanation. What, in principle, distinguishes *hokmah* (if originally a goddess) from "wickedness," "justice," "earth," "fire," or "wine" for whom no goddess status is claimed? Though an original goddess myth is possible, no direct parallels have been found.[10]

---

8. James L. Crenshaw, "The Acquisition of Knowledge in Ancient Israelite Wisdom Literature," *Word and World* 7:3 (summer 1987), 246–47.

9. Lang, *Wisdom and the Book of Proverbs*, 132.

10. It is well known that Proverbs draws (heavily at times) upon Egyptian wisdom sources. Christa Kayatz notes that in Egyptian wisdom, *Maat* is not only the principle of order, justice, and truth but is also the name of a goddess who is associated with the king, is pictured as a divine child at play, and preexists the creation of the world, all of which has striking similarities to Woman Wisdom. See her *Stu-*

Even if the language were originally goddess language, what substance does that add to our interpretation of these texts? In earlier
chapters, we sought to understand the texts as we have them,
rather than substitute a reconstructed original, and we shall do so
here, especially since little is gained for our present understanding
by reverting to a prior original. In either case, the text offers the
reader a female figure, Woman Wisdom, who is powerful, deeply
interested in teaching and learning, and highly desirable. How are
we to understand her and her role in these texts?

Claudia Camp turns from searching for origins to examining
the present poetic function of this feminine imagery, tracing the
"system of commonplaces associated with 'the feminine' in Israel"
to illumine that imagery. Biblical women were deeply grounded
in everyday experience, managed households, and like Woman
Wisdom (Prov. 9), they prepared meals for others. Women were
lovers, harlots, and wise ones. Women were regarded as an authority within the home, though often authority had to be exercised
indirectly. Biblical women offered counsel or wise practical advice to their husbands, who often listened and followed it, from
Eve, to Sarah (Gen. 16), Rebekah (Gen. 27), Abigail (1 Sam. 25),
Bathsheba (1 Kings 1), Esther, even Job's wife.[11] This traditional
picture is confirmed and expanded in the portrait of the strong
woman in Proverbs 31. In addition, many biblical women used
persuasion, indirection, or even trickery to effect justice and even
God's own ends, for example, Rebekah, Tamar (Gen. 38), Moses'
mother and sister (Exod. 2), Michal (1 Sam. 19), Ruth, the Wise
Woman of Tekoa (2 Sam. 4), and Esther. "In every case the indirect
but effective action taken by the woman is done without any instructions or aid from Yahweh and yet nonetheless serves to effect
the deity's purpose," and in every case, that requires "disruption
of the established hierarchies of society."[12] In doing so, they helped
preserve and became part of the tradition. Such women, like sages,
had the authority of insight and experience, but they did not have
the means or power by which they could coerce others to do their
will, so they acted indirectly.

dien zu Proverbien 1–9: eine form- und motivgeschichtliche Untersuchung unter
Einbeziehung ägyptischen Vergleichsmaterials (Neukirchen-Vluyn: Neukirchener,
1966), 76–134. Others have seen Canaanite influences as more determinative; see
William McKane, Proverbs: A New Approach (Philadelphia: Westminster, 1970),
344.
    11. Camp, Wisdom and the Feminine, 86–90.
    12. Ibid., 124.

In Proverbs 1–9 Woman Wisdom is engaged in a contest between two competing sets of values for the loyalty and understanding of the young and the wise. Here the sages have pictured
the right path (which includes righteousness, justice, fear of the
Lord, and self-discipline) as a beautiful woman and the wrong
path (which includes thievery, disloyalty to parents, adultery, for-
nication, murder, stupidity, and lying) as a band of thieves and
as a seductive prostitute. The good path leads to life, wealth, and
honor, while the wrong path leads to death.

By personifying these paths as women, the poet invites readers to an imaginative exercise in which the allure of each path
is graphically depicted; thus, reader-learners can more nearly feel
their seductive appeals. In several of these texts, Woman Wisdom
speaks in first-person address to reader-learners, so they must learn
to read accurately their claims. Indeed, in the diatribe of Proverbs
7, the description and "smooth words" of the adulteress, seeking to
lure a "young man without sense," are so vivid that reader-learners
may sense this author has "been there — done that." Thus reader-
learners are led more fully into the experience of having to choose
one's own path.

There is a playful as-if quality to both poetic personification and
this contest that appeals to the imagination: Think of Wisdom *as
if* she were a beautiful woman, with whom every young person
would want to be on intimate terms. Then her benefits become
more clear:

> Hug her to you and she will exalt you;
> She will bring you honor if you embrace her.
> She will adorn your head with a graceful wreath;
> Crown you with a glorious diadem. (Prov. 4:8–9, NJPSV)

> Long life is in her right hand;
>   in her left hand are riches and honor.
> Her ways are ways of pleasantness,
>   and all her paths are peace.
> She is a tree of life to those who lay hold of her;
>   those who hold her fast are called happy. (Prov. 3:16–18)

The promises held out to those who choose rightly in this contest are long life, wealth, peace, honor, and the tree of life, which
resonates with the divine blessings of the Garden of Eden. That
these resonances with the creation and with divine activity are no
accident is confirmed by the very next verse:

> The LORD by wisdom founded the earth;
> by understanding he established the heavens. (Prov. 3:19)

This theme is found as well in Job 28, where wisdom is not so much a person as a "thing." The thematic question, Where is wisdom to be found? leads to a lengthy search through mines and seas (as though wisdom were precious metals or jewels; Job 28:1–19), among the birds and beasts, even among the mythological creatures (Job 28:20–22), but only God knows the way to wisdom:

> "God understands the way to it,
> and he knows its place.
> . . . .
> And he said to humankind,
> 'Truly, the fear of the Lord, that is wisdom;
> and to depart from evil is understanding.' " (Job 28:23, 28)

At this point in the text of Job, humans cannot find true wisdom; only God can, but the wisdom that humans can attain is the conventional "fear of the Lord" and "to depart from evil."

Proverbs 8 develops this creation theme more fully and differently answers the question, Where is wisdom to be found? Here Woman Wisdom is raising her voice (intemperately?), calling to all people (in public?), "Listen, for I speak noble things … my mouth utters truth" (8:6–7, NJPSV). Then she lists her credentials (8:6–21), showing why her words should be taken seriously by every reader-learner. She not only offers wealth (8:21) but what is better than silver and gold — instruction, insight, strength, and wisdom (8:10–14):

> "By me [Wisdom] kings reign,
> and rulers decree what is just;
> by me rulers rule,
> and nobles, all who govern rightly.
> I love those who love me,
> and those who seek me diligently find me." (Prov. 8:15–17)

While this is remarkably direct speaking, Woman Wisdom seeks to persuade reader-learners of her authority, not coerce them by her power:

> "The LORD created me at the beginning of his work,
> the first of his acts of long ago.
> Ages ago I was set up,
> at the first, before the beginning of the earth.

> When there were no depths I was brought forth,
>   when there were no springs abounding with water.
> Before the mountains had been shaped,
>   before the hills, I was brought forth —
> When he established the heavens, I was there." (Prov. 8:22–27)

As Job also observed, God must have used wisdom in creating the universe — therefore, she was there in God's presence. (Genesis 1:26 has God speaking reflexively in the plural.)

Woman Wisdom speaks boldly but does not describe herself, nor does any biblical author. She remains mysterious. Such reticence is also found in biblical accounts of encounters with God. For example, Isaiah described his call, saying: "I saw the Lord sitting on a throne" (Isa. 6:1). Then Isaiah described the hem of Yahweh's robe, the seraphs who surround him, the smoke that filled the temple, but said nothing about what God was like. Rather than describe God or Woman Wisdom directly, such texts show how human beings and the divine relate. *Sophia* is personified as active during creation but not as creator. She says, "I was there. . . . "

> "when he marked out the foundations of the earth,
>   then I was beside him, like a master worker;
> and I was daily his delight,
>   rejoicing before him always,
> rejoicing in his inhabited world
>   and delighting in the human race." (Prov. 8:29–31)

In this passage, most translations have used the term "rejoicing" for the Hebrew *shahket*, perhaps because that seems "a more pious"[13] or ecclesiastically suitable word. Yet everywhere else in the Hebrew Bible, this term is translated "play." It is used of children playing with toys and games, of people playing musical instruments and dancing (1 Sam. 18:7; 2 Sam. 6:5), of the Lord playing with Leviathan (Ps. 104:26), and even of the love-play between Isaac and Rebekah (Gen. 26:8).[14] Lang translates it as "frolicking,"[15] and even the usually cautious McKane translates it as "jesting."[16] (The careful reader will also notice that the margins of most translations indicate that "master worker" can as well be translated as "little child.") Here are the same verses in the Jerusalem Bible translation:

---

13. Samuel Terrien, *Till the Heart Sings: A Biblical Theology of Manhood and Womanhood* (Philadelphia: Fortress, 1985), 98.
14. Ibid.
15. Lang, *Wisdom and the Book of Proverbs*, 78.
16. McKane, *Proverbs*, 223, 356–58.

> "I was by his [Yahweh's] side, a master craftsman,
>   delighting him day after day,
>   ever at play in his presence,
> at play everywhere in his world,
>   delighting to be with the sons of men."

In this picture, while God was creating the universe and declaring it good, she was God's "delight," playing at God's side, giving God delight, or joy. This word "play" is also the word used in Ecclesiastes in the phrase, "eat, drink and be merry" (*euphraino*, LXX), which is urged as one of the God-given ways to live in a universe that no longer seems coherent (Eccles. 2:10; 3:12). Luke then uses that exact same playful "merrymaking" word for the joyous celebration ordered by the father of the reconciled prodigal son (Luke 15:23–24, 29, 32), which so rankled the self-righteous elder son. (Jesus' way of eating and drinking also was a source of great irritation to his self-righteous critics.)

In the Proverbs 8 text, the childlike play of Wisdom goes beyond giving delight and pleasure to God; her playfulness was also evident in her "delighting in the human race" (8:31). In Samuel Terrien's words, "play becomes the bridge between the Sovereign of the universe" and lonely humanity![17] Not only is this a strikingly positive portrayal of a woman's role in Israelite religion; this playful Woman Wisdom, who delights in humankind, is linked directly to pedagogy in the very next verses:

> "And now, my children, listen to me:
>   happy are those who keep my ways.
> Hear instruction and be wise,
>   and do not neglect it.
> Happy is the one who listens to me,
>   watching daily at my gates,
>   waiting beside my doors.
> For whoever finds me finds life
>   and obtains favor from the LORD;
> but those who miss me injure themselves;
>   all who hate me love death." (Prov. 8:32–36)

Listening, study, discipline, and eager anticipation are educational practices and virtues that are the way to happiness and life, and ignoring these leads to death. Because humans were not there at the beginning of the universe, we must learn about such matters from the traces left within the created order and from those who

---

17. Terrien, *Till the Heart Sings*, 98.

are wiser than we. Such learning is both a source of joy and a serious life-and-death matter! Notice that this portrayal yokes learning with blessing and joy and not learning with death! Does this suggest something about the mood of education? Should it be deadly dull? Is this making too much of a verse or two from a seldom-used portion of an ancient biblical text? Let us see how these themes are picked up and amplified in Sirach and the Book of Wisdom.

WOMAN WISDOM IN SIRACH

Sirach begins his book with reflections on wisdom and the fear of God in which wisdom is again personified (*Sophia* now, since the text was translated into Greek). She is said to be "created with the faithful in the womb"; she abides faithfully among human beings; "she inebriates mortals with her fruits; fills their house with desirable goods"; and she "rained down" knowledge, discerning comprehension, and long life (Sir. 1:14–20). Sirach, like Proverbs, considers her a teacher who brings joy, love, and blessing:

> Wisdom teaches her children
> and gives help to those who seek her.
> Whoever loves her loves life,
> and those who seek her from early morning are filled with joy.
> Whoever holds her fast inherits glory,
> and the Lord blesses the place she enters.
> Those who serve her minister to the Holy One;
> the Lord loves those who love her. (Sir. 4:11–14)

As we saw earlier, Sirach identifies Wisdom with Torah, and they come together in the pedagogical enterprise. While Torah is teaching and following the teaching is the right path, Sirach's imagery is far too erotic and festive to fit comfortably into contemporary notions of a classroom:

> Whoever fears the Lord will do this,
> and whoever holds to the law will obtain wisdom.
> She will come to meet him like a mother,
> and like a young bride she will welcome him.
> She will feed him with the bread of learning,
> and give him the water of wisdom to drink.
> He will lean on her and not fall,
> and he will rely on her and not be put to shame. (Sir. 15:1–4)

This portrait of teaching and learning, like the father's pleading in Proverbs 4, seeks a more intimate and lasting connection between the learner and the teacher/subject matter.

In chapter 23 Sirach teaches self-discipline and self-control, especially of the tongue and of sexual or adulterous passions. Immediately following this, he breaks into a hymn of praise for *Sophia*, who speaks in the first person. Here she is not just a witness at creation but helped lead Israel out of bondage in Egypt, and not only speaks in public but "in the assembly of the Most High...and in the presence of his hosts she tells of her glory" (24:2):

> "I came forth from the mouth of the Most High,
>   and covered the earth like a mist.
> I dwelt in the highest heavens,
>   and my throne was in a pillar of cloud.
> . . . .
>   and over every nation and people I have held sway.
> Among all these I sought a resting place;
>   in whose territory should I abide?
>
> Then the Creator of all things gave me a command,
>   and my Creator chose the place for my tent.
> He said, 'Make your dwelling in Jacob,
>   and in Israel receive your inheritance.'" (Sir. 24:3–8)

Sirach's *Sophia* was not only present at creation in the mist (cf. Gen. 1:2) but also was enthroned in the "pillar of cloud" that led Israel through the wilderness. Thus *Sophia* affirms her importance both in creation and in Israel's history and then goes on to claim she was with God from the beginning and will be for all time (24:9; cf. John 1). *Sophia* takes up residence in Jacob and Israel, affirming her historical and geographical particularity, living specifically in the holy tent (24:10–12; cf. Exod. 25–26) and in Jerusalem, where she put down roots.

Sophia thus assumes historical and cultic priority. She grew tall and blossomed, and the exuberant descriptions of the abundance of her growth, her fragrance, and the glorious and graceful delights of her abundant blossoms and fruit (24:13–17) evoke for the attentive reader both the luxuriant abundance of the descriptions of the Song of Songs (Song 3:6; 4:6, 14; 5:15), the incense of the holy tabernacle,[18] and the invitations to the feast by Woman Wisdom in Proverbs 9. She invites the reader-learner to participate in her abundant feast:

---

18. See the helpful comments by Patrick W. Skehan and Alexander A. DiLella, *The Wisdom of Ben Sira*, AB 39 (New York: Doubleday, 1987), 334–35.

"Come to me, you who desire me,
  and eat your fill of my fruits.
For the memory of me is sweeter than honey,
  and the possession of me sweeter than the honeycomb.
Those who eat of me will hunger for more,
  and those who drink of me will thirst for more.
Whoever obeys me will not be put to shame,
  and those who work with me will not sin." (Sir. 24:19–22)

(This passage resonates with Johannine passages dealing with the sacrament and with the significance of Jesus; see John 4:14; 6:35.) This feasting imagery is part of Sirach's larger pedagogical vision in which learning is satisfying because it enables the learner to participate in the right path, in the covenant, and in the glories of temple religion. Sirach equated the fear of the Lord with the commandments (6:37): "Torah is fear of God, and wisdom is Torah."[19] For Sirach, covenant, Torah, wisdom, and temple were all a single whole — and they fused together in the personification of *Sophia*, who brings divine blessings to all who diligently seek her:

All this is the book of the covenant of the Most High God,
  the law that Moses commanded us
  as an inheritance for the congregations of Jacob. (Sir. 24:23)

Here Sirach reinterpreted Torah within the sphere of wisdom. Wisdom includes Torah, not the other way around.[20] Wisdom is the primary topic for this teacher of wisdom.

As we saw earlier, Sirach rejected the narrow exclusivism of Ezra and those who would jealously guard the boundaries of Israel's God in order to guard her purity and holiness. For Sirach, wisdom (which includes Torah) flowed beyond the boundaries of Israel:

It overflows, like the Pishon, with wisdom,
  and like the Tigris at the time of the first fruits,
It runs over, like the Euphrates, with understanding,
  and like the Jordan at harvest time.
It pours forth instruction like the Nile,
  like the Gihon at the time of vintage. (Sir. 24:25–27)

Mythical rivers flood the whole world with pedagogical nutrients! The mythical rivers of the Garden of Eden (Pishon and Gihon, Gen. 2:11, 13), Israel's river (Jordan), and the major rivers of

---

19. Gerhard von Rad, *Wisdom in Israel* (Nashville: Abingdon, 1972), 245.
20. Ibid., 245–47.

the world (Tigris, Euphrates, and Nile, whose annual flooding is the source of agricultural abundance) all show how continuous and abundant the blessings of Torah (teaching) will be. The blessings of wisdom and of Torah, like the blessings of the Most High God, naturally run over all human-made national, ethnic, and religious boundaries. What are these blessings that overflow the banks of the world's rivers? Wisdom, understanding, and teaching (Gk. *paideia*) — a remarkable pedagogical vision!

Sirach believed this abundance has always been so, though it has not always been recognized:

> The first man did not know wisdom fully,
>   nor will the last one fathom her.
> For her thoughts are more abundant than the sea,
>   and her counsel deeper than the great abyss. (Sir. 24:28–29)

Naturally, if wisdom includes Torah, "the first man" (Adam) could not have known it since it was not yet revealed, but since the last one will also not know, the barrier here is not chronology but human understanding. Pedagogy is necessary! Someone who understands must help others drink in this abundance. So Sirach devoted himself to teaching (24:30–33). He saw his teaching (and writing) as an overflow of that divine abundance personified in *Sophia*, and like her, he invited others to come and partake of that abundance (51:23–30).

In portraying *Sophia*'s central place in yoking the wisdom tradition and the historical events of Israel's experience with a liberating Lord and with the Jerusalem temple worship and prayer life, Sirach most fully expressed his own vision of what would help Israel remain faithful to the Lord while living under the domination of a Hellenistic culture that threatened to overwhelm Israel's particular vision of God. In this vision, teaching and learning were vitally essential. In the next chapter, we will see Sirach's fusion of traditions expressed again in the pedagogical vision and actions of a Galilean peasant.

SOPHIA IN THE BOOK OF WISDOM

The fusion of wisdom with cultic and historical traditions in Sirach was carried further in chapter 10 of the Book of Wisdom, where the mighty acts of God were explicitly described as the work of *Sophia*. Yet the most remarkable and distinctive aspect of *Sophia*

in the Book of Wisdom is how she is pictured in the invitations
from 6:12 to 9:18:

> I will tell you what wisdom is and how she came to be,
> and I will hide no secrets from you,
> but I will trace her course from the beginning of creation,
> and make knowledge of her clear,
> and I will not pass by the truth. (Wisd. 6:22)

When this author begins to tell what *Sophia* is, it feels like he
cannot get his words out fast enough, nor find adjectives enough to
do her justice. This is not neutral description offering dispassionate
knowledge. Rather it is a hymn of praise, enticing reader-learners
to fall in love with this wonderful woman. In this text, *Sophia*
perhaps has gone beyond poetic personification to take on divine
characteristics.[21] This may be best seen in the piling up of five
metaphoric hyperboles describing her divine attributes (echoed in
Colossians, Ephesians, and Corinthians, but attributed to Jesus):

> For she is a breath of the power of God,
> and a pure emanation of the glory of the Almighty;
> . . . .
> For she is a reflection of eternal light,
> a spotless mirror of the working of God,
> and an image of his goodness. (Wisd. 7:25–26)

In Sirach, *Sophia* was linked exclusively with Israel, but here
Sophia has a more cosmic reach.[22] She is "the fashioner of all
things" (7:22) or the mother of "all good things" (7:11–12). "She
reaches mightily from one end of the earth to the other, and she
orders all things well" (8:1). This cosmic "power of God" at the
same time "goes about seeking those worthy of her" (6:16). How
does one meet this desirable woman? The king says he prayed to
God, and "the spirit of wisdom came to me" (7:7). She taught him
"what is secret and what is manifest" (7:21–22).

What is even more remarkable and pedagogically significant
about this text is the degree of personal intimacy being urged here
between an individual and cosmic divinity. Job reminisced about
the good old days when he and God were close, using the word
"friendship" to describe their relation (Job 29:4). But Job knew
that in asking to speak face-to-face with God, he risked his life
(13:13–15). And even as he warmly described God's friendship,

---

21. David Winston, *The Wisdom of Solomon*, AB 43 (Garden City, N.Y.:
Doubleday, 1979), 34.
22. Terrien, *Till the Heart Sings*, 111.

Job maintains a prudent distance, saying the "friendship of God was upon my tent" (Job 29:4). Proverbs and Sirach maintain a similar reserve. Woman Wisdom is to be loved and embraced (Prov. 4:6, 8), yet while called "bride" in the Book of Wisdom, in Proverbs she was more guardedly called "sister" or "your intimate friend" (Prov. 7:4). In Sirach also, the reader-learner was urged to love Woman Wisdom, but even in the most detailed descriptions (Sir. 24), she came to live with the whole people more in corporate solidarity than in individual intimacy.

The Book of Wisdom, however, introduced *Sophia* as one who reaches out "to make herself known" to those who seek her, and she "graciously...meets them in every thought" (6:12–16). Then, in the sorites we explored earlier (6:17–20), *Sophia* and pedagogy lead to intimacy with God. This linkage of education and intimacy with God invites reader-learners into a pedagogical possibility quite different from objective mastery of a body of facts or a computer modem connection. Here is promise of a kind of learning in which a holy spirit enters into people's souls

> and makes them friends of God, and prophets;
> for God loves nothing so much as a person who lives with wisdom
>   (*Sophia*). (Wisd. 7:27–28)

The imagery here is the language of love and marriage:

> I loved her and sought her from my youth;
> I desired to take her for my bride,
> and became enamored of her beauty.
> She glorifies her noble birth by living with God (*symbiosis*)
> and the Lord of all loves her.
> For she is an initiate in the knowledge of God,
> and an associate in his works. (Wisd. 8:2–5)

Again, borrowing a theme from Proverbs 8:30–31, *Sophia* is portrayed as the link of love between the Lord and the king, and since (borrowing the language of commentator David Winston) she "lives in love with God" (or perhaps the author borrowed the language of the Hellenistic mystery religions, especially that of Isis), she is an "initiate in the knowledge of God," and thus she is in perfect position to bring mortals into this immortal relationship.[23] Therefore, the king boldly avows, "I determined to take her to live with me" (Gk. *symbiosis*, 8:9). She will bring him good advice and

---

23. See Winston, *The Wisdom of Solomon*, 37, who offers additional bibliography as well.

consolation in grief (8:9), glory and honor (8:10), immortality and being remembered (8:13), and intimate "rest with her,"

> for companionship with her has no bitterness,
> and life with her has no pain, but gladness and joy.
> . . . .
> in kinship with wisdom there is immortality,
> and in friendship with her, pure delight,
> ... wealth,
> ... understanding,
> and renown. (Wisd. 8:16–18)

What more could reader-learners hope for?

A SIGNIFICANT FIGURE IN BIBLICAL AND THEOLOGICAL HISTORY?

Where do these ideas about Woman Wisdom come from, and why do they emerge? Are they important, or are they more like an imaginative footnote in a distant history and a dead literature? Woman Wisdom in these texts is clearly more than simply a useful poetic illustration or "motivational enticement for recalcitrant schoolboys."[24] She may be a form of response to the presence of non-Israelite goddesses of love, but more positively Woman Wisdom is a mainstream response to a series of crises in nascent Judaism: the fall of Jerusalem, the destruction of the temple, the loss of the Promised Land, exile and captivity, the loss of the king as symbol and mediator of divinity, and eventually the encounter with Hellenism. Instead of an autonomous kingdom, Israel had become an oppressed, tribute-paying, priest-governed province under someone else's royal power. As we have seen, these crises were sometimes experienced as the silence or even the enmity of God, a threatened collapse of faith in a God who had earlier promised to protect Jerusalem forever. These crises coincided with the profound shift from oral transmission of tradition to written texts. In these transitions, wisdom, sages, and texts assumed a symbolic centrality once held by the king and his court.[25] Gerald Sheppard has even argued that in the process of compiling the texts, exilic and postexilic sage-redactors used procedures similar to Sirach's to sapientialize nonwisdom traditions of the Torah.[26]

---

24. Camp, *Wisdom and the Feminine*, 286.
25. Ibid., 290–91.
26. Gerald T. Sheppard, *Wisdom as a Hermeneutical Construct: A Study in the Sapientializing of the Old Testament* (Berlin: de Gruyter, 1980).

Into these crises, poets brought "Wisdom at play" as a feminine figure who challenged the exclusive and imperial assumptions of both apocalyptic and priestly expectations, with their masculine and cultic superiority.[27] Instead of prophetic condemnation and reassurance, Woman Wisdom offers playing, singing, dancing, feasting, and making love as ways of being with God and presents "delight" as a divine-human relation! Yet Israelite religion, as well as early Christianity and early Judaism, remained profoundly androcentric, especially in their theological treatment of the divine-human relation. Does this mean that this imaginative leap was ignored or bypassed? Yes and no.

The Hebrew Bible and the intertestamental literature (especially the later, more Hellenistic works) provided the conceptual framework for much of orthodox religious thought of the New Testament period. It is striking that all the attributes of *Sophia* we have just reviewed in this literature are subsequently applied to Jesus and the Holy Spirit in the New Testament. Paul calls Jesus "the wisdom of God" (1 Cor. 1:24), and the author of Colossians and Ephesians freely used the language of chapter 7 of the Wisdom of Solomon to describe Jesus. The same is true of the Gospels (e.g., cf. Prov. 8; Sir. 24; Wisd. 7; John 1). We will explore these matters more fully in the next chapter.

In addition, the descriptions of *Sophia* were also taken up in rabbinic and medieval Judaism, especially with the development of the notion of *Shekhinah*, the feminine term derived from the Hebrew *shakhan*, "to dwell": "God's presence, what in the Bible is called His 'face,' is in Rabbinical usage His *Shekhinah*."[28] *Shekhinah* is used frequently as a synonym for the immanence, the divine presence in the world and among God's people, the "created light, the first of all creations," and is later synonymous with the "glory of God" or the "great radiance" or the "holy spirit."[29]

Perhaps all these interpretations just stretch a few insignificant words, verses, and themes out of proportion. If these are so important, why has the church not made Woman Wisdom more important in teaching and theology? That is an interesting question to ponder, especially in the light of church history. Jaroslav

---

27. Terrien, *Till the Heart Sings*, 100. The ecumenism of the biblical wisdom tradition reaches out to other cultures and religions as well.

28. Gershom Scholem, *On the Kabbalah and Its Symbolism* (London: Routledge and Kegan Paul, 1965), 105.

29. Gershom Scholem, *Major Trends in Jewish Mysticism* (New York: Schocken, 1941), 111.

Pelikan, historian of Christian doctrine, observed that "the development of the doctrine of the Trinity...was decisively shaped by the use of Proverbs 8:22–31 (LXX) as a passage dealing with the relation between the preexistent Logos and the Father."[30] Indeed, the whole "Arian controversy broke out over the exegesis of Proverbs 8:22ff."[31] This passage about Woman Wisdom was the central feature of the discussions, exegeses, and debates among Origen, his pupil Dionysius of Alexandria, Athenagoras, Hippolytus, Theophilus, Irenaeus, Tertullian, Justin, Hilary, Athanasius, and Arius himself. The issue concerned ontology and metaphysics, but it was debated by means of competing exegeses interpreting the relation of Woman Wisdom with God. Was she (and by analogy, Jesus) "created" or "acquired" or "born" or "begotten" of God? Each possibility was (and is) a legitimate translation of the Hebrew and Greek terms.[32]

In this debate, Proverbs 8 was used to make two points simultaneously: like Woman Wisdom, Jesus was eternal and thus distinct from humans, but also like Woman Wisdom, Jesus was created and thus distinct from God. Arians and others insisted that this latter distinction meant that God and Jesus were not of the same substance and that, therefore, Jesus was also subordinate. The anti-Arian faction eventually rejected the notion of Jesus being "created" or "acquired" (and thus subordinate) and substituted "begotten."[33]

It is important (but difficult) to remember that in the early days of the church, people were trying to make sense of events that seemed quite unique in history. Who was Jesus, and how were he and his activities to be described? They sought language that would, on the one hand, be in continuity with Israel's monotheism yet would, on the other, acknowledge that Jesus is also God. The idea that a human could be called the *son* of a transcendent God was not as familiar then as it sounds to us today. While we shall return to some of these issues later, for now we note that

---

30. Jaroslav Pelikan, *The Christian Tradition: A History of the Development of Doctrine*, vol. 1, *The Emergence of the Catholic Tradition* (Chicago: University of Chicago Press, 1971), 61.

31. Ibid., 193.

32. Each of these translations still has its advocates today among contemporary biblical translations.

33. The familiar phrase "only-begotten" (Gk. *monogeneis*) in the creed is also found in the King James Version's rendering of John 1:14; 1:18; and 3:16. It is more than coincidence that "only-begotten" occurs originally in Wisdom of Solomon 7:22, in my view.

(a) the early church used descriptions of *Sophia* to describe Jesus and the Holy Spirit and (b) the orthodox understanding of the doctrines of Christology, Trinity, creation, sin, and soteriology[34] were all originally hammered out in disputes over the interpretation of the relation of Woman Wisdom with God as portrayed in Proverbs 8. Therefore, what we make of Woman Wisdom is hardly insignificant or peripheral.

THE PEDAGOGICAL SIGNIFICANCE OF THIS *SOPHIA*-TEACHER

When we put all these texts together and see how the trajectory of Woman Wisdom progresses through them, we find a rich and vivid pedagogical vision of how people come to know and understand God.

Learning and Metaphoric Playfulness

In each of these texts, the reader-learner has been invited to explore the realm of this female figure by means of metaphoric, poetic personification. Woman Wisdom herself invites playing with ideas and images that could even become realities. As we have seen before, such imaginative play is intrinsic both to the poetic and the educational process and finds frequent expression in wisdom literature.

The sages frequently extol listening, study, discipline, eager anticipation, and other virtues as the way to happiness and life. For the sages, learning was a matter of life and death. But if it was so serious, why should it be called *play?* How do we put together their emphasis upon instruction and discipline (including physical punishment as pedagogical strategy) with this playful use of poetic language and gender, as well as the emphasis upon playful delight in the presence of God? Woman Wisdom plays as though a child; invites reader-learners to instruction, discipline, and listening; and promises "favor," "blessing," and "life" because "finding her" is a life-and-death matter (Prov. 8:32–36). Then she immediately invites everyone to a party!

> "Come, eat of my bread
>   and drink of the wine I have mixed.
> Lay aside immaturity [simpleness], and live,
>   and walk in the way of insight." (Prov. 9:5–6)

---

34. See Pelikan's lucid discussion, *The Christian Tradition*, 1:172–225.

Then the text turns to reflection upon correction and rebuke in teaching and learning, which only the wise take willingly (9:7–12). Why do these juxtapositions of play and instruction, or of serious life-and-death matters with banquet feasting, appear? Johan Huizinga observes that "in the very nature of things the relationship between feast and play is very close. Both proclaim a standstill to ordinary life." In both, mirth and joy dominate, though both can be serious; both are limited in time and space; and both combine strict rules with genuine freedom.[35]

Perhaps we need to take Woman Wisdom's words literally, "Lay aside immaturity [or simpleness]" (Prov. 9:6), and take a more complex and mature look at the notions of play and discipline, especially in education, if we are to grasp how the serious and the playful can be so completely intertwined in these texts. Reflection on the links between play, seriousness, and education is not restricted to Israel's sages. Plato was also serious about play, and some of Jesus' critics contended he feasted too much and was not serious enough about the rigors of law and purity.

Play often requires practice, and practice is a form of learning. Play also requires self-discipline and following rules, as does education, and both can be full of surprises. Perhaps it is not surprising that sages played with both the language and the ideas that gave expression to their understanding of how to steer through life. We shall return to these notions in our final chapter.

Learning and Gender

One of the ideas the sages played with is the notion of gender. These texts are the products of an androcentric culture, and most were written by men for men. Yet one of the central ways of evoking the divine-human relation in these texts relies upon the use of a female figure.

We noted above that the notion of *contest*, which reaches well back into pedagogical prehistory, has been shown to be gender related. Adversative or contest behavior plays a much larger role in male than it does in female behavior, in both animal and human realms.[36] Thus, if education was seen as a contest, perhaps it is not surprising that early schooling in both Greek and Hebrew cultures was essentially for males. Or was education seen as a contest because it was only for males?

---

35. Johan Huizinga, *Homo Ludens: A Study of the Play Element in Culture* (Boston: Beacon, 1950), 22.
36. Ong, *Fighting for Life*, chap. 2: "Contest and Sexual Identity," 51–96.

Why do these texts portray wisdom as a woman? Is it a pedagogical device to hold the attention of adolescent males, as Crenshaw suggests?[37] It is even more puzzling if we take later tradition into account. In Judaism, the house of study and synagogue worship were by definition limited to men, yet they thought of themselves as the "female spouse of a masculine God."[38] Similarly the Fathers of Christianity refer to the church primarily as "she." Is this no more than traditional personification or the use of biblical metaphors (Israel and church as "brides" of God)? Arthur Green suggests provocatively:

> In the search for the kind of intimacy, tenderness and warmth that such people wanted to express in talking about the relationship between God and Israel [or church], they could not remain in the domain of the all-male universe where they lived their public lives. There is no way, without turning to images of the feminine, or without thinking of the relationships between men and women, that most men can express the degree of love, passion and warmth that the spiritual life may arouse in them.[39]

If there is any truth in that observation, it suggests that one of the values of playing with ideas and texts like these is that it opens up possibilities that allow people to transcend the limits of what is taken to be culturally or conceptually acceptable at some particular time and place. That in itself is a valuable contribution to pedagogical procedures, one still needed and useful today. We constantly need assistance in breaking out of the confines of our familiar concepts.

This raises another important question: If men designate their own activities using the feminine gender, then surely these feminine images are not only for the sake of women. The practice suggests the images are needed by men as well. Are they not needed especially by heterosexual men who insist upon a masculine gender for God?[40] If people form images to give expression to thoughts and feelings, or to discover thoughts and feelings by using various images, then to delimit the images one might use (e.g., images for God) restricts the path and scope of one's learning.

37. Crenshaw, "The Acquisition of Knowledge," 246–47.
38. Arthur Green, "Bride, Spouse, Daughter: Images of the Feminine in Classical Jewish Sources," in *On Being a Jewish Feminist: A Reader*, ed. Susannah Heschel (New York: Schocken, 1983), 249–50.
39. Ibid., 250.
40. Ibid., 248.

A learner can only discover the potential fruitfulness of a metaphor, an image, an analogy, by trying it out, using it, seeing what it leads to and where it will not permit one to go. That is how one's learning grows and is tested. But historically, most schools, created by and for men, were an institutionalized form of controlling (exercising power over) others (learners) because schools were a means by which some people learned how to govern others.[41] That is, knowledge is power. Seldom have such schools exhibited a playful spirit or allowed the kind of learning we have been describing that requires practice in real, ordinary, everyday living. Women have seldom had public power as have men, so they worked indirectly or persuaded rather than coerced or governed. Perhaps just as *Sophia* assumed importance in an Israel in crisis, evoking different ways of seeing the divine-human engagement, ways in which reeducation played a very large role, alternative gender imagery might also help us reimagine educational ministry today. Perhaps it is not merely an accident that one of the contemporary world's greatest sages, Gandhi, gave high priority to alternative styles of teaching and learning in the process of social and political transformation and also spoke of himself as a maternal figure. He clearly used power and pedagogy, but in unusual (more feminine?) ways. We will return to these issues.

Can Education Be a Way of Being in the Presence of God?

These texts about Woman Wisdom often link education with the fear of the Lord and with being in God's presence, which are not a familiar way of thinking today. Is this just poetic hyperbole, or is there something here yet to be fully appropriated?

We have noted how often reader-learners have been exhorted to physical participation in this relationship, ranging from seeking to embracing, to living together (*symbiosis*), and to feasting. (For an imaginative and evocative portrayal of how such feasting might be a spiritual experience of the presence/absence of God, view the film *Babbette's Feast*.) In other words, if play is a way of being joyous in the presence of God, it is not just spiritualized play but is embodied in and through the physical body and senses. In one sense, this is consistent with what we saw of the joyous sensuality in the Book of Wisdom (and in the Song of Songs as well), where

---

41. See Robert Holmes Beck, *A Social History of Education* (Englewood Cliffs, N.J.: Prentice-Hall, 1965); and G. H. Bantock, *Studies in the History of Educational Theory*, 2 vols. (London: Allen and Unwin, 1980, 1984).

the relation with *Sophia* has been pictured as an intimate relation, even as marriage. While today we may talk this way about one's individual (private) spiritual life, do such images really seem appropriate for the educational process? Yet these texts repeatedly connect learning, education, intimacy with *Sophia* and with God. Today education is usually regarded as part of the public realm, which requires interpersonal distance, while intimacy, spiritual life, and nearness are relegated to the realm of the private. Yet, even as we read these texts, we sometimes sense that they do not share our familiar cultural notions of how different and distinct the private and public are. This is another reminder both of how recently in human history we have constructed today's private versus public assumptions[42] and that it is possible to construe things differently.

We observed above that as texts took on Hellenistic features, they tended to adopt Greek dualistic notions that denigrated the physical, especially as a means of religious expression. The body, in the Greek concept, was clay from which it was best for the soul to leave. The soul had been "sent down" (from heaven) for a time, "to act as an administrator to the murmurous and fertile province of the body."[43] This supports a tendency to regard the physical or sensuous as less worthy than the spiritual, and we observed the pedagogical corollary that concrete and particular is lower, and the greater the abstraction, the better.

All these texts, whether Hebrew or Greek, presume that the educational process has less to do with what or how much one knows and more with who one is becoming. The concern has less to do with what today we might call the shape of one's mind and more to do with the shape (and forming) of one's character. Character is formed in relationships, including intimate relations.

The imagery and metaphors used of Woman Wisdom are later adapted for use in describing another teacher, Jesus, and another figure, the Holy Spirit, so we turn now to the writings of the New Testament.

---

42. See the multivolume work edited by Philippe Ariès and Georges Duby, *A History of Private Life* (Cambridge: Belknap, Harvard, 1987).

43. Peter Brown, *The Body and Society: Men, Women, and Sexual Renunciation in Early Christianity* (New York: Columbia University Press, 1988), 26.

CHAPTER SIX

WHY DIDN'T JESUS TELL BIBLE STORIES?

Telling Bible stories has long been a favorite mode for the church's educational ministry. Storytelling was also a frequent activity of Jesus. So it is not surprising that many believe that if teachers are to teach as Jesus did, they must tell Bible stories. But Jesus did not tell "Bible stories." The Bible Jesus knew (the Hebrew Bible) contained many stories, and it is safe to assume he knew many of them. Jesus did tell stories, especially parables. Indeed, many scholars claim that was part of his distinctive contribution. Yet seldom do the Gospel writers portray Jesus as telling a story chosen from among the stories of Israel, though he does occasionally refer to some. Why?

The sages and Jesus alike made virtually no use of historical narratives. The sages turned to the created order rather than historical events to understand God, and Jesus' sayings about God are filled with sparrows, fig trees, vineyards, lost sheep, mustard seeds, lilies of the field, and so on. Much of Jesus' teaching is portrayed as responses to questions and persons, speaking the right word at the right time, in the manner of the sages. The ancient sages insisted that one's wisdom is seen in his deeds, not just in words, and Jesus reportedly railed out at the hypocrisy of those whose actions contradicted their speech. Jesus challenged the conventional order as did Job, Ecclesiastes, and the prophets, and he refers to covenantal traditions in a manner quite like Sirach's fusion of traditions (yoking creation, redemption, covenant, Torah teaching, and temple cult with *Sophia*).

While Jesus' sayings and stories later became part of what was called the *Bible*, his stories are distinctly different from the stories of the Hebrew Bible, including those of the wisdom tradition we have been tracing. Like the sages of old, Jesus was a teacher whose sayings and actions, collected in the Gospels, seem to affect reader-learners in ways similar to the wisdom texts we have been studying.

We have seen the back-and-forth "dialogue" in the wisdom traditions. The Book of Proverbs used proverbial sayings and imperatives to help establish and confirm the right way, or what has been called a *conventional order*. Then Job and Ecclesiastes challenged this order (especially retribution). Qohelet quoted conventional proverbs in order to challenge them and the traditional status quo and offered his own distinctive aphorisms, which suggest quite a different counterorder. Then Ecclesiasticus and the Wisdom of Solomon reaffirmed the conventional order and retribution, using proverbs. However, if we accept the views of Crossan, Williams, and Perdue, as described above (p. 123) neither book contains a single aphorism. In the Gospel texts, we see another shift. Jesus used conventional-order proverbial sayings to affirm the status quo. But he also offers parables and aphorisms that question the status quo and evoke a counterorder view.

In our earlier texts, the meaning, use, and truth of each of those texts did not depend upon historical verification or authenticity of either its central figure or its author. When we come to the New Testament, we have no text from the hand of Jesus. Rather, we have four texts focusing upon a single historical person, yet their primary intent is not just transmitting news (*gospel* means "good news") about this person but, in John's words, "so that you may come to believe that Jesus is the Messiah, the Son of God, and that through believing you may have life in his name" (John 20:31). Here the pedagogical intent is secondary to the primary intent of believing. However, readers must learn something about Jesus in order to believe, and Jesus himself did much teaching, so our pedagogical interest can also be explored.

Still, the only other "person" assuming similar importance in our earlier texts was *Sophia*, and she was a poetic figure. Now historical questions (who Jesus was and what we know about him) become more important, and having multiple texts offers readers differing (historical and/or theological) views of Jesus and his significance, and these differences affect our pedagogical inquiry. For example, if Jesus is seen primarily as a healer or as a magician, then what he said or how he taught is far less central than if he is seen as a prophet or as a sage-teacher or as "the wisdom of God." Whereas earlier we could treat historical issues as matters of context, now our pedagogical inquiry is more complicated by the way these historical and theological issues impinge on the task.

In chapter 5, we reviewed how the sage-poets described *Sophia* or Woman Wisdom. While the accounts offered in Proverbs 8 and in the Wisdom of Solomon 7–9 claim to be about the same figure, the portrait is different, partly because the literary and cultural framework has changed. The same holds true for each New Testament account and also for each contemporary scholar's account of the historical Jesus. Each portrays the figure of Jesus within a frame, and thus we see the picture differently. For example, contemporary historians look at Jesus, each having read the same texts. Yet E. P. Sanders insists the Jewish prophet is the best overall frame, while Morton Smith sees Jesus as a magician, Geza Vermes sees a Jewish *Hasid* or *zaddik* (a holy or righteous man) who heals, John Dominic Crossan sees a Mediterranean peasant healer with radically egalitarian ideas gleaned from Cynic philosophers, Marcus Borg sees a spirit-possessed sage, John Meier sees a "marginal Jew," Elisabeth Schüssler Fiorenza sees "Sophia's prophet," and Stevan Davies sees a "spirit-possessed healer" who used dissociative techniques (hypnosis) to induce a healing trance in his associates.[1] Each offers historical and textual evidence to support his or her view. What does this mean for our task?

HOW SHALL WE PROCEED?

Do we simply say, "We seek Jesus the sage-teacher," and then go looking for him? I raise this issue because in the early twentieth century, many religious educators and some biblical scholars studied Jesus as the master teacher, searching the Scriptures for clues about how Jesus taught. The "answers" they found sometimes made Jesus look more like a Protestant American disciple of John Dewey than a Jewish Galilean in first-century Palestine.[2]

---

1. E. P. Sanders, *Jesus and Judaism* (Philadelphia: Fortress, 1985); Morton Smith, *Jesus the Magician* (New York: Harper and Row, 1978); Geza Vermes, *Jesus the Jew: A Historian's Reading of the Gospels* (Collins, 1973; Philadelphia: Fortress, 1981); John Dominic Crossan, *The Historical Jesus: The Life of a Mediterranean Jewish Peasant* (San Francisco: HarperSanFrancisco, 1991); Marcus Borg, *Jesus: A New Vision: Spirit, Culture, and the Life of Discipleship* (San Francisco: Harper and Row, 1987); John P. Meier, *A Marginal Jew: Rethinking the Historical Jesus*, 2 vols., Anchor Bible Reference Library (New York: Doubleday, 1991, 1994); Elisabeth Schüssler Fiorenza, *Jesus: Miriam's Child, Sophia's Prophet: Critical Issues in Feminist Christology* (New York: Continuum, 1994); Stevan L. Davies, *Jesus the Healer: Possession, Trance, and the Origins of Christianity* (New York: Continuum, 1995).
2. For example, see Luther Weigle, "The Ideal Teacher: Jesus," in his classic *The Pupil and the Teacher* (New York: Hodder and Stoughton, 1911), 210–17;

In part, this was the product of their methodology, which abstracted the biblical texts from their historical and cultural settings. Newer historical-critical methods offered needed correctives. We must modify the approach used in previous chapters to allow for the differences we have described, while skirting the swamp of endless methodological discussion. How can we deal with texts constructed with theological (or christological) interests centered upon a historical person, yet keep our focus upon our pedagogical interests without distorting the texts?

The New Testament calls Jesus many names (prophet, priest, lamb, teacher, preacher, etc.). Jesus is called *prophet* or *priest* for good reason — his activities are similar to the activities of the Hebrew prophets and priests. Yet with Jesus, as with every person, no one name or role exhausts the whole. Can we, with careful scrutiny, discern similarities between Jesus and the sage-teachers we have been reading? Jesus was a teacher, but what kind of teacher? The names, titles, and descriptions often serve theological agendas. Might how Jesus was described and addressed also offer clues about what kind of teacher he was?

HOW WAS JESUS DESCRIBED?

Throughout Jesus' ministry and after his death, people asked, "Who is this man?" Many descriptions and characterizations were offered to try to make sense out of words and actions that seemed unprecedented, even astonishing. In every account we have, we see people trying on labels, making comparisons with previous figures (e.g., Moses or Elijah or Melchizedek), and borrowing language from many sources in their attempts to make sense of what they saw and heard. Many descriptions of Jesus that legitimately fit the prophetic and priestly traditions of Israel's heritage, such as Son of man, Son of God, Suffering Servant, prophet, priest, and king, have been thoroughly examined by scholars.[3] We turn instead to

---

or George H. Betts, "Jesus the Embodiment of All Scientific Pedagogy," in *How to Teach Religion: Principles and Methods* (New York: Abingdon, 1919), 217–20. Even the more sophisticated studies by biblical scholars we now see as inadequate, e.g., C. T. Craig, "Modern Values in Jesus," in *Jesus in Our Teaching* (New York: Abingdon, 1931), 114–41.

3. Most scholars agree that these honorific titles are products of the early church and cannot be claimed to have been used by or of Jesus during his lifetime, with the possible exception of "prophet." For a brief survey of the arguments, see W. Barnes Tatum, *In Quest of Jesus: A Guidebook* (Atlanta: John Knox, 1982), 113–22; or for a more extended treatment, see Vermes, *Jesus the Jew*.

several texts that describe Jesus in language earlier seen in wisdom texts. How good is this fit?

Jesus as the Wisdom of God

Several authors explicitly identify Jesus as "Wisdom" (*Sophia*), while others adopt descriptive language for *Sophia*, using it to describe Jesus without actually calling him the name.

PAUL. We begin with the earliest New Testament texts, the Epistles of Paul, written twenty to thirty years after Jesus' death.[4] Paul, a Jew raised in a Hellenistic environment, was trained as a Pharisee (2 Cor. 11:22–29; Phil. 3:2–7; Gal. 1:13–14). Like the author of the Wisdom of Solomon, Paul used Hellenistic concepts and culture to make another point of view (Christianity) plausible and persuasive.

In his first letter to the Corinthians, written in approximately 55 C.E., Paul clarified his own mission and message using *sophia* (wisdom) in relation to Jesus. There had been quarreling and divisions among the congregation's members (1 Cor. 1:10–16). Paul wanted unified loyalty to Christ, not competing allegiances to church leaders and teachers. Paul wrote that he was sent "to proclaim the gospel, and not with eloquent wisdom (*sophia*), so that the cross of Christ might not be emptied of its power" (1:17).

The text invites the reader to consider two different ways to make the Christian message known and persuasive: one way uses human standards of eloquence, "lofty words" (2:1), or what today we might call *creative packaging* or *marketing strategies*. The other way speaks of "Christ crucified," which is foolishness to those who think of marketing. Who would be attracted to a leader who died in humiliation among criminals? The text contrasts two paths: the way of wisdom (using human standards, 1:26) and the way of the cross (using God's standards): "Has not God made foolish the wisdom (*sophia*) of the world? For since, in the *sophia* of God, the world did not know God through *sophia*" (1 Cor. 1:20–21). Paul claimed that instead of using worldly wisdom, he came preaching Christ crucified, which to the Greeks is a scandal and foolishness (1:22–23), but to believers is "Christ the power of God and the *sophia* of God" (1:24). What Paul takes away with one hand, wisdom as a way of knowing God, he quickly gives back with the

---

4. Specifically, in chronological order, 1–2 Thessalonians, Galatians, 1–2 Corinthians, Romans, Philippians, and Philemon.

other — for Christ is how we are to know God and Christ is
Wisdom (*Sophia*).

How are reader-learners to understand this? How can Paul assert both? We recognize a familiar tactic of wisdom texts, creating
perplexity that requires a reader to stop, go back, and read again,
perhaps more carefully, noticing how the concepts are used to shift
the reader-learner's understanding. On a second reading, we see
more clearly that Paul did not deny *all* wisdom, but specifically
that Christ is "human wisdom." Rather, as *Sophia*, Christ is God's
gift. This resonates with Proverbs, where "the LORD gives wisdom" (2:3–6), brings riches and happiness, and is "a tree of life"
(3:13–18). Paul also affirms, "He is the source of your life in Christ
Jesus, who became for us *sophia* from God" (1 Cor. 1:30).

Those who identify with human leaders or causes, and who
then argue over their differences, are actually praising their own
theological perception, as learned from their leader.[5] What is at
stake here is literally theology: knowing God does not abide by
human standards (worldly wisdom). Paul claims God made this
path foolish (as did the counterorder wisdom of Job and Qohelet).
In this path, all one can have is not knowing (1 Cor. 1:21). In
its place, Paul affirms a reversal of human expectations, Christ as
God's *Sophia*, resonating with the revelations heralded in Proverbs 8, Sirach 24, and the Wisdom of Solomon. Here, as in Job
and Qohelet, Paul has embedded the crucial insight of his theology
within the pattern of his text so that if reader-learners discern the
reversals in the text correctly, they will also discern that a reversal
is required when looking at the cross. What seems humiliation is
actually power! What seems defeat is actually victory! Sometimes
what seems a poor sermon or a confused argument may be God's
wise eloquence! The reader-learner will have to discern wisely.

In Paul's text, Wisdom (*Sophia*) is personified, not as a woman,
but as Jesus the Christ, who brings a renewed understanding of
God and thus new life. Possibly Paul, a Hellenistic Pharisee, found
the conceptual step from Torah teaching to Jesus as the *Sophia*
of God easier since his Jewish and Hellenistic predecessors —
Proverbs, Sirach, and the Wisdom of Solomon — had already personified wisdom as *Sophia*, yoking Torah teaching with *Sophia*

---

5. Peter Lampe, "Theological Wisdom and the 'Word about the Cross': The
Rhetorical Scheme in I Corinthians 1–4," *Interpretation* 44:2 (April 1990), 120–
21.

as the cosmic principle linked with creating and ordering the universe.[6]

Paul's text uses a modified diatribe (a Hellenistic form used in the Book of Wisdom) or perhaps even quotes those on both sides of the quarrel. Then the text shows how to resolve such disputes, by a reversal of values: Real wisdom, that is, God's *sophia*, is found in acts of humility and worldly impotence, rather than in jockeying for positions of power in human communities. This, again, echoes a familiar wisdom theme: one's wisdom shows more in what one does, one's attitudes in action, than by affirming the right propositions. Peter Lampe observes that Paul does not refer directly to party strife in the text of 1:18–2:16, but instead the concealed argument is like a "Trojan horse, it at first pleases its listeners until they are shocked to discover that they are themselves criticized by the same text."[7]

First Corinthians is not exceptional, for wisdom language and motifs used of Jesus occur all through the Pauline corpus, including 2 Corinthians 3–4; Philippians 2:6–11; Colossians 1:15–20; Ephesians 1, 5 (if those two are Pauline); and Romans 9–11.[8]

MATTHEW. Matthew and Luke depict Jesus' chastising hypocrites, yet their quotes differ. In Luke, Jesus addressed lawyers, saying,

> "Woe to you! For you build the tombs of the prophets whom your ancestors killed.... Therefore also the Wisdom of God said, 'I will send them prophets and apostles, some of whom they will kill and persecute.' " (Luke 11:47, 49)

Here, Luke's Jesus speaks of the *Sophia* of God in the third person, as one who sent prophets and apostles, adopting language similar to that of the Wisdom of Solomon 7:27 and 11:1. Matthew's Jesus addressed scribes and Pharisees, rather than lawyers, saying,

---

6. W. D. Davies argued that in Paul, Jesus replaced Torah as the center and organizing principle of his life. See his *Paul and Rabbinic Judaism: Some Rabbinic Elements in Pauline Theology* (London: SPCK, 1962), esp. 147–76. This is confirmed by Eckhard J. Schnabel, *Law and Wisdom from Ben Sira to Paul: A Tradition Historical Enquiry into the Relation of Law, Wisdom, and Ethics*, WUNT Reihe 2:16 (Tübingen: Mohr, 1985).

7. Lampe, "Theological Wisdom," 128.

8. One of the earliest works to treat wisdom influences in the New Testament extensively was Robert L. Wilken, ed., *Aspects of Wisdom in Judaism and Early Christianity* (Notre Dame, Ind.: University of Notre Dame Press, 1975). See especially the articles by James M. Robinson, Elisabeth Schüssler Fiorenza, and Birger A. Pearson. More recent works provide additional bibliography: Ben Witherington, *Jesus the Sage: The Pilgrimage of Wisdom* (Minneapolis: Fortress, 1994), esp. 249–334; and E. E. Johnson, *The Function of Apocalyptic and Wisdom Traditions in Romans 9–11* (Atlanta: Scholars, 1989).

"Woe to you, scribes and Pharisees, hypocrites! For you build the tombs of the prophets and decorate the graves of the righteous. . . . Therefore I send you prophets, sages, and scribes, some of whom you will kill and crucify." (Matt. 23:29, 34)

In Matthew, Jesus speaks in the first person saying, in effect, "I am the Wisdom of God," resonating with Pauline usage. This is only one of many instances where Matthew depicts Jesus as embodied *Sophia* and teacher.[9]

Matthew uses a variety of images with which to make sense of Jesus and his significance, each resonating with wisdom texts. For example, in Matthew 11:2 Jesus was teaching when John's disciples asked, "Are you the one?" Jesus responded, "Tell John what you hear and see." In other words, "Look at what I say and what I do" (11:3–6). Then the text portrays Jesus as reflecting upon expectations that shape what people are prepared to see and therefore learn. By this means Matthew asks reader-learners as well what they (we) expect to see when looking at John and Jesus. Do we look for a teacher (11:1) or prophet (11:5, 13–14) or a royal figure (11:8; suggesting John and Jesus are important figures)? Are they nobodies (a "reed" in 11:7) or children (11:16–18), or do we look for works or deeds (11:19)? This profusion of images in one chapter leaves reader-learners to sort out which picture is the most appropriate, though the order in which they are presented could imply that the latter — more humble — images are the more fitting (esp. 11:7–19).

But there are always some who refuse even to engage in the process. They would rather sit on the sidelines and criticize those who risk playing. Matthew's Jesus portrays it thus:

"But to what will I compare this generation? It is like children sitting in the marketplaces and calling to one another,

'We played the flute for you, and you did not dance;
we wailed and you did not mourn.'

For John came neither eating nor drinking, and they say, 'He has a demon'; the Son of Man came eating and drinking, and they say, 'Look a glutton and a drunkard, a friend of tax collectors and sinners!' Yet wisdom is vindicated by her deeds." (Matt. 11:16–19)

---

9. M. Jack Suggs first highlighted these wisdom motifs in Matthew's portrayal of Jesus in his *Wisdom, Christology, and Law in Matthew's Gospel* (Cambridge: Harvard University Press, 1970).

This picture of wisdom as children playing resonates with Proverbs 8:30–31. Some children cry, "Let's play the dancing game," but when the flute is played, no one moves. So they try the opposite: "Let's play the funeral game!" Yet when the dirge is played and the wailing begins, no one joins in. This generation would rather watch or criticize than risk participating in "the seriousness of children's play":[10] "Yet wisdom is vindicated by her deeds." (Luke's parallel in 7:35 reads, "Nevertheless, wisdom is vindicated by her children.") No risk, no action, no wisdom. Talk will not do it.

The reader can feel the frustration in this text. Nothing provokes response from a jaded audience, which is even less responsive than the pagan inhabitants of Tyre, Sidon, or even Sodom. Indeed, here Jesus-*Sophia* is so hidden that he can only be seen by those who have been given the gift directly from God (Matt. 11:25–27)! Yet in verse 5 Jesus had said that anyone who opened his eyes could see what is going on here — it is so plain even Gentiles see it — yet it is so hidden that the wise and intelligent cannot see! Recall that Sirach summarized his activity as a sage and teacher and invited reader-learners:

> Draw near to me, you who are uneducated,
>
> . . . .
>
> Put your neck under her yoke,
> and let your souls receive instruction;
>
> . . . .
>
> See with your own eyes that I have labored but little
> and found for myself much serenity. (Sir. 51:23–27)

In Matthew 11:28–30 Jesus, speaking as Wisdom, echoes those thoughts:

> "Come to me, all you that are weary and are carrying heavy burdens, and I will give you rest. Take my yoke upon you, and learn from me; for I am gentle and humble in heart, and you will find rest for your souls. For my yoke is easy, and my burden is light."

In Matthew, Sirach's "her yoke" becomes "my yoke." Thus the "serenity" or "rest" (same Greek word) comes from Jesus as *Sophia*. In this way, Matthew affirms that Jesus makes himself central in his teaching, so what the reader-learner must see is Jesus, a sage-teacher-*Sophia* and, as such, the source of wisdom and rest.

JOHN. John's prologue (1:1–14) sees Jesus as the "Word" (Gk. *logos*) in phrases that echo the language of Woman Wisdom: "He

---

10. Joseph A. Fitzmyer, *The Gospel according to Luke*, AB 27 (New York: Doubleday, 1981), 1:678.

was in the beginning with God. All things came into being through him" (1:2–3), echoing Proverbs 8:22–31 and Sirach 24. "What has come into being in him was life, and the life was the light of all people. The light shines in the darkness" (John 1:3–5). Proverbs also says of Woman Wisdom, "Long life is in her right hand; . . . She is a tree of life to those who lay hold of her" (Prov. 3:16, 18), and she says, "Whoever finds me finds life" (Prov. 8:35). The Wisdom of Solomon describes *Sophia* as unceasing radiance or a "pure emanation of the glory of the Almighty . . . a reflection of eternal light" (Wisd. 7:10, 25–26). John says that the "Word became flesh and lived among us, and we have seen his glory" (1:14). *Sophia* also was commanded by the Creator, " 'Make your dwelling in Jacob' " (Sir. 24:8–12).[11] *Sophia* invited people to come feast at her table, to "eat of my bread and drink of the wine I have mixed" (Prov. 9:1–5; Sir. 24:19–21), and John's Jesus makes wine (John 4), offers bread and fish, even the "bread of life," and says, "Those who eat my flesh and drink my blood have eternal life" (6:54).

In other words, New Testament writers, seeking to make sense of the events of Jesus' life, death, and resurrection, events that stretch ordinary speech, adopted language and concepts from the various texts of the wisdom tradition (alongside language from prophetic and priestly texts) to convey the significance and effects of Jesus upon their own understandings. Why would these authors borrow and adapt language from a female figure to describe the male Jesus? That they were willing to risk misunderstandings in a gender-conscious culture may suggest they saw strong resemblances between their understandings of Jesus and *Sophia*.

Jesus as Teacher

According to the Gospel accounts, what Jesus did most often was heal and teach. The Gospels describe Jesus performing twenty-six healings and exorcisms (not including various summaries), while they describe Jesus using numerous proverbial sayings and telling twenty-seven parables (not including summaries). The Greek word *didaskein* (to teach) and cognates occur ninety-nine times in the first three Gospels alone, virtually all relating to Jesus' activity. Teaching language is used in relation to Jesus more than twice as often as either preaching language (*kerusso*, *euangelizomai*, and

---

11. For additional "borrowings," see Raymond E. Brown, *The Gospel according to John*, AB 29 (New York: Doubleday, 1966), 1:cxii–cxvii.

cognates)[12] or prophecy language (*propheteuo* and cognates). John never writes of Jesus as preaching, while the Synoptics stop designating Jesus' activity as "preaching" very early in their Gospels (Matt. 11:1, 5; Mark 1:39; Luke 8:1, unless we include Luke 20:1, where he says Jesus was "teaching the people in the temple and telling the good news"). Yet in each of the Gospels, including John, Jesus teaches from beginning to end.

Recent historians have almost universally agreed that Jesus' teaching and healing activity is historically reliable, though some play down the significance of the teaching.[13] Marcus Borg and Ben Witherington agree with Bernard Brandon Scott's claim that it is an "undoubted fact that Jesus was a teacher in the wisdom tradition," and they call Jesus a sage-teacher.[14] Even historian Vermes observes, "Whatever else he may have been, Jesus was unquestionably an influential teacher."[15] On the other hand, Davies acknowledges that "practically all historical scholars engaged in Jesus research" agree that Jesus was a teacher, but since these scholars are all teachers themselves, Davies suspects their findings reflect their own interests. He points out that Paul finds Jesus as teacher of little interest, while Q, Thomas, Mark, Matthew, Luke, and John do not agree about the content of Jesus' teaching, which Davies thinks we ought to expect if teaching were important. Thus Davies contends that "it may well be that the very idea that Jesus was primarily a teacher came into being only after his death."[16]

---

12. The distribution of synoptic usage of teaching and preaching language is intriguing: All three Synoptics describe Jesus as preaching or proclaiming, teaching, and healing. But while Jesus is frequently described as teaching and healing all through each of the Gospels, he is less often described as preaching. Matthew used preaching language (*kerusso* and *euangelizomai*) of Jesus only five times, the last of which is in 11:5, while he used "to teach" nine times of Jesus in all parts of his Gospel. Mark used preaching language of Jesus only three times, the last in 1:39, while the teaching verb is used fifteen times of Jesus spread throughout the Gospel. Luke used preaching language eight times of Jesus, seven before 8:2 and once in 20:1, while "teaching" occurs fourteen times of Jesus in every part of the Gospel.

13. Smith, Crossan, and Vermes see Jesus' magiclike healing activity as central; see Smith, *Jesus the Magician*, 89, 115; Crossan, *The Historical Jesus*, 137–58; Vermes, *Jesus the Jew*, 58–80. Sanders acknowledges that both healing and teaching are historically valid, but they are part of a more central picture of Jesus as an eschatological prophet; see his *Jesus and Judaism*, 158–73.

14. Bernard Brandon Scott, *Hear Then the Parable: A Commentary on the Parables of Jesus* (Minneapolis: Fortress, 1989), 21; also Borg, *Jesus: A New Vision*, 97–124; and Witherington, *Jesus the Sage*, chap. 4.

15. Geza Vermes, *The Religion of Jesus the Jew* (Minneapolis: Fortress, 1993), 46.

16. Davies, *Jesus the Healer*, 9–21, 120–50. For a quick summary of other views, see Sanders, *Jesus and Judaism*, 1–13, where he rehearses how scholars differ

What do we expect to see when we call Jesus a *teacher*? If one sees teaching as a credentialed expert presenting formal, technical lectures to hundreds of students in a classroom setting, would occasional parables and folksy proverbial sayings by an itinerant even count as teaching? Interestingly, even as Davies denies the importance of Jesus' teaching, he and many other scholars seem to agree on what counts as teaching. Davies writes, "If he [Jesus] had a coherent message and neither we nor his known near contemporaries know for sure what it was, he ought not to be thought, first and foremost, to have been a great and challenging teacher."[17] Then he quotes Cadbury approvingly,

> I...propose...Jesus probably had no definite, unified, conscious purpose, that an absence of such a program is *a priori* likely and that it suits well the historical evidence....My impression is that Jesus was largely casual. He reacted to situations as they arose but probably he had hardly a program or a plan.[18]

What is being assumed here about teaching? First, Davies (and many others) assumes that teaching equals "teachings," the content or "what" is taught. Davies further assumes that such content, if it is to qualify as great or challenging ought to be coherent rather than casual, situational, or self-contradictory and that it ought to be part of a "definite, unified, conscious purpose" or "program." (Other historical-Jesus researchers also seek Jesus' central purpose or mission.) Davies's assumptions about what counts as teaching become quite explicit when he recommends "Jesus the Healer" as a better paradigm for the historical Jesus. Davies suggests, "Start with the question 'how did he heal' rather than the question 'what did he teach' and many things become clear."[19] In other words, Davies assumes teaching, unlike healing, has to do with *what*, not with *how*.

After surveying the teaching offered by biblical sages, reader-learners may well be puzzled by such assumptions. Indeed, Cadbury's comments fit the sages we have studied quite well. Their coherence was not located in the logical consistency of what they

---

on what kind of teacher Jesus was, but not that he was a teacher. Sanders himself is unwilling to say that Jesus was "first and foremost" a teacher (see p. 158), a judgment with which I agree. That view is too reductionist to fit the evidence of the texts.

17. Davies, *Jesus the Healer*, 13.

18. Ibid., 14, citing Cadbury, *The Peril of Modernizing Jesus* (London: SPCK, 1962), 141.

19. Davies, *Jesus the Healer*, 15.

taught, so much as in their desire to understand by whatever means necessary. Indeed, Davies's claim that Jesus cannot be called a "great and challenging teacher" because he did not have a coherent message and his hearers neither comprehended it nor agreed about it is a curious claim at best. If that were true, what are we to say about the author of Job, about the collectors of Proverbs, or about Qohelet, to say nothing of such great and challenging teachers as Kierkegaard and Wittgenstein? There has been vigorous discussion and disagreement about the coherence and comprehension of all these authors, in part because what they teach and how they teach are so closely yoked that *both* must be considered if there is to be comprehension. Perhaps Davies does exactly what he accuses others of doing, that is, bring his own notions of teaching to his reading of the text in a way that distorts understanding. If we approached Jesus' teaching with the expectations gleaned from the biblical sages, we would not expect to reduce teaching to what is taught, nor would we expect a twentieth-century notion of coherence and program.

Still, these scholars are rightly reluctant to say too much about the *how* of Jesus' teaching since the texts show no interest in accurate descriptions of pedagogical practices. This makes it difficult if not impossible to use the sources to reconstruct with historical reliability how Jesus taught.

Historians are agreed that teaching was important in Jesus' activity, though we do not have a clear picture of Jesus' teaching methods or what kinds of activity count as teaching in the Gospel texts. This means, at the least, that we must be wary of importing notions of teaching based upon contemporary schools, classrooms, lectures, assignments, tests, and so on. What we do have is texts that seek to evangelize readers, as in John 20:31, or, as Paul Achtemeier has argued for Mark, to persuade readers that Jesus was a teacher whose power as a teacher was made known by his miracles and his confrontation with authorities.[20] But if the texts are to succeed, readers must first become learners, come to know something about Jesus, and discern or comprehend in and through these texts what significance these events and beliefs might offer for steering through their own daily living.

---

20. Paul Achtemeier, " 'He Taught Them Many Things': Reflections on Marcan Christology," *Catholic Biblical Quarterly* 42:4 (October 1980), 474–75.

HOW WAS JESUS ADDRESSED?

In some cultures, people call each other by name, while in other cultures that is regarded as too familiar or even as disrespectful, so acquaintances are addressed by their titles or roles. For example, instead of saying, "Hello, Mr. Smith," one might say, "Hello, Professor." How do the Gospels portray people addressing Jesus?

Kyrie or Lord

In the synoptic Gospels, Jesus is most often addressed as *kyrie*, often translated in English as "lord" or "master" (the Greek *kyrie* translates the Hebrew *adon*, often with a suffix in *adonai* to mean "my lord"). In Aramaic, the equivalent is *mar* or *mari* for "my lord" (in 1 Cor. 16:22, see *Maran atha* or "Our Lord, come!"), which conveys respect, honor, or deference from the speaker to the one addressed. This was not a relation of equals. The one addressed as *Kyrie* was in charge, as when Luke describes the owners of a donkey as the donkey's *kyrioi* (plural for *kyrios*) or when Mark refers to the "master (*kyrios*) of the house" (Mark 13:35).[21]

Kyrie could be used as a form of address to a teacher, not to describe teaching but to show honor, so it would be a natural form of address by disciples to a master. In the first century, *mar/adon* was used as a title of respect for a holy man or miracle-worker.[22] Yet even here, as Vermes shows, the Aramaic and Greek have begun to interpenetrate by the first century, and "lord" became extended, especially in Matthew and Luke, to include "teacher."[23]

---

21. These terms of honor can be used of a human "lord" or a divine "Lord," and translators sometimes show the distinction by using capitalization. For example, since the Jews did not speak God's name (*YHWH*), when reading aloud, they said *adonai* or "my Lord" whenever YHWH appeared in the text. What cannot be inferred from the usage of the Greek *kyrie* is the theological conviction that whenever it is used of Jesus, it refers to his status as Son of God, and thus "Lord" in an ultimate sense, as it is sometimes used outside the synoptic Gospels. Aaron Milavec, *To Empower As Jesus Did: Acquiring Spiritual Power through Apprenticeship*, Toronto Studies in Theology 9 (Toronto: Mellen, 1982), 96–101.

22. Vermes, *Jesus the Jew*, 113–21.

23. Ibid., 122–26. Vermes' conclusion seems supported by Luke's substitution of the more deferential *epistate* (master) in miracle contexts where Matthew had *kyrie* (Lord) and where Mark has either *rabbi* or *didaskale* (teacher). It is difficult to know how much to make of these terms as historical evidence, since Matthew's and Luke's emendations of Mark may have christological import. For example, Matthew and Luke never allow "teacher" to be a term of direct address to Jesus by his disciples, and so they substitute "lord" or "master" where Mark has "teacher" in the mouth of disciples. Many have suggested this has christological significance, though Vermes' discussion posits that there are numerous linguistic and historical considerations to be accounted for as well.

The pedagogical potential of *kyrios* may be more easily seen in another common English translation, "master." For example, note how differently translators render the same word and add capitals (not in the Greek) to try to capture the flavor of the texts:

Jesus said to him, "Away with you, Satan! for it is written,

'Worship the Lord (*kyrion*) your God,
and serve only him.' " (Matt. 4:10)

She said, "Yes, Lord (*kyrie*), yet even the dogs eat the crumbs that fall from their master's (*kyrion*) table." (Matt. 15:27)

While the title *kyrios* may only hint at Jesus' actual teaching activity, it is consistent with the respect accorded teachers in first-century culture and with reports of the hearers' sense of Jesus' authority. It may also carry some pedagogical import in ascribing authority and in recognizing some degree of mastery or being in charge of others.

Didaskale *or Teacher*

"Teacher" is the second most frequently used form of address to Jesus in the Synoptics.[24] Twelve times Mark has Jesus addressed as "Teacher" (Gk. *didaskale*). Matthew deleted seven of these, and Luke deleted five, but each added seven or eight more uses. In Matthew and Luke, *only* nondisciples addressed Jesus as "Teacher" (*didaskale*), while the disciples never did. Matthew amended Mark's text in two ways: either he deleted *didaskale* and used no direct address form, or he substituted *kyrie* for *didaskale*. Luke often used *epistata* (often translated "master") in place of *didaskale*, a term used in the LXX of the "taskmasters" of Egypt overseeing Israelite slaves (Exod. 1:11; 5:14), of overseers in the building of the temple (1 Kings 5:16; 2 Chron. 2:2), and of officers in command of soldiers (2 Kings 25:19; Jer. 52:25). Perhaps Luke used it to suggest Jesus' authority.[25] Yet sometimes one is appointed "taskmaster" or "overseer" or "officer" because one has "mastered" the tasks that one now oversees. Clearly Matthew and Luke had a particular "agenda" of their own regarding the use of "teacher" as direct address (and also for *didaskalos*,

---

24. Jesus is often addressed as "Teacher" in each Gospel, although never as "Preacher."

25. James Donaldson, "The Title Rabbi in the Gospels — Some Reflections on the Evidence of the Synoptics," *Jewish Quarterly Review* 63:4 (April 1973), 289.

"teacher" used as a descriptive term), though that agenda was not christological.[26]

Is this difference in usage significant? Did Matthew and Luke prefer honorific to functional forms of address? Since they were written later than Mark, do they reflect a greater sense of honor or authority attributed to Jesus? Still, *didaskale* could be used as a title of honor, so its use reveals little about the nature of Jesus' teaching activity, except that he was respected. So what kind of teacher was he? The Gospels also call Jesus a *rabbi*, yet with a difference.

Rabbi

The Gospels depict Jesus as being called *rabbei* (or *rabbounei*, "my rabbi"): Matthew (four times: 23:7, 8; 26:25, 49), Mark (four times: 9:5; 10:51; 11:21; 14:45), and especially John (eight times: 1:38, 49; 3:2, 26; 4:31; 6:25; 9:2; 11:8), but never in Luke, who avoided Hebrew terms with which his Greek readers would be unfamiliar. Interestingly, the direct-address uses in Mark and Matthew never imply a link with teaching, nor do they occur in teaching settings, since "rabbi" could be used as a term of respect for any exalted person, whether he actually taught or not.[27] The Gospel of John does connect Jesus as teacher with the term "rabbi," yet John's usage is much later and is usually filled with christological significance (see esp. John 1:49; 3:2), so it cannot be treated simply as historical description.

There is another problem. Solomon Zeitlin flatly asserts that "the title rabbi was not used by the Judeans at the time of Jesus" and thus is an anachronism.[28] Despite the existence of considerable literature from the period, such as the Apocrypha, Josephus, Philo, and the tannaitic literature prior to the destruction of the temple in 70 c.e., "in none of this literature does the word Rabbi occur."[29] Thus the founders of the two most important rabbinic schools, Hillel and Shammai, both contemporaries of Jesus, were not themselves called *rabbi*. Zeitlin concludes that while the Gospel writers used the term, it was unlikely to have been available as a

---

26. Achtemeier, " 'He Taught Them Many Things,' " 473–74.

27. Karl H. Rengstorf, "didaskalos," in *Theological Dictionary of the New Testament* (Grand Rapids: Eerdmans, 1964), 3:153.

28. Solomon Zeitlin, "The Pharisees," *Jewish Quarterly Review* 51:2 (1961), 122.

29. Solomon Zeitlin, "The Title Rabbi in the Gospels Is Anachronistic," *Jewish Quarterly Review* 59:2 (October 1968), 158.

form of direct address for Jesus within his lifetime. On the other hand, while Hershel Shanks agrees that "rabbi" was first used later than Jesus' time as a title for a formal office, it is possible some variant (such as *rav*) could have been used as a title for an itinerant preacher such as Jesus, even before it became used as a title for ordained scholars and official leaders.[30] Martin Hengel argues that while some variant of "rabbi" may have been used as a form of address to Jesus, still use of the term is now "extremely misleading," for "rabbi" was not yet "the established title of an ordained scribe."[31]

After the destruction of the temple in 70 C.E., the title "rabbi" carried specific parameters: the rabbi was ordained, after having been the disciple or pupil (Heb. and Aramaic *talmid*) of a rabbi. This rabbi then taught "seated" (cf. Matt. 23:2; "seated on the chair of Moses") indicating that even creative teaching fulfills the law's "chains of transmission" from Moses through the master to the new rabbi and into the future.[32] Yet there is no evidence Jesus studied with a learned teacher, nor that he was ordained. Indeed the reports that the crowds were surprised at his authority may well imply they saw him as "unauthorized."[33]

Still, Jesus seems to have acted something like a rabbi: he was a teacher; he had disciples; he offered theological, civic, and ritual opinions on controversial matters; and his opinion was sought.[34] Perhaps the ambiguity leads to attempts to redefine Jesus in light of later rabbinic ideals. As Jacob Neusner notes, when Jesus asked people what they thought he was, he asked them to "reframe everything they knew in the encounter with the one they did not know."[35] Ernst Käsemann observes that the portrayal of Jesus as

---

30. Hershel Shanks, "Origins of the Title 'Rabbi,'" *Jewish Quarterly Review* 59:2 (October 1968), 152–55.

31. See Martin Hengel's discussion in footnotes 19, 20, and 22 in *The Charismatic Leader and His Followers* (New York: Crossroad, 1981), 42–44.

32. Safrai, *The Literature of the Sages* (Philadelphia: Fortress, 1987), 184–85. During this later period, sages and scribes became more sharply distinguished. Sages created oral Torah teaching and made legal decisions, whereas scribes were elementary Bible teachers and clerks or Bible copyists (148–53).

33. Donaldson, "The Title Rabbi in the Gospels," 290. See also Ephraim E. Urbach, *The Sages: Their Concepts and Beliefs* (Cambridge: Harvard University Press, 1987), 593–603.

34. Gunther Bornkamm, *Jesus of Nazareth* (New York: Harper and Row, 1960), 56–60; David Abernethy, *Understanding the Teaching of Jesus* (New York: Seabury, 1983), 124–25.

35. Jacob Neusner, *Judaism in the Beginning of Christianity* (Philadelphia: Fortress, 1984), 37.

"the teacher of wisdom accords but ill with that of the rabbi, because the former lives by the immediacy of contemplation, such as is familiar to us from the parables of Jesus, while the latter's existence is determined by meditation and by the bond which keeps him tied to Scripture."[36]

So the forms of address ("Master," "Teacher," or "Rabbi") offer little solid information about what kind of teacher Jesus was. Can we find some clues in how the disciples are described?

WHAT KIND OF DISCIPLES

According to the synoptic picture of Jesus, he sought and called his own disciples, whereas a rabbi's disciples sought him.[37] The sage-teachers also expected learners to seek teachers (Prov. 4:1–9; 7:1–4; Sir. 6:34, 36; Tob. 4:18), yet *Sophia* took the initiative calling people to turn aside, feast, learn (Prov. 1:20–33; 8:1–36; 9:1–12; Sir. 24:19; Wisd. 6:12–16), and Sirach invited learners to come to his school and learn (51:13–26).

Two linguistic puzzles concerning disciples, discussed by the British scholar T. W. Manson, are of particular interest. Manson observed that the term "disciple" (Gk. *mathetes*, literally "learner") is very common in the Synoptics (over 150 uses), yet occurs only five times in Jesus' sayings.[38] The usual Hebrew and Aramaic word for "disciple" when referring to a rabbinic learner is *talmid*. The Hebrew Bible often emphasized teaching (Moses was called a teacher, and Israel learns; Deut. 5:1; 6:1), yet *mathetes* (disciple, learner) never appears in the Greek translation of the Hebrew Bible, and *talmid* appears only once, in 1 Chronicles 25:8.[39] If teaching and learning were so important, especially learning the commandments, why was there so little use of the

---

36. Ernst Käsemann, *Essays on New Testament Themes* (London: SCM, 1964), 41.

37. Celia Deutsch, *Hidden Wisdom and the Easy Yoke: Wisdom, Torah, and Discipleship in Matthew 11:25–30* (Sheffield: JSOT, 1987), 143.

38. T. W. Manson, *The Teaching of Jesus: Studies of Its Form and Content*, rev. ed. (Cambridge: Cambridge University Press, 1935), 237.

39. In this passage, David's officers selected 288 persons for special work and sought to insure that their skills were passed on to their sons. Some were trained in prophecy; some, in lyre playing; and some, in singing — "teacher and pupil alike" — or we could say as well, father and son alike.

term "learner"?[40] And why does *talmid* appear so frequently in the rabbinic writings after 70 C.E.?

This lack of usage cannot be attributed to the use of the Greek language, for the teacher-learner relation (*didaskalos-mathetes*) was well known in Greek culture. The Sophists used the master-disciple relation as like an apprenticeship, with a disciple dependent upon and showing allegiance to a teacher, which fits the descriptions of Jesus and his disciples. Socrates, Plato, and Aristotle vehemently rejected use of the term *mathetes*, apparently because of their contempt for the Sophists, who taught for money. Socrates insisted his teaching was not for sale. He also insisted that since he offered fellowship in an intellectual life, his role was not "master" but the first among equals in inquiry.[41]

On the other hand, in the first century, "fellowship" increasingly was used to describe the master-disciple (*didaskalos-mathetes*) relations among the Epicureans and the Neo-Pythagoreans and especially with Apollonius of Tyana. In these groups, the person and words of the teacher, as well as the communal fellowship and its traditions played a large role and took on a religious quality.[42] Yet if the Synoptics found these terms appropriate in describing Jesus' disciples, why did they depict Jesus as using the terms so seldom? Was loyalty to master or to tradition not important to Jesus? Jesus' disciples were not initiated into an intellectual fellowship or modes of philosophical argument. There seems to have been no insistence on mastery of texts, on memorization, or on faithful transmission of Jesus' sayings. What kind of master-disciple relation was this?

The second linguistic puzzle Manson noticed occurs in a Gospel saying in both Matthew and Luke (therefore Q) that has perplexing variations:

> "He who loves father or mother more than me *is not worthy of me* ... and he who does not take up his cross and follow me *is not*

---

40. Rengstorf, "*mathetes*," in *Theological Wordbook of the New Testament*, 4:426–27. Rengstorf cannot be followed uncritically, for he often allows his theological convictions to shape his linguistic observations, a temptation described by James Barr, *The Semantics of Biblical Language* (London: Oxford University Press, 1961). For example, Rengstorf contends that the reason for this linguistic absence is that Israel had no special learner and no tradition linked to a person who thus called forth disciples *because* theirs was a religion of revelation, and thus they were all subject to the will of God. It is far from clear that theological explanations determine linguistic development.

41. Rengstorf, "*mathetes*," 4:417–20.

42. Ibid., 4:420–26.

worthy of me." (Matt. 10:37–38, emphasis added, Manson's own translation)

"If anyone comes to me and does not hate his own father and mother . . . *he cannot be my disciple.* Whoever does not bear his own cross and come after me, *cannot be my disciple."* (Luke 14:26–27, emphasis added, Manson's translation)

Manson attempted to account for this variation by trying to reconstruct what might have been the original Aramaic version of these sayings, assuming that "disciple" was *talmid,* to see if a copyist might have misread the original. It did not work. Then he noticed that "not worthy of me" in Aramaic is *shewe lyi* and there is another Aramaic word for "disciple" or "learner" — *shewilya.* If that is the word used for "disciple," it becomes easy to see how the words "not worthy of me" might be mistaken for "disciple."[43] Manson contends these two different Aramaic words for disciple or learner had different connotations: *talmid* meant "student-learner," as used of one who studied texts in a school or classroom, whereas *shewilya* meant "apprentice-learner," as used in reference to a weaver's apprentice, a blacksmith's apprentice, or a carpenter's apprentice.[44] Apprenticeship "is personal, hands on, and experiential" and is used "where there is more to performing the role at hand than reading a description of its content can communicate."[45] "All in all, the education that apprentices receive has as much to do with how to behave as it has to do with mastering specific tasks."[46]

If a disciple is an apprentice, then the teacher is the master, not just of texts and sayings but of the practices that are learned, not so much by reading about them, but by engaging in them. Apprentice learning requires observation, imitation, trial and error, learning from mistakes, formation of habits and skills, reflection on why things happened as they did and what could be done differently next time, and so on:[47] "A master seeks to progressively

---

43. Manson, *The Teaching of Jesus,* 237–38. Critical readers will observe that the saying is from Q, which was likely in Greek. Thus Manson still offers no satisfactory explanation for how the variance occurs if both Matthew and Luke were using a Greek source. Still, the observations concerning two different terms for disciples are appropriate, even if they do not suffice to explain these particular texts.

44. Ibid., 238.

45. Michael W. Coy, ed., *Apprenticeship: From Theory to Method and Back Again* (Albany: State University of New York Press, 1989), 1–2.

46. Ibid., 3.

47. See the study by Milavec, *To Empower As Jesus Did,* 83–91. While Milavec's study lacks today's historical rigor, his presentation of apprenticeship as

alter his/her disciples' habits of perception and standards of judgement."[48] Finally, apprentice learning cannot be done by a solitary
individual; it requires collaboration, a sharing of practices.

Michael Goldberg has argued persuasively that even later rabbinic discipleship consisted not alone in attending lectures, reading
texts, and mastering the material. It focused upon personal service
to the master as a way of "getting to know a particular rabbi's way
of life." This was a practical course of study, because "the rab-
bis' knowledge could only be taught from life to life."[49] Goldberg
warns that "what we look for" in teaching has been profoundly
shaped in recent years by the modernist rationalization of social
institutions, so in educational settings today we hear much about
discipline and disciplines but seldom about disciples. This leads us
to see teaching and learning as following a method or a subject
matter, rather than following the life of another human being.[50]

While no single designation may be adequate by itself (Jesus
is also fittingly called an eschatological prophet, a renewer of Israel, and a healer of the ill), we can call Jesus a sage-teacher
with some historical confidence. But as we do so, we must beware of imposing twentieth-century notions of classroom teaching
onto a first-century apprenticeship. Perhaps Manson's linguistic
puzzles lead to a new and more appropriate picture of what kind
of teaching and learning these texts presume.

We now turn to ask our three pedagogical questions directly of
the texts. Will they confirm what we have just proposed?

HOW TO READ AND BE READ

The sages taught not only how to read texts but also how to read
or discern the creation and human behavior. In Luke, the first fully
described act of ministry is an act of reading, which can also be
read as an act of teaching others to read and be read.[51] Luke paints

---

applied to Jesus' relation with the disciples is faithful to what is known of that
relation.

48. Ibid., 91.

49. Michael Goldberg, "Discipleship: Basing One Life On Another — It's Not
What You Know But Who You Know," in *Theology without Foundations: Reli-
gious Practice and the Future of Theological Truth*, ed. Stanley Hauerwas et al.
(Nashville: Abingdon, 1994), 290–94.

50. Ibid., 289–90.

51. A lucid description of various reading strategies for the Gospel texts can be
found in Robert M. Fowler, *Let the Reader Understand: Reader-Response Criticism
and the Gospel of Mark* (Minneapolis: Fortress, 1991), chaps. 2–3. The reading or

the following picture: Jesus returned to Galilee (Luke 4:14–15) "with the power of the spirit" and taught in synagogues, attracting praise "by everyone." He then went home to Nazareth, to the synagogue "as was his custom." He stood up to read from the scroll of Isaiah:

"The Spirit of the Lord is upon me,
    because he has anointed me to bring good news to the poor.
He has sent me to proclaim release to the captives
    and recovery of sight to the blind,
    to let the oppressed go free,
to proclaim the year of the Lord's favor."
                                        (Luke 4:18–19; cf. Isa. 61:1–2)

Thereupon Jesus "sat down" (the customary way to teach) and said, simply, "Today this scripture has been fulfilled in your hearing" (4:21). Matthew (13:53–58) and Mark (6:1–6) omitted the Isaiah quotation but had the people respond to Jesus' teaching saying, "Where did this man get this wisdom?" (Matt. 13:54; par. Mark 6:2). Luke, on the other hand, omitted all reference to wisdom here. Instead the neighbors were "amazed" at Jesus' "gracious words" (Luke 4:22).

By his example, Jesus affirmed that his hearers should attend to the text. But did he himself attend to the text in a conventional way? While we have no way of knowing what else he might have said, Luke's Jesus claimed no control of this text. Instead, *the text has read him!* According to Luke, Jesus said, in effect, "This Isaiah text has told me who I am and what I am to do with my life. The spirit is upon me, and I am sent — with good news, release, sight, recovery, freedom, and the Lord's favor!" In other words, as an exemplary reader, teaching others how to read, Luke's Jesus showed his hearers that a proper reading might well mean (require?) allowing oneself to be read so that one might come to know who one is and what one is to do.

How did Luke depict the response of Jesus' hearers? Initially, they were very enthusiastic: "All spoke well of him and were amazed at the gracious words that came from his mouth. They said, 'Is not this Joseph's son?'" (Luke 4:22). To what were they responding? We do not know. But it does not seem they were learn-

---

interpretation of the Luke text that follows is indebted to the provocative reading of this text by Stephen D. Moore, *Mark and Luke in Poststructuralist Perspectives: Jesus Begins to Write* (New Haven: Yale University Press, 1992), 125–26.

ing to read as Jesus had suggested, that is, reading as "being read." They seemed to hope he would do what they had heard of him doing in Capernaum (4:23). They wanted to be spectators (recall Matt. 11 and Luke 7!). They were willing to see good news done for others. But if, instead, they were to receive the good news themselves, they would have to allow themselves to be read as those who were among the poor, the blind, the captives, and the oppressed. Yet Luke depicted Jesus' hometown folks as unwilling to let the text read them into the story. Instead, "they were filled with rage" (4:28), and so Jesus left them.

While the text Jesus read (and was read by) was from the prophet Isaiah and not from a wisdom text, Proverbs 1:24–28 describes how Woman Wisdom will deal with learners who refuse her offer: she will not answer when calamity strikes them and will even laugh and mock them. This sounds harsh, but apparently neither Woman Wisdom nor Jesus (according to Luke) was willing to assume responsibility that rightly belonged to learners.

What does the text do with or to reader-learners? Luke claimed to be writing an "orderly account" of eyewitness reports (1:2–3). Notice the alternation of visual, tactile, and oral detail in this text: the Isaiah text was read aloud, but Jesus specifically "unrolled the scroll" (4:17) — a vivid visual detail. The text makes touching (by the spirit, being anointed, release of bonds), blindness, and seeing ("recovery of sight") central, and when Jesus sat down, "The eyes of all . . . were fixed on him" (4:20). The text evokes reflection on those who *look* but do not *see*. Then Jesus said, "Today this scripture has been fulfilled in your hearing" (4:21). Yet all they could *see* was Joseph's son, and all they could *hear* were "gracious words."

Did they, do reader-learners, hear the words, allow them inside so they can do their work and be fulfilled? Or do reader-learners, with the listeners, only notice what is outside, for example, how remarkable it is that Joseph's son should be able to do this! Readers who hear can become aware that to be free and to see require that they let go of their blindness and see differently, more truthfully, their own need as well as that of others. This is to read with one's whole being — eyes, ears, sense of touch, and an open spirit that lets reading inside so that learning can take place in a way quite different from the grasping mastery of an external text. Is this the kind of reading that Luke's text itself evokes and expects?

WHAT IS WORTH LEARNING?

Many scholars have described the content of Jesus' teaching, that is, what he and the Gospels want people to learn. We cannot do an exhaustive treatment, so we will focus especially upon what is most central in the texts that we can affirm with some historical confidence and that is of pedagogical interest.

God's Ruling (The Kingdom of God)

Jesus used the motif of the "kingdom of God" frequently to show what God's way of ruling or governing is like.[52] Does this image carry on and reframe the sages' ongoing discussion of God's just governance of the universe and the fear of the Lord?

WHO IS GOD, AND HOW DOES GOD ACT? Before the time of Jesus, "the Lord is King" most often referred to God as Creator, "Master of the Universe," the victor over chaos, sustaining the earth.[53] In the creation story, God gave dominion to humans, not absolute rule but a stewardship on behalf of God. "We have no King but the Lord" likely had covenantal roots and may have served as a battle cry in the period before the monarchy, thus confirming God's claim. This claim was repeated even in the monarchy, often by prophets. For example, Nathan bluntly concluded his parable to David (2 Sam. 12:7) with "You are the man!" reminding King David to rule in accord with the Lord's standards, not only his own. Through the centuries, Israel hoped for a Davidic successor, a "shoot from the stump of Jesse" who might end the reign of foreign oppressors. Thus the "kingdom" image became linked with expectations of ethical behavior consistent with that of God — in a mood of hope.

The Book of Proverbs referred to kings and how to behave in their presence, and we saw those sayings could as well be used metaphorically for ordinary people. Jesus' approach was more striking. Rather than use the imagery of kings to speak of ordi-

---

52. The phrase "kingdom of God" does not come from the Hebrew Bible (although the concept of God's kingly ruling appears often), and it appears rarely in other Jewish literature prior to Jesus. (The phrase does occur once in Wisd. 10:10.) Prior to the New Testament, kingdom language occurs mostly in poetic contexts, especially in the Psalms and the Prophets, and "even in the narrative books, God's kingship is a poetic metaphor." See Meier, *A Marginal Jew*, 2:238, 245.

53. I shall not rehearse the extended scholarly discussion of Jesus' use of the "kingship" of God, though for those who are interested, I find the approach offered by Bruce Chilton and J. I. H. MacDonald in *Jesus and the Ethics of the Kingdom* (London: SPCK, 1987) to be both highly compatible with my understanding of Jesus' approach to teaching and especially instructive in dealing with the issues of eschatology and ethics.

nary people, Jesus used images of ordinary people or images from creation to talk about God as King! For example, in the parable of the prodigal son (Luke 15:11–32), a father, following traditional laws, perhaps against his own better judgment, gave his younger son a cash inheritance (since the elder son would inherit the property). The parable does not invite hearers and reader-learners to empathize with the younger son, for not only did he leave home, but he squandered his inheritance in "dissolute living" (15:13). Then he suffered the natural consequences, being forced to feed pigs (unclean) and "dying of hunger." That is justice — he got what he deserved. The father also treated his elder son completely fairly. Despite that, the elder son finds it difficult to share his father's exuberant joy at the younger son's return. Here, contrary to convention, father/King/God's "compassion" (15:20) and love refused to exclude, separate, and reject, even when the son had made himself alien. Did the son deserve it? Did the son repent? The reader knows the younger son's thoughts, but the father had compassion "while he was still far off." Reader-learners are offered a simple, realistic, yet complex picture of love and justice juxtaposed — both honored, yet in natural tension. Is this analogous to the disputed issues of Job?

In the parable of the prodigal son, Jesus offers a human father as a worthy model for a king or a King, as he does also in the parable of the owner of a vineyard who hires workers at various times in the day, yet pays those hired last, who only worked an hour, as much as those who worked all day (Matt. 20:1–15). This owner has honored his contract with those hired earlier (thus acting justly), yet he was quite generous to those hired last. In this parable, the doctrine of retribution is not exactly denied, as in Job, yet it also is not the determining principle in the owner's actions. There is both order and also a counterorder. The owner is both fair and generous, which is within his rights. There is no strict formula by which one could predict or calculate his actions, just as Qohelet insisted with his "who knows" refrain.

Another parable points in the same direction, and it is the only parable in which a king is the central character. This king behaves strangely (Matt. 18:23–34). A debtor who cannot pay is condemned to jail, pleads for mercy, and to his surprise, the king changes his mind, not only showing mercy but generously canceling his whole debt. Reader-learners might ask if it is fair or just that the king demands payment? Yes. Is it just that he then cancels the debt? No, for while it is a merciful or compassionate act, strictly speaking it contravenes the doctrine of reciprocity (which a king has authority and power to do). Does this suggest that justice or retribution is not the only principle to be considered in governance? The Lord's speeches in Job led us to suspect that when it comes to things like snow, ice, and ostriches — creating and sustaining creation — retribution may not be as useful as some other kind of wisdom. In this parable, a king decides it is wise to give his slave another chance and cancels his debt, only to have him tortured shortly thereafter. Why? The slave, having been shown compassion, did not himself show compassion to those who owed him money (Matt. 18:34). Strict formulas of retribution do not explain everything. Sometimes suffering is not brought on by sin, and sometimes there is undeserved mercy. Jesus' parables not only use ordinary people as models for kings but also suggest that ordinary people ("subjects") act (compassionately) like kings.

Ironically, Matthew applies this parable to the later church as well, but in so doing, Matthew's Jesus tells Peter, in the verses immediately preceding this parable, to forgive seventy times seven (Matt. 18:21–22), yet the king did not. Which is right? Is this another instance of juxtaposing contradictory sayings (e.g., Prov. 26:4–5), thus requiring reader-learners to discern what it is time for?

Jesus' sayings seem to invite the hearers and reader-learners into an imaginative space where they can see God's ruling. In that space, conventional standards are seen in the light of strikingly different standards — and we catch a glimpse of how things might work out if ordinary people were to live within God's way of working.

WHO ARE SUBJECTS OF THE KING, AND HOW SHOULD THEY ACT? Where there is a king, there must be subjects. In the Gospel portrayals of Jesus' teaching, either there is an ambiguity in "being a subject" of the King, or else there is a reinterpretation of "subject" that is pedagogically very important. The ambiguity begins with the King's behavior being portrayed using ordinary people and continues with the expectation that merciful acts might be appropriate for both King and subject.

Jesus often drew attention to the link between what people say and what they do and the link between their role or status as subjects of a King and how they actually behave. For example:

> He [Jesus] began to tell the people this parable: "A man planted a vineyard, and leased it to tenants, and went to another country for a long time. When the season came, he sent a slave to the tenants in order that they might give him his share of the produce of the vine-

yard; but the tenants beat him and sent him away empty-handed."
(Luke 20:9–10)

This parable invites reader-learners into a familiar space: a lease
relation, which defines the roles and responsibilities of owner and
tenants. The parable expects reader-learners to assume that this
owner character (God?) is acting justly, both in setting up the
agreement and in expecting the tenants to behave according to its
terms. The tenants are subjects in a double sense. They are not
objects but subjects expected to act on their own initiative, for example, in maintaining the property given to their care. It is in their
own best interest (as well as the owner's) to see that the vineyard
flourishes. But their being tenants also defines and delimits some of
their actions, for they are also subject to the owner of the vineyard
and thus must provide him a fair share of the profits. When the
tenants deny the owner his share, they also deny (in deed) their
own status. Their behavior shows they regard themselves as no
longer tenants, subject to the owner's ruling authority. They are
acting as if they were owners! When reader-learners reach the end
of the tenth verse, already the thought has surfaced: "They can't do
that! That isn't right!" This concrete story focuses reader-learners'
attention upon the tenants' self-contradiction and creates a desire
in reader-learners to take the side of the owner character (God).
Again we see the similarity with the parable of Job. The Lord affirmed Job's speaking the truth about God (being a subject and
expressing his agency truthfully) and also challenged Job for assuming too much agency, that is, accusing God of injustice despite
Job's having only a finite understanding.

The parables of the vineyard and the prodigal son, as well as
Job and Qohelet, picture God's ruling as including justice but not
only that. The owner of the vineyard sent four messengers, including his own son, whom the tenants killed, before he finally
gave them what they deserved. The parable also reveals the foolishness of subjects who act as what they are not. Thus did Jesus'
teaching (like the sages') simultaneously affirm justice, unmask self-
deception, and demonstrate that actions speak as loudly as words,
whether for good or ill. Still, justice is not the only motif worth
learning.

If it is important to learn the nature of a subject in the kingdom, it is equally important pedagogically. One can easily forget
that a subject is intrinsically relational, with responsibilities and
limits as well as rights. Tenants, a king's subject, and learners are

all necessarily subject to someone or something other than themselves, especially if learning takes the form of an apprenticeship.
As a teacher is a subject, both a responsible actor and also subject to the subject matter, so also the subject matter acts upon
teacher and learner, yet is subjected to what the teacher does with
it. The learner is an actor in her own learning, yet subject to the
teacher and/or the subject matter. In each instance, the parables
suggest that subjects are to become more like that to which they
are subject. Jesus made a similar claim with a proverbial saying:
"A disciple is not above the teacher, nor a slave above the master;
it is enough for the disciple to be like the teacher, and the slave like
the master" (Matt. 10:24; par. Luke 6:40). Jesus also said, "Whoever does not receive the kingdom of God as a little child will never
enter it" (Mark 10:15). A child knows more completely what it
means to be a subject and accepts that condition more naturally.
Adults must often learn to recapture that sense.

History has taught us that there are dangers in adopting the
"kingdom" metaphor. People imagine power, authority, and domination and try to act like lords rather than as subjects. Educators
like Paulo Freire have rightly insisted that such contests of power,
authority, and domination are pedagogically unhealthy and ethi-
cally untenable,[54] so the words of both justice and of being subject
are important. In many families, schools, churches, universities,
and theological institutions, patterns of power and domination are
deeply embedded in institutional structures, in teaching practices,
in administrative structures, and even in interpersonal relations,
despite democratic and collegiality talk. (Language is revealing. In
such institutions, teachers are often described as "serving" on com-
mittees, yet teaching itself is almost never described as "serving"
students.)

In making the metaphor "kingdom of God" central and defining
humans as subjects becoming more and more like the King, Jesus
gave numerous concrete examples of what God's kingdom might
look like in daily living. As subjects in God's ruling, or children in
God's family, in observing how God rules we learn not only something about God but also something about how we can become
more fully what we are: both just and loving.

---

54. See especially Paulo Freire's *Pedagogy of the Oppressed* (New York:
Seabury, 1970). Many religious educators and others have been heavily influenced
by him, including myself.

Love God, One Another, Your Neighbor, Your Enemies

Like the Proverbial sages, Jesus could be very traditional, quoting texts and using imperatives in his teaching, but often he added his own twist. For example, sometimes Jesus quoted traditional biblical commands, such as Deuteronomy 6:5, "You shall love the Lord your God with all your heart, and with all your soul, and with all your mind" (Matt. 22:37; par. Mark 12:30).[55] Then he refocused tradition by joining it with another quote from Leviticus 19:18, "You shall love your neighbor as yourself" (Matt. 22:39; par. Mark 12:31).[56] Similarly, he quoted and then sharpened the tradition so that his hearers (and later reader-learners) could focus upon what distinguishes God's rule, making the subjects' role explicit: "You have heard that it was said, 'You shall love your neighbor and hate your enemy.' But I say to you, Love your enemies and pray for those who persecute you, so that you may be children of your Father in heaven" (Matt. 5:43–45). To be loving is to be like the ruler of the kingdom, or a father, not just part of a love-ethic program, unless we consider the nature of God to be a program for humanity.[57]

Are Jesus' imperatives rules? Jesus refused repeatedly to play the familiar game of "tell me the rules to get the prize." He rejected calculation. Even in commanding love of neighbor and enemy, he specified no particular behaviors: "Jesus nowhere prescribes regular church attendance or the tithe. He did not issue detailed instructions on sexual morality for his followers or whether they should drink wine or dance. He *does* tell them that they are to love their enemies."[58] For example, Jesus' parable of the good Samaritan (Luke 10:30–37) provides no list of neighborly actions or rules for neighbors, even when Jesus was asked for one. Rather he depicts an occasion for choosing a specific loving action (take the

---

55. In the Gospels, the Hebrew versions of these commands were combined and adapted to Greek thinking in adding "with all your mind." There is no way to tell whether that adaptation and addition was done by Jesus or by oral tradition or by the Gospel writers.

56. Luke puts these commands in the mouth of a lawyer (Luke 10:27), but Jesus agreed. While each evangelist used the love commands in a manner suited to his own interests and while scholars differ on which form was more original, all agree that such teachings are characteristic and authentic with Jesus. See, e.g., Victor Furnish, *The Love Command in the New Testament* (Nashville: Abingdon, 1972), 24; and E. P Sanders, *The Historical Figure of Jesus* (London: Penguin, 1993), 202.

57. Chilton and MacDonald, *Jesus and the Ethics*, 37; Pheme Perkins, *Love Commands in the New Testament* (New York: Paulist, 1982), 45.

58. William Klassen, *Love of Enemies: The Way to Peace* (Philadelphia: Fortress, 1984), 7.

wounded man to a hospital) based upon what is needed at that
moment. Indeed, in this parable, it is not even immediately clear
which is neighbor or which is enemy, since for a Jew a Samaritan could be either. Jesus provided little basis upon which people
could study what is required and then calculate whether the effort
was worth it. Rather Jesus seems to have reflected upon God, who
God is, what God has created, and how God acts and thus decided what are God's intentions for humans and how humans can
become more like God.[59]

Many today see teaching as mastering right thinking or training
in right behavior. Such an emphasis has led to extended ethical,
psychological, and theological debates about heteronomy versus
autonomy. Educators ask, Is learning from the outside in (heteronomy) or from the inside out (autonomy)? Jesus seems to agree with
both because the pedagogical task is more basic than what one
thinks or does but has to do with who one is. Who am I becoming?
Whose subject am I? Who am I becoming like?

Jesus' love command is communal as well as individual. Unless
one has been loved, one does not even survive physically, let alone
learn to be loving. For loving to come to seem natural, it must be a
natural part of one's experiential world. Loving one's enemies not
only requires courage, but such courage must be communal, even
when expressed by an individual. Since the command to love one's
enemies runs contrary to so much social convention, it requires
communal support to work.[60]

Strikingly, Jesus is portrayed as confronting those with whom
he disagreed, *but he is never depicted as coercing others or as defending himself in any way* — a remarkable omission since he lived
within a culture of enforced imperial oppression. The commands
to love suggest that one's identity is not defined primarily by op-
positions. There is evil in Jesus' world — threats abound — yet
there is little sense of defending oneself against such evil; rather,
the image is of engaging the evil with love. What is gained by insisting on how different "we" are from "them"? Jesus' parable of
the good Samaritan undermines simplistic polarities by challenging
what we take for granted about us and them. Similarly, the parable
of the prodigal son affirms that both sons are good and bad, so
clear lines cannot be drawn unequivocally. Identity is formed, not

---

59. Perkins, *Love Commands in the New Testament*, 6–7.
60. This is what the radical new attempt in South Africa, using the Truth and
Reconciliation Commission to heal the enmity of apartheid, is learning.

by maximizing our differences from those unlike ourselves, but by becoming more like the one who rules.[61]

Holiness and Compassion, Words and Deeds

If Jesus urged loving one's enemies, why is he depicted as so often in conflict with the Pharisees over issues of Torah teaching about holiness and purity? There is much misunderstanding about these matters.[62] The Gospels' portrayal of the conflicts over holiness and ritual purity may reflect later conflicts as the early church separated itself from Judaism.[63]

The Torah teaching does command, "You shall be holy, for I the LORD your God am holy" (Lev. 19:2), and spells out behaviors that are human reflections of the behavior of the Holy One. Jesus

---

61. Pheme Perkins, *Jesus as Teacher* (New York: Cambridge University Press, 1990), 101.

62. Early church disagreements surrounding holiness continue, often with the following stereotypes: "pharisee" appearing as a synonym for "hypocrite" and "legalism" describing the Jewish religion. Prejudicial judgments occur within biblical scholarship as well, so we must use the scholarly sources with critical care. See the review of scholarly views by Sanders in his *Jesus and Judaism*, 18–58. Also see E. E. Urbach, *The Sages*, 4–16. As Urbach and Sanders have both shown, often groups or scholars allow theological convictions to override historical judgments or lack sufficient familiarity with historical data about early Jewish movements and figures. In many ways, Jesus and the Pharisees were natural allies. The Pharisees were a largely lay group (though including some priests) who sought to make fulfillment of the law important and practical in daily living. What distinguished the Pharisees among other Jewish groups was their insistence upon observing ritual purity laws (for sanctification) *outside* the temple, and the strong bond of community forged by their commitments and practices. ("Pharisee" means "separated," yet their separation was never as extreme as the Essenes, who formed a physically separate community away from other Jews in order to remain "pure"; Neusner, *Judaism in the Beginning of Christianity*, 58.) For a fuller description of what is known about Pharisees by historians, see the following: Shaye J. D. Cohen, *From the Maccabees to the Mishnah* (Louisville: Westminster, 1987); Helmut Koester, *Introduction to the New Testament*, vol. 1, *History, Culture, and Religion of the Hellenistic Age* (Philadelphia: Fortress, 1982); Neusner, *Judaism in the Beginning of Christianity*; and James D. Newsome, *Greeks, Romans, Jews: Currents of Culture and Belief in the New Testament World* (Philadelphia: Trinity Press International, 1992).

63. See the careful discussion in chap. 14, "Contention and Opposition in Galilee," in E. P. Sanders's *The Historical Figure of Jesus*, 205–37. Sanders allows that Jesus may have debated these practices, but Jesus denied neither the validity nor the divine origin of these laws. Sanders observes that the chief points of contention — circumcision, sabbath, and food — were ways to distinguish Jew from Gentile, but were not "hot topics" within a Jewish community (222). Sanders also asks, if Jesus explicitly rejected the Torah teachings about clean and unclean, why did Peter not seem to know that in Acts 10, and why did Paul not remind Peter of Jesus' teaching (Gal. 2)? Witherington thinks Sanders understates the conflict between Jesus and the Pharisees and discusses Sanders's account in *The Jesus Quest: The Third Search for the Jew of Nazareth* (Downers Grove, Ill.: InterVarsity Press, 1995), 127–29.

agreed, saying, "Do not think that I have come to dissolve [abol-ish] the law [Torah teaching] or the prophets; I have come not to dissolve but to fulfill" (Matt. 5:17).[64] Two contemporary scholars, one Christian and one a Jewish rabbi, have recently discussed these conflicts.

Marcus Borg claims Jesus did not call the Pharisees hypocrites because they were insincere, for they were "good, devout people," sincerely committed to an "ethos and politics of holiness." According to Borg, this dispute is about fundamentally conflicting visions of human community and how God is to be reflected in that community. The Pharisees, according to Borg, used a strategy of exclusion with their stress upon separating the pure from the im-pure and thereby "created division within society."[65] Jesus, on the other hand, according to Borg, insisted that his "counter-cultural politics of compassion" required "internal transformation," a spir-itual revitalization that expressed itself by including the poor, the outcasts, and women. Rather than divide the people, Jesus called people to "an alternative community with an alternative consciousness" and to peace through loving their enemies.[66]

Jacob Neusner insists the Pharisees and Jesus had profound sim-ilarities and, like Borg, denies the Pharisees were hypocrites.[67] For Neusner, if there were differences between Jesus and the Phar-isees, it was because the Pharisees saw ritual purity as defining clean *space*, while Jesus seems to have confused that with *moral* cleanness.[68] According to Neusner, for Jews "pure" means "ac-ceptable in the holy place" (the temple), and thus "impure" means "unacceptable." He explains,

> purity is simply not a category that has anything to do with ethics. Not only is there no tension between rite and right, there is no point of intersection. Contrasting "inner" in purity with "outer" purity, meaning an unethical private life joined to a ritually correct exter-

---

64. Following Ulrich Luz, *Matthew 1–7: A Commentary* (Minneapolis: Augs-burg, 1989), 256. Luz and others have shown that this verse is fully Greek in origin and cannot be a translation of Jesus' Aramaic original. Still the thought itself is con-sistent with Jesus' words and actions elsewhere. See Luz's discussion on pp. 257–65; and Sanders, *Jesus and Judaism*, 260–64.

65. Borg, *Jesus: A New Vision*, 158.

66. Ibid., 131–42.

67. See Neusner, *Judaism in the Beginning of Christianity*, chap. 4: "The Pharisees: Jesus' Competition," 45–61.

68. Jacob Neusner, *A Rabbi Talks with Jesus: An Intermillennial, Interfaith Exchange* (New York: Doubleday, Image Books, 1993), 121.

nal life, is incomprehensible. The issue of "purity" does not concern ethics.[69]

Neusner is correct that purity regulations originate with concerns for holy space (the temple as a location of the presence of a holy God) and holy times (sabbath and feasts) and that holiness requires an ongoing disciplined life. Only a caricature could reduce this to a code of petty, priestly regulations about purity, as is too often done. Still, Neusner's distinction is too sharp even for the levitical Holiness Code. For example, while Yahweh tells Moses (Lev. 19:2), "You shall be holy, for I the LORD your God am holy," what immediately follows is the Ten Commandments and detailed instructions about social and ethical behavior that is consistent with reverence toward a holy God (Lev. 19:3–20:26). And, as John Gammie explains, "in contradistinction to the priests of Israel, the prophets clearly taught that the holiness of God required the cleanness of social justice."[70]

While the sages sometimes expressed wariness of the cult (see Eccles. 5:1–7), they also insisted that there was a "point of intersection" between purity and ethics, as can be seen in Proverbs 16 and 22:11 and most especially in Job.[71] Indeed, Job 31, the culmination of Job's defense, is an extended affirmation of his ethical integrity, not of his sinlessness, for Job claims he did not hide his sins in silence (31:33–34). Job's "Code of A Man of Honor" in chapter 31, which the Jewish biblical scholar Robert Gordis deems "the noblest presentation of individual ethics in the pages of the Bible," "like important sections of the Holiness Code in Leviticus," deals with external behavior as well as with "inner attitudes" and "sins of thought and feeling."[72] Here, in the words of Gammie, "holiness lays claim to conscience."[73]

Neusner and Borg both seek to counteract a popular anti-Jewish bias that reads Gospel accounts of conflict between Jesus and the Pharisees as "Jesus against the Jews." Such a view implicitly denies that Jesus was a Jew of his time and place. Both scholars do so polemically, in either-or terms, so if one side is right, the other must be wrong, which is not wholly inconsistent with the picture painted in the Gospels of Jesus and the Pharisees. Can an

69. Ibid.
70. John G. Gammie, *Holiness in Israel* (Minneapolis: Fortress, 1989), 100.
71. Ibid., esp. chaps. 5–6.
72. Robert Gordis, *The Book of Job: Commentary, New Translation, and Special Studies* (New York: Jewish Theological Seminary, 1978), 542.
73. Gammie, *Holiness in Israel*, 147.

either-or conflict (Borg's "politics of "holiness" versus "politics of compassion" or Neusner's "purity" versus "ethics") be reframed? As C. S. Lewis wisely warns, "Images of the Holy easily become holy images — sacrosanct. My idea of God is not a divine idea. It has to be shattered time after time. He shatters it Himself. He is the great iconoclast. Could we not almost say that this shattering is one of the marks of His presence?"[74]

Elisabeth Schüssler Fiorenza sees a similar polarizing among those who claim Jesus as a feminist by setting him in opposition to patriarchal Judaism, and she suggests another path.[75] Fiorenza attributes Jesus' departure from John the Baptist to a shift in Jesus' understanding of the coming kingdom. John stressed the wrath and judgment that will precede the coming kingdom, calling for repentance, while Jesus stressed not only the yet-to-come kingdom but that it is also already here: "Go and tell John what you have seen and heard" (Luke 7:22; notice the tense). This difference, according to Fiorenza, leads to fundamentally different lifestyles, which put Jesus into conflict with the Pharisees and their dietary concerns. John was ascetic while Jesus came "eating and drinking." According to Fiorenza (and Crossan), one of the central symbols of the coming and now-present kingdom of God is, not ritual purity, but the "sumptuous, glorious banquet celebration," whether it is a marriage feast (John 2), the feast for the prodigal son (Luke 15), or the banquet to which are invited "the poor, the crippled, the blind, and the lame" (Luke 14:15–24). In this vision, according to Fiorenza, "the power of God's *basileia* [kingdom, rule] is realized in Jesus' table community with the poor, the sinners, the tax collectors, and prostitutes — with all those who 'do not belong' to the 'holy people,' who are somehow deficient in the eyes of the righteous."[76] Within this vision, as with the sages, "everydayness . . . can become revelatory, and the presence and power of God's sacred wholeness can be experienced in every human being."[77] This means also that holiness is linked with wholeness and healing, especially healing the brokenness of community.[78]

An ethic of holiness (as wholeness) offered both friends and enemies a place at the table, communion making community whole,

---

74. C. S. Lewis, *A Grief Observed* (New York: Bantam, 1976), 76.
75. Elisabeth Schüssler Fiorenza, *In Memory of Her: A Feminist Theological Reconstruction of Christian Origins* (New York: Crossroad, 1983), 106–7.
76. Ibid., 121.
77. Ibid., 120.
78. Ibid.

including, as God does, all God's children. Jesus, Sirach, and *Sophia* invited all, but especially learners, to come to the banquet feast, where what is taken in becomes part of one's being. What is taken in at the feast is not only food but communion across divisive boundaries and a kind of learning akin to character formation. The joy of the feast is a good metaphor for what a teacher offers.

If this is what Jesus holds to be worth learning, then education must express the fact that learners become compassionate by being in the presence of compassionate characters, teachers, and learners — by taking in the banquet benefits and regularly trying on and coming to value loving attitudes and behaviors. While the apprentice may never give up study of the law, the study is *so that* the law may become part of who one is: one becomes the law, becomes love, joy, truth, and life.

Humility and Courage

Jesus' reformulation of Israel's heritage and his quest to evoke new and deepened understanding and behavior in noncoercive ways required courage, for history confirms that those who seek to reformulate a tradition and to enable others to act accordingly will meet resistance. Jesus not only said what truth demanded but also showed in his actions how to walk loving and life-affirming paths. Jesus' humility finds expression in many ways. He refused honorific labels. He lived simply and is reported to have even washed the disciples' feet (John 13:5). He also demonstrated courage in facing arrest, trial, and the threat of death.

Learning to be courageous or humble is important but not often talked about because courage and humility may have less to do with *what* one knows or does than with *how one is.* Courage and humility are discerned in deeds that flow from one's character. These two virtues are especially important pedagogically.

Matthew's Jesus reminded the disciples of the need for humility. Even as teachers they ought not be concerned with places of honor and respectful titles, not even "instructor," for "you are all students. . . . The greatest among you will be your servant. All who exalt themselves will be humbled, and all who humble themselves will be exalted" (Matt. 23:8, 11–12). Luke places the same saying in a different context: not taking the place of honor at a wedding banquet but waiting to be invited to move up higher (Luke 14:7–10; echoing an imperative proverb in Prov. 25:6–7). Luke then added a descriptive proverb at the end of the parable: "For all who exalt themselves will be humbled, and those who humble themselves will be exalted" (14:11). Joachim Jeremias asks, Is this saying "intended to be a piece of practical wisdom, a rule of social etiquette? Surely not!" He insists it speaks an "eschatological warning" or a "call to renounce self-righteous pretensions and to self-abasement before God" in the face of the reversal of values brought about by God's eschatological activity.[79] Surely one can acknowledge that God humbles and lifts up without denying the self-evident facts that this *is* a piece of wisdom and it *does* have to do with social etiquette. Indeed, Jeremias's denial helps hide another motif in this text. Jeremias rightly wants to avoid reading this text as etiquette, lest it encourage calculating or strategically wise actions ("sit at the lowest place"). But is "eschatological warning" the only other option? When the Lukan parable is coupled with the proverb, reader-learners may also read the whole as an invitation to reflect upon two kinds of character. What kind of person exalts himself, and what kind of person acts humbly? Which does a host (God) favor? But that invites the reader-learner not only to find a theological point in this text but also to look at one's own character, allowing herself to be read by the text: Who am I? What does my behavior say about who I am? What sort of character is appropriate to a subject or a servant?

That is why the path requires both courage and humility at the same time: courage to follow a path in which the agent is a subject, which grounds the humility. Jesus' vivid images help reader-learners see the King and the path, and therefore themselves, more clearly.

Why are humility and courage important for education? Learning requires humbly acknowledging that one does not yet know or that one misunderstands and needs to relearn. Often it requires courage to follow where truth leads — out beyond what is accepted as normal and conventional — as Job, Qohelet, the prophets, Jesus, and many others have demonstrated.

HOW WAS LEARNING EVOKED?

Having outlined some of the Gospels' portrayal of what is worth learning, we will now consider how it was to be learned. Remember, we do not seek historical reconstruction of Jesus' teaching methods, as though we could then "teach as Jesus did." If the

---

79. Joachim Jeremias, *The Parables of Jesus*, rev. ed. (New York: Scribner, 1963), 191–93.

Gospels are not primarily interested in historical accuracy, neither are they textbooks in pedagogical methods. Rather we focus upon the literary patterns characteristic of these texts (which historians say are forms characteristically used by Jesus). Here the historical question is not so much, Did Jesus actually say this? but more, Did Jesus typically use these kinds of saying forms (e.g., proverb and parable)? Then we examine the pedagogical function of such forms. How do those forms act upon hearers and upon reader-learners (a literary judgment). In addition, we shall also look at how Jesus is said to have acted, since teaching is much more than talking.

Many forms of wisdom sayings are attributed to Jesus, such as folk and literary proverbs; antithetical, synthetic, and comparative proverbs; better sayings; numerical sayings; riddles; rhetorical and impossible questions; beatitudes; admonitions and instructions; disputations; and aphorisms.[80] We will focus on three forms distinctive of Jesus' usage: proverbs, aphorisms, and parables.

Learning with Conventional Proverbial Sayings

All the Synoptics, as well as other independent sources, report that Jesus taught using proverbial sayings. Charles Carlston counts approximately 102 wisdom sayings in the Synoptics, Max Küchler counts 108, and Crossan counts 133 aphorisms.[81] (None included parables in the count.)

In Proverbs, two-line literary, indicative proverbs invite reader-learners to observe — to see what is and reflect — or they evoke imagination and wonder. Many of Jesus' indicative proverbs do the same, though they are often single-line oral (folk) sayings:

"Today's trouble is enough for today." (Matt. 6:34)

"The eye is the lamp of the body." (Matt. 6:22)

---

80. Leo G. Perdue, "The Wisdom Sayings of Jesus," *Foundations and Facets Forum* 2:3 (1986), 3–35. Kloppenborg has recently considered Q in detail and finds its formative material to be sapiential and instructional in character, though other material (some prophetic) has been interpolated. See John S. Kloppenborg, *The Formation of Q: Trajectories in Ancient Wisdom Collections*, Studies in Antiquity and Christianity (Philadelphia: Fortress, 1987), 263.

81. Charles E. Carlston, "Proverbs, Maxims, and the Historical Jesus," *Journal of Biblical Literature* 99:1 (1980), 91; Max Küchler, *Frühjüdische Weisheitstraditionen* (1979) cited in Claus Westermann, *Roots of Wisdom: The Oldest Proverbs of Israel and Other Peoples* (Louisville: Westminster/John Knox, 1995), 114; John Dominic Crossan, *In Fragments: The Aphorisms of Jesus* (San Francisco: Harper and Row, 1983), viii-ix, 330–41, 369–71.

"If one blind person guides another, both will fall into a pit." (Matt.
15:14)

Sometimes a saying includes an added interpretation (added by
whom?):

"No one can serve two masters; for a slave will either hate the one
and love the other, or be devoted to the one and despise the other."
(Matt. 6:24; Luke 16:13)

These describe what is so, what has been learned by observation and experience, and they require no supernatural revelation
to guarantee their truth. Similarly, many of Jesus' sayings draw
upon images and observations of the created world of plants and
animals, as did the proverbs of the sages of old:

"Look at the birds of the air." (Matt. 6:26; Luke 12:24)

"Consider the lilies of the field." (Matt. 6:28; Luke 12:27)

"If your child asks for bread, will [you] give a stone?" (Matt. 7:9;
Luke 11:11–12)

"Are grapes gathered from thorns, or figs from thistles?" (Matt.
7:16; Luke 6:44)

So many of Jesus' sayings begin with concrete observations the
truth of which no one can deny; they would be quite at home
among the sayings of Proverbs and Sirach, where God's rule is
found in the created order, governed by justice. This order is maintained by the authority of parents and sages who seek to transmit
and awaken learning in the young.[82] Were we to read only these
sayings, Jesus could be seen as just another conventional proverbial sage. These proverbial sayings take for granted that there is
order and that it expresses divine care. For example, "If your child
asks for bread, will [you] give a stone?" presumes a parent neither
demands that children earn their food nor responds to a child's
need heartlessly. Of course, lilies do not worry (Matt. 6:28), and
birds do not farm (Matt. 6:26); everyone knows that! But notice
how these indicatives act upon reader-learners, especially within
their literary context: we are invited not only to face these ordinary facts but, in accepting them, to acknowledge the trust implicit
in them. The trust a sparrow or lily shows could be the trust that a
subject shows for the king. Anxious striving is chasing after wind.
Rather, trust the king's care.

---

82. This summary is from James G. Williams, *Those Who Ponder Proverbs:
Aphoristic Thinking and Biblical Literature* (Sheffield: Almond, 1981), 17.

Conventional sayings not only affirm traditional order; they can also nudge the reader to see order from other angles. We noted that in Luke's version of Jesus' first reading in Nazareth, the people responded to Jesus with astonished approval, yet wondering, "Is not this Joseph's son?" (Luke 4:22). Jesus took the initiative then, telling them they would respond to him with an imperative proverb: "Doubtless you will quote to me this proverb, 'Doctor, cure yourself!' " (Luke 4:23). He then countered with his own indicative proverb: "Truly I tell you, no prophet is accepted in the prophet's hometown" (Luke 4:24). Both proverbial sayings claim the authority of long observation of human behavior verified in experience, yet they invite different conclusions. Jesus' response acknowledged and confronted his neighbors' skepticism yet did not do so simply on his own individual authority. In using the proverb, he claimed the support of communal tradition and experience, differing with his neighbors yet providing them with a conventional proverb to explain their response. That leaves neighbors (and later reader-learners) to choose. Which proverb best suits the situation? Both reader-learners and neighbors are deeply implicated by the form of the text itself — who else is to decide?

Jesus, like the sages of Proverbs, also used imperatives that invite obedience:

> "Do not judge, so that you may not be judged." (Matt. 7:1; Luke 6:37)

> "In everything do to others as you would have them do to you." (Matt. 7:12; Luke 6:31)

Jesus' imperatives are strikingly strong, and some invite a radically different way of seeing the world and quite *unconventional* obedience:

> "Do not worry about tomorrow, for tomorrow will bring worries of its own." (Matt. 6:34)

> "Love your enemies, do good to those who hate you." (Luke 6:27; Matt. 5:44)

> "Be perfect [merciful], therefore, as your heavenly Father is perfect [merciful]." (Matt. 5:48; Luke 6:36)

There is a certain irony here. Conventional imperatives offered by a teacher with authority invite reader-learners to be subject to or obey the authority figure, yet to obey many of Jesus' commands would be quite subversive of conventions. Jesus' sayings can awaken self-reflection ("Why do you see the speck in your neighbor's eye?"), stimulate unusual vision ("Consider the lilies"), and even create ethical dilemmas ("Love your enemies") that invite reader-learners to a counterorder vision of human behavior. Conventional wisdom urged prudence or moderation, yet the sayings of Jesus more often turn to hyperbole or extreme sayings.[83] Jesus also set traditional imperatives alongside new imperatives, just as Qohelet did:

> "You have heard,... 'You shall love your neighbor....' But I say to you, Love your enemies and pray for those who persecute you." (Matt. 5:43–44; Luke 6:27–28)

> "You have heard,... 'You shall not swear falsely....' But I say,... Do not swear at all." (Matt. 6:33–34)

> "You have heard,... 'An eye for an eye....' But I say,... Do not resist an evildoer." (Matt. 5:38–39)

While the new imperative does not contradict the tradition, it extends or intensifies it to be more expressive of the heart of the matter. The tension between the two invites reader-learners to self-involved reflection and perhaps new ways of behaving as well.

This tension is present as well in Jesus' use of conventional proverbial sayings, using ambiguity to involve hearers and reader-learners in interpreting their meaning and to evoke something radically new.[84] For example, Jesus used a familiar farming image of planting seeds that grow: "When the grain is ripe, at once he goes in with his sickle, because the harvest has come" (Mark 4:29). The farmer does not make the seed grow but must use his judgment to discern when it is ripe, a judgment learned from his own farmer-father and his previous experience. But here the image is applied to the coming of the kingdom! The reader-learner is invited to see the kingdom as growing seeds and ripening plants, but how does one judge that a kingdom is ripe? If it is ripe, a harvest requires cutting down and threshing. What does that expect of reader-learners?

Learning with Aphorisms

Jesus' use of the aphorism is perhaps closest to Qohelet's quoting and questioning of conventional wisdom,[85] but unlike Qohelet, Jesus' contrasts are often positive:

---

83. Ibid., 54; and Carlston, "Proverbs, Maxims, and the Historical Jesus," 91–99.
84. Crossan, *The Historical Jesus*, 350–51.
85. Hengel, *The Charismatic Leader*, 7.

"For all who exalt themselves will be humbled, and those who humble themselves will be exalted." (Luke 14:11)

The first line is a popular hope for reversal, that the mighty will be brought low, but the second line runs against conventional expectation. The effect here is disorientation, which invites the hearer or reader to stop and reconsider — and perhaps to hope? We see this frequently in Jesus' sayings:

"For those who want to save their life will lose it, and those who lose their life for my sake, and for the sake of the gospel, will save it." (Mark 8:35)

"I am sending you out like sheep into the midst of wolves; so be wise as serpents and innocent as doves." (Matt. 10:16)

"It is easier for a camel to go through the eye of a needle than for someone who is rich to enter the kingdom of God." (Mark 10:25)

No wonder the Gospels report that Jesus' teachings stirred up astonishment at his authority and opposition. His conventional wisdom seems obvious, but, like Qohelet, then he offered his own vision of a counterorder, which turned conventional expectations on their head.

As a pedagogical strategy, aphorisms are guaranteed to provoke thought and discussion among hearers and reader-learners. How learners respond to provocation will depend significantly upon how open they are to reconsidering what they have been taught and take for granted. That is not always easy. And the use of aphorisms is not a starting point for teaching but is designed to challenge what is familiar and has already been settled, thus presuming adult learners. Yet a challenge will as likely evoke resistance as readiness to change.

Aphorisms, because of their brevity, are more evocative than definitive. They do not so much provide a picture of an alternative vision as they hint at it or suggest a few of its features. Given their fragmentary character, their primary intent is to arouse, provoke, or argue, not to give a blueprint. Relying upon aphorisms presumes that much of the responsibility for learning, for making sense of what is evoked, lies with the subjects, the reader-learners, trusting their willing and active participation based on the clues offered.

Learning with Parables

Jesus' use of parables calls for more extended treatment, especially because the use of parables in educational ministry has often betrayed a fundamental misunderstanding of the nature of the parable. Since the word "parable" (from the Greek *parabolé*, literally, "to throw alongside" or "compare") suggests "this is about that," many have assumed the stories are illustrations used to deliver moral lessons. Amos Wilder counters this view directly:

> It is not enough to say that Jesus used the parable only as a good pedagogical strategy. It was not merely to hold the attention of his hearers that he told stories or took good illustrations out of his file. . . . In the realism and the actuality of the parables we recognize Jesus the layman. . . . This is a world in which as a matter of course things happen, men and women do things, one thing leads to another . . . Jesus, without saying so, by his very way of presenting man [*sic*] shows that for him man's destiny is at stake in his ordinary creaturely existence, domestic, economic and social. This is the way God made him. . . . A man is a toiler and an "actor" and a chooser. The parables give us this kind of humanness and actuality.[86]

C. H. Dodd's definition of parable is often quoted: "At its simplest the parable is a metaphor or simile drawn from nature or common life, arresting the hearer by its vividness or strangeness, and leaving the mind in sufficient doubt about its precise application to tease it into active thought."[87] This definition should strike several familiar resonances by now, for the sages frequently draw their imagery from nature and common life and loved vivid, concrete language. And what could better describe the sage's intent than teasing "into active thought"?

A parable is a combination of metaphoric and narrative form that must be more fully understood if we are to see how parables evoke learning. Usually longer than a proverbial saying or an aphorism, a parable takes the form of a "short, narrative fiction."[88] Some parables may be as short as one sentence, while others are longer, even as long as the Book of Job. Jesus' parables rarely are longer than a single paragraph. As a narrative form, a parable has some sort of story line or a plot with characters, a setting, and a time sequence. Stories provoke insight, not by abstract generalization, but by means of concrete thinking.[89] As fiction, the parable

---

86. Amos N. Wilder, *Early Christian Rhetoric: The Language of the Gospel* (Cambridge: Harvard University Press, 1971), 71, 74. One can affirm these descriptions by Wilder while remaining "agnostic" about his convictions concerning metaphysical realism in these texts.

87. C. H. Dodd, *The Parables of the Kingdom*, rev. ed. (New York: Scribner, 1961), 5.

88. Scott, *Hear Then the Parable*, 35.

89. Ibid., 37.

raises the issue of truth in a most interesting and pedagogically important manner. First, the truth of a parable, as a story, has little to do with whether or not it actually happened. Historical truth has no relevance to the truth of a parable.[90] Even if there never was a real Job or a real prodigal son or an actual good Samaritan on the Jericho road, the parables are true, the characters real. Secondly, a parable is essentially a metaphoric device, using this (seed) to talk about that (kingdom). Thus, a parable only works when the hearer or reader-learners recognize that it is both true and *not* true at once.

Donald Davidson helpfully compares metaphors with telling lies: "The parallel between making a metaphor and telling a lie is emphasized by the fact that the same sentence can be used, with meaning unchanged, for either purpose."[91] For example, consider "She's a witch." To recognize the metaphoric use (and thus, that it is true), one must recognize that the sentence is not literally true. That is, only by not being literally true can it be metaphorically true, for only then can we use the image "witch" as a lens with which to see or frame the woman. Yet one could use the exact same sentence as literally true, and then it could become a lie, as it did in the Salem witch trials late in the seventeenth century.

Parables are closely related both to similes and metaphors. A simile compares by saying, "That man is *like* a wolf," or "The kingdom of heaven is *like* a mustard seed" (Matt. 13:31, emphasis added). A metaphor goes further — it compares by saying, for example, "That man *is* a wolf." In other words, "a simile tells us ... what a metaphor merely nudges us into noting."[92] Similarly, each parable only works if it is not true in one sense (it is to miss the point to ask the name of the owner of the vineyard), yet the discrepancy stimulates imagination and insight by the reader-learner

---

90. Knowing historical and cultural "facts" can add to the richness of understanding and even help those from different times and cultures see the point of a parable, which may presume culturally specific information. For example, the protagonist is a Samaritan, and knowing that Jews denigrated Samaritans is important in interpretation, for it "gives the parable its edge." Robert W. Funk, *Language, Hermeneutic, and Word of God: The Problem of Language in the New Testament and Contemporary Theology* (New York: Harper and Row, 1966), 213.

91. Donald Davidson, "What Metaphors Mean," in his *Inquiries into Truth and Interpretation* (Oxford: Clarendon, 1984), 258.

92. Ibid., 253. Most interpreters affirm that what seems literal cannot be taken literally, though often for different reasons and with different consequences. See the interpretations by Searle, Black, Davidson, and Levin in the classic collection by Andrew Ortony, ed., *Metaphor and Thought*, 2d ed. (New York: Cambridge University Press, 1993), chaps. 2–8.

(What does "wolf" suggest about this man? What is the behavior of that vineyard owner like?).

Parable and metaphor are forms of "seeing as." Davidson explains, "Seeing as is not seeing that. Metaphor makes us see one thing as another by making some literal statement that inspires or prompts the insight. . . . But in fact there is no limit to what a metaphor calls to our attention, and much of what we are caused to notice is not propositional in character."[93] The same is true for parable. The parable paints a picture in story, but the reader-learner must then see for herself. Interpretation can prompt or stimulate seeing, but it cannot substitute for it.

A parable makes sense of a thing not well known (e.g., God) by seeing it as another that we know more concretely (e.g., a father or the owner of a vineyard). That is essential to metaphoric process and to all human knowing. By the nature of it, each reader-learner must judge for herself — using her own experience or by doing some historical investigation or by asking, "Suppose I adopted that view, what would it make possible? Suppose I were to see myself as a neighbor or as a father awaiting a prodigal son?" Matthew's Jesus tells the disciples, speaking about understanding parables, "Blessed are your eyes, for they see" (Matt. 13:16).

Strictly speaking, can there be one right view of a particular parable? As Crossan observes, "Polyvalence is not the parable's failure or betrayal, but rather its victory and success."[94] It is made for multiple interpretations. "Let whoever has ears hear" implies that this one might hear differently from that one (read commentators or listen to preachers for confirmation of this point). This undermines the drive to certainty and the need for one right answer or a moral lesson that have been so common in the educational use of parables. Hearers and reader-learners are fundamentally important in the interpretation of what a parable comes to mean and how it is to function in their understanding and living. Here teachers cannot do all the work and cannot rule for learners the one right understanding. However, teachers can, and should, help learners discern that some understandings may be less adequate than others, for various reasons.

Parables evoke a cognitive understanding, but they may also evoke an emotional experience, an aesthetic awareness, new motivations, altered behavior, or all the above. Too often parables

---

93. Davidson, "What Metaphors Mean," 263.
94. Crossan, *In Fragments*, vii.

are construed narrowly as a means to cognitive attainment. Earlier we considered the parable of the vineyard and noted that reader-learners would likely be moved to an intuitive sense of outrage that these tenants behaved quite unjustly. Similarly, we observed in the story of the prodigal son that the parable expects the reader to feel a tension between the claims and expectations of the two sons and to feel surprise at the response of the father. Evoking such feelings might well lead a reader-learner to reconsider his own motives (allowing the text to read the reader) and/or to discover possibilities that lead to altering his own behavior.

The story of the good Samaritan (Luke 10:25–37) has sometimes been called not a parable but an *example story*.[95] An example story supposedly is less metaphorical, telling more directly how or how not to behave. Scholars have argued whether Jesus told this as an example story or whether Luke or the early church changed a parable into an example story ("Go and do likewise"). Crossan claims this story was a parable that Luke has changed into an example story by creating a new literary context for the parable proper (vv. 30–35). In Crossan's view, this means that the literary context thus "cannot be used to interpret the meaning of the parable for Jesus."[96] Crossan's interpretation may provide a good test of the pedagogical function of parables offered here. Does metaphoric "seeing as" occur only within or by use of the parable itself, or might the narrative account of Jesus' actions and interactions with others assist the metaphoric process, encouraging them to see differently?

Luke sets this story in the context of a lawyer's test or question of Jesus: "What must I do to inherit eternal life?" Jesus answers with a question that does not seek to expose the lawyer-learner's weakness but appeals to his strength — the lawyer's own legal expertise. The lawyer answers that one is to love God and neighbor (he knew the "right answer" all along). Jesus then shifts responsibility back to the lawyer by suggesting, "Do this and you will live." Then the lawyer asks another legal question, perhaps trying, as do many learners, to shift responsibility back to the teacher: "And who is my neighbor?" (In other words, "let's play the legal definition game.") Jesus responds by telling a short narrative fic-

---

95. Bultmann first classified the good Samaritan as an "example story," but he is followed in this by others. See the discussion in Crossan, *In Parables: The Challenge of the Historical Jesus* (San Francisco: Harper and Row, 1973), 55–66.

96. Crossan, *In Parables*, 58.

tion, which invites the lawyer to see this story as a response to his question (shifting responsibility back to the lawyer-learner).

What are we to make of this story as a way of "seeing as"? Many conventional interpretations draw connections between loving God and neighbor and the loving behavior of the Samaritan to the wounded man and thus conclude that the answer to the lawyer's question is that our neighbor is anyone in trouble or need — a conventional lesson. The behavior of the priest and Levite heighten the reader-learner's empathy for the poor wounded "neighbor," who was being ignored. This interpretation confirms (or assumes?) this is an example story, since it recommends helping behavior, not metaphoric "seeing as."

Suppose we slow down our reading and notice some of the ways Luke's account invites "seeing as." If we start with the lawyer, what might he have come to see? (Luke does not specify; thus, reader-learners are invited, indeed required, to use their imagination — "seeing as though" they were the lawyer, and not only as readers.) What the lawyer expected is embedded in his question: "Who is my neighbor?" He expects the neighbor to be someone out there, so he might see the wounded man as his neighbor. But as the parable proper ends, Jesus changes the question, ignoring the wounded man: "Which of these three, do you think, was a neighbor?" This new way of seeing changes what the lawyer is to expect, inviting him (and reader-learners) to look, not for someone out there who needs help, but at the Samaritan, the priest, and Levite so that he can see himself. Can you see yourself as a neighbor now that you have seen how a neighborly person acts? (Again, the text invites the reader to be read: Will I, as agent, act lovingly, as a subject of a loving King?) While this sounds like a metaphoric challenge, still Jesus' final word, "Go and do likewise," sounds like an example story. Crossan sees these divergent uses of "neighbor" as a discrepancy or a clue that Luke or earlier tradition had combined "divergent sources" rather than reported an actual dialogue of Jesus.[97]

Part of what makes this way of seeing a difficult experience for Luke's fictional lawyer is that he, a Jew, is being asked to see himself acting like a Samaritan! He is being invited (as Jesus seems to have done regularly) to break down barriers between insiders and

---

97. Ibid., 60–61. Crossan does then argue that Jesus' question ended the original parable and provided a parable of reversal, which was later combined with an example story.

outsiders, which were so strong in those cultures.[98] This parable actually excludes the Jew from being the hero. Unless the hearer were to change age-old Jewish cultural convictions, the only other way a Jew could find a way into this parable is to see himself as *the victim!*[99] No wonder Jesus' listeners were offended by his parables!

Luke's Jesus allowed the lawyer to make his own sense of the story, and his "Go and do likewise" can be read as an invitation to the lawyer and to later reader-learners. If this is so, it undermines Crossan's separating the parable proper from Luke's literary context, for it is precisely the parable in the narrative context of the teacher-lawyer exchange that invites the lawyer to "see himself as" a possible neighbor. As the sages insisted, the lawyer's new "seeing as" would be as or more evident in his actions and attitudes than in his verbal productions. The same is true of later reader-learners.

Pedagogically, the use of parables and metaphors is an age-old form of indirect communication that allows and invites reader-learners to new seeing and to change their mind, feelings, and behavior. Yet the parable does this — without explicit argument, persuasion, or coercion — by gentle invitation, as though saying, "Whoever has ears to hear, hear." But as everyone since King David has learned, if one hears, a parable may evoke a radical reorientation in hearers and in reader-learners.

Learning from Stories, Actions, and Reading

The sages insist wisdom is expressed in practices as well as in words. Learning from experience can come by paying careful attention to the sayings, by paying careful attention to one's own actions, or by reading stories about what others do. Therefore, we now ask, How do we learn from Jesus' actions and the narrative accounts of those actions? How do those accounts engage reader-learners?

Narratives use characters, plots, settings, and sequences of time to invite reader-learners to join in the story, as we saw in the Book of Job. Narratives also help shape, limit, and evoke metaphorical meaning. We will briefly sample selected narrative accounts of three of Jesus' practices, ones about which there is consensus as to historical reliability and that are intrinsically related to

---

98. See Bruce Malina, *The New Testament World: Insights from Cultural Anthropology*, rev. ed. (Louisville: Westminster/John Knox, 1993), for further description of these cultural dynamics. Also Bruce Malina and Richard Rohrbaugh, *Social-Science Commentary on the Synoptic Gospels* (Minneapolis: Fortress, 1992).

99. Scott, *Hear Then the Parable*, 200.

the *what* of his teaching: Jesus' calling and sending disciples, his healing practices, and his eating practices. Then we turn to the narratives as texts, asking what these narratives expect of implied reader-learners.

CALLING AND SENDING DISCIPLES (AND READER-LEARNERS). Early in each Gospel, the authors depict Jesus' calling men to leave home and follow him as disciples. Reader-learners are given very little description of these calls. The narrator in Mark begins by saying that Jesus is the "Son of God," that John the baptizer came "before him" as predicted by Isaiah, and that as John baptized Jesus, a "voice from heaven" confirmed that Jesus was "my Son," "Beloved," and one with whom "I am well pleased" (Mark 1:1–11). Thereafter Jesus approaches four fishermen, presumably strangers, and says, "Follow me and I will make you fish for people." Mark tells us their response: "And immediately they left their nets and followed him" (Mark 1:16–20; Matt. 4:18–22). This may not surprise reader-learners — who would not follow the Son of God? But the disciples have not read Mark's text! The narrator prepared reader-learners to recognize Jesus' authority, and at this point readers knows more about Jesus than do these new disciples. Mark and Matthew offer readers no explanation why these disciples' respond so immediately and totally. Luke, on the other hand, does, describing Jesus' using the disciples' boat as a place to sit while he taught people at the edge of the lake, after which he asked the fishermen to push out and let down their nets for a catch. They protested that they had caught nothing all night, but they did as he asked and were rewarded with a great shoal of fish (Luke 5:1–7). No wonder they leave everything and follow (Luke 5:8–11)! Reader-learners see the disciples have both heard Jesus teach and witnessed an event that seemed miraculous. In contrast, readers of Matthew and Mark are left to supply motivations for the disciples.

The Gospels go on to portray Jesus as an itinerant teacher, speaking as people gathered, all the while trying to help his disciples comprehend what he was doing and why. This seems consistent with what today we might call *coaching*,[100] as is done with apprentices. Apprentices listen and watch the master, then are given small tasks to develop skills and understandings of their own. They are gradually given greater responsibilities and opportunities

---

100. See Donald A. Schön, *Educating the Reflective Practitioner* (San Francisco: Jossey-Bass, 1987).

to try it out for themselves. Then they review their experiences with the master for evaluation and instruction.

Jesus' authority as master appears again when he sent his apprentice-disciples on their first mission to preach and to heal (Matt. 10; Mark 3; 6; Luke 9), though no mention is made of teaching. The disciples were given detailed and explicit directions. They were to take no money, no bag, no food, only the clothes they were wearing. In their itinerant poverty, they were to be dependent upon the hospitality of others and each other (Luke 10:4–11; Matt. 10:12–14; Gosp. Thom. 14:2).[101] While the Gospel accounts sometimes portray the disciples as objecting to something Jesus said or misunderstanding him, they do not object to his stringent conditions for their mission. They are depicted as responsive and obedient.

Assuming some positive response to these accounts, reader-learners might expect some description of what the disciples did and how it turned out. Yet reports are limited, and there is more detail about the disciples' failures than their success. This is quite natural in an apprenticeship, where misunderstandings and mistakes are important learning opportunities.

But the absence of success stories may have another effect on reader-learners, who have been told things the disciples cannot have known. For example, in Matthew's text, the disciples responded unambiguously to Jesus' call to follow. Then they heard Jesus' teaching (chaps. 5–7); they witnessed miracles (8:1–17); yet Jesus rebukes them for their "little faith" (8:26); and when he calms a storm, they ask, "What sort of man is this?" (8:27). Similarly, just after the disciples are described as "understanding" what Jesus is teaching (13:51–52), they again were terrified in a storm (14:22–33). Thus reader-learners are invited to observe both the loyalty and the failures of the disciples, seen from the vantage point of Jesus' corrections.[102] Richard Edwards observes, "The disciples

---

101. There are similarities between these ideals and those of the Cynics, a Hellenistic philosophical movement known in Galilee prior to Jesus' time. Crossan and others have claimed Jesus was influenced by the Cynics (Crossan, The Historical Jesus, esp. chap. 4). It is possible, but unproven. Even if true, the Cynic adopted poverty both as a protest to conventional culture and morality and as a sign of one's self-sufficiency, while Jesus taught interdependence not self-sufficiency. (See Dennis C. Duling and Norman Perrin, The New Testament: Proclamation and Pareness, Myth and History, 3d ed. (Fort Worth: Harcourt Brace, 1994), 67–68, 527–28. In addition, neither Jesus nor any other peasant needed to adopt poverty as a protest against cultural convention. Poor is just what they were.

102. See Richard A. Edwards, "Uncertain Faith: Matthew's Portrait of the Disci-

never live up to Jesus' standards. Given the effect on the reader, discipleship will be viewed as a situation that is never completed, is likely to be in constant flux, and cannot be idealized."[103] On the other hand, these failures may entice reader-learners to view Jesus more sympathetically ("He has to put up with so much!"). And since reader-learners cannot rely on the disciples as models, they will have to rely even more on Jesus "to learn what it means to live a life obedient to God."[104]

HEALING THE ILL. Were Jesus' healing activities connected with his teaching? There is an emerging consensus, in Meier's words, that the historian must admit that "Jesus performed deeds that many people, both friends and foes, considered 'miracles,'" and that is a key to much else in these accounts.[105] Meier asserts that the historical attestation to Jesus' miracles is so impressive that (a) total fabrication by the early church is impossible and (b) "if the miracle tradition from Jesus' public ministry were to be rejected *in toto* as unhistorical, so should every other Gospel tradition about him."[106] While some healing accounts can be traced back to events in Jesus' ministry, "however much they may have been reworked and expanded by Christian theology," others were clearly fabricated later.[107] Thus, while we cannot say with complete confidence that any one of these accounts reports events exactly as they oc-

ples," in *Discipleship in the New Testament*, ed. Fernando F. Segovia (Philadelphia: Fortress, 1985), 47–61.

103. Ibid., 52.

104. David B. Howell, *Matthew's Inclusive Story: A Study in the Narrative Rhetoric of the First Gospel*, JSNTSup 42 (Sheffield: JSOT, Sheffield Academic Press, 1990), 247.

105. Meier, *A Marginal Jew*, 2:3.

106. Ibid., 630. It is virtually a consensus view among historians these days that Jesus' healing activity "is recognized as characteristic, even central to his mission." See Robert Webber, "Jesus the Healer: History, Hype, and Hope" (convocation lecture at Lancaster Theological Seminary, Lancaster, Pa., 26 September 1996). The historians disagree about the significance and meaning of these healings. Some use the supposedly neutral term "magic" to describe them (Crossan, Davies, Smith), while others speak of "miracle" (Meier), but none, as historians, judge their historical or medical validity, nor do they draw "faith-portraits" based on them. See Sanders, *The Historical Figure of Jesus*, chap. 10; Crossan, *The Historical Jesus*, chap. 13; Smith, *Jesus the Magician;* Davies, *Jesus the Healer;* and especially the extensive (500 pp.) discussion of many views in Meier, *A Marginal Jew*, vol. 2, chaps. 17–23.

107. Meier, *A Marginal Jew*, 2:726. Even Meier, willing to credit Jesus with having performed healings and exorcisms, still finds that of the twenty-six or twenty-seven healing stories reported in the Gospels, only twelve could be credited as "reflecting events in Jesus' ministry," and many of those cannot be taken simply as given. See the extended discussion and brief summary in *A Marginal Jew*, 2:646–970, 968–70.

curred, we can say with confidence Jesus "did this sort of thing."[108] Even within the Gospel accounts, there are several attempts to denigrate or question Jesus' healing activity. For example, Jesus is asked by what authority he does these things or is charged with doing these things by the power of Beelzebul, yet, strikingly, *never* does either friend or foe deny that Jesus heals. Similarly, later in the era of the early church, still there is no attempt, even by detractors, to claim that Jesus did no miracles or healings. That he did such is accepted.

Here we are more interested in whether these healing accounts have anything to do with learning and teaching and, if they do, the nature of the connection. On these matters the scholars are more divided. Smith sees the relation between healing and teaching as one-way: Jesus' healing attracted crowds for his teaching. Smith accepts that it is plausible that a miracle worker like Jesus attracted crowds, which he then taught, and thereby came to be known as a prophet, an authority, and a possible messiah, which aroused turmoil among those with whom he disagreed, thus leading to his death.[109] On the other hand, Smith argues, it is hard to image a teacher becoming a threat. As we observed earlier, that judgment will depend in part upon what counts as teaching, for certainly teachers from Socrates to Paulo Freire have been seen as threats to those in authority.[110] Meier asserts that "Jesus obviously appreciated the value of miracles for pedagogy," not just to attract crowds but more as "the present enactment of the powerful rule of God," thus confirming a central theme in his teaching.[111] Here again contemporary assumptions shape historical discussion.

How does a reader-learner see or envision Jesus? Is he seen as a teacher who also heals, or is he seen as a healer who also teaches, or as a prophet and reformer who also teaches? While such notions often frame the contemporary discussion among scholars, do they anachronistically presume some manner of specialization in first-century Palestine? For example, Jesus has traditionally been portrayed as a carpenter, but that is unlikely to have been anything like today's professional specialist. In small-town Galilee (Nazareth had fewer than a thousand residents), each family raised some crops, some cattle perhaps, maybe a single cow, did some carpen-

---

108. Ibid., 646.

109. Smith, *Jesus the Magician*, 9–23.

110. Authorities in Athens made Socrates drink poison, and authorities in Brazil exiled Freire from the country in fear of his work in teaching peasants to read.

111. Meier, *A Marginal Jew*, 2:1043–44.

try, some masonry, and so on. Even if someone excelled at one craft, it was unlikely he could support his family doing only one thing, nor did that preclude him from doing many other things as well, either cooperatively with others in town or for others on a barter system.

While Jesus likely related with his disciples as a master with apprentices, that would hardly suggest he was preparing them for a trade or specialty. The question of which trade Jesus was preparing his apprentices for — prophet, reformer, healer, or teacher — misses the mark altogether. Since Jesus was a sage-teacher, what was more important by far is what kind of persons they were to become. What allegiances, loyalties, and convictions formed their characters and were expressed in their practices and daily living? Still, we can ask what Jesus' healing practices reveal about the convictions that underlie his own practices.

First, Jesus' healings were not those of a trained medical specialist. Indeed, healing was not a secular matter but was seen as part and parcel of what we now call *religious convictions* and *social practices* (see Sir. 38). A healer dealt not only with the physical but also with the social, communal, and spiritual dimension embodied in a person's need.[112] This is not just what we now call *holistic medicine*, for it might as well be called *holistic teaching* or *holistic preaching* or *holistic communal health* or even, by extension, *holistic social policy*. All of these descriptions, in Jesus' practice, are related to his teaching about King/God's ruling activity and human participation in that rule.

Second, Jesus responded to a need, no matter what the nature of the need. Where there is hesitation, it never took the form of saying, "Sorry, I am a teacher (or prophet, preacher, reformer). You need a physician." Jesus' use of the Samaritan is illustrative, for the neighborly action was neither spiritual nor specialist — he took the wounded man to an inn, cleaned him up, tended his wounds, and hired help for his recuperation.

Third, Jesus' healings were seen by the Gospel writers as evidence of his compassion, and they write that Jesus attributed them to God's compassion (e.g., Luke 7:11–17). God was seen as the source of Jesus' power to heal, a claim that forges an important pedagogical link. When Jesus urges hearer-learners to become

---

112. See Crossan's distinction between disease (a medical condition) and illness (a psychosocial and cultural condition) in *The Historical Jesus*, 336–37; and Meier's discussion of miracles and modern minds and ancient minds in *A Marginal Jew*, vol. 2, chaps. 17–18.

"mature" or "complete" or "perfect" or "merciful," it is because they are to become like God (Matt. 5:43–48; Luke 6:27–36). In other words, in healing and teaching alike, Jesus expected those he healed or made whole and those he taught to become more God-like. Jesus, in sending his disciples out to heal, in effect commands them to live in constant expectation of God's compassionate ruling activity and to express a like compassion themselves.

Lastly, Jesus, like the sages, cares not only about mental activity but also about bodies. One cannot become whole exercising only one's head or only one's body. Human beings, as creatures, are embodied beings. Yet it is equally true that bodies are also minds and hearts. So often our contemporary approach to both medicine and education assumes a specialist who deals with cases or with a problem child. In the accounts of Jesus' healing activity, reader-learners encounter bodies touched, imaginations stirred, families reunited. These accounts portray marginalized persons, bleeding women, leprous outcasts, the blind, beggars, paralytics, the demon-possessed, even the dead, restored to family and community, from which their illnesses had made them social outcasts. These portraits stretch a reader-learner's imagination of inclusive community and of sovereign, compassionate power, yet keep it very concrete![113] By analogy, what could be more important to the pedagogical endeavor than stretching the imagination? What could be more pedagogically healthy than including more and more of the human (physical and spiritual) community in imaginative learning? Thus it is not surprising that Jesus healed, nor is it surprising that his healing restored community, just as did his eating practices.

Walter Wink has demonstrated that while these texts can be read as descriptive accounts of what some person named Jesus did in Palestine nearly two thousand years ago, one can also read them as questioning the reader-learner: "What is it in you that needs healing?"[114] What Wink says of parables is just as true of many of the healing stories: "Parables have hooks all over them; they can grab each of us in a different way, according to our need."[115] To do this reader-learners need to shift how they see the stories, and the texts often invite reader-learners to do just that. For example, John 9 provides a lengthy account of Jesus' healing of a blind beggar in which religious authorities find themselves asking, "Surely we are

113. Webber, "Jesus the Healer," 9.
114. Walter Wink, *Transforming Bible Study*, 2d ed. (Nashville: Abingdon, 1989), see esp. 136–42.
115. Ibid., 161.

not blind, are we?" (John 9:40). Are they also finding themselves being read?

FEASTING WITH THE POOR, OUTCASTS, AND SINNERS. In sending his apprentice-disciples out, Jesus commanded them to rely humbly on those who received them for their food. Presumably, this also is as he had done. Despite this commitment to itinerant poverty, many accounts depict eating, controversies about food, hospitality, who is invited, and so on, which indicate the importance of meal practices in Jesus' teaching (Acts 10; Gal. 2:11–14; 1 Cor. 8; 10:14–33; 11:17–34; James 2:14–17). Why were food and eating so important, and have they any pedagogical significance?

Food and eating are not only a biological necessity but have social and cultural significance. The history of food reflects and is reflected in cultural patterns, including familial, religious, and political patterns.[116] Especially in antiquity, meal practices helped confirm (or challenge) existing social structures. Eating together implied that those with whom one eats were part of one's in-group, sharing common ideas and values.[117] One of the features of Jesus' ministry that was claimed to be offensive to some was that Jesus ate and drank with those who were religiously unacceptable or ritually impure. Similarly, when Jesus sent disciples out to preach and heal, he commanded them to take no food but to accept the hospitality of those they met. Does that command implicitly require them to eat what was offered them without regard to purity laws (recall Sir. 31:16)?

Crossan argues that Jesus' ignoring traditional ritual regulations concerning eating is evidence for Jesus' participation in an egalitarian peasant mind-set. For Fiorenza and Crossan alike, these meal practices were centrally important expressions of Jesus' new vision.[118] In Crossan's words, this shared table is "the heart of the original Jesus movement, a shared egalitarianism of spiritual and material resources."[119] The disciples, in their journeys, "share a miracle and a Kingdom, and they receive in return a table and a house."[120] While this judgment may assume more contemporary ideological clarity than the evidence of the texts will bear, it seems right in spirit.

116. Maguelonne Toussaint-Samat, *The History of Food* (Cambridge, Mass.: Blackwell, 1992).
117. Malina and Rohrbaugh, *Social-Science Commentary*, 191.
118. Fiorenza, *In Memory of Her*, 120–21; Crossan, *The Historical Jesus*, 340.
119. Crossan, *The Historical Jesus*, 341.
120. Ibid.

Mealtime has long been seen as an occasion for both informal learning and formal instruction. What could be learned by eating together? Participating itself was and still is a way of learning social roles. One's social status was discerned in whether or not one was allowed to participate, where one was allowed to sit, who assigned one's seat, what one was given to eat, how that compared with what others were given to eat, whether one washes, whether a servant offers washing or actually washes the guest, and so on.[121]

Not only did an individual learn at meals; food was a potent tool for teaching about how wealth and political power affect social divisions. In a society of limited goods, especially one such as Palestine where food shortages and malnutrition were common, wealth and power showed in control of food — so some ate well, and many only dreamed of abundance. There was a

> pervasive linking of status and diet. Power was the power to eat. The divisions of society coincided transparently with gradations of access to foodstuffs: more food, more varied and better-prepared at the top; less food and less varied towards the bottom. [Meat and cooked food were largely beyond the scope of the poor.] ... This is an age where thought about eating was, inevitably, a form of second thought about society and its blatant divisions.[122]

This helps explain why the image of a banquet with an abundance of food and wine and thrown open to those from the hedges and byways came to be such a powerful image for the coming kingdom.

Tracing how the Synoptics portray women and meals with Jesus and the disciples shows that Luke retains traditional roles for women while Mark and Matthew offer more gender-inclusive portrayals.[123] Yet Luke also depicts Jesus' using the notion of "service at meals" (Gk. *diakoneo*), typically a woman's role, as a model for learning the authority appropriate to discipleship, suggesting *all* disciples should be serving others.[124]

Especially in Mediterranean cultures, mealtime has long been an opportunity for direct instruction. In Israel, the weekly sabbath rituals as well as such annual festivals as Passover either

---

121. Ibid., 192.

122. Peter R. L. Brown, "Response," in Robert M. Grant, *The Problem of Miraculous Feedings in the Graeco-Roman World* (Berkeley, Calif.: Center for Hermeneutical Studies in Hellenistic and Modern Culture, 1982), 19.

123. Kathleen E. Corley, *Private Women, Public Meals: Social Conflict in the Synoptic Tradition* (Peabody, Mass.: Hendrickson, 1993).

124. E. Jane Via, "Women, the Discipleship of Service, and the Early Christian Ritual Meal in the Gospel of Luke," *St. Luke's Journal of Theology* 29:1 (December 1985), 37–60.

occurred over meals or prescribed public rituals involving eating and fasting. In Hellenistic cultures, Plato's *Symposium* and later Plutarch's *Table Talk* demonstrate the use of a meal or a banquet with wine as an important occasion for teaching. As we have seen, both Proverbs and Sirach offer directions about how to behave on such occasions. In *Laws*, Plato uses two whole sections (over fifty pages!) describing "Drinking Parties as an Educational Device."[125] Many scholars have observed that Luke in particular, in keeping with these practices, uses the Hellenistic symposium as a literary format for describing several of the meals shared with others, during which Jesus offered observations, proverbial sayings, and parables to the guests at the meal (see esp. Luke 14).[126]

Finally, notice the vocabulary used to depict the mood that accompanies such occasions. We observed earlier that Woman Wisdom was graphically depicted (in Prov. 8:30–31) as playing in the presence of God, bringing God delight or joy, and sharing that playful joy with humankind as well. The Hebrew word used there was *smch* (verb) or *simchah* (noun), variously translated as "laugh," "play," "dance," "jest," or "rejoice." The LXX translates this with the Greek *euphrosune* (noun) and *euphraino* (verb), which suggest a mood of joy, especially associated with feasts and festivals and with the processes of intellectual and spiritual life.[127] The same word (*euphrainesthai*) is used frequently in the LXX translation of Ecclesiastes (3:12, 22; 5:18–20; 8:15; 9:7) when Qohelet urges the readers to "enjoy" or "have joy" in work or to "find joy" in eating, drinking, making love, and working. Similarly, the word is found in Sirach's description of the fear of Yahweh:

> The fear of the Lord is glory and exultation,
> and gladness and a crown of rejoicing. (Sir. 1:11)

Interestingly, this word appears again in Jesus' parable of the prodigal son, where it is used to depict the mood of the father upon the return of his son, expressed in joyous feasting (Luke 15:23–24, 29, 32).

---

125. Plato, *The Laws* (New York: Penguin, 1970), 63–116. See also the treatment by Werner Jaeger, *Paideia: The Ideals of Greek Culture* (New York: Oxford, 1943–44), 2:174–97 and 3:213–31, showing the link of eros and friendship with education and especially the ideal of self-control rather than control by others, which is tested by consuming wine.

126. Dennis E. Smith, "Table Fellowship as a Literary Motif in the Gospel of Luke," *Journal of Biblical Literature* 106:4 (1987), 613–38.

127. Rudolf Bultmann, in *Theological Dictionary of the New Testament*, 2:772.

Jesus' and his disciples' (including those normally excluded) festive behavior eloquently taught God's kingly and loving ruling even
when nothing was *said* directly. Crossan's affirmation is sound:
"the Kingdom is at hand or near in the sense . . . of presence and
. . . its power is made visible in the commonality of shared miracle
and shared meal."[128]

READING AND LEARNING WITH NARRATIVES ABOUT ACTIVITIES. Let us now turn from
what these texts tell us about what Jesus and others might have
done, and look more closely at how these narrative texts and readers intersect pedagogically. How do these texts help reader-learners
not only to learn *about* Jesus (as though a reader were only gathering information) but also to learn *of* Jesus or to encourage
believing participation, as is made explicit in John 20:31.

Each narrative necessarily has a narrator — someone who guides
reader-learners through the text, much as a teacher guides learners.
Sometimes the narrator tells readers directly how to make sense
of the text, as we observed above when reader-learners are told
in Mark 1:1 that Jesus is the Messiah (that is, Christ), the Son of
God, which is then confirmed in the story by a voice from heaven.
But no character in the story (other than possibly Jesus, who goes
to the wilderness) reacts to this voice, so perhaps it is for reader-
learners to react. Apparently the disciples have not heard this voice
either, nor could they have read Mark's introductory verse, and
several chapters later they are still asking, "Who then is this?"
(Mark 4:41). Further, Jesus repeatedly cautions his disciples and
those he heals to "say nothing to anyone" (Mark 1:44; 5:43; 7:36;
8:30; 9:9) but to keep it a secret. But it is a secret only for the
characters in the story, not for reader-learners! In other words, the
story is explicitly constructed to "let the reader understand" (Mark
13:14) what the characters in the story do not understand, thus in-
suring that reading the story is a very different experience for the
reader-learner than it is for the characters enacting the story. This
is exactly what we saw earlier in the Book of Job! Robert Fowler
contends, "The Gospel is designed not to say something about the
disciples or even to say something about Jesus, but to do something
to the reader."[129]

---

128. Crossan, *The Historical Jesus*, 345. In this quotation, I have chosen to leave
out "not of promise but." Crossan consistently denies that there is any eschatological significance or future reference in these texts, but in the judgment of many,
myself included, the textual and historical evidence does not support his denial.
Still, what Crossan affirms is valid.

129. Fowler, *Let the Reader Understand*, 79.

How the Gospels handle the disciples as characters in the story also guides reader-learners, but much more subtly and indirectly. Many scholars have noted how readers in the early church might well have found themselves identifying with the disciples as they, too, struggled with faith and sought to understand their relation with Jesus.[130] Matthew's Gospel is quite explicit about this connection: in Matthew, the disciples understand Jesus (Matt. 13:51–52). The sending of the disciples (chap. 10) focuses more on early-church persecution than on the difficulties experienced by the original disciples, and the closing command-promise in Matthew 28:19–20 applies for all disciples, early or late. In Matthew, the disciples are the insiders who understand Jesus, while all others are outsiders who do not understand (see Matt. 13). Thus the reader might be expected to want to be like the disciples.

Mark's handling of the disciples in the story is more ambiguous and does something quite different with reader-learners.[131] As Ted Weeden first demonstrated, Mark's picture of the disciples (especially when compared with Matthew's and Luke's treatment) shows them unable to perceive who Jesus is, then they misconceive who he is, and finally they abandon Jesus.[132] Mark's narrative focuses upon Jesus' activities, and from the beginning, the disciples are eyewitnesses and recipients of Jesus' teaching (chaps. 2–4). When opposition arises, Jesus defends the disciples from attack (chap. 2) and even calls them his brothers and sisters (3:31–35). Yet when a storm arises rocking their boat, the sleeping Jesus is wakened by the disciples with a rebuke, "Teacher, do you not care that we are perishing?" Having just read several descriptions of closeness between Jesus and his disciples, including his having "explained everything in private to his disciples" (4:34), the reader is bound to be surprised at this outburst. Reader-learners have been led to infer up to this point that these men understood Jesus and knew he cared for them. Even granting that the disciples were frightened, why should Jesus' sleeping be seen as an uncaring act? Jesus responds to their charge, "Have you still no faith?" (4:40). Within the story, the disciples' accusation triggers Jesus' counteraccusation, and reader-learners may feel distance growing between themselves

---

130. See, for example, the collection of essays edited by Fernando Segovia, *Discipleship in the New Testament* (Philadelphia: Fortress, 1985).
131. The interpretation that follows is indebted to Fowler, *Let the Reader Understand*, 67–70.
132. Theodore J. Weeden, *Mark: Traditions in Conflict* (Philadelphia: Fortress, 1971), 23–44.

and the disciples. Yet the use of "still" invites hesitation: "We are inclined not to be too critical of them at this early stage in the Gospel, for perhaps they will yet arrive at understanding and faith."[133]

Two chapters (or eighty-nine verses) later, there is another sea story, which Mark handles quite differently. In the storm story of Mark 4:35–41, the narrator is an outside reporter of the event. Now, having just read of an exorcism, raising a girl from the dead, and feeding five thousand people, reader-learners are invited to enter the story of Mark 6:47–52 from the point of view of Jesus, seeing the disciples "straining at the oars" as he was walking on the water. We are even told Jesus' intention (which only an insider can have known) to "pass them by." Just here (6:49) the narrator abruptly switches, and reader-learners find themselves inside the point of view of the disciples: what they saw, what they thought, their feelings of terror and astonishment. Again the narrator switches point of view (6:51b) and becomes an outside reporter, explaining the disciples' lack of comprehension of the loaves as a case of "their hearts were hardened." Here the reader is invited to stand apart from the disciples and pass judgment on their lack of understanding. Fowler comments,

> Having seen astonishing or frightful things through their (the disciples') eyes, we are often inclined to forgive their lack of insight. When we are offered the opportunity to see things through their eyes and we cannot do so, however, because our knowledge and understanding is greater than theirs, in those moments the reader is closer to Jesus than are the disciples. The narrator has opened up the distance between Jesus and his disciples and inserted the reader into the space between them.[134]

This distance between Jesus and his disciples grows as Mark's story unfolds, until at last the disciples abandon Jesus just before the crucifixion, which means that "the burden of discipleship now falls squarely upon the shoulders of the only remaining candidate for discipleship — the recipient of the narrator's discourse, the reader of the Gospel."[135]

In other words, the Gospel writer has used the storyteller's art to do exactly what the earlier sages and Jesus did with their proverbial sayings and parables — entice hearers and reader-learners into

---

133. Fowler, *Let the Reader Understand*, 67.
134. Ibid., 70.
135. Ibid., 70–71.

a puzzle or enigma and then shift to them (us) the responsibility for making sense of it and responding appropriately. As Jerry Camery-Hoggatt observes about Mark's uses of narrative dissonance, "it is not that Mark sought to combine dissonant story elements into a more or less coherent narrative, and that he failed in that attempt. Rather, it is that he deliberately generated dissonance in an attempt to force the reader to take a position, and thus come to faith."[136]

WHY? WHAT IS THE POINT OF LEARNING THIS WAY?

Congruence between the *what* and the *how* (content and method) is pedagogically striking in Jesus' teaching and in the Gospel texts. Jesus talked of the kingdom, the compassionate and just rule of God, what it was like to be a subject, and he enacted that in his interactions with people. The texts not only portray Jesus' sending apprentice-disciples to do as he did but effectively invite later reader-learners to find themselves sent as well. What then can we infer about the purpose of expecting hearers and reader-learners to learn this in this manner? Then we also ask, How does this understanding of pedagogy fit with Jesus' death? for it does not seem plausible to hold that the Gospels show that teaching was focal to Jesus' mission in life but unrelated to his death. Why is that important?

Reform and Renewal, Tradition and Experience

The Gospels' portrayal of Jesus' teaching and activities seems to weave together the diverse strands of the previous texts we have surveyed. Like Proverbs, Jesus' teaching was thoroughly grounded in the everyday realities of common life, and it incorporated Israel's historical traditions with wisdom interests in a manner quite similar to Sirach and the Wisdom of Solomon. Jesus used these traditional materials to propose a fresh reading of who God is, how God acts, and how humans are to be within that rule. Like Job and Qohelet, Jesus' manner of teaching questioned older conventions even as it invited and evoked radical new ways of seeing and participating in God's coming kingship. The Gospel writers and Paul recognize this fusion of old and new, order and counterorder, in using the language about and from Woman Wisdom in their texts about Jesus.

---

136. Jerry Camery-Hoggatt, *Irony in Mark's Gospel: Text and Subtext* (Cambridge: Cambridge University Press, 1992), 180.

Continuity with one's heritage and the ability to adapt or change it are significant issues for the pedagogy of any religious community.[137] They are issues of individual and communal identity and are contestable and controversial because they are political in the deepest sense: communities deciding what they want to be and become — together. Recent historical studies confirm that Jesus was a Jew thoroughly steeped in Israel's traditions and convictions.[138] He embraced Israel's traditions, urged their restoration, enhanced their claims on everyday life, and used them to point to God's ruling so that people could see. Yet, pedagogically, his parabolic approach to learning focused less on recitation and more on performance.

How very different all this is from what we expect of teachers today! We are so engrossed in getting it right and whether it really happened that we often wander off the path, lose our imagination, and can no longer see. In today's world, these texts of Jesus' actions and sayings seem distinctly odd. He did not tell Israel's stories; he invented new ones. Is it possible that Jesus, like our earlier authors, was convinced that the only way to preserve and renew a tradition is to reinvent it?

Is Learning Character a Gift?

Jesus' sayings seem so simple, yet so profoundly true. Why is the metaphoric so dominant in his approach to learning? Why does he keep saying, "Let whoever has ears hear"? Perhaps the problem, to paraphrase the Bard, is not in our stars, but in ourselves.

Metaphoric or figurative texts are not "real." We (like Jesus' hearers?) too readily assume that the world is a given. Do we assume that "given an incompatibility between the utterance and conditions in the world, the conditions are to be taken as fixed, and it is the utterance that must be construed"?

> Now this is not a logically necessary position. We may, if we like, in the face of an incompatibility between what is asserted in an utterance and conditions as they obtain in the world, regard the utterance as fixed and construe the world. Instead, that is, of construing the utterance so that it makes sense in the world, we construe the world

---

137. See the collection of essays edited by Padraic O'Hare, *Transformation and Tradition in Religious Education* (Birmingham, Ala.: Religious Education Press, 1979); and Mary Elizabeth Moore's *Education for Continuity and Change: A New Model for Christian Religious Education* (Nashville: Abingdon, 1983).

138. See E. P. Sanders, *Jesus and Judaism;* and more recently, James H. Charlesworth, ed., *Jesus' Jewishness: Exploring the Place of Jesus within Early Judaism* (New York: Crossroad: 1991), esp. the chapter by Meier, "Reflections on Jesus-of-History Research Today," 84–107.

so as to make sense of the utterance. On this account, "defectiveness" is located in the world (i.e., the actual world), not in the utterance. "Deviant" utterances are taken literally; they mean what they say — what gives is the world.[139]

The metaphoric way of learning used by Jesus and by the texts we have been exploring invites learners to see the world under another picture than that given by "reality." Reader-learners are asked to suppose we can learn to be a subject, can assume a relation with the King even in ordinary daily living. If we did that, might the world as we know it become different? Jesus' pictures reshape our imaginations, and when we act according to those pictures, then we reshape the world. Jesus (an unschooled layman) and these Gospel texts neither reject nor presume a sacred space or a religious ritual or a liturgical season or a religious expert and certainly nothing like a classroom, printed curriculum materials, or a church program. With this approach, any time and place is the right time and place. If we have accurately described what is to be learned and how it is to be learned from Jesus and these texts, what reader-learners are invited to is a continuous mindfulness of being governed by God, so that one's character and actions show oneself increasingly a subject (in the double sense described above).

Some ways of thinking about character presume that it is a defined or predefined social role — much like a character in a play. Others presume that character is a quality of the person, created by and possessed by the person in interaction with significant others. We speak of someone "being a character" or "having character." But these texts invite reader-learners to assume a particular character — that of a subject. This is an invitation into a relation, for one cannot be a king's subject without a king, and one's "being a subject" is not something one has so much as it is something one is given in relation to the king. The point here is not just to follow the King's laws but to become holy as the King is holy, to become caring and compassionate as the King is caring and compassionate, to be just as the King is just, and so on. To be a subject, one must become it, for it shapes one's character.

A teacher knows that to master complex and difficult subjects, the learner must begin with simple skills that build toward future mastery. Before one can act a Shakespearean character well, one

---

139. Samuel R. Levine, "Language, Concepts, and World: Three Domains of Metaphor," in *Metaphor and Thought*, ed. Andrew Ortony, 2d ed. (New York: Cambridge University Press, 1993), 121.

must learn to read and then to comprehend Elizabethan linguistic and cultural patterns. Those basic skills must then be combined with oral and dramatic performance skills. Nor will those skills be sufficient or fruitful if one does not also acquire attitudes such as patience, persistence, self-discipline, and a love for language, theater arts, and history. And all that is needed only to act as a character. This may sound schoollike, but it is an ancient and ordinary human experience. A child learns to become a member of a particular family. An infant born into the Smythe family has the genetic potential to *become* a Smythe, not just in the physical sense, but in the more important sense of one whose living can express the attitudes, values, and behavior appropriate to the Smythe clan and heritage. If the learning is faulty, other Smythes might say, "Well, he surely doesn't act like one of us."

Learning to be a member of the family or kingdom of God means more than knowing the stories and the heritage or believing the right doctrines. If God, who created and sustains this family, desires peace and love because they are essential qualities of God's character, then a family member will also come to desire those qualities and embody them in her character. To stay in character, we have to stay in touch. In this apprentice-disciple-learning, both "kingdom" and "learning to participate" are simultaneously present and not-yet fully realized.

When one is learning how to be a family member or a subject, what we are to become is already given in one sense, yet we must reform what we are given to become ourselves. The tradition is a gift to the new character — they do not create it; they re-create it. Thus these texts serve, not so much as lessons to be mastered and then applied in daily living, but more as reminders. They call a reader-learner's attention back to the heart of the matter, to the gifts, to the subject, and thus to God.

Did Jesus Practice Noncoercive Learning?

"Loving God, loving neighbors, and loving your enemy" would include most sources of conflict. Might it also suggest a nonviolent, even noncoercive, approach to daily living and to pedagogy? Violence begins from a premise that there are some (often children) who can be coerced or must be coerced, legitimately. Some reason, for example, "They must come to believe or to behave in certain ways which are contrary to their own self-interest and/or against their will, so for their own good and for the good of all, they must be coerced."

What would the history of pedagogy be without coercion? Even in an enlightened modern world, we are so immersed in structures and practices of pedagogical coercion we can hardly imagine another possibility. We have compulsory schooling laws. We use patterns of discipline that compel "acceptable behavior" by the use of threats, sanctions, punishments, and inducements. We use grading to compel activity by students and to assure control by teachers. The rationale often offered for using coercion on learners is that it is done for their sake and in their own best interest. This usually presumes two corollary beliefs: (a) that the teacher knows what is best for learners and (b) that learners cannot be trusted to do what is best for themselves. Let us also admit that many find substantial empirical and experiential evidence (of the sort that the wisdom tradition would admire) that these corollary beliefs may be justified.

If we grant that Jesus was a wise teacher and seems to have shown above-average insight and ability, then perhaps he was in a better position than most to decide what is good for others. Who better to coerce people into what was best for them? Yet he did not. Why? All the teacher-inquirer exchanges portrayed in the Gospels involving Jesus are between adults. We have no reports that Jesus ever engaged in learning activities with children, which is not surprising given the limited nature of the educational enterprise in that culture. Sometimes the coercive practices that an adult teacher uses with children would create offense if used with adults. Does that explain why Jesus did not use such tactics in his teaching?

If, as scholars contend, the Gospels sometimes shape their accounts of Jesus' sayings and activities to suit controversies in the church, where there was much competitive strife over doctrinal issues, then we might expect to find accounts of Jesus' insisting upon doctrinal agreement. Yet he is not portrayed as having pressured his opponents to agree with him. One of his most characteristic refrains was, "Let anyone with ears listen!" This seems to invite hearer-reader-listeners both to make sense of the saying or parable in question and to make up their own minds. For example, the account of Jesus' encounter with a rich young man records that the young man heard Jesus' advice, and Jesus "loved him." Yet the young man may have left without accepting the advice, and Jesus reportedly let him go without comment (Matt. 19:16–22; Mark 10:17–22; Luke 18:18–23).

Despite Jesus' lack of coercive effort, his teaching was perceived as having authority, even by those with whom he disagreed! Indeed, were this not the case, it would not have been necessary to take official action to hinder his influence. So his influence and authority were not grounded in his power to coerce agreement in his hearers.

Jesus' image of the kingly rule of God, creating loyal subjects, might even support coercive tactics, for kings coerce subjects and others often and in many ways, including violence and war. A few of the characters in Jesus' parables even used coercion or violence, such as the king who imprisoned and tortured the servant whose debt he first forgave (Matt. 18:34) and the owner of the vineyard who destroyed the tenants (Luke 20:16).

Is a loving disposition the product of coercion? What are the means by which one's character becomes dominated by compassion and concern for what is good for other people? Is it not the case that both coercion and violence incite defensive and self-protective behavior, not loving concern for others? Being a loyal subject, being responsible, being caring, being educated, being loving — when all these ways of being are expressed, they require not having been coerced. Perhaps Jesus did not engage in coercive behavior because it was incompatible with what he sought for others. Could today's teachers "go and do likewise"?

Wisdom as Both Act and Word: Embodied Character

Clearly Jesus was a teacher, and much of his teaching is portrayed in a manner quite consistent with the wisdom tradition we have examined. But the Gospels are so thoroughly imbued with theological and christological interests, that it is almost impossible to distinguish between the parts of the portrayal of Jesus as teacher as Christology and the parts that reflect the historical Jesus' activities. Yet Mark's depiction of Jesus as teacher did not originate with him, for he is using traditional material that portrays miracles and confrontations as teaching, thus linking his teaching to his death.[140] While we cannot know for sure, we might ask if this link is just Mark's construction, or could we imagine a plausible way this link might have played itself out historically?

Jesus' reminders of God and Israel's traditions were not just reminders about ideas. Education has been so associated with schools, books, and ideas that we become misled — so we need to be reminded, for example, of apprentice-disciples and of learning from seeing others do things. If learning to love your enemies

---

140. Achtemeier, "He Taught Them Many Things," 480–81.

is an idea or theory, dismissal can come easily: "Well, that's all fine in words or in theory, but it won't work in real life." But when I see someone act it out in the real world (e.g., Gandhi, Dorothy Day, Martin Luther King, Mother Teresa) or when I learn by trying it out myself, it is harder to dismiss. Also, when people can watch and feel what it is like when someone starts *acting* differently, innovations might catch on even among those who do not often think carefully about ideas and their long-term implications. Seeing a vision acted out demonstrates that it is more than abstraction — living this way might change how people relate one with another. Sometimes that is taken to be threatening.

As a vision is lived out, it can also become harder to recant under threat. We have numerous examples of people other than Jesus (even teachers) who faced a demand to recant their views under implied or explicit threat of death (Socrates, Joan d'Arc, Luther, Galileo, Gandhi, Martin Luther King, Paul Freire). For such, to deny their convictions to save their own skin would contradict what they had stood for and would betray the trust of their community of learners-disciples-supporters. On such a view, a particular individual is less important than the life of the vision and message, providing hope and new life for a community. The teacher teaches for the sake of the larger community and in hope for the future, not just for self.

This is not an unfamiliar experience for teachers. In teaching, inevitably, a teacher professes what she believes, even if only implicitly. Sometimes a teacher will even discover what she believes on some subject as it is discussed. It is also not unusual, especially for the teacher of adults, for learners to suggest that she more fully act out her beliefs: "Practice what you teach!" (Indeed, one good reason for stating publicly what you believe is to invite others to help you live out or correct those beliefs.)

Suppose Jesus experienced just that in the hearings before the elders and Pilate. The Gospel texts show that Jesus had become a subject, as displayed in the consistency between his actions and sayings. Being confronted with what he had said and done, and with what others had said of and about him, perhaps he saw with new clarity where his own convictions were leading. Rather than deny those convictions, change his character, or contradict his teaching, he allowed events to unfold. When a teacher has worked closely with a particular group for a long time, gained their trust, changing one's mind is no longer a solely individual matter.

This scenario need not imply that Jesus' teaching was the direct cause of his death in a strong sense. His teaching was not so different from Israel's tradition to warrant death on theological grounds, nor was Rome (Pilate) that concerned about his teachings. Still, his teaching role played a significant part, for if the choice was to live by taking back his teaching and denying his actions to make people and community healthy, whole, and joyous or to die misunderstood — Jesus chose death. If this is so, here is another indicator that teaching and learning both have fundamentally to do with one's character and not simply with ideas. Or, to adapt a theological convention, Jesus demonstrates pedagogical incarnation, just as biblical texts witness to theological incarnation. In doing so, these accounts resonate again with Job: suffering neither has a fixed meaning, nor need it be the last word.

CHAPTER SEVEN

WHAT COUNTS AS EDUCATION IN A WISDOM APPROACH?

> A neighbor went to Nasrudin, asking to borrow his donkey, "It is out on loan," said the Mulla. At that moment the donkey was heard to bray, somewhere inside the stable. "But I can hear it bray, over there." "Whom do you believe," said Nasrudin; "me or a donkey?"[1]

It might be wise to stop right here, to end the book; first, to allow the particular wisdom figures and texts to speak for themselves and, second, to allow space and opportunity for the present reader-learners to create their own synthesis. It would be foolish to expect the author of Job and the author of the Book of Wisdom, in different cultures, different historical circumstances, facing different questions, to approach teaching and learning in the same way simply because both were "sages."

Still, we should ask, So what? If we cannot reproduce today the conditions under which these sages taught or even the conditions in which these texts were created, what has all this to do with contemporary educational ministry? What follows are some musings of my own — one person's attempt to respect the spirit of these sages of old and their texts, while reflecting on contemporary educational concerns.[2] I invite you to assess my attempts ("Whom do you believe, ... me or a donkey?") — may they prompt your own.

We begin by repeating our three questions. Then we ask, What counts as education in a wisdom approach? Could it be a single, coherent pedagogical approach, or is it a collection of divergent

---

1. Idries Shah, *The Sufis* (New York: Doubleday, 1964; Anchor Books, 1971), 88–89.

2. I have been teaching courses in the wisdom materials and courses in educational theory and philosophy, side by side, for over twenty years by now, so I can no longer be sure whether what I now see in these texts originated in the text or in my understandings of educational ministry. Be that as it may, here is what I see. See if you see it too.

approaches? We conclude with a few observations about what is required of one who teaches and some whimsical musings.

WHAT IS WORTH LEARNING?

The sages often used dualities (two paths, two women, wise and fool, etc.) to call attention to the simple complexity that is one of biblical wisdom's gifts to pedagogy.

Learning to Slow Down

The study of texts is vitally important, but texts are, not ends in themselves, but a means to learning how to steer a path through life. Ultimately what is worth learning is how to live. Too often teachers use texts as a substitute for dealing with life itself. (I've done it myself.) To see reading texts as reading for life, especially in today's mass-media and computerized world, we must slow down our reading (the opposite of what is often recommended) — make it more reflective. Slower reading not only allows us to absorb the many layers of the texts, their richness; it allows time and space for the text to begin to read the reader-learner. It allows time for resonance — time for a reader to become aware of and explore the ways one text has echoes in another that enrich and enliven the messages of both. Still, being read by a text is more a matter of receptivity (than of time and space), and one is more receptive if one sees that these texts really can and do address our knowing how to live with one another as subjects.

In our contemporary world, we are also misled by two common beliefs (usually enacted, sometimes even verbalized). The first is that religion is different from everyday life. For example, many seem to believe that religion happens in church and education happens in school. (A "separation of church and state" is unimaginable both in biblical times and through most of history.) This emerges innocently enough when, for example, Christians falsely say, "It is time to go to church." In Christian practice, the people *are* the church. We mislead ourselves by fragmenting life. The second belief is that religion has primarily to do with what you believe, things spiritual, or faith, not external behavior. What is affirmed here is correct, but so is what is denied. Learning to think well can help one live well, but sometimes we act better than we know, and sometimes we use our ignorance as an excuse for not practicing even what we do know. These texts affirm that what is worth learning is worth living, what one lives shows what one has learned.

What is worth learning? Learning to read texts and life or, better, becoming readers for life. Becoming a reader for life, the Gospel texts remind us, also means letting the text read the reader. To be an active subject relating to a text is also to be subject to the text, much as to a king. After being read, the role of the reader is, in the words of al-Hasan ibn al-Haytham, an eleventh-century Egyptian scholar, to render visible "that which writing suggests in hints and shadows."[3]

Experience and Tradition

At the end of the school day, the children came and sat on the flour sacks. Jacob would sit across from the children, and they would talk.

As Jacob told his stories, he would from time to time shut his eyes. It was as if he were remembering what to say, not by searching through his mind, but by remembering what he saw. . . .

"What do you see when you shut your eyes, Jacob?" asked a little girl.

"Well, Jacob said, "once upon a time there was a man who had a vision and began pursuing it.

"Two others saw that the first man had a vision and began following him.

"In time, the children of those who followed asked their parents to describe what they saw.

"But what their parents described appeared to be the coattails of the man in front of them.

"When the children heard this, they turned from their parents' vision, saying it was not worthy of pursuit."

Jacob leaned toward the little girl who had asked the question.

"So, what do we discover from this story?"

The children were quiet.

"I'll tell you," said Jacob.

"We discover children who deny what they have never experienced.

"We discover parents who believe in what they have never experienced.

"And from this, we discover the question is not 'What do I see when I shut my eyes' but 'What do you see when you open yours?' "[4]

---

3. Quoted by Alberto Manguel, *A History of Reading* (New York: Viking, 1996), 39.

4. Noah ben Shea, *Jacob the Baker* (New York: Villard, 1989), 29–31.

Jacob the baker's story and commentary highlight the sages' pervasive concern for both tradition and one's own direct experience, which is also basic in educational ministry.

Without a tradition, we would never know what an experience is. We cannot do without traditions, nor can we rely on them alone. To remain alive and to become alive for each of us, traditions must be absorbed and tried on but also questioned and reshaped, as all these texts attest. Like a living language and like one's clothing, a tradition must not only be lived in; it must also change and grow as the community's understanding changes and grows, or else it will die. Traditions make life work.

Some say the best way to preserve a tradition is to repeat it exactly as received. But what if the tradition stays the same while the culture and language change around it? Consider an actual translator's dilemma: how does one translate "the bread of life" into a language and island culture that has never had grain and thus knows nothing of bread? The point of the metaphor is that the bread of life is common and basic to survival, not that it is strange, unknown, or imported. A literal translation of the traditional "bread of life" image would actually change its meaning in a culture that operates with a different paradigm of what is basic to survival. The traditional rendering literally could do no work in that setting. The translator had to change the metaphor to keep it the same, using "the sweet potato of life." On the other hand, sometimes new paradigms will not permit essential values of a tradition to work either, as when media and the hurry of society inhibit reflective quiet.

No formula reveals when a tradition needs adapting and when the adaptation has gone too far. There will necessarily be differences of judgment; arguments; controversy; reassessing evidence; appeals to different experts, sources, and versions; dialogue; trial and error in lived experience — all familiar pedagogical tools for apprenticed reader-learners. Wise judgments are called for, as well as both humility (being subject to the tradition) and also courage (an active subject daring to revise the heritage).

As Jacob the baker observes, the essential question is not what the expert sees when his eyes are closed, but what the reader-learner sees when her eyes are open. Tradition insists there is something to see — *if* one's eyes are open.

Answers and Questions

Sometimes when people talk about questions, it seems the only reason for having a question is to get an answer. When one arrives at an answer, one is finished with the question and can throw it away. But when contemporary experience and tradition engage, which question one asks can make all the difference. Each of our texts has dealt with traditions, but they have asked different questions: How can we preserve tradition? How can we get rid of the tradition's rigidity? How can we deal with both our tradition and this new culture? And so on. It may be more important to learn how to ask fruitful questions that give rise to truth yet honor essential mystery.

The sages teach us to seek questions and answers not only in written texts and mountain-top revelations but also in the creation and in everyday life around us. As Elizabeth Huwiler says,

> Seems to me that the most wonderful thing about wisdom for contemporary religion is precisely that it does not come from times of specific Israelite revelation. It's one thing to have an idea of how to live as God's people when your leader is on the Holy Mountain receiving tablets inscribed by "the big Y" in person; or when you are transported into the divine council. But when that isn't happening, how do you know how to live? The sages seem to me to treat all creation as revelatory: not just the emphasis on primordial creation, but the willingness to look into the created world, at the ways of ants and crocodiles, to gain insight.[5]

There are risks. Job insisted, for example, that God was responsible for Job's suffering — and the author so constructed the book that reader-learners are inclined to agree with Job. Many insist God is responsible only for good things and someone else must be responsible for all that is bad. Yet Job insists God is his enemy, even his abuser, and God admits responsibility.

Are there questions that cannot be asked? Are there times when asking questions is itself misleading? Ludwig Wittgenstein suggested that sometimes a seemingly obvious question cannot sensibly be asked without leading to hopeless muddles. Asking the question may create a problem where there should be none. Qohelet also suggested that always asking, "What is gained?" or "What's in it for me?" misleads. Is that why Job gave up his questioning? "I lay my hand on my mouth... and I will not answer"

---

5. Elizabeth F. Huwiler, letter to author, 10 July 1991.

(Job 40:4–5), and "I have uttered what I did not understand, things too wonderful for me" (42:3).

What are questions for? Among our texts, some seem to prefer answers (Proverbs, Sirach, and Wisdom of Solomon), while others prefer questions (Job and Ecclesiastes), and some offer answers that act more like questions (Jesus?). Or did Qohelet suggest there are answers (gifts) for which there are no questions? To the sages, this is a matter for judgment, and making such judgments wisely is precisely what constitutes shrewdness, understanding, discernment, and prudence and insight into enigmas (see Prov. 1:2–6). Acquiring sound judgment requires instruction and study, patience, extensive practice, dialogue within the community, and careful, reverent reflection.

Indeed, too much focus upon questions that only lead to answers can mislead us to expect that learning and teaching have primarily or even solely to do with verbal matters, answers to questions. If the wisdom tradition seeks primarily to guide one's path in living, then perhaps God offers a much wider range of gifts than either questions or answers.

God's Gifts and Human Achievements

We have noted repeatedly how little explicit attention the sages pay to the major historical events of Israel's tradition. Yet, according to the sages, those who engage their ordinary life and their daily bread and work with their eyes and ears wide open more clearly see the minutiae of mundane living, and in the mundane, they see intimations of more.

We also noted the sages pondered less about what God is doing and more about what kind of God this is. Is God omnipotent? Is God just? Is God omniscient? Does God allow injustice and innocent suffering? Why? What kind of God would do that? Is God caring? Is God present? If so, in what manner and to what end? Jesus also seems to consider the character of God. And if we are to be subjects in God's ruling, what kind of character need we be? How can we become more compassionate, more loving, more just, more attentive to what we have been given, and thus more full of joy?

Educational institutions, secular or sacred, are places of *work*. Children may be allowed to think of their work as play, but the higher one travels in educational circles, the more stress is placed on hard work. In one sense this is quite natural, for educational attainment requires hard work, even drudgery. Every scholar, every scientist, and every athlete knows how much plodding along and grinding it out is necessary for accomplishment. This is not new. Long ago the redactor of Ecclesiastes observed, "Of making many books there is no end, and much study is a weariness of the flesh" (12:12).

Yet the sages also counsel, "Happy are those who keep my ways; Hear instruction and be wise . . . whoever finds me, finds life" (Prov. 8:32–35); "whenever a man does eat and drink and get enjoyment out of all his wealth [and work], it is a gift of God" (Eccles. 3:13, NJPSV). Sirach urges bending to *Sophia*'s yoke, chains, and bonds, searching and seeking, and thus "you will find the rest she gives, and she will be changed into joy for you" (Sir. 6:28; cf. Matt. 11:28–30). The Wisdom of Solomon testifies that "life with her [*Sophia*] has no pain, but gladness and joy" (Wisd. 8:9–16). And Jesus came feasting. Jesus' words in John ring true in spirit, "I came that they may have life, and have it abundantly" (John 10:10).

Promises of extrinsic reward motivate when the work itself is not rewarding. Yet the sages do not use joy and pleasure as rewards or inducements but as the very spirit in which the learning and teaching are engaged. The key here, I believe, lies in seeing mundane, daily living as a gift *and* seeing the educational process itself, not as an arduous and onerous task, but as one of many gifts. To adapt Sirach, how can a community help the giftlike quality of learning ("A-ha!") more fully come to expression so that the spirit full of wonder, respect, excitement, and eagerness flows through all pedagogical rivers (Sir. 24:24–34)?

HOW CAN THESE BEST BE LEARNED?

Pedagogical know-how is twofold: methods and manner must be congruent. Teachers know that using the right method in the wrong manner can be just as counterproductive as speaking words of affection in a tone of contempt.

Real-Life Teaching and Learning

Each of the wisdom texts uses language skillfully to enlist reader-learners in their own quest for understanding, for skill to discern, for guidance on the path. Yet reader-learners must also practice, try things out for themselves, much as apprentices do with a master-teacher. Jesus' apprentice-disciples learned concepts and beliefs but also shared emotions, attitudes, dispositions, behaviors, anxieties, uncertainties, hopes, and loyalties. All these were intertwined with certain smells, the taste of bread and fish, the rocky road beneath the feet, the rocking of the boat, and the still quiet at night. Learning in this manner would reach more levels of character and consciousness than the linguistic mastery of contemporary schooling and church education. Must we become itinerants then? If we are to be apprentices, can we be apprentices to daily living?

Barbara Myerhoff, an anthropologist whose book *Number Our Days* provides vivid descriptions of life among elderly Jewish people in a senior center, puzzled about why "as a group, the men seemed more worn out and demoralized than the women."[6] While women live longer than men, Myerhoff suggested the difference in daily vitality can be traced to a "complex combination of physiology and culture," including their different religious experiences.[7] These seniors all grew up in Eastern European Jewish shtetls, amid sharply distinguished gender roles in family life, in social and economic life, and in religion. Religion was important to everyone, but it was the specific responsibility and privilege of the men. For example, it took ten men to form a minyon for a prayer service (women did not count). Women were facilitators of men's activities, supporters, and nurturers, following men's instructions and interpretations. Women were "subjected," modest, and devoted to family, and they prepared the sabbath meals, even worked outside the home to make more time for men to study Torah. These women dealt with government officials and peasants, managed the household budget, and organized family schedules coordinating religious, familial, and public demands. They also cared for the sick, collected money for orphans and refugees and for needy Jews all over the world.[8] These activities revolved around the necessities of everyday life, so the women continued them into old age, whereas when the men retired from their work, they gave up a portion of their active identity.

These men and women had also experienced starkly different methods of learning Jewish religious activities. The men studied Talmud and Torah in Hebrew (which the women often did not understand), scrutinizing and arguing about great ideas, while the women baked bread, lighted candles, sang, and prayed — orally in

---

6. Barbara Myerhoff, *Number Our Days* (New York: Simon and Schuster, Touchstone, 1978), 248.

7. Ibid., 242.

8. Ibid., 242–53.

Yiddish.[9] Myerhoff vividly evokes these differences in the words of two of the women,

> We girls had what you could call domestic religion, that means it comes to you through the rituals. I will explain to you. We had a grandmother who gathered us seven girls around. The two boys went off early in the morning to pray. For us, we had to say the morning prayers.... Now I knew the Hebrew words already by heart, I knew about the washing of the hands, the prayer for the bread, keeping separate the meat and milk, all these things Grandmother taught us. But not what anything means. But it was our habit and it was beautiful. God wants it so, that's all.... I think the boys didn't have it that way. They knew what the sacred words meant so they could argue and doubt. But with us girls, what we knew we couldn't doubt because what we knew came without understanding. These things were injected into you in childhood and chained you together with that beautiful grandmother, so since infancy you can't know life without it. The boys in cheder could learn the words and forget them, but in this domestic religion, you could never get rid of it.... You could not just set it aside when you don't agree anymore. *When it goes in this way...Jewish comes up in you from the roots and it stays with you all your life.*[10]

This early learning was deeply yoked with family affection, with smells, tastes, a warm hearth, and candles, so sometimes later candlelighting ceremonies evoked emotional memories. Basha said:

> Do you know what it meant to me when I was called to the candles last Friday? I'll tell you. When I was a little girl, I would stand this way, beside my mother when she would light the candles for Shabbat. We were alone in the house, everything warm and clean and quiet with all the good smells of the cooking food coming in around us. We are still warm from the mikva. My braids very tight, to last through Shabbes, made with my best ribbons. Whatever we had, we wore our best. To this day, when the heat of the candles is on my face, I circle the flame and cover my eyes, and then I feel again my mother's hands on my smooth cheeks.[11]

These accounts strongly resemble an informal apprentice-style learning, yoked to the traditions of the community but embedded in direct sensory experiences that carry deep affective and symbolic significance. One could infer that the women's method of learning religion enabled them to be more fully subjects (in the dual sense

---

9. Ibid., 256–57.
10. Ibid., 234–35, emphasis added.
11. Ibid., 256.

described in the previous chapter) in later life. Myerhoff suggests that this helps account for the differences in vitality in the lives of the women compared with the men.[12]

Using Simple Stories

One of the purposes of sayings and stories (whether told by these texts or by other sages such as Confucius, Lao-tzu, Jochanan ben Zakkai, Nasrudin, or Jacob the baker) is to preserve in memorable and useful form the accumulated experience of the community and of wise persons. The hoped-for effect is that the hearer will recognize its truth — "Oh, I knew that" or "Of course, that is so obvious! Why didn't I think of that?"

Sometimes the simple is quite complex. Jacob does not claim there were actual parents and children like those described in his story, yet the story is surely true, just as are the parables of the good Samaritan and the prodigal son. Poetry and fiction often tell the truth. The Book of Job is fiction as truth, with the power to stir imagination and emotions to arouse continued engagement with the existential issues the story evokes.

Stories, proverbs, aphorisms, and poetry evoke more than they tell. Good educators, especially teachers of young children, have long known the power of poetry and story or a pithy saying repeated at the right time. And authors such as Katherine Paterson can tell a complex story with theological sophistication yet communicate effectively to young people.[13] Recently theologians have also made much of narrative structures, a helpful corrective to the tendency to see biblical material within the frame of doctrinal propositions. Yet there are also dangers here. For example, often when the biblical material is portrayed using narrative frameworks, portions of the canon that are not narratives (often the wisdom texts) drop out of the portrayal.[14] And wisdom's critical

---

12. Similar observations can be made about the apprentice manner in which doctoral students are mentored and by the various mentoring approaches and programs being tried today. See, for example, the confirmation program developed by William H. Willimon, *Making Disciples* (Inver Grove Heights, Minn.: Logos, 1990).

13. Katherine Paterson's award-winning children's novels are more "simple" than the complex novels written for adults, but they are powerful because they are truthful about life and portray grace and hope in everyday form. See *The Great Gilly Hopkins* (New York: Crowell Junior Books, 1978); and *Jacob Have I Loved* (New York: HarperCollins, 1990). See also her essays about her own and others' books: *A Sense of Wonder: On Reading and Writing Books for Children* (New York: Plume, 1995), esp. "Hope and Happy Endings," "Do I Dare Disturb the Universe?" and "Yes, But Is It True?"

14. For example, Walter Wangerin's *The Book of God: The Bible as a Novel,*

strain can poke fun at such large overarching narrative structures (see Job 28). Sages know that no matter how good the story, theology, or ideology, there always will be loose ends, and living usually does not wait until we find the master narrative or the ultimate explanation.

Ralph Waldo Emerson recommended "embracing the common" — where our lives are played out.[15] One of the themes of the doctrine of the incarnation is that Jesus came as a common man and blessed common bread and wine and died as a common criminal. Yet many regard his life as extraordinary. Simple stories and simple sayings evoke much more than they tell.

Metaphor, Learning, and Indirect Communication

In the Jacob the baker story above, as well as in Job, Ecclesiastes, and the Gospels, "seeing" is used as a metaphor for a learning that is experiential, rather than vicarious. In these texts, "seeing" and "sight" connote not only a visual experience but the ability to *perceive* more than what is actually visible. Job affirmed in his concluding profession that hearsay was insufficient, "but now my eye sees you" (Job 42:5). Qohelet frequently reported what he saw, yet seeing seems to undermine his confidence that he knows what God is doing, except as he sees that bread, wine, love, sunlight, are God's gifts for joy. In the Gospels, Jesus is said to teach in parables because the people see but do not perceive, and when John's disciples ask Jesus if he is the one they are waiting for, Jesus answers, "Go and tell John what you hear and see" (Matt. 11:4). This is seeing, but in a metaphoric sense "commonly associated with the apprenticeship experience."[16]

Teachers ask, "Do you see it?" or they suggest, "Look at it this way." They want learners to see the point. Yet teachers cannot coerce seeing, nor can teachers see for students. Socrates insisted he could not or would not make others see, but he could act as midwife to help others give birth to their own ideas. Jacob the baker reminds us that seeing is crucial and is easier when we have our eyes open. Such metaphors remind teachers that de-

---

2d ed. (Grand Rapids: Zondervan, 1996), must leave out the wisdom texts in order to make a novel of the Bible.

15. See especially Stanley Cavell, *This New Yet Unapproachable America: Lectures after Emerson after Wittgenstein* (Albuquerque: Living Batch Press, 1989), 9; citing Emerson's "The American Scholar."

16. Michael W. Coy, ed., *Apprenticeship: From Theory to Method and Back Again* (Albany: State University of New York Press, 1989), 2.

livering the message is preparation, which evokes something that must be completed or put together or discovered or appropriated by the learners. Judgment cannot be taught directly; one cannot understand something for another.

Humans use metaphors freely and familiarly, though we do not always understand how important metaphorical processes are in pedagogy.[17] Metaphors help us see one thing as another; or to use Piaget's language, they allow us to *assimilate* something new or strange into an old or familiar conceptual framework, just as Job first assimilated his suffering into the notion of punishment. But when something is really new or strange, in assimilating it to the old, we also stretch (accommodate) our old concept (what we already know) to what is new and strange. Job came to recognize that if he forced his losses to fit into the traditional concept of retribution, it challenged his concept of the divine. Something had to give. Qohelet recommended changing metaphors for how we think about food, drink, love, and work. By changing the framework with which we see, we change reality. In this case, the nonliteral (metaphor) changes the literal facts.[18] This is what Jesus' sayings and parables about the king's rule and the king's subjects do for human notions of how to be in this world with one another. This view of metaphor is closer to what Max Black has called the *interactive* level of metaphor, where metaphors not only compare but actually create the similarity or act as a bridge between the new and the old.[19]

Indirect communication is not new in pedagogy, though it is not widely understood. We see it already in Socrates' conversations and in Plato's allegory of the cave.[20] Nathan used indirect communication with David (2 Sam. 12), enabling David to see his actions

17. I explored these issues in "An Exploration in the Presuppositions of Objective Formation for Contemporary Protestant Educational Ministry" (Ph.D. diss., Yale University, 1969) and in "The Significance of Marc Belth for Religious Education," *Religious Education,* 64:4 (July–August 1969), 261–65.

18. This formulation is indebted to the article by Hugh G. Petrie and Rebecca S. Oshlag, "Metaphor and Learning," in *Metaphor and Thought,* ed. Andrew Ortony, 2d ed. (Cambridge: Cambridge University Press, 1993), 579–609, though the language used here is adopted from Thomas Green's article in the same volume, "Learning without Metaphor," (614), which is both a critique and affirmation of Petrie's article in the first edition. Specifically, Green affirms, "It seems to me that the paradigm case of learning something radically new in Petrie's sense would occur in the case of religious teaching" (611).

19. Max Black, *Models and Metaphors: Studies in Language and Philosophy* (Ithaca, N.Y.: Cornell University Press, 1962), 37–47.

20. Plato *The Republic* 25.7.514A–521B.

truthfully and judge himself. Israel's sages used it frequently, as we have seen. Indirect communication is described and used extensively by Søren Kierkegaard and by others since.[21] Kierkegaard insisted it was necessary, in part, because we, like David, tend to live with illusions (especially about ourselves) that prevent us from seeing truthfully. When that is so, direct communication is ineffective. Direct communication can also lead reader-learners, as well as teachers, to think about the message itself, objectifying it. Even teachers sometimes need a reminder that the religious message is self-involving. The concern is not just about how best to communicate to others, to learners, but how teacher and learners alike can hear and respond.[22]

In the Manner of Love and Mystery

We observed that the most frequently recurring phrases in wisdom texts had to do with "the fear of the Lord is the beginning of wisdom" (and variants). Jesus offered sayings that made response to a loving God central. Subjects who are loved want to be more loving. Sometimes the sages and Jesus have been portrayed as offering two opposing pictures of God and human response to God, as though the God of the Hebrew Bible is a judge to be feared and the God of the newer covenant is loving and affectionate. As we have seen, this is a misunderstanding of the meaning of "the fear of the Lord" as used in the Hebrew Bible.

In both Testaments, God initiates love and grace to humans, who respond with love, loyalty, and awe. In both Testaments, human awe is evoked not only by divine power but also by a sense

---

21. See Søren Kierkegaard's *Philosophical Fragments* (Princeton: Princeton University Press, 1985); *Concluding Unscientific Postscript* (Princeton: Princeton University Press, 1941); and especially his *The Point of View for My Work as an Author: A Report to History* (New York: Harper, 1962). See also C. Stephen Evans, *Kierkegaard's "Fragments" and "Postscript": The Religious Philosophy of Johannes Climacus* (Atlantic Highlands, N.J.: Humanities Press, 1983), 9–11, 95–113.

More recently, Sara Little expanded Kierkegaard's approach for educational ministry in chap. 7 of her *To Set One's Heart: Belief and Teaching in the Church* (Atlanta: John Knox, 1983), and Maria Harris expands Little by recommending aesthetic or artistic modes of indirect instruction in her *Teaching and Religious Imagination* (San Francisco: Harper and Row, 1987), though perhaps Harris's reading of Kierkegaard is actually closer to Buber. See as well the persuasive treatment of both indirect communication and of Kierkegaard's writings as a curriculum in Pamela Mitchell's "Unconcluding Scientific Postscript: A Kierkegaardian Reconceptualization of Christian Education Curriculum" (Ed.D. diss., Presbyterian School of Christian Education, 1986).

22. Evans, *Kierkegaard's "Fragment" and "Postscript,"* 112.

of wonder that God (or anyone) could continue to love others who are unlovely and who have betrayed that love over and over again. That is a mystery time does not diminish. If such awe were simply a response to overwhelming power, submission or trembling would be an appropriate response, but awe regularly gives rise to worship in which humans affirm that steadfast divine faithfulness and love are worthy of awe and gratitude.

In like manner, learners repeatedly "get it wrong" or "take the wrong path." The master-teacher expects this of apprentices and finds ways to make the mistakes occasions for more learning. When an apprentice makes a mistake, the master evokes respect, even awe, by showing how to take the right path instead of the mistaken path. The master cracks open a door and shows the learner how to walk through it, and a trace of the awe can be heard in the familiar responses, "Oh, now I see!" or "Aha!!" or "How'd you know to do that?" When that happens, a learner is likely to regard the one who teaches as "worth her salt."

Mistakes need not be occasions for punishment. Punishment may awaken learning, if used sparingly and wisely under the right conditions. But most often what is learned is how to avoid punishment, rather than the way to a better path. Sometimes punishment is less a design for learning and more a sign of a teacher's frustration, either because the teacher lacks self-control or because the one teaching thinks there is something wrong with mistakes. Punishment has the potential to kill education. It can kill the desire for learning and may lead the learner to avoid occasions where learning might be called for or where mistakes might occur. That is a dangerously high price to pay.

If the fear of the Lord is the beginning of wisdom, and that is a lifelong condition, then it is just as true for the one who teaches as it is for the learner. Both make mistakes. And the mistakes of both can become opportunities for further learning and wisdom. How? Both mistakes and getting it right, both teacher and learner, must be seen within the context of something larger and deeper than both, that is, within the context of the divine source and ruler of life itself, the source of what is of worth.

It is no accident that Sirach and Jesus spoke repeatedly about the importance and regularity of prayer and worship and that the Wisdom of Solomon incorporated ritual into the notion of wisdom as holy. These later sages are critical (either implicitly or explicitly) of the misuse of ritual, but they also demonstrate how ritual and prayer show attentive learners new responses to mistakes in living and thereby can become a means to seeing the way to the right path. Ritual is a regular reminder of the basics that are so easily forgotten when we are not paying attention. My pastor-father once observed that one function of using the same liturgy every week is to ensure that the gospel is present no matter what the preacher says or does. The rituals can help remind us that God is central and humans are subjects, in the full sense.

WHY LEARN IN THIS WAY? WHAT IS THE POINT?

Creation, Creating, and Creatures

The sages turned primarily to the created world and ordinary human behavior for their imagery and lessons. Even when, late in the tradition, Sirach and the Wisdom of Solomon incorporated God's actions in history into wisdom, they attributed it to *Sophia* and used it more as illustration than as foundation.

Interestingly, while inferring God's ways from the created world (see, e.g., Wisd. 13–14 or Job 12:7–10), the sages never once speak of "nature," for that concept grows out of assumptions the sages are unwilling to grant. Nature is something that is not the product of artifice or is not produced, made, or constructed. Instead, what is natural is what has always been or has grown, evolved, or reproduced from what is itself natural. The sages, on the other hand, see the created order itself as God's artifice or creating. Nothing is natural — all is created and "creature" and, therefore, as it naturally stands, is in a relation with the Creator.

This view also implies that what is created can reveal something about the Creator, as assumed in Jesus' use of lilies, sparrows, mustard seed, and so on. As Walter Brueggemann notes, Proverbs is already

> an example of a style of life in which men really ask about the mes
> sage given in their environment. In such a dialogue nothing is trivial
> or safely ignored. Each small turn of events speaks a word to us and
> discloses a freshness about the world in which we live. The word
> spoken is often a new word, unexpected, not in conformity with
> how we thought it should be and always was.[23]

By implication, this also means there can be no neutral stance from which to describe or use nature. Rather the basic given from which

---

23. Walter Brueggemann, *In Man We Trust: The Neglected Side of Biblical Faith* (Atlanta: Knox, 1972), 115. This comment is in a chapter titled "Uneasy Reflections from a Son of Neoorthodoxy."

everything proceeds is that all are creatures, created, related, and thus all must be disciples (i.e., learners) to discern what can be learned. As expressed by Gerhard von Rad:

> in the case of the wise men's search for knowledge, even when they expressed their results in a completely secular form, there was never any question of what we would call absolute knowledge functioning independently of their faith in Yahweh. This is inconceivable for the very reason that the teachers were completely unaware of any reality not controlled by Yahweh...the sentences teach a truth to which one has already committed oneself; one could even call it a truth which has to do with character rather than with intellect.... A man was considered to be wise only when he allowed his whole way of life to be modeled on these insights which put their emphasis on values.... One has to "walk" in wisdom.[24]

When someone creates an understanding of life and behavior, are they creating, or are they re-creating or discovering truth and value that has already been built into the created order by the Creator? This has been argued both ways. If we only discover what is already there, why do different cultures find such different things there, and why does one culture's notion of what is there change so much over time? On the other hand, if we are created in the image of the Creator, it is proper to think of ourselves as creating as we construct these lessons, though that carries a corresponding responsibility not to forget that we create as creatures. The intrinsic humility of that double recognition is a very important aspect of the pedagogy of the wisdom traditions. This double recognition is also a source of wonder as new understandings and insights emerge through the centuries. If these feelings are attended to, there can be no end to the joy of discovery, the wonder of the new that is found in the midst of the old and the familiar, and no end as well to the excitement of learning.

Learning Judgment, Wisdom, and Love by Practice

The wisdom texts place responsibility upon the reader-learner, beginning with the necessity of making sense out of enigmatic proverbial sayings. The Books of Job and Ecclesiastes raised the level of enigma almost to the breaking point, but the responsibility was still placed upon the reader-learner, not the author, as it similarly was with Jesus' "Let anyone with ears listen." Readers often want the Gospel writers to fill in the blanks so we know how

---

24. Gerhard von Rad, *Wisdom in Israel* (Nashville: Abingdon, 1972), 64.

the stories come out or how people responded. For example, in Luke's story, the rich young ruler asked, "Teacher, what must I do to inherit eternal life?" He had kept the Commandments, so the reply was, "Sell all that you own and distribute the money to the poor...then come, follow me" (Luke 18:18–25). Did he do it? The reader-learner is only told that the young man became sad, for he was rich. The text remains open ended, just like Jesus' parables. Therefore, the story not only tells about an event in the distant past but can pose a challenge for any reader.

The most vital step is what reader-learners do next, for the only way a reader-learner can know if a story or saying is true is to try it on and see if it works as suggested or promised. Just as life experience offers opportunities to practice making judgments and thus to discern the benefits and liabilities of that practice, so these sayings convey their truth value and worth to those who try them. This not only limits how much responsibility the one who teaches can assume; it also suggests that such learning must be extended in time, which is especially true of the attitudes, behaviors, and dispositions recommended in wisdom texts. The authors of Job or Ecclesiastes depict life-wrenching insights — did they learn these suddenly? Jesus urges, "Love your enemies," but one does not just fall in love with them. One must first learn to talk with them in a civil manner before beginning to explore the issues that have given rise to the enmity, let go of our own prejudices, and seek mutual interests or their best interests. Since what is called for is an alteration or modification of character, the kind of learning required by wisdom often calls for extensive and extended self-reformulation, a lifelong practice.

Facing Uncomfortable Questions

There seems to be a history of desire for religion to produce a picture-perfect, postcard world. That may be the realm of Hollywood or magic, but it is not the world of the sages. The sages do use aesthetic devices, but not to make things pretty or beautiful. Rather it is to help reader-learners face reality and truth, even when they are uncomfortable.

Jesus' parables are art, but not art for art's sake. Here art serves truth because the issue is *how to live*. The same is true in our teaching. The point is not just to appreciate the brilliance with which the author has used his aesthetic resources to move the reader along certain lines, no matter how fascinating and valid such study may be. Yet just as there is no one right way to live, so there is no one right way to move reader-learners to discern truth.

Acquiring the Discipline for Success, Righteousness, Justice, and Equity

One theme that can be traced consistently through the writings of the sages is a quest for righteousness and justice. We noted that the sages' concern with justice was not always consistent. Job, even in the depths of his suffering, retains an aristocratic disdain for society's outcasts who mock him, calling them those "whose fathers I would have disdained to set with the dogs of my flock" (Job 30:1). Qohelet, similarly, cries out against injustice, but he never seems to have to face the question about where his own next meal is coming from or whether he should use his leisure and affluence on behalf of the poor, as Jesus did. Still, these sages faced hard questions about justice and showed concern for how their community handled injustice. Never do they treat injustice as though evil will either go away or is separable from God. They were convinced that God cares about justice and so should God's people.

For the sages, becoming wise necessarily included learning to engage life with a concern for justice. Here again, practice in ordinary life is pedagogically important. For example, in both family and school settings, one often observes children running to parent or teacher with complaints that others are not being fair. These are potential moments for the children's acquiring judgment and wisdom by learning how to recognize and cope with injustice and justice, if the parent or teacher refrains from settling the issue too quickly. The children themselves might be asked to describe, re-describe, and work through the injustices toward justice — with prescriptions for their own and others' behavior. This requires more time than does a simple arbitrary adult decision that settles the dispute, and time is not always available. Thus adults also must exercise wise discernment about how children will best learn justice.

The Importance of Pedagogical Hope

The sages wrestled with profoundly unsettling questions, yet they circled back again and again to joy and happiness and blessing and pleasure and long life. These sages felt that understanding was a necessary part of attaining such joy. Joy cannot be commanded directly, but it can be evoked:

> Happy are those who find wisdom,
>   and those who get understanding,

for her income is better than silver,
  and her revenue better than gold.
She is more precious than jewels,
  and nothing you desire can compare with her.
Long life is in her right hand;
  and in her left hand are riches and honor.
Her ways are ways of pleasantness,
  and all her paths are peace.
She is a tree of life to those who lay hold of her;
  those who hold her fast are called happy. (Prov. 3:13–18)

These are very strong promises. It is striking that these affirmations arise amidst some of the most troubling (experientially and theologically) dilemmas described in biblical texts. Job and Qohelet never give up hoping. They may be confused or tormented or uncomprehending, but they hope. Their texts also lead reader-learners on in a state of aroused expectation — each new glimpse of truth leads one to expect more.

Pedagogy is intrinsically founded upon such hope. If either teacher or learner gives up hope, education comes to an end. Sometimes teachers must carry enough hope for both themselves and their learners, and sometimes learners must muster enough hope to overcome their teachers' lack of it. The hope upon which pedagogy is based is a communal hope. Parents and teachers share their resources because they are witnesses to the value of what they have been given, what they have received from their own parents and community. They also share because they hope: they hope to contribute to the community as well as to the individuals in their care so both will be better. And teachers and parents are also motivated by a hope (even if not always fulfilled) that someday injustice and torment will give way to a life filled with justice, love, and joy.

Is Wisdom a Post-Postmodern Strategy?

Strictly speaking a tradition that reaches so far behind the invention of the modern is only anachronistically called either *pre-modern* or *postmodern*, let alone *post-postmodern*. Yet the wisdom traditions address the major concerns of many postmodernists. Biblical wisdom fosters understanding of one's own tradition, while also honoring and using other traditions. These texts respect the created order rather than dominate it. They eschew violence. They favor particularity and avoid universalizing and rely more on concrete, lived experience and narrative than on abstract or theoretical principles.[25] Further, these traditions honor communal tradition while engaging it critically. They deny that one can be an individual apart from a community and its traditions or that one can be an individual without engaging in critical reflection about one's communal traditions.

Part of what makes these texts so puzzling to many readers is that they seem to operate on the reader's consciousness by *deconstructing* themselves. First, conventional proverbial sayings, such as those in Proverbs, take what is familiar to all of us, the simple events of our ordinary life, and handle it linguistically so that it no longer looks quite so familiar. With the familiar made strange, we can see new things in it. Similarly, Job and Qohelet take familiar doctrines, essential to the tradition that they themselves inhabit and upon which they depend, and make them strange with their hard questions and probing. In the process, the reader-learner may become disoriented and gain new insights that conventional thought will not allow.

The wisdom texts are suited for lifelong learning. There are times when individuals, communities, and traditions need some shaking up and reorienting, even moving backward in order to find a way forward again. Both the prophetic and the wisdom traditions excel at this kind of reorientation.

WHAT COUNTS AS "EDUCATION" IN THE WISDOM TRADITIONS?

Can we speak of the "way of the sage," or must we speak rather of the "ways of the sages"? On the face of it, looking at the variety of texts, I find it hard to imagine that the diverse range of doctrines and questions, emotions and anxieties, literary techniques and philosophical convictions, we have encountered can be pulled together into a single coherent concept or pedagogical approach. Still, there are resemblances among them. All use proverbial sayings to sum up communal experience. All invite readers to considerable agency or responsibility in learning to become wiser. They expect learners to see.

The sage-teacher, like prophets and priests, has great authority, but it is not established by priestly heredity or by the prophetic

---

25. See Stephen Toulmin, *Cosmopolis: The Hidden Agenda of Modernity* (New York: Free Press, 1990); and Albert Borgmann, *Crossing the Postmodern Divide* (Chicago: University of Chicago Press, 1992). For fuller treatment of these issues, see my article, "Pluralistic Religious Education in a Postmodern World," *Religious Education* 90:3–4 (summer-fall 1995), 346–59.

disclaimer, "The word of the LORD came to me." Rather a sage's authority is established by experience, age, integrity, standing in the community, and perhaps especially by a recognition of accumulated knowledge and sound judgment. In other words, the authority of the sage is neither conferred, nor does it come with an office. Rather the authority seems inherent in what the sage says and does and how that works among those who receive the sage's counsel.

Since the sages each address such different cultures and issues, we cannot assume they share the same concept of education. In what follows, I identify five different concepts of education found in the wisdom traditions we have examined. While each may be more prominent in one or another text (or is more needed at a particular time and place), all are found (explicitly or implicitly) in each of our texts.

Education as Dialogue or Conversation

In the wisdom traditions, pedagogy is intrinsically and necessarily dialogical. The conversation goes on between texts and living; between the divine and the human; between tradition and experience; between critiquing and creating; between thought and deed; between love and justice; between young and older; among divergent visions of the divine, even divergent religions; between women and men; between the past and present; between critique of the past, despair in the present, and lively hope.

In this approach to learning, the respective roles of teachers and learners are almost infinitely flexible. If there is to be true dialogue, there must be attentive listening — from those who teach as from those who learn. The Job text reminds us forcefully how not listening prevents hearing, learning, growth, and virtually everything essential in education. Like wisdom, education requires, not a listening as impatiently waiting for a chance to speak, but the kind of listening that seeks to discern and understand that which is other.

Many a teacher knows that while the young are born avid learners, often by the time they arrive in the presence of those who are formally designated as teachers, those same young have not been listened to for a long time. In contemporary societies, many of the young have absorbed one of the fundamental lessons offered by television: "You, the viewer, will never be listened to. Your task is to listen, watch, and want (to consume). We will do the work for you." Such persons must be listened into becoming active learners, and that is no small task, for teachers will have to fight expectations such learners bring with them. Listening persons into active learning is a challenging task. But if it is not done, learners not only remain dependent; their ability to become subjects in the senses described in the previous chapter is inhibited, and their education is stunted, for they will be available to be controlled by others.

Education as Apprenticeship for Steering through Life: Acquiring Self-Discipline

An apprenticeship can be quite dialogical, though clearly the apprentice is subject to and dependent upon, even controlled by, the master. Historically, apprenticeship functions as a mediating structure (similar to the institution of schooling today) between family and kin relations and wider social or public and economic relations.[26] Within a family, children learn as though apprentices to the family — listening, imagining, playing, conversing, trying to imitate, and experiencing correction. Elders (and/or older children) set the agenda, and while a child's range of participation and responsibility is limited by his age, he gradually picks up (learns) the family's values and standards without reading or formal study.

Formally becoming an apprentice both replicates family patterns yet also calls into question the prior standards, for now there is a new master with different ideas. When Jesus called disciples, he took them away from their families (Mark 1:16–20; Matt. 4:18–22) and offered new sisters and brothers — a family governed by different values and standards (see Mark 3:31–35; Matt. 12:46–50; Luke 8:19–21). This seemed to have been a source of continuing puzzlement or tension — both for the families left behind and for the disciples themselves.

The new apprentice replicates family roles: he is obedient and subservient, must show respect, and only gradually assumes a greater role in the work. He begins by watching, performing routine tasks, gradually learning to understand the materials and technology and the premises underlying how they are combined. Often this cannot be taught, yet must be learned: "It seems that where what is to be learned is a blend of mental and physical representations and skills of widely varying levels of specificity this cannot be transmitted in a purely verbal manner. There are things which only 'make sense' when they have already been mastered."[27]

26. Esther N. Goody, "Learning, Apprenticeship, and the Division of Labor," in *Apprenticeship: From Theory to Method and Back Again*, ed. Michael W. Coy (Albany: State University of New York Press, 1989), 236–39.
27. Ibid., 247.

The apprentice, like a child in a family, is allowed to be inept. He is more or less expected to be ignorant until he proves otherwise.[28] The task of the master is to arrange, assign, and monitor tasks in a fashion based on increasing complexity.[29]

While apprenticeship may be dialogical, it focuses attention less upon the dialogue itself and more upon where that dialogue is leading or what it makes possible. The master-apprentice conversation is not a value in itself so much as it is a necessary means to a valued end — learning a craft. Still, the relation between apprentice and master often has very strong affective and moral dimensions, again not unlike family relations. Apprenticeship "is a means of learning things that cannot be easily communicated by conventional means. Apprenticeship is employed where there is implicit knowledge to be acquired through long-term observation and experience."[30] The master works with apprentices not only to create or craft things but also to help the apprentice-learners eventually become able to make mature and skillful judgments and value decisions as the master does. This is perhaps especially true when what is being crafted is not just a piece of wood or clay but a life. An apprentice learns in dialogue with the master and other apprentices but even more by practice and more practice. In this process, learning self-discipline is very important.

In an apprenticeship, when a master offers guidance in steering a right path through life, the master recognizes both that the learner is doing the steering and that steering is intrinsically normative. That steering must continue when the master or teacher is no longer present. How can a teacher help a reader-learner come to make good judgments? Sometimes they do it by saying directly, "Go right" or "Go left." Often they use what we have called *indirect approaches*. They help learners look ahead, offering different pictures or visions with which to guide their steering. They tell stories or use metaphors that evoke choices or suggest alternative paths that could be taken.

While education as apprenticeship is both dialogical and creative, it also is associated in our minds with hard work in ways that may sometimes be misleading about the spirit of these sages and their texts. Perhaps another metaphor would better express

28. Ibid., 250.
29. Ibid., 247.
30. Coy, *Apprenticeship*, xi-xii.

the spirit in which the work of religious learning-apprenticeship best occurs.

Education as Play or Teasing into Truthful Lives

Roland Murphy, speaking of how the sages use comparisons and analogies, observes that the pedagogy of the wisdom traditions "does not command so much as it seeks to persuade, to tease the reader into a way of life."[31] That language evokes a concept of education that fits both the sages of old and contemporary educational ministry.[32] Rather than do an exhaustive or analytic description of this concept of education (as I have in the past),[33] allow me to play with you, the reader — to tease out a concept by slightly more indirect means.

Education as play is hardly a new idea,[34] but when it has been used in religious education circles, it usually applies only to children.[35] In what follows, I offer a playground more than an argument — to tease you (and myself) into reflection on educational ministry. It will be best if we take our time and amble along.

IS EDUCATION SERIOUS? IS IT HARD WORK? Education is often regarded as serious business, even work. This is especially true of education that

31. Roland E. Murphy, *The Tree of Life: An Exploration of the Biblical Wisdom Literature* (New York: Doubleday, 1990), 15.

32. This section is based upon the unpublished paper "Teasing Out Truthful Lives" (presented at a Research Interest Group at the annual meeting of the Association of Professors and Researchers in Religious Education, Boulder, Colo., November 1990).

33. See, for example, early articles, "Does the Church Really Want Religious Education?" *Religious Education* 69:1 (January–February 1974), 12–22; reprinted in John Westerhoff, ed., *Who Are We? The Quest for a Religious Education* (Birmingham, Ala.: Religious Education Press, 1978), 250–63; "What Is Religious Education?" *The Living Light* 14:3 (fall 1977), 339–52; reprinted in Jeff Astley and Leslie Francis, eds., *Critical Perspectives on Religious Education: A Reader on the Aims, Principles, and Philosophy of Christian Education* (Leominster, U.K.: Gracewing, 1994), 48–60; and "What Is the Educational Ministry of the Church?" *Religious Education* 73:4 (July–August 1978), 429–39.

34. The connection between playfulness and education is at least as old as Plato and Confucius, and the link with human living and religion has been treated by many since Johan Huizinga's *Homo Ludens: A Study of the Play Element in Culture* (Boston: Routledge and Kegan Paul, 1949), first published in 1939.

35. See, for example, Roger Gobbel and Gertrude Gobbel, *The Bible: A Children's Playground* (Philadelphia: Fortress, 1986); and Jerome Berryman, *Godly Play: A Way of Religious Education* (San Francisco: HarperSanFrancisco, 1991). Ironically, Berryman's practices with children seem more playful than his articulation of theory in the book. See also Diane Hymans, "The Role of Play in a Cultural-Linguistic Approach to Religion: Theoretical Implications for Education in the Faith Community" (Ed.D. diss., Presbyterian School of Christian Education, 1992), a thoughtful exploration of play as a way of understanding educational ministry with adults as well as children.

concerns religion or Christianity. For some, this is serious because salvation is at stake. But, if that is so, and if salvation is a gift, why should the pedagogy feel like work? Might talk of work in educational ministry mislead?

What does it mean to be serious? It need not mean that we go about our task, our learning and teaching, in a somber mood or with a perpetually straight face. Plato wrote, "Swear with a seriousness that is not out of tune combined with the playfulness that is the sister of seriousness."[36] For Plato, seriousness and playfulness are not opposites, strangers, or even distant acquaintances, but intimately related. It is intriguing that both Plato and Proverbs, where Woman Wisdom plays in the presence of God, not only speak of an intrinsic link between play and education but speak of it using the female gender.

Plato spent fifty years writing about law, yet in his mature years he saw laws as play. He also called literature and the new art of philosophy play, yet for him it was a lifelong aesthetic passion. He also viewed human life as a play and spoke of humans as God's playthings, and thus God was worthy of our most serious endeavors.[37] But all his writing and his philosophy was also self-consciously a form of education, a *paideia:*

> Education is in our view just about the most important activity of all. So each of us should spend the greater part of his life at peace, and that will be the best use of his time. What, then, will be the right way to live? A man should spend his whole life at "play" — sacrificing, singing, dancing — so that he can win the favor of the gods.[38]

For Plato, nothing is more serious than playing in the presence of God — and education, play, and religion are related. Plato says, in effect, "Grow up and play!"[39] For Plato, playing in the presence of the gods helps sort out what is important so we can "sail through this voyage of life successfully."[40] Plato sounds like the Hebrew sages in this passage, as he metaphorically describes education for character forming as laying down the "character-keel" of a ship so that we can "play our part" and "order our life." No

---

36. Plato *Letter VI* 323D; quoted from Paul Friedländer, *Plato: An Introduction*, 2d ed. (Princeton: Princeton University Press, 1969), 123.

37. Plato *Laws* 803.

38. Ibid. The selection here is quoted from the Trevor Saunders's translation, rev. ed. (Harmondsworth, U.K.: Penguin, 1975), 292.

39. This felicitous phrase was suggested to me by Ginny Deneka.

40. Plato *Laws* (Saunders's trans.), 291.

one plays with his own and his companion's ideas more deftly than Plato, until confusion and clarity are spun round and round into contemplation and commitment to truth.[41]

Both Plato and the ancient Hebrew sages knew that the kind of education that fully engages people, that transforms their whole way of seeing the world, is a kind of education that gets under the skin and gradually becomes a part of one's way of being. Indeed, one way of reading many of Plato's dialogues is to see them as playing around with ideas and with the mind of the reader. Plato's questioning skillfully keeps the dialogue partners unsettled, and if the reader hangs on too tightly to fixed notions that cannot be questioned, the dialogue evokes defensiveness and anger. In thinking of teaching and learning as a form of playing, we picture ourselves holding ideas rather lightly in our grasp so that they can be turned around and looked at from different angles. If we grasp too tightly, we cannot easily let go long enough to see things from the other side. Proverbial sayings and riddles call reader-learners to similar activities. We saw earlier that enigmatic texts like Job and Ecclesiastes also invite us to look at things differently. Perhaps part of Job's problem was that, in his pain, he was obsessed with only one question ("Is God just?") and thus could not hear or see that there might be other answers that do not address that question.

Some years ago, Johan Huizinga observed that the two most prevalent images used for the human being have been *homo sapiens* (human as rational or "one who reasons" or even, to take the Latin literally, as "wise") and *homo faber* (human as "maker" or "producer"). Both images take human constructive activity very seriously. Huizinga proposed rather *homo ludens* (human as "player") as a more complete description since "civilization arises and unfolds in and as play."[42] Huizinga commented that "seriousness seeks to exclude play, whereas play can very well include seriousness."[43] He agrees with Plato.

---

41. See Paul Friedländer, *Plato,* 2d ed. (Princeton: Princeton University Press, 1969), 1:116–25.

42. Huizinga complains in his forward to *Homo Ludens: A Study of the Play Element in Culture* that he means "the Play Element *of* Culture" though some want to "correct" his title to read "the Play Element in Culture." He insists he did not intend to see play as one element within a culture, but "rather to ascertain how far culture itself bears the character of play." Did his translator and publisher not listen, or did they "play around" with his text and intention? Is this a form of irony that is not play?

43. Ibid., 45.

BECOMING LIKE CHILDREN.

"Truly, I say to you, unless you change and become like children, you will never enter the kingdom of heaven." (Matt. 18:3)

We educate children. We make them work. But we *know*, even as we teach them, that they learn many things that are not true. Some say a child's work is play. Are they playing with what we teach them? Can play be true or false?

Woman Wisdom plays in the presence of God. What was Jesus' own manner? Was Jesus playing in telling the parables? Was he teasing? Did he have a twinkle in his eye as he told his stories? Why is becoming "like children" held up as a key to the kingdom? What does it include? (Why didn't Jesus explain that?) What is the pedagogical significance of becoming like children? Did Jesus himself model that? Was he childlike?

PLAY, HUMOR, AND EDUCATION. In my view, education is sometimes killed by the manner or spirit in which it is conducted, and that is often done in the name of discipline, order, and patience. Education has too often been tied to hierarchical notions about who is better than whom. And to protect those notions (and ourselves), shame, coercion, sanctimony, embarrassment, and punitive notions of work have been used to elevate some and exclude others. There is such a fine line between guidance, on the one hand, and domination, coercion, and control, on the other.

How do we combat such abuses? Do we fight them, or does that just replicate what we seek to eliminate? Humor is a more playful way to expose pretensions and thus begin liberation, teasing things into the open without violence. But this presumes we see clearly the log in our own eye before we try to lift the speck in another's eye (Matt. 7:3–5). Can we become the subject of our own laughter? Can we learn to tease ourselves? Might we make less use of sarcasm and more of irony?

Irony has not been much used in educational ministry, perhaps because education is so often assumed to be for children. Yet empirical research shows that children as young as three years old understand metaphors and that those as young as six understand irony.[44] The prevalence of irony in biblical texts (not only in wisdom texts but in the prophets, Mark, Luke, John, and Paul)

---

44. Ellen Winner and Howard Gardner, "Metaphor and Irony: Two Levels of Understanding," in *Metaphor and Thought*, ed. Andrew Ortony, 2d ed. (Cambridge: Cambridge University Press, 1993), 425–43.

suggests it may be too important to ignore.[45] In fact, Kierkegaard, a great lover of irony, claimed that "no authentic human life is possible without irony."[46]

Recognition of the discrepancies between how we appear or want to appear and how we actually act may best come by means of humor or parable, especially when the irony touches us personally. We can discover our incongruence in being entrapped by a story (Nathan's with David), in which or through which we see ourselves from an unfamiliar angle — and see a truth (or a falseness) about ourselves we had missed. Such discoveries are a means to correction and a move toward more truthful ways — a move basic to education and being religious. Observe how playfully Kierkegaard treats Socrates' claim that all he knew was his ignorance:

> In the last analysis the ironist must always posit something, but what he posits in this way is nothingness. Now it is impossible to take nothingness seriously without either arriving at something (this happens when one takes it speculatively seriously), or without despairing (this happens when one takes it personally seriously). But the ironist does neither of these, and to this extent one may say he is not really serious about it. Irony is the infinitely delicate play with nothingness, a playing that is not terrified by it but still pokes its head into the air. But if one takes nothingness neither speculatively nor personally seriously, then one obviously takes it frivolously and to this extent not seriously.... [Socrates] does not take this ignorance any further to heart; on the contrary he feels quite properly free in this ignorance.... Socrates knows nothing at all, and to this extent it is an irony over the state when it deprives him of life and thinks by his death to have inflicted a punishment upon him.[47]

Might the same be said of the death of Jesus? Or would that not be irony?

---

45. For example, on the Hebrew texts, see Edwin Good, *Irony in the Old Testament* (Philadelphia: Westminster, 1965); on Mark, see Fowler, *Let the Reader Understand: Reader-Response Criticism and the Gospel of Mark* (Minneapolis: Fortress, 1991); and Jerry Camery-Hoggatt, *Irony in Mark's Gospel: Text and Subtext* (Cambridge: Cambridge University Press, 1992); on Luke, see James Dawsey, *The Lukan Voice: Confusion and Irony in the Gospel of Luke* (Macon, Ga.: Mercer University Press, 1986); on John, see Paul D. Duke, *Irony in the Fourth Gospel* (Atlanta: John Knox, 1985); and on Paul, see Karl A. Plank, *Paul and the Irony of Affliction* (Atlanta: Scholars, 1987).

46. Søren Kierkegaard, *The Concept of Irony: With Constant Reference to Socrates* (Bloomington: Indiana University Press, 1965), 338.

47. Ibid., 285–88.

PLAY AND GETTING THE PEDAGOGICAL MOOD RIGHT. Education is a practice, or practices, in which it is critically important to get the mood right. I do not pretend to grasp this matter fully, but it needs exploration.[48]

Educators have long talked about setting a climate or creating an environment for certain things to happen. The atmosphere of a lecture giving didactic exposition is different from a group engaging in shared, open-ended inquiry. Different educational practices have their own mood. Is it possible that one reason the liberal or progressive religious educators of the early twentieth century were never well understood was, not just that they had a different theology, but that their educational intentions and procedures with learners required creating quite a different educational mood than was desired among the evangelists who preceded them and among the neoorthodox educators who succeeded them?

Imagine two kinds of journey. In one, we know the destination from the beginning, and there is some urgency in getting there as directly and immediately as possible. In the other journey, we know only that we are going in a certain direction, and while our journey is purposeful, we are in no great hurry but expect interesting surprises along the way that may be just as exciting as finally arriving: "One is responsible for finding the journey's end in every step of the road, in one's own gait."[49] Is the mood of these two journeys the same? Would both be hospitable to the same kinds of learning? Would teaching be directed to the same things in both trips? Would teasing be evaluated the same in both?

Different biblical texts have different moods. Do sound hermeneutical principles include a concern with getting the mood right? If so, should teaching such texts not also concern itself with teaching them in the proper mood? Is one misinterpreting a text if it is taught in a different mood?

Do education and Christianity have different moods? Can they have the same mood? For example, is it possible to compel or coerce either education or Christianity into existence? Would that not

---

48. What follows has been suggested by the work of three oft-misunderstood authors: Søren Kierkegaard, Ludwig Wittgenstein, and Stanley Cavell. Each has attended carefully to the congruence between what is being said or written and how it is being communicated in a concern to get the mood right. I share their concern, but have often failed at the task. See Kierkegaard's *The Point of View for My Work as an Author.* See Cavell's reading of both Kierkegaard and Wittgenstein in *Must We Mean What We Say?* (Cambridge: Cambridge University Press, 1969); and especially his rereading of Thoreau and Emerson in *The Senses of Walden,* expanded ed. (San Francisco: North Point Press, 1981.)

49. Cavell, *This New Yet Unapproachable America,* 17.

be getting the mood wrong? Can one be coerced into living? Or would coerced living be less truthful or less abundant? Or do education and religion each have multiple possible moods that might overlap?

Can our manner of living, our actions, our moods, be judged as more or less truthful? Actions can be dishonest. What about moods? Can such things be approached directly, or do they call for indirection? Can truthful acts be teased into life?

Clearly I have more questions than answers, but the issue has fundamentally to do with the spirit within which teaching, learning, and education take place.[50] Is mood a form of presence? If the point or purpose of education in the wisdom traditions has to do with life, with abundant living, with new life, new creation, and vitality, then the methods and content of the educational processes should hardly be boring or tedious or uninteresting. How can we ensure that teaching and learning are vital and alive and bring forth life?

Education as Forming Persons of Integrity

One of the oldest persistent themes in these wisdom traditions is a critique of hypocrisy. Some of the most biting satire within the biblical texts (Job, Jesus) and beyond (see the Akkadian text "A Pessimistic Dialogue between Master and Servant") focuses on this theme.[51] This need remains.

Contemporary life has been so fragmented that we find it easy to teach high ideals with little thought about how we practice those ideals ourselves. Teachers commute to schools (or church schools) where they meet students, whom they seldom see elsewhere, teach highly specialized subjects, using materials prepared by distant experts (who know neither the teachers nor the students nor the community where the materials are to be used). In such conditions, it is easy, even necessary, to separate the pedagogical process from the teacher's daily living and from the daily life of the learners. Thus learners seldom see teachers struggle with their own experience and their own faithfulness (or questions) with the tradition.

---

50. See Max van Manen, *The Tact of Teaching: The Meaning of Pedagogical Thoughtfulness* (Albany: State University of New York Press, 1991), whose work addresses some of these concerns.

51. James B. Pritchard, *Ancient Near Eastern Texts: An Anthology of Texts and Pictures* (Princeton: Princeton University Press, 1958), 1:250–52.

Integrity has to do with being integral, that is, whole, unified, or complete. Yet we say: Politics and religion don't mix, and the church budget is a financial concern not a spiritual matter, and mathematics has nothing to do with sports, and our choice of friends has nothing to do with race, and our automobile has nothing to do with ethics, and so on. We even do this to people. We deal with the mailman, not as a person, but as a mail-delivery function, and the grocery clerk is an extension of the checkout counter. What do we know of what goes on in their lives? Why should we? We do not have time for it. We do not even notice how little of our world we notice, and soon our not noticing becomes a self-deception:

> The range of what we think and do
> is limited by what we fail to notice.
> And because we fail to notice
> that we fail to notice
> there is little we can do
> to change
> until we notice
> how failing to notice
> shapes our thoughts and deeds.[52]

To put together what we have long held apart is not easy. Here human community and agency play complementary roles. I need others to help me see myself for what I am — not to collude with me in not noticing, but to join with me in a common search for truth and for life. Just as peace will not be attained until it is founded upon justice, so also authentic and eternal life must be founded on truth.

One of the most enlivening aspects of the ways of the sages is the hope that every little learning leads to something else, a piece of the puzzle called life. Qohelet has taught us we may never see the completed picture. We may even doubt there is or will be a complete picture. We do know, with Qohelet, that "the same fate happens to everyone" (Eccles. 9:3). Death cannot be denied, for paradoxically without death a life will never be complete or whole. Qohelet reminded us that we do not have to hold on so tightly to all those little discrete pieces as though our striving could put them back together again!

Earlier we noted that education in the path of wisdom requires both humility and courage. It entails taking risks: "The Book of

---

52. R. D. Laing, *Knots* (London: Penguin, 1971).

Proverbs is about letting go as much as it is about holding firm," but in letting go, one also takes hold of the hand of Woman Wisdom; thus the "silent son has become a responsible citizen of the community."[53] Job must let go not only of the security of patriarchal norms but his family as well, and Qohelet let go of finding meaning. Jesus let go of life itself. Yet each found integrity as a simple gift.[54]

Do we have the humility to let go? Can we find the courage it takes? Is that too much playing — perhaps playing with fire? Or is letting go an absence playing with presence?

Education as Death and Resurrection

Life and new life are familiar images, and in the wisdom tradition, they are often offered by *Sophia* or Woman Wisdom, usually as an alternative to the threat of death. In the previous chapter, we explored the plausible connections between Jesus' teaching and death. The Gospel texts exist, not because people took a historical interest in Jesus, but because believers saw Jesus' death as leading to new life. Believers "see" Jesus "as" Christ, which is a faith judgment or a theological conviction, not a historical claim. Jesus' death became the lens through which Jesus' activities and life were reinterpreted as an expression of God's love.

Paul used "death and resurrection" as a metaphor for the Christian life and for the shape of ethics. Can the two also be a fruitful metaphor for education? To learn, one must let old ways of thinking, being, and behaving die, for unless they do, they prevent the emergence of new possibilities. But, in education as in other arenas of life, humans often use tradition, custom, and doctrine to avoid or deny death. Even preaching and consoling others are sometimes used to deny or avoid death itself.

Job's friends not only were unwilling to allow the notion of retribution to die; they were even unwilling to admit it might be "sick." As a result, they learned nothing new about themselves, about Job, or about God, and they ended up "speaking falsely for God." Job, on the other hand, let retribution die as a notion that explained his situation and thus opened the way for new possibilities. Job also laments, for when something important dies, grieving is called for. But Job and Qohelet both show that even in the midst

---

53. William P. Brown, *Character in Crisis: A Fresh Approach to the Wisdom Literature of the Old Testament* (Grand Rapids: Eerdmans, 1996), 152, 155.
54. Ibid., 155–57.

of the turmoil, when death and despair are pressing hard, there is a residue of hope — something new is possible. Might refusing to let go deny hope or trust?

Teachers walk between twin temptations. The first is the temptation to stress affiliation or nurture too strongly: Teachers want to support and protect the learner from pain and hurt, so sometimes they avoid conflict. But does that not affirm (in actions) that one should not have to die or that the death of a cherished idea or action will not harm or hurt? Can protecting learners from pain also protect them from learning? Can a teacher's well-meant affection control the learner in ways that subvert education? Is such "caring" loving? The other temptation is to use the teacher's power to coerce death, eagerly, forcefully, imposing the death of old ideas and ways of thinking and behaving. Teachers who succumb to this temptation (usually men?) distort the needed death in another way, for what is called for is not murder but a letting-go kind of dying *by the learner*, a giving-up-the-old. While this is painful, the learner eventually must see it as necessary. What the teacher can do in this situation is recognize the pain, help learners with the needed burial and grieving, which takes more time, energy, and sharing than teachers sometimes allow.

The educator's task is both to allow the needed death of the old and then to use one's caring to sustain and support the learner in finding and shaping new truth and thus new life. There are even times when a teacher has to do the hoping for a learner, for experience has taught the teacher there is a path on the other side of the pain, without taking away the learner's agency.

We have explored five pictures or concepts or approaches to education that are compatible with the biblical wisdom traditions. Each enables one to see a facet of education more clearly than the others, but like a diamond, each helps make the light shine more luminously. We see less if we do not use them all. Or to change the metaphor, rather than seek single, clear notes, we might consider using a chord. Then, to mix our metaphors, together these five form a richer, fuller picture, which may be more true because it is more harmonious.

WHAT DOES ALL THIS REQUIRE OF ONE WHO TEACHES?

Can teachers be sages? Must they? What is required of teachers by these approaches?

Age and Life Experience

The wisdom traditions presume that the teacher has lived long enough to have acquired experience and knowledge worth passing on to others. How long is long enough? The texts never say.

Some people manage to live a long life and gather little wisdom from their experience, while others are, proverbially, "wise beyond their years." The issue is not simply chronological longevity but what one does with one's time. One who teaches would be wise to consistently reflect upon her or his experiences. Listening to one's elders and the community, studying texts, reflecting upon what makes things whole or reminds us all of the humility and courage it takes to keep on — all are ways of using experience well. But to use experience, or life, well also means keeping a sense of perspective — spending some time out under the stars...or in a cathedral...or singing in a chorus. There are many ways to help encourage absence and presence to stay in conversation.

Being Backward as a Way Forward

Often we must look backward in order to see forward. We have to turn ourselves around, front to back, so we can see our tradition more clearly than those captivating TV images. We must face backward to see clearly and to learn to listen with our whole being to those sights, sounds, tastes, smells, and caresses that define how God loves us and those to whom we are called to minister.

Being seen as backward is not popular. Educators often rely on technical expertise, using sophisticated theological, psychological, and pedagogical jargon. Educators could as well speak in more common ways, using little simple stories and sayings that they have proven to be true, seeking constantly to find the right, simple truth for the right time. It is my experience that sometimes when you do that, some people look at you as a little simple or as conservative or as just not very with it. I confess I sometimes feel slightly embarrassed at being considered backward or out of touch. Some assert their backwardness with pride and confidence, even certainty, since only a return to the familiar paths and doctrines of prior generations will preserve the heritage of God. Job's friends and Jesus' opponents argued thus. How do we discern the right kind of backwardness?

The sages did not respond to their sense of the absence of God with the backward positivism of the TV preacher or with pride about their differentness. While experience sometimes left them in the dark, unable to see clearly, they also found that traditional pictures could mislead as well. They discovered that their intense feelings, while exceedingly real, could lead them to misunderstand. They affirmed the validity of their experience but learned they could no more make experience absolute than others could make tradition absolute.

In holding both their own experiences and honored traditions with a light grip, they sometimes sensed the divine presence was closer than traditional pictures of a transcendent God would suggest. Often the sages highlighted an aspect of the tradition that had been forgotten, thus finding a source of hope. So Job turned from argument and logic to silence. Qohelet turned from anxious striving and trying to gain an advantage to enjoying bread, wine, and work. Sirach and the Wisdom of Solomon insisted that the new philosophy (Hellenism) need not be an enemy but might become an ally of faith and tradition. Jesus turned to a new emphasis on God as one who loves not only the pure but also the least, the common, even the unclean amidst a banquet feast! Each seems to have found something in his experience that questioned the tradition, yet each also found in the tradition a way to challenge, refresh, and renew his experience.

Be What You Teach

These texts call reader-learners to go beyond intellectual appropriation of experience and tradition to "practice what you teach." Loving and being truthful are not put on. They are not professional roles but are to be part of one's character. One who teaches can start by adopting more loving professional manners with students and by telling the whole truth, and then through constant and attentive practice, one can gradually let those manners permeate one's being. Each person is many things at once. I am simultaneously son, father, teacher, husband, friend, learner, lover, alien and ally, strong and weak, and so on. Even within the teaching function, there are many roles and tasks, some in tension with others. We learn early how to hold aspects of our selves away from one another and thus find it difficult not only to be whole but even to be in dialogue with our selves. In this respect, as in others, teaching itself is a lifelong apprenticeship. Perhaps if we want to learn to live with or overcome some of these separations, we can find ways to put young and older more fully in touch with one another's lives and with how one's own experiences and the communal traditions are critically and creatively engaged in daily living.

SO WHAT?

Times today are drastically different from those of ancient Israel or of the Palestine of Jesus' day or even of the later New Testament authors. Have these ancient wisdom texts anything to offer in a modern world?

Jacob the baker, that canny, playful spiritual guide, tells this story:

> There was a terrible banging on Jacob's front door. From the intensity of the hammering and shouts, it became clear to Jacob he had been unaware of the noise for some time. This awareness did not disturb him. He appeared rather to enjoy it.
>
> When the door was opened, a man with a puffy red face shouted at Jacob, "What were you doing?" Two others stood behind the inquisitor.
>
> "Thinking," said Jacob, giving very little notice to the man's anger.
>
> "Thinking?" repeated the man as if he were measuring Jacob's sanity.
>
> "Yes," said Jacob, who now closed the door behind him and headed off to work.
>
> The three agitated, middle-aged men stood blankly facing each other, and then, determined not to be left behind, they began after him.
>
> Moments later, Jacob stopped without warning and then, to himself as much as to them, answered the question they had asked earlier.
>
> "I was thinking about how many doors there are and how seldom we use them."
>
> Then, again, he set off.
>
> In order to catch up and talk with Jacob face to face, the men had to increase their pace to almost a run. When they did approach him, they were too out of breath to speak.
>
> Jacob stopped and waited.
>
> "Thank you," said the men, half-bent over, their hands on their hips.
>
> When the men captured their breath, they also revived their anger. The leader tried to bring all his authority to bear in his voice.
>
> "Look, Jacob! I've seen you for a long time. You're just Jacob the baker. Now everyone wants to ask you questions, and the children come to learn from you. What do you tell them?"
>
> Jacob was missing the warmth of the huge bakery oven. The sunrise was painting orange cracks in the gray sky.
>
> He searched his mind for a door these men might pass through and then spoke.

"I will be glad to tell you what I have been teaching the children," he began, "but first you must all agree to put your fingers in your ears."

The men did as they were told and stood as a jury opposite Jacob who began speaking.

After a few minutes, the men waved and shouted, trying to draw Jacob's attention.

"Jacob," they said, "we can't hear what's being said when our fingers are in our ears!"

"That," answered Jacob, "is what I have been telling your children."[55]

Is there a door we can walk through? Do we have fingers in our ears? Do we already know what questions must be answered? Or are we open to discovering new questions?

If we begin with the assumption that what we are now doing cannot be changed, there is little need to learn. There is good reason for believing that it is hard to bring about change. Denominations and publishers have produced attractive, popular, and extensive curriculums and educational programs. They lay out designs for teachers and administrators that are easily implemented and that promise discernable results. Of course, this has been going on for years, and yet there are fewer participants, and religious communities have less influence in the social order.

If only the sages could offer an alternative "program" that would reverse these trends. Unfortunately, these texts do not lead us to expect such a program. These texts expect reader-learners to find their own voice, not just imitate. There are many doors through which we can pass to wisdom. Perhaps the problem is not that there are many doors but how seldom we use them.

In concluding our pedagogical journey together, I offer some playful pedagogical maxims.

Some Pedagogical Aphorisms

Aphorisms can seem trite and simplistic, like proverbial sayings, yet each might also be a door to walk through or a window to freshen one's seeing. Want to try some of your own?

To become wise, open your eyes.

Acting what you know is better than knowing how to act.

To teach well, listen well.

---

55. Ben Shea, *Jacob the Baker*, 65–68.

Evoke more than you tell.

Expect to learn from the unexpected; be open to surprises.

Question what you know, and trust what you question.

Humility goes before learning.

Being right is a matter of time.

Become a reader for life and you will be read.

Deceive yourself; dig your own grave.

To move forward, be backward.

Education is too serious to be anything other than play.

Embrace the common.

Take time to wander and ponder.

To live life fully, be at peace with death.

Love your enemies; fear God.

Embody your teaching.

Loving God is the beginning of wisdom.

The last words belong to a friend of mine, a woman who teaches:

Hear instruction and be wise,
    and do not neglect it.
Happy is the one who listens to me,
    watching daily at my gates,
    waiting beside my doors.
For whoever finds me finds life
    and obtains favor from the LORD. (Prov. 8:33–35)

INDEX OF
BIBLICAL REFERENCES

INDEX OF
SUBJECTS AND AUTHORS